Negation in Baroja

Negation in Baroja

A KEY TO HIS NOVELISTIC CREATIVITY

LEO L. BARROW

THE UNIVERSITY OF ARIZONA PRESS
TUCSON   ARIZONA

About the Author . . .

LEO L. BARROW has addressed himself frequently to the subject of creativity in writing as evidenced by two of his books released during the 1960s, *Creative Spanish* and *Creative French* (Harper & Row). He spent the summer of 1970 in close contact with the people about whom Pío Baroja writes, in the Basque region of the Pyrenees in northern Spain. The 1968–69 sabbatical year he spent in Brazil studying and writing about the works of Machado de Assis. In 1961 Barrow joined the faculty of the University of Arizona, teaching courses in Spanish and Brazilian literature and literary criticism. He taught previously at the University of California in Riverside, St. Louis University, and for several summers at the University of Arizona summer school in Guadalajara. A graduate of the University of New Mexico, he received his M.A. in Madrid and a Ph.D. in Spanish at UCLA, applying the writer's observing eye to the contemporary scene as a Los Angeles taxi driver while in graduate school. Additionally in press for 1971 was Barrow's *Aspectos de la Literatura Espanola* (Xerox Publishing Co.).

THE UNIVERSITY OF ARIZONA PRESS

A mi profesor
JOSE RUBIA BARCIA

Contents

Preface

DON PÍO BAROJA — Don, in this case, is charged with the affection and respect Spaniards feel for this eccentric, sincere, and very human writer who stands easily in the company of Spain's greatest novelists, Cervantes and Galdós. Many English readers share these sentiments, and writers like Hemingway and Dos Passos have been generous in their praise of el maestro Don Pío.

Probably more of his books have been translated into English than those of any other Spanish author except Blasco Ibáñez whose popular and sensational literature has not stood the test of time. Also there have been scores of books published about Baroja, dealing with his life, his political thought, and his style, but thus far no significant volume of a critical nature published in English.

Baroja himself writes with a clarity and precision that leave no need for critical aid to understand. Nevertheless readers of his novels often feel more is there than they see at first glance — an extra something that they have trouble putting into words. There is indeed an extra something. Understanding of it may hopefully provide the key to Baroja's creativity and how he worked, leading in turn not only to fuller appreciation of this novelist but of others in the so-called "Generation of 98."

This generation derives its name from the date of Spain's defeat in the Spanish American War. The loss of the last of Spain's once great empire caused writers and intellectuals to take a new and hard look at Spain and reappraise her values. They rejected Spain's old values of God, King, and Country, her old traditions and myths — the Don Juan myth for example — the old Cervantine style, and, each in his own way, embarked on a quest for the essence of Spain, of the Spaniard, and finally of man himself. Azorín coined the name, but it is the concept of negation which binds these disparate writers together as the "Generation of 98." Also this was a generation that resisted being tagged or classified. Baroja himself objected to generic classification of his work. Application of the timeworn labels used to describe literature will not serve — almost by definition — to instruct the reader on the aims and methods of Baroja and his contemporaries.

Among the many critics of Spanish literature interested in Baroja, a large number have concerned themselves with his life, believing that knowledge of the creator leads to understanding of what has been created. Yet it is a truism — in Spanish a *perogrullada* — that the study of an author's life is *not* a substitute for a study of his works, effective though biography is in casting sidelights.

Study of Baroja's works as distinct from his life has largely been confined to articles, essays, and reviews, in newspapers and journals. An exception might be Juan Uribe Echevarría's *Pío Baroja: técnica, estilo, personajes*. But the attempt to compress the three elements of Baroja's voluminous and unorthodox work into 160 pages eliminated in this instance the possibility of comprehensive treatment.

Among articles, García Mercadal's anthology of magazine pieces about Baroja and his works has been a considerable contribution (José García Mercadal, *Baroja en el banquillo*. Zaragoza: Librería General, 1947). A number of other short pieces have served to stimulate interest in Baroja, but they have been limited in space and time.

On a comparative basis, the critics who have studied several members of the Generation of 98 in one work have made a valuable contribution — pointing out similarities and differences among these writers. Such works include Laín Entralgo's *La Generación del 98,* Hans Jeschke's *La Generación de 1898 en España,* Díaz-Plaja's *Modernismo frente a 98,* and César Barja's *Libros y autores contemporáneos.*

However this collective approach permits no concentrated study of any one phase of any one author's work. Yet it is in concentrated study of a single phase that a key is often found to the unique creativity of a particular writer or a literary period.

This study, therefore, proceeds in terms of a hypothesis generated by a single phase: the belief that there is an intimate and vital relationship between negation and literary creativity in many twentieth-century authors, and specifically in the members of the Generation of 98. Applied to Baroja, the hypothesis calls for investigation of the role that negation has played in his creativity as a novelist.

A comprehensive study of negation should reveal with clarity those values that Baroja has retained, throwing them into relief through a process of elimination of the values rejected. It is hoped also that the study may make the reader more aware of Baroja's efforts to isolate, penetrate, and portray novelistically the essence of humanity.

From an investigation of limited scope, there is hope for findings of greater depth; hope also of inspiring additional single-phase studies, their results eventually combining in a portrait of Baroja's creativity that should be significant in detail as well as truthful in outline.

José Camilo Cela calls for this type of phase-by-phase contribution in his *Recuerdo de don Pío Baroja:*

> For Pío Baroja I would like to ask — and precisely here and at this time — the homage of our dedication. If each one of us, according to our strength and our true knowledge and understanding, takes up our pen and sketches a corner of our man and of his characters, we will have contributed jointly to raising something much more enduring — and much more serious also — than a statue. At this moment, all of us feel that Don Pío Baroja deserves it. The important thing is for us not to weaken. Ladies and gentlemen, let's get to work! (México: Ediciones de Andrea, 1958.)

In the following pages, therefore, negation will be studied as a fundamental aspect of Baroja's style, showing forth in his dialogue, his creation of atmosphere, his revelation of character and delineation of minor characters, his evocation of landscape, his poetical interpretation of all these phases, and finally his total novelistic world.

Among the primary aims will be to determine the extent to which negation is used; its relationship to Baroja's theory of the novel; its importance relative to the totality of his production, and finally, how and why negation is used at all.

In each chapter the method will include four main parts: an objective starting point, a listing of negative or creative factors involved; examples of these factors, and corroboration of them by Baroja and his critics. Application of the method will vary in detail with the varying material in the chapters. In most cases a comparison will be the objective starting point, but in one chapter a basic idea found in Granjel's *Retrato de Pío Baroja* will serve the same purpose. In each chapter, examples of the major factors of negation in Baroja will be taken from each of the four decades of his novelistic production. This division into decades is arbitrary — a pragmatic ordering of a large mass of novelistic material, possible because of the overall consistency of Baroja's work.

In a study thus ordered, one may hope to trace a continuity of artistic devices in Baroja's writing. There should emerge also a basis for comparison, not only between Baroja and other members of the Generation of 98, but between this Spaniard and twentieth-century novelists in the English language, for some of whom negation has seemed almost a *modus operandi* — such writers as Sherwood Anderson, Hemingway, and John

Dos Passos. It is in the interest of these broader applications by students of comparative literature that the passages from Baroja's novels and the comments from his Spanish critics are presented here in English translation. For the most effective exposure to Baroja's style there is of course no substitute for reading and re-reading the novels themselves in the original Spanish.

ACKNOWLEDGMENTS

BRINGING INTO EXISTENCE a book about an author as prolific and profound as Pío Baroja requires a lot of reading, some serious thought about oneself and mankind in general, and considerable patience. Along the way one encounters a number of people, in person or through correspondence, who know and admire, or discover and admire, Don Pío Baroja. These people have helped the writer in his research and encouraged him in his writing. I am grateful to all those who so generously helped me and so willingly extended to me the honor and pleasure of their intellectual and human friendship.

Here is a partial list of those who have contributed to the publication of a book which should shed some light on what Don Pío Baroja had to say about mankind and how he said it: the Graduate College Research Committee of the University of Arizona gave me a grant to do research at Baroja's personal library in Itzea, Spain, in the summer of 1967. My research there and my lengthy and fascinating talks with Baroja's nephew, Don Julio Caro Baroja, provided a wealth of additional information and spurred me on to the completion of the book. Since that time the committee has sponsored me in a number of research projects, even though publication of the final results has been painstakingly slow. This manifests, I believe, the committee's firm conviction that original research, aside from publication, produces better teaching and more knowledgeable and enthusiastic guidance.

Don Julio Caro Baroja deserves special thanks for permission to quote without restriction from Baroja's works and for the wealth of information and insight he gave me about his uncle, Don Pío Baroja.

Marshall Townsend, director of the University of Arizona Press, and Elizabeth Shaw, associate editor who has done most of the editorial work on the book, deserve special credit, first for believing in the book — the *sine qua non* of publication — and then for working hard to make it more meaningful and readable for people who don't know Spanish.

The difficult problem of designing pages for adjacent Spanish and English text was well solved by Doug Peck, production manager of the Press.

I thank the following writers and publishers for permission to quote from their works: José Suárez Carreño, *Las últimas horas,* Ediciones Destino, S. L.; Joseph Conrad, *Three Great Tales,* Random House, Inc.; Ortega y Gasset, *Obras Completas,* W. W. Norton Company, Inc.; Juan Uribe Echevarría, *Pío Baroja, técnica, estilo, personajes,* Ediciones de los Anales; Camilo José Cela, *Recuerdo de don Pío Baroja* and *La colmena,* Editorial Noguer, S. A.; Marguerite Rand, *Castilla en Azorín,* Revista de Occidente; Carlos Bousoño (my professor at the University of Madrid to whom I owe a considerable debt for the formation of my own modus operandi for literary criticism) *Teoría de la expresión poética,* Editorial Gredos; Sherwood Anderson, *Winesburg, Ohio,* Viking Press; Luis Granjel, *Retrato de Pío Baroja,* Editorial Barna; García Mercadal, *Baroja en el banquillo,* Librería General; R. W. B. Lewis, *The Picaresque Saint,* J. B. Lippincott Company; James Joyce, *Dubliners,* The Viking Press.

LEO L. BARROW

1. *Introduction*

> *Esas tardes del Retiro,*
> *en pleno mes de noviembre,*
> *me dan la impresión romántica*
> *de un mundo que desfallece.*[1]

BAROJA'S NOVELS, like the November afternoons in the Retiro, give the impression of a world that is dying; their total impact is pessimistic and antivital. The feelings, ideas, and sensations received from reading and studying his novels are quite different from those produced by literary artists of other times. Reading Cervantes, one is somehow filled with a great enthusiasm for life and with an indomitable courage and faith to master all its obstacles. Adventure stories of the past century, such as those of Melville and Poe, awaken the reader's desires for adventure, and arouse an optical avidity for new and strange lands. The gentle creaking of the timbers and the rolling of Vasco da Gama's ship as it gets under way makes of the most sedate reader an explorer and conqueror of new worlds. These novels, adventure stories, and epics whet the appetite for a more intense participation in life.

Baroja's novels produce the opposite effect. The world Baroja creates fills the reader's sensibility with a sense of dejection and lifelessness, making him more critical and pessimistic.

R. W. B. Lewis has stated, "Twentieth Century literature began on the note of death."[2] The line refers to the first story in *Dubliners* by James Joyce. It could have easily referred to Pío Baroja's first novel, *La casa de Aizgorri,* published in 1900. Don Lucio, master of the house of Aizgorri, is dying, and the atmosphere of the entire novel centers around his death. James Joyce's Father Flynn and Pío Baroja's Don Lucio become symbols of the paralytic dying world of the Twentieth Century depicted by so many writers. From the beginning of the century the world has been depicted thus. "And the world or Europe or some fragment of Europe or

America is depicted thereafter as maleficent and sinful, paralyzed and dying," continues R. W. B. Lewis.[3] He adds that the very titles of works such as *Death in Venice* and *The Wasteland* suggest the fascination and the importance of death in the literature of our century. Baroja's titles, *Las agonías de nuestro tiempo* and *César o nada* are as suggestive. Ernest Hemingway, self-confessed debtor to Baroja in the art of writing,[4] was fascinated by titles and themes dealing with death. According to Auerbach, such writers as Joyce, Proust, and Virginia Woolf show a hostility to the reality that surrounds them and a tendency to turn away from the will to live.[5] For writers quite different from Joyce, Proust, and Thomas Mann — for Camus, Silone, Moravia, Faulkner, and Graham Greene, death and negation of their world also have played an important role.[6]

The pall of death and devitalization in Baroja's novels links them to the works of the aforementioned writers of our century. These same qualities weld his works to the writers of Baroja's own generation. The most cursory of glances at the literary production of a group of writers later to be known as the "Generation of 98"[7] will show their intense preoccupation with the twilight hours of life. The poetry of Antonio Machado, the languishing and abulic world of Azorín, the frequency of executions, suicides, and macabre scenes in Valle-Inclán and Unamuno, are enough to suggest the important role of death in this generation.

Negation nourishes the spiritual, intellectual, and philosophical roots of the Generation of 98. The Krausista movement in Spain and later the Institución Libre de Enseñanza stand as overt manifestations of the tendency to question, criticize, and reevaluate some of the traditional Spanish values. Indications of the denial of the status quo in Spain are found also in the writings of Echegaray, Campoamor, and Galdós, according to Azorín: "Unite then, the passionate cry of Echegaray, the subversive sentimentalism of Campoamor, and Galdós' vision of reality, and you will have the factors that were to be embodied in the Generation of 1898."[8] (A) These writers helped to set the stage for a literary creation impregnated with negation of the traditional values of Spain and Spanish life.

In the year 1898, defeat in the war with the United States and the loss of the last of the holdings of Spain's once great colonial empire made the Generation of 98 fully aware of the existence of a Spain and a Spanish way of life they could no longer accept. Thus the tendency to question, to criticize, to be preoccupied over the problems of Spain, to deny many of its traditional values, became general, or as Azorín expressed it, "A spirit of protest, of rebellion, animated the youth of 1898. Ramiro de Maeztu wrote impetuous and flaming articles, tearing down traditional values and manifesting his eager desire for a new and powerful Spain."[9] (B) The critical, questioning attitude seemed to be one of the few things that the members of this so-called generation had in common.

As one critic expressed it, "No matter how singular those individual attitudes might be, they were all similar in one fundamental note: they all began negatively with a violent rejection of the historical Spanish life then in progress."[10] (C) Alfonso El Sabio's sweeping praise of Spain, "¡Ay, Espanna, non a lengua nin engenno que pueda contar tu bien!" (Oh! Spain, no tongue nor wit can tell of your greatness!), was turned into an all-encompassing criticism of contemporary Spain. Every facet of Spanish life — religion, pedagogy, politics, philosophy, sociology, etc. — was criticized. This group of young Spanish writers, influenced perhaps by the tragic outcome of the war, was forced to view its world through the same critical lenses used by Joyce, Proust, Mann, Camus, Silone, Faulkner, and Hemingway.

More important for placing Baroja within the currents of literature, the novel of his day, especially, is the consideration of the answer given by each artist to the hopeless and dying world that surrounded him. R. W. B. Lewis has set up a useful dichotomy between the answers given by what he calls the first generation — Proust, Thomas Mann, Virginia Woolf — and the second generation: Moravia, Camus, Pietro Spina, Faulkner. The difference pointed out between the two generations gives insight into one of the basic directions and purposes of Baroja's novels. Referring to the first generation, Lewis states, "For the latter, perhaps the simplest adjective would be 'artistic.'"[11] For the second generation his key adjective is quite different:

> But for the world of Silone and Camus, of Faulkner and Moravia and Greene and Malraux, perhaps the best single word is "human." It is a world in which the chief experience has been the discovery of what it means to be a human being and to be alive.[12]

Lewis points out just what form this humanity takes in each individual author and work. In each of the novelists of the second generation, the answer to the dying, negative world that surrounds him is a human

---

(A) Unid, pues, el grito de pasión de Echegaray al sentimentalismo subversivo de Campoamor y a la visión de realidad de Galdós, y tendréis los factores de un estado de conciencia que había de encarnar en la generación de 1898.[8]

(B) Un espíritu de protesta, de rebeldía, animaba a la juventud de 1898. Ramiro de Maeztu escribía impetuosos y ardientes artículos, en los que se derruían los valores tradicionales y se anhelaba una España nueva, poderosa.[9]

(C) Por muy singulares que sean estas actitudes individuales, todas ellas se asemejan en una nota fundamental: todas comienzan negativamente, por una violenta repulsa de la vida histórica española entonces en curso.[10]

answer. In Moravia the thing that gives meaning and humanity to such meaningless and inhuman things as money and politics is *eros;* in Ignazio Silone's works it is the power of human sympathy.

For the moment three observations can be made about Lewis' appraisal of these six authors. First, their worlds are still essentially pessimistic and retain a close relationship to death. Second, out of their negative and dying cosmos springs a hopeful reaffirmation of humanity and a sense of the meaning and direction one may give to life. Third, these reaffirmations are not all-encompassing but rather minute and carefully delimited values that have been salvaged meticulously from the chaos of the nihilistic ambients created by the authors.

These three observations could apply partially to the Generation of 98. Principally because of their spiritual origins, the worlds created by the literary artists of the Generation of 98 — by artists in different media as well, if one considers the painting of Zuloaga and others — could not be worlds of vital optimism. These creators began by criticizing many aspects of Spanish life; they sought new, more real values or a reaffirmation of the old. Out of their negative worlds come new values or old ones reaffirmed. These values and reaffirmations seem more carefully selected and more stringently delimited, as are those of the second generation mentioned by Lewis.

Criticism in Spanish letters has not pointed out all these new values and reaffirmations of the generations, but it is safe and reasonable to mention a few that have received notice from the very beginning. In keeping with the selectivity and delimitation already mentioned, some of the members of this generation have been noted for their interest in and keenly poetic portrayal of the minutiae of Spanish existence. With the broad concepts of Spain's *raison d'être* undergoing criticism and reevaluation, Valbuena Prat points out that many of these writers turned toward less grandiose, more immediate, and perhaps more tangible things for the substance of their literary creations.

In the face of an affirmative position towards the Spanish past and present, and the tendency toward generalization of commonplaces in the novel and criticism, one attunes his sensibilities to small details, to intimate self-communion, and adopts a critical attitude toward the Spanish problem.[13] (A)

One of the most positive of the new values and affirmations is the rediscovery of the Spanish landscape which becomes an integral part of the existence of the men of 98.[14]

Furthermore, an intimate and binding relationship exists between the negative dying worlds created by these authors and the very process of the artist's creativity. In all the novelists mentioned, and in many more of the twentieth century, the paralytic, agonizing world seems to become more than just the substance with which they must work or choose to work. This world seems to become inextricably part of their creative *modus operandi,* a part of the style and form, as well as of the background. It is not difficult to observe many suggestive instances of indivisibility of form and content in the works of these writers. A glance of their vocabularies may suggest the possible validity of the conjecture. A few lines from one of Joyce's short stories in *Dubliners,* called "A Painful Case," indicate the role reiterative negation plays in the formal aspects of his prose.

He had neither companions nor friends, church nor creed. He lived his spiritual life without any communion with others, visiting his relatives at Christmas and escorting them to the cemetery when they died. He performed these two social duties for old dignity's sake but conceded nothing further to the conventions which regulate the civic life. He allowed himself to think that in certain circumstances he would rob his bank but, as these circumstances never arose, his life rolled out evenly — an adventureless tale.[15]

Carlos Baker has pointed out another use of negation in the creative technique of Ernest Hemingway.

Several other stories among the first forty-five — perhaps most notably the one called "A Way You'll Never Be" — engage the *nada*-concept. And whoever tries the experiment of reading "Big Two-Hearted River" immediately after "A Clean Well-Lighted Place" may discover, perhaps to his astonishment, that the *nada*-concept really serves as a frame for what is ostensibly one of Hemingway's happiest stories.[16]

In the Generation of 98 there are more definite guides to link the writers' negative conception of the world to the literary form of the conception. Hans Jeschke has outlined many of the negativistic attitudes of the Generation of 98 as reflected in the formal aspects of its literature. One such attitude is the rejection of the traditional Spanish sentence with its complex subordinate clauses and concomitant logical connectors. This was replaced by the simple or the coordinated sentence.[17] The vocabulary of the generation was specifically and drastically affected. Members of the generation often used an unintensified series of commas to produce a steady monotonous intonation. They were drawn irresistibly to negative words, words indicating the decadent, the crumbling, the infirm.[18] The frequent use of colors, principally black, white, and yellow, to suggest sadness and decadence, is another indication of the workings of this pessimism on author vocabulary.[19] In conclusion Hans Jeschke states:

(A) Frente a una posición afirmativa ante el pasado y presente españoles, y una tendencia a la generalización de tópicos en la novela y la crítica, se afina una sensibilidad del pequeño detalle, del íntimo recogimiento, y una postura crítica ante el problema español.[13]

Therefore the generation's abandonment of the traditional construction of sentences which, especially oriented towards a strong Latin syntax by Renaissance influences, was characterized by its artistic connecting words and phrases and its complex dependent clauses, didn't remain merely a theory but became a reality which they practiced. From a stylistic-esthetic point of view, the fact that the writers of 98 preferred the paratactic construction of sentences and avoided complex formations led to a new art of sentence construction typical of the generation. The sentences are no longer developed, as in the "pure Spanish style," in a well-balanced form with a pompously bombastic tone, but sometimes short and sometimes long, they follow one another in rapid and energetic succession and produce the strongest physic and rhythmic effects with their simple and uniform structure.[20] (A)

Because the strong feeling of death and negation in Baroja's novels relates him closely to other novelists of his century and more particularly to his fellow members of the Generation of 98, it seems worthwhile to search out and to study carefully and define the other tendencies common to the other writers of his day.

These writers were seeking an answer to what appeared to them as the inhuman chaos of their times. Their artistic creations, to a large degree, have been this answer. Spread falteringly and sporadically, but nevertheless penetratingly, throughout their works, in most cases is a *human* answer to the inhumanity that they felt surrounded them. Even those works that don't give an answer as such, those filled with nihilism and inhumanity, cry out for a touch of humanity they do not or cannot possess. In some of these authors the answer takes a somewhat concrete and almost definable form; in others it remains esoterically ineffable. The answers frequently appear to be fractional; the human or esthetic values established in their works seem to be disconnected, minute, piecemeal, and without order. The values salvaged from the nihilistic cosmos of this generation seem to be flickerings of human truth that reflect a mere hope of man's salvation rather than a dogmatic assurance.

In none of these writers has the answer been given in capital letters on every page. In some cases, through a combination of careful study, appraisal, and intuition, the answer has been discovered and at least partially defined, although the nature of the problem tenaciously resists reduction and definition. Baroja too may have given a positive answer enveloped in the nihilistic world he created. The fact that Baroja's positive answer is not evident at first glance makes the effort to discover it more interesting and challenging.

The consideration of negation, not only as a basic element in the content of artistic works of our century, but also as a vital and directing force in their formal aspects (style and technique) is highly suggestive. Such critics as Carlos Baker and Hans Jeschke have prepared the way for more intense investigation of this in one twentieth century writer. Baroja stands almost without paragon in his ability to write pessimistic lines, create nihilistic orbs, and to people them with quasi nonentities. The scope and penetration of his pessimism, the almost flawless consistency of his rejection of everything and everybody, makes his art potentially a rich field for such investigation. Paradoxically, the extremity of his negation almost assures finding the concealed positive. The systematic damnation of all ideologies presupposes some hidden spark of an ideal.

Negation as a key to the understanding of a literary art is not without literary precedent in Spanish letters. Américo Castro in his chapter on "El judío en la literatura y pensamiento‑españoles" suggests that the fundamental bitterness, lack of true faith, pessimistic attitude, and the desperate existence of the converted Jewish man of letters determined the form of his artistic production.[21]

The predilection for a negative, failing world is clearly marked in many of the contemporary novelists of Spain, who in several ways followed in Baroja's steps. The Madrid of 1942 represented in Camilo José Cela's novel *La colmena* is clearly such a world. This land also is peopled with quasi entities who spend the dead hours thinking " . . . vaguely, about that world that, alas! wasn't what it could have been, about that world in which everything has been slowly failing, without anybody being able to explain it, probably because of some insignificant little thing."[22] (B)

Many contemporary novels draw the greater part of their substance and their complete artistic ambience from nonpositive sources of Spanish life. To be counted among these are such works as *Nada* by Carmen Laforet, *Las últimas horas* by José Suárez Carreño and *La noria* by Luis Romero.[23]

Because the negative factor plays an important role in the contem-

---

(A) Por consiguiente, no siguió siendo mera teoría, sino que se realizó prácticamente, como acabo de mostrarlo, el abandono que hizo la generación de 1898 de la tradicional construcción de períodos que, especialmente orientada con fuerte sentido latino por las influencias renacentistas, se caracterizaba por sus artísticos encadenamientos y oraciones dependientes complejas. Desde un punto de vista estético-estilístico, el hecho de que los noventayochistas, prefirieran la construcción paratáctica de los períodos y eludieran las formaciones oracionales complicadas, condujo a una nueva tectónica de las oraciones típica de ellos. Las oraciones ya no se desarrollaban, como en el "estilo castizo," en una forma bien equilibrada de acento ampulosamente patético, sino que se siguen unas a otras ya más breves, ya más largas, en un cambio a veces rápido y enérgico y producen los más fuertes efectos anímicos y rítmicos con su estructura uniforme y sencilla.[20]

(B) " . . . vagamente, en ese mundo que, ¡ay!, no fué lo que pudo haber sido, en ese mundo en el que todo ha ido fallando poco a poco, sin que nadie se lo explicase, a lo mejor por una minucia insignificante."[22]

porary novels of Spain, Pérez Minik lists it as a primary requirement for the novelist:

> We have already repeated several times, in the course of this debate, that the novel in order to be authentic must say "no" to the world that surrounds it. This "no" lends credence to its existence and individuality, force to the incitements received and reality to the critical answers emitted.[24]

Baroja assuredly is one of that group of writers who, as the first step in his creative process, said "no" to the world around him.

2. *Style*

COMPARISON OF A PAGE of prose written by one of Baroja's contemporaries and a page of prose by Baroja points the direction his prose style will take. Comparison and study in this chapter will be limited to certain formal and rather traditional aspects of style such as rhythm, vocabulary, sonority of words, figures of speech, syntax, sentences, and paragraphs.[1]

The comparison also indicates partially the devices used by Baroja and the devices he rejects in order to achieve his highly personal and individualistic style. A selection from one of Ricardo León's novels was chosen here because León's ideas about writing were diametrically opposed to those held by Baroja and many members of the Generation of 98. Ricardo León tried to imitate the style of the writers of the Golden Age of Spanish literature, as he states in his prologue to *El amor de los amores.*

And although it may not be in keeping with the humility of my project, already in an advanced stage, of coming out with a book of this kind — outside modern taste, contrary to the ideas and customs in use, cordial enemy of what they call life and art — I am pleased to have recourse to the canons and pragmatic sanctions of the Muses, taking for light, authority, and delightful company that of those greatest of all poets of the Golden Age who coined their medals in pure gold, in that noble metal of the language of Castile, so hard and so resistant to vile thoughts, so harmonious and soft for the divine die of chaste thoughts.[2] (A)

(A) Y aunque no se ajuste a la humildad mi propósito, llevado ya muy adelante, de salir con un libro de este jaez, fuera de los gustos modernos, contrario a las ideas y hábitos en uso, enemigo cordial de lo que llaman ahora vida y arte, soy servido de acogerme a los fueros y pragmáticas de las Musas, tomando por luz y autoridad y sabrosa compañía las de aquellos altísimos poetas del siglo de oro que en oro puro acuñaron sus medallas, en este noble metal de la lengua de Castilla, tan duro y tan rebelde a pensamientos viles, tan armonioso y blando para el troquel divino de los castos pensamientos.[2]

The selection that follows is from Ricardo León's *Casta de hidalgos.*

A *fellow countryman* of *Gil Blas, dreamer, rebel, poet,* and *lover,* was Jesús de Ceballos, a *young man* of *handsome cast, tall* in *stature, lean* of *limb,* and *grave* in *speech.* He had dark pale skin, big flashing eyes, an *aquiline* nose, a humid and sensual mouth, and a *proud head* with *romantic locks.* He was the son of a *mountain nobleman* — one of those *firstborn sons* that still exist, *carved out of the old stone,* in the far corners of Cantabria — *said nobleman* lived, *for many long years,* in his *ancestral home* in Santillana, forgotten by the world. Jesús, born and educated in that silent village, his thoughts nurtured by *ancient memories,* and his fantasy by *books* of *adventure,* began to culti- vate slowly the desire to see new things, to *let his spirit soar freely, like a lark,* and flee from that tomb of the dead and the living where he *leisurely dwelled.* That night he put his thought in practice, furtively *abandoning* the village and leaving behind him the *calm* serenity of his home to ride at will over *distant lands.*

It was a balmy and peaceful night, a summer night in Asturias de Santi- llana. *Mounted on a diminutive nag,* Jesús went along, his heart *spurred* on by his eagerness to see the adventures he *had dreamed* of become a reality. Although he was riding alone along the deserted road, with no other *arms* than an old pistol, nor more *money* than thirty poorly counted silver coins, enough to frighten away any anxiety were his *few years* and that *wild young madness* that had launched him upon *unknown roads,* leaving behind his *soft* and *idle* bed *to ride up one trail and down another.*[3] (A)

The following selection is taken from Pío Baroja's *Zalacaín el Aven- turero.*

In this country house Martín Zalacaín de Urbía, the one who later was to be called Zalacaín el Aventurero, was born and spent the first years of his childhood; in this country house he dreamed his first dreams and tore his first britches.

The Zalacaín family lived a few steps from Urbía; but neither Martín nor his family belonged there; their house was a few yards outside the village.

Martín's father was a farmer, a somber man and not very talkative, he was killed by a smallpox epidemic; neither was Martín's mother a woman of character; she lived in normal psychological obscurity among the country people, and went from a maiden to a wife, and from a wife to a widow with complete unconsciousness. When her husband died she was left with two children, Martín and a young girl called Ignacia.

The farm house where the Zalacaíns lived belonged to the Ohando family, Urbía's most ancient, aristocratic, and richest family.

Martín's mother lived almost on charity from the Ohando family.

Under these wretched and poverty-stricken conditions, it seemed logical that, because of his inheritance and the action of his environment, Martín would be like his father and mother: somber, timid, and humble; but the young man turned out to be determined, fearless, and audacious.[4] (B)

There is a sharp opposition between the two styles. The respective vocabularies of the two authors form opposites. The words that Ricardo León uses, Baroja avoids. Ricardo León's passage seems a study in tradi- tional Spanish rhetoric and figures of speech; Baroja's passage seems an effort toward a precise and graphic use of the language of the street. Ricardo León's syntax and grammatical usage seem carved and elaborated after the fashion of what he believes to be traditional Spanish prose. His sentences are long, with many parenthetical expressions and subordinations. Baroja's sentences are shorter, and there is a definite preference for coordination over subordination and parenthetical expressions. Closely related to the difference in syntax is the difference in the cadence, rhythm,

---

(A) *Compatriota* de *Gil Blas, soñador, rebelde, poeta* y *enamorado,* era Jesús de Ceballos un *mozo* de *gallarda estampa, alto de estatura, enjuto de miembros, grave de expresión.* Tenía la tez morena y pálida, los ojos grandes y ardientes, la nariz *aguileña,* la boca húmeda y sensual y una *altiva cabeza de melenas románticas.* Era hijo de un *hidalgo montañés* — uno de esos *mayorazgos* que aun quedan, *tallados en viejo pedernal,* en los rincones de Cantabria —, *el cual hidalgo* vivía, de *luengos años,* en su *casa solariega* de *Santillana,* olvidado del mundo. Nacido y educado Jesús en aquella villa silenciosa, nutrido el pensamiento de *antiguas memorias* y *excitada* la fantasía con *libros de aventuras,* fué poco a poco cultivando el deseo de ver cosas nuevas, *de echar el alma a volar, como una alondra,* y huir de aquel sepulcro de muertos y vivos en que *moraba ocioso.* Aquella noche había puesto en práctica su pensamiento, *saliendo* hurtadamente de la villa y dejando el *blando* sosiego de su casa para cabalgar a su gusto *tierras adelante.*
Era la noche templada y apacible, noche de verano en las Asturias de Santillana. *Jinete en menguado rocín* iba Jesús, *espoleado* su corazón por el ansia de ver realizadas sus *soñadas aventuras.* Aunque iba solo por la desierta carretera, sin más *armas* que una vieja pistola, ni más *dineros* que treinta duros mal contados, bastaban para ahuyentar toda zozobra sus *pocos años* y *aquella brava locura juvenil* que le lanzaba a *ignorados caminos,* dejando el *blando* y *ocioso lecho* para *correr por trochas* y *veredas.*[3]

(B) En este caserío nació y pasó los primeros años de su infancia Martín Zalacain de Urbía, el que más tarde había de ser llamado Zalacain el Aventurero; en este caserío soñó sus primeras aventuras y rompió los primeros pantalones.
Los Zalacain vivían a pocos pasos de Urbía; pero ni Martín ni su familia eran ciudadanos: faltaba a su casa unos metros para formar parte de la villa.
El padre de Martín fué labrador, un hombre oscuro y poco comunicativo, muerto en una epidemia de viruelas; la madre de Martín tampoco era mujer de carácter; vivió en esa oscuridad psicológica normal entre la gente del campo, y pasó de soltera a casada, y de casada a viuda, con absoluta inconsciencia. Al morir su marido quedó con dos hijos, Martín y una niña menor llamada Ignacia.
El caserío donde habitaban los Zalacain pertenecía a la familia de Ohando, familia la más antigua, aristocrática y rica de Urbía.
Vivía la madre de Martín casi de la misericordia de los Ohando.
En tales condiciones de pobreza y de miseria, parecía lógico que, por herencia y por la acción del ambiente, Martín fuese como su padre y su madre; oscuro, tímido y apocado; pero el muchacho resultó decidido, temerario y audaz.[4]

and intonational patterns of the two prose selections. Baroja's paragraphs are short, and Ricardo León's are long. Ricardo León's prose exudes a vitality, a varied intonational pattern, a ringing sonority, an assertative conclusiveness, while Baroja's prose seems flat, sometimes inconclusive, and almost without inflection.

In short, Ricardo León's prose is the result of a long and careful study and assimilation of what he considers classic Spanish literature, and an attempt to recreate, to give new life to this rich tradition.

A comparison of the respective vocabularies of the two authors, immediately bears out certain factors. Ricardo León's vocabulary shows a tremendous predilection for four constellations of words and phrases: words and phrases dealing with patriotism, such as *compatriota;* names of literary figures and places, such as *Gil Blas, Santillana;* words and phrases lifted from Spain's literary tradition, such as *soñador, poeta, mozo de gallarda estampa, melenas románticas, tallados, enjuto, luengos, solariega, moraba, como una alondra, cabalgar;* words that have an artistic flavor such as *gallarda, grave, altiva, hidalgo, montañés, mayorazgos, armas.*[5]

To show the preponderance of all these words, they have been italicized where they appear in the Spanish text. Although some of them do not have the indicated connotation apart from the text, they all do have it, within the text. In essence, all the words in the quoted passage fall into one or more of these four categories.

Furthermore, Ricardo León's prose shows a certain delight in the beauty and sonority of words, a certain faith in their intrinsic worth. It reflects the attitude that these words carry within themselves a creative potential and a somewhat immortal vital reality. It reflects a belief in words as such.

Baroja quite evidently avoids these four constellations of words. "Those words," he states in his *Discurso de ingreso en la Academia Española,* May 12, 1934 (and he could well be referring to those words used by Ricardo León), "those words that screech and whose use for some constitutes the desideratum of literature, produce a very disagreeable and grotesque effect for me."[6] Baroja's attitude toward the literary lexicon of the past, commonly called *lenguaje castizo,* although by far the most extreme, is shared by Valle-Inclán and others of his own generation.

> For many years now, day by day, in that which concerns me I have been at work digging a hole to bury this hollow and pompous Castilian prose which can no longer be ours when we write, if we feel the demands of the hour. Apparently, such a manner still exists because we look at words as if they were shrines and not living souls. We love them more and they seem more beautiful to us when they preserve bones and ashes.[7] (A)

Azorín joins Baroja and Valle-Inclán in their criticism of *el lenguaje castizo* or pure Spanish:

Among the majority of those given to literature — not among true artists — it is believed that a style is pure Spanish when it is shaped by turns of phrase, words, and expressions of the writers of three or four centuries ago. Such an idea, in turn, implies another: the idea that languages do not evolve, that they don't progress.

Sensibility evolves and language evolves; if we were to admit the concept of pure Spanish that we are censuring, the Castilian language would have stopped centuries ago.[8] (B)

Baroja declares that he has always had a poor memory for the sound of words. "En la infancia tenía una buena memoria de cosas vistas, pero mala para palabras oídas."[9] The sound of words or their musicality is of no importance to Baroja.[10] They are all too often a cover for a vacuum of ideas and feelings. "The literary novice learns words and turns of phrase before he has ideas or impressions and wants to write to have the pleasure of using them and of hearing them sound in the air."[11] (C)

If Baroja feels that certain words have no intrinsic value and are of no use to him in his writing, he feels even more strongly about their use in the vital affairs of life.

The span, the structuralization, the volume of events, the horizontality of life, the eçumenical factor, vertical syndicalism, astronomic sums . . . All that, which might give a vague impression, if it were dealing with literary and subjective matters wouldn't be important, but when it deals with vital questions it produces confusion, a sort of mystic and obscure haze which gives things false perspective and presents concepts which aren't concepts and justifies the unjustifiable. This reminds one of the sentence by Feliciano de Silva, quoted in *Don Quijote:* "The reason of the non reason that is my reason

---

(A) Desde hace muchos años, día a día, en aquello que me atañe yo trabajo cavando la cueva donde enterrar esta hueca y pomposa prosa castiza, que ya no puede ser la nuestra cuando escribamos, si sentimos el imperio de la hora. Aparentemente, tal manera perdura porque miramos las palabras como si fuesen relicarios y no corazones vivos: Las amamos más, y nos parecen más bellas cuando guardan huesos y cenizas.[7]

(B) Entre la generalidad de los afectos a cosas literarias — no entre los verdaderos artistas — se cree que un estilo es castizo cuando se plasma sobre giros, voces, maneras de decir de los escritores de hace tres o cuatro siglos. Tal idea implica otra a su vez: la de que las lenguas no evolucionan, no marchan. . . .

Evoluciona la sensibilidad y evoluciona el lenguage; de admitir el concepto de casticismo que censuramos, el idioma castellano se hubiera detenido hace siglos.[8]

(C) "Este literato novicio aprende nombres y giros antes de tener ideas o impresiones y quiere escribir para tener el gusto de emplearlos y para que suenen en el aire."[11]

presents itself in such a manner that my reason weakens, that with good reason I complain of your beauty."[12] (A)

In the same essay he denies the intrinsic value of neologisms (non-scientific ones, of course) and of the renovation of the lexicon.[13] "The lexicon was renewed, but the ideas weren't. The idea that all you have to do to modify ideas is to change the words is pure fantasy."[14] (B) Baroja seems to believe that the sound and the orthography may vary but the idea and the substance remain the same.

Many passages in Baroja's novels point out the intangibility and the arbitrariness of words. In *Aurora roja,* Juan has taken Manuel, Salvadora, Canuto, and others to a *merendero*. The owner, symbolic of the atmosphere of the place and of all of Madrid, has greeted them with these words:

> Gentlemen: I am the master of this establishment, in which you have taken a seat so intimate and you will be served nourishment with good condiment, for here there is good sentiment although little ornament, and if one thirst after merriment he will be brought refreshment, so have a look at this document — and he showed a list of prices — and let's get on with the action.[15] (C)

In the same novel Manuel, upon hearing a speech by an anarchist called Caruty, suspects that there exists some strange relationship between revolutions, anarchy, and literature. "¡Anarquía! ¡Literatura! Manuel encontraba una relación entre estas dos cosas; pero no sabía cuál."[16] In this passage Baroja indicates that revolutions, anarchy, and literature are related because they are all composed of words.

Baroja is fully aware of the fact that certain words when used constantly and indiscriminately lose their power and meaning.

> Today, thanks to the diligence of the Director of the Editorial Society in the publication of perfectly useless scientific and literary works, and aided by the young artist Videgain, we can give the public a resume of the interesting (that's the word used for everything) work by Doctor Guezurtegui.[17] (D)

The word *interesante,* as illustrated by the passage, has lost its power.[18]

Baroja also believes that adjectives are not especially precise.

> The same thing happens to adjectives; they carry beforehand and in a veiled manner an idea of praise or disdain, but they are never the result of a judgment that is clear and without passion.
> Believing the contrary is for me the error of all dogmatic persons. Human sentiments don't have a clear and definite label in our language. Definitions and adjectives are no more than approximations.[19] (E)

Baroja feels that adjectives, besides being approximations, depend almost entirely on the person who utters them. He illustrates the point with the character Afsaguin in *El mundo es ansí.*

Afsaguin came up to Sacha and warmly praised his ape-like friend, said that he was a true Russian and a true socialist.

Since this praise coming from Afsaguin had become a constant commonplace they didn't pay much attention to his friend.[20] (F)

Intention is the most important factor in determining the true meaning and significance of adjectives according to Baroja.

Baroja pays little heed to the etymology of words. He believes it has little significance in regard to their present meaning. Usage is what interests him. He categorically states in one of his essays called *Arbitrariedad y*

(A) La envergadura, la estructuración, el volumen de los acontecimientos, la horizontalidad en la vida, lo ecuménico, el sindicalismo vertical, las cifras astronómicas . . . Todo esto, que da una impresión vigorosa, si se tratara de cuestiones subjetivas y literarias, no tendría importancia, pero tratándose de cuestiones vitales produce una confusión, una especie de bruma oscura y mística que da falsas perspectivas a las cosas y presenta conceptos que no son conceptos y justifica lo no justificable. Esto le recuerda a uno la frase de Feliciano de Silva, citada en *Don Quijote*: «La razón de la sinrazón que a mi razón se hace de tal manera mi razón enflaquece, que con razón me quejo de la vuestra fermosura.»[12]

(B) "Se renovó el léxico, pero no se renuevan las ideas. Eso de que basta que cambien las palabras para que se modifiquen las ideas es una fantasía."[14]

(C) Señores: soy el amo de este establecimiento, en donde han tomado ustedes asiento y se les servirá el alimento con un buen condimento, que aquí hay muy buen sentimiento, aunque poco ornamento, y si alguno está sediento, se le traerá un refrescamiento; conque vean este documento — y enseñó una lista de los precios — y ande el movimiento.[15]

(D) Hoy, gracias a la diligencia del director de la Sociedad Editorial para la impresión de los trabajos científicos y literarios perfectamente inútiles, y ayudados por el joven artista Videgaín, podemos dar al público un resumen del interesante (es la palabra que sirve para todo) trabajo del doctor Guezurtegui.[17]

(E) Así pasa con todos los calificativos; llevan de antemano y de una manera velada una idea de elogio o de desdén, pero no son resultado de un juicio limpio y sin pasión.

El creer lo contrario es para mí el error de todos los dogmáticos. Los sentimientos humanos no tienen en el lenguaje una etiqueta clara y definitiva. Las definiciones y los calificativos no son más que aproximaciones.[19]

(F) Afsaguin se acercó a Sacha e hizo un elogio caluroso de su simiesco amigo, de quien dijo que era un verdadero ruso y un verdadero socialista.

Como este elogio en boca de Afsaguin se había convertido en un lugar común constante, no hicieron del amigo mucho caso.[20]

estilización found in *Vitrina pintoresca* that, "Estas puerilidades etimoló-gicas no demuestran gran cosa."[21]

Baroja never resorted to what he considered cheap words to elicit erotic responses. Although he made no big issue of that practice in his critical writings, his works are almost completely devoid of the sensation-arousing terms that seem to be so necessary to many of his fellow writers of this century. José M. Salaverría, in an article published in the *A B C* of Madrid, pointed out a constant restraint in the use of erotic words by Baroja. He speaks of the restraint in these delicate matters as *el pudor vasco.*[22] Although Salaverría's article was written in 1935, Baroja remained true to this code of writing throughout his novelistic career.

Baroja's cry echos Hamlet — words, words, words. In *La caverna del humorismo,* Savage, maddened by the tremendous pedantry, repeats the cry: "Nature capriciously makes men gelastic or agelastic. There are also hypergelastic men — words, words, words — murmurs Savage, like Hamlet."[23]

Comparison of León's and Baroja's writing shows how León has exaggerated oratorical and rhetorical tones, and how Baroja has tried to avoid such tones, or at least to subdue them markedly. Rejecting much of Spanish rhetoric in the formation of his style, Baroja, in his *Divagaciones apasionadas,* explains and justifies this rejection. "It is not strange that I have abominated oratory and rhetoric in a country like Spain, super-saturated with a rhetoric that does not let it see reality."[24]

A continuous preoccupation with avoiding rhetoric is found in Baroja's essays and also throughout his novels. In *El mundo es ansí,* Sacha, worthy of a better fate, is wooed and won by mere empty words, by rhetoric:

Sacha let herself get carried away by Nature's charm and by the charm of words.
There is in love, as in everything expressed by human lips, a skillful and artificial rhetoric which gives signs of life to that which is dead and a brilliant aspect to that which is opaque.[25] (A)

Baroja's characters often profess a dislike for *el tono mayor,* or rhetoric. Larrañaga, in *Los amores tardíos,* confesses a liking for the modest and the unpretentious, even in regard to women. "Naturally, because you look at it from a woman's point of view; you prefer an elevated style, but I don't."[26] Arcelu, in *El mundo es ansí,* expresses a dislike reflecting Baroja's for pure verbiage, rhetoric, and obscurity for obscurity's sake.

"Yes," he was saying the other day — "one keeps looking for the truth, keeps feeling hate for wordiness, for exaggeration, for everything that brings obscurity to ideas. One would like to squeeze the language, cut it down, reduce it to its quintessence, to something algebraic; one would like to suppress every-thing superfluous, all the flab, all the excess foliage."[27] (B)

Ortega y Gasset praises the absence of rhetoric in Baroja's style and his refusal to imitate others in *El espectador.*[28] Further comparison of León's and Baroja's syntax and León's preoccupation with grammatical niceties demonstrates a marked contrast. Unlike León, Baroja does not have much respect for strict adherence to grammatical rules. He and others have had a great deal to say about his disrespect for the sacred idol, grammar. In a letter to Federico García-Sanchiz, Baroja writes:

> Therefore, in everything I write there will always be a touch of sadness and a couple of insults to grammar. I don't dominate all the means of expression and I always tend, by temperament, to say things graphically and without adornment.[29]

Baroja states at the beginning of *Las inquietudes de Shanti Andía,* "Besides, like a good Basque I have always been just a little disrespectful to that respectable and chaste lady they call grammar." [30]

Emilio Carrere referred to Baroja's antigrammatical qualities in this manner, "Visions of a little misogynous and misanthropic burgher, with the paradoxical soul of a vagabond, stumbling at times through grammar and at catch-as-catch-can with rhetoric." [31]

Baroja's syntax, along with his grammar, has been the subject of many comments.

> Critics have quibbled with Baroja's syntax and language. We have seen that sometimes he does give new meanings to his words or at least slightly different meanings. In this event, he has the excuse of being only one of many. But must one really accept as carelessness, such sentences as: don't call
> — For luck is cruel to me! — Or did he introduce them deliberately to see what the pedants would say about them?[32]

Ignacio de Areilza, Cristóbal de Castro, and Peseux-Richard are among the many who have praised Pío Baroja for consistent rejection of the traditional Spanish sentence. Ignacio de Areilza quotes from Baroja's own character, Doctor Guezurtegui: "That sentence," he says, "always cut in the same way, in which a number of parenthetical phrases are

---

(A) Sacha se dejaba llevar por el encanto de la Naturaleza y por el encanto de las palabras.

Hay en el amor, como en todo lo que se expresa con labios humanos, una retórica hábil y artificiosa que da apariencias de vida a lo que está muerto y aspecto de brillantez a lo que es opaco.[25]

(B) —Sí — decía él el otro día —, uno va buscando la verdad, va sintiendo el odio por la palabrería, por la hipérbole, por todo lo que lleva oscuridad a las ideas. Uno quisiera estrujar el idioma, recortarlo, reducirlo a su quinta esencia, a una cosa algebraica; quisiera uno suprimir todo lo superfluo, toda la carnaza, toda la hojarasca.[27]

mounted and which always ends in a theatrical manner, depresses me,"
and adds his own criticism:

> Reading this automatically brings to mind that eagerness to swell end-
> lessly the sentence or to give it exaggerated dimensions, that hail of adjec-
> tives, that external high-flown language and musical thrilling, so much in favor
> with so many Spanish novelists, that it has reached a more than annoying
> degree in some.[33]

Following the same procedure, Cristóbal de Castro quotes from Baroja:
"The author" — he says in *The Wax Figures* — "rejects the pure Spanish
sentence, the idiomatic turn of phrase. All this undoubtedly strikes him
as excess foliage, a putrified commonplace, something pestiferous from
which one must flee." Then he comments, "And, actually, his sentence
is rapid, brusque, intermittent. The turn of phrase, hurried, invertebrate,
reportesque, authentic writing as the pen moves, without reflection. Baroja
prefers naturalness to finesse; sacrifices exactitude to vividness."[34] Peseux-
Richard states: "No rhetoric, no display of empty eloquence. Not one of
these ready-made phrases which stud the periods of the best Spanish
writers and which, clinging to the thought, are carried along by it and
hinder its expression.[35]

Reading the selections from León and Baroja aloud demonstrates
that the difference in the pattern of the sentences and the paragraphs causes
an even greater difference in the rhythm and moving speed of the prose.
Ricardo León's sentences, being long and complex, flow smoothly, easily,
and assuredly, rising gracefully to the intonational peaks at the end of
the inconclusive subordinate clauses and falling decisively at the end
of the conclusive clauses. The rhythm of these sentences is not slow or
tortuous but rather steady, flowing, and musical. Baroja's sentences are
short; most of them are simple sentences or independent clauses connected by a semicolon.[36] The many abrupt stops, occasioned by the
periods and the semicolons, cause his prose to move with a somewhat
punchy and telegraphic rapidity.[37]

Baroja considers this restless, uneven rapidity of his prose one of its
salient qualities. In *Juventud, egolatría* he enlightens those who attribute
the peculiar flavor of his prose to the lack of grammatical knowledge or to
a Basque syntax.

> Principally what I lack in order to write Castilian isn't pure grammatical
> correction nor is it syntax. It is the timing, the rhythm of style. This is what
> disturbs one who reads my works for the first time; he notices something that
> doesn't sound right, and a manner of breathing that isn't traditional.[38]

The rapidity of movement in Baroja's prose is, in a sense, a rejection
of the literary tradition of lingering upon certain subjects. Baroja refuses
to dwell upon any one phase or subject. He seems to have only a certain
amount of time for each character presentation, each description, each

narrative episode. None of these individual parts swell with importance; none seem lulled or static. All parts of Baroja's novel are subject to the dynamic movement of his brisk sentences and paragraphs. His style has been likened by Juan de la Encina to the rapid flame of Jamaican rum that licks at everything but never seems to slowly devour or turn its objects into ashes.[39]

Jean Cassou considers this rapidity a curse to Baroja's style, an act of desperation and an indication of emptiness. "In reality, the velocity which circulates through one of Baroja's novels leaves a painful impression of emptiness, and in regard to novelistic invention it is nothing more than an act of desperation."[40]

Ramón Sender also becomes impatient with Baroja's rapidity.[41] Julio Laborde, in an article that appeared in the *Comoedia* of Paris, thinks it is pernicious. He feels that Pío Baroja has tried, rather unsuccessfully, to imitate Pierre Loti. "But his own sentence, so short, so contrary to Spanish style, where did he find the model, if not in Pierre Loti. What am I saying? The short verbless sentences of Pierre Loti are, at times, less rapid than Baroja's complete ones."[42]

Most critics, however, consider this quickness one of Baroja's greatest virtues and one of the most individual characteristics of his style. ". . . our thought is pleased by the facility and freeness of his expression, and we are drawn into the novelistic farce, because of its realistic tone, with instantaneous rapidity. . . ."[43]

Baroja, in his "Prólogo casi doctrinal sobre la novela" to *La nave de los locos* says: "Heaviness, slowness, slow time cannot be a virtue. Slowness is antibiological and anti-vital."[44] In this rejection of slow-moving prose rhythms, he hints that the justification for his own rapidity is to be found in its vital, biological relationship to himself. He seems to be indicating that a drive within him forces him to perceive life at a certain quick pace and record it thus. His repeated comment "I think that writing is like walking,"[45] emphasizes this point of view.

PURE STYLE

While Baroja's critics usually mark and praise his striving for a more natural mode of communication and his rejection of traditional literary artifices, some of them have exaggerated it, and this exaggeration has hindered complete understanding of Baroja's prose technique. These critics suggest that an exact parallel exists between the man and his expression — the man and his style. They imply that no stylistic device is used, that Baroja, simply does not know how to write, that he doesn't think the business of how one says things is important, and therefore he carelessly flings words, phrases, and sentences at a piece of paper. The promoters and perpetuators of this viewpoint — the writer himself, ironically, is sure to be counted among them — imply that Baroja, through genius, black magic, or just pure orneriness, has been able to create a system of communication all his own which disregards all systematic conventions in expression.[46]

The following anecdote has been cited many times by those who wish to prove that Baroja finds difficulty in saying things correctly and therefore doesn't particularly care how he expresses them. Many writers, including Miguel de Unamuno and Ortega y Gasset, have told the little story. Baroja and Ortega have gone on a hiking excursion in the Sierra de Gata. At night, Baroja looks up from a stack of papers where he is laboring over the exploits of Aviraneta and says,

> You see? There is nothing worse than to start to think about how to say things, you end up losing your mind. I had written here "Aviraneta came down in slippers (*de zapatillas*)," but I asked myself if it is right or wrong, and now I no longer know if I should say "Aviraneta came down in slippers (*de zapatillas*)," or "he came down (*con zapatillas*)," or "he came down (*a zapatillas*)." [47]

This anecdote has given certain critics a great feeling of liberty in their disparaging comments on Baroja's style. Federico García Sanchiz has likened it to an emotional babbling. "With an unfinished style, intense and poor like an emotional babbling, he tells about Sacha, the daughter of a barbarous general of the Czar." [48]

Some critics simply speak of a pure style. Francisco de Miomandre thinks this will speed his hour of recognition in France.

> If you add to this the fact that he possesses a clean incisive, direct style, as pure as crystal, you can't help but conclude as I have that, because he has waited much longer than many many others for his hour of success in French, Pío Baroja perhaps will know it more completely, still more perfectly.[49]

Still others comment on the complete lack of adornment. "Stylistic trappings always grow old faster than the man himself, but Baroja's literary garb doesn't go out of style, because his style is nudity itself." [50] Baroja's own description of natural style becomes a little more complex. He speaks of an absolute parallelism between the psychic movement of ideas, sentiments, and emotions, and the movement of style. This idea, together with the idea that style is a means of self-portrayal, is expressed by Doctor Quezurtegui in *La caverna del humorismo*.

> For me, the absolute in art is to arrive at an absolute parallelism between the psychic movement of ideas, sentiments and emotions, and the movement of style. The more precise this relation is, the better. I believe that here it should be like it is with a portrait: the more it looks like the man being painted, and not how much more beautiful it may be, the better it is as a portrait (not as a work of art).

Thus, the simple, humble, and careless man will reach perfection in a simple, humble, and careless style, and the rhetorical, high-sounding, and gongoristic man in a rhetorical, high-sounding and gongoristic style.[51] (A)

Gregorio Marañón treats this statement as the whole truth of Baroja's stylistic success.

For years now I have had this paragraph marked as the key to Pío Baroja's literary esthetics and, in part, to his psychology; also, as an argument against the nonsense that has circulated about his style, about his lexicon and about his supposed anti-academic attitude. It is evident that Baroja is the same "simple, humble, and careless man" of the words transcribed.[52] (B)

Baroja divides style into two parts: that which is interior and spontaneous and that which is exterior and artificial. "Style, from a psychological point of view, can be of two classes: interior, a spontaneous product of the imagination, of the sensibility, of the temperament of the author or artist that gives form to his ideas and a characteristic nuance to his sensations, and exterior, maneristic, made with artificial and studied formulas."[53] (C)

A friend, Azorín, echoes this idea in the introduction to Baroja's *Obras completas*. "Why isn't a prose that is vital and not fictitious, that is a product of physiology and not of a formula, going to be read?"[54] (D)

(A) Para mí, el *summun* del arte literario es llegar a un paralelismo absoluto entre el movimiento psíquico de ideas, sentimientos y emociones y el movimiento del estilo. Cuanto más exacta sea esta relación, mejor. Yo creo que aquí debe pasar como en un retrato: que es mejor como retrato (no como obra artística) cuanto más se parezca al retratado, no cuanto más bonito esté.

Así, el hombre sencillo, humilde y descuidado, tendrá su perfección en el estilo sencillo, humilde y descuidado, y el hombre retórico, altisonante y gongorino, en el estilo retórico, altisonante y gongorino.[51]

(B) Hace años que tengo anotado este párrafo como clave de la estética literaria de Pío Baroja y, en parte, de su psicología; también, como argumento contra los despropósitos que han venido circulando acerca de su estilo, de su léxico y de su supuesto antiacademicismo. Es evidente que Baroja es el propio «hombre sencillo, humilde y descuidado» de las palabras transcritas.[52]

(C) El estilo, desde un punto de vista psicológico, puede ser de dos clases: interior, producto espontáneo de la imaginación, de la sensibilidad, del temperamento del escritor o del artista que da a sus ideas una forma y reviste sus sensaciones de un matiz característico, y exterior, manierista, hecho con fórmulas artificiales y estudiadas.[53]

(D) "¿Cómo no ha de ser leída una prosa que es vital y no ficticia; que es producto de una fisiología y no de una fórmula?"[54]

All this can be accepted as a poetic description of his style, but it can never be an exact, scientific description. What Baroja feels and desires to express may well be interior and spontaneous, but the expression of these feelings and sensations of the printed page must be achieved through an artifice. There is no natural style, as José Sánchez Rojas claims. "And he lets it glide along thus, smoothly, in a transparent, clear, simple, natural spontaneous style. He writes as if he had been born writing. With Baroja style is nature, not a robe. A theologian would call it a grace.[55] (A)

In the criticism of Edmundo González Blanco there is a flickering of recognition of the fact that Baroja is nursing this legend of the natural, spontaneous style. Blanco admits in an article that appeared in *La Esfera* of Madrid that Baroja is a stylist and that some of the defects of form serve directed and purposeful ends.

> Defects in form? . . . Yes, his work has them and in great numbers. But somehow they are conscious defects, characteristics of a stylist who takes too many liberties with language, because he knows it well enough to abuse it, and who begins by saying that his way of writing isn't the classic or academic but rather the anarchic or romantic which is based upon the imitation of nature without worrying about any rule and interpreting life capriciously.[56] (B)

Peseux-Richard sounds just a note of caution in regard to taking Baroja's pure and antigrammatical style seriously, in the following comment:

> Autodidactic — at least in literary matters — and an irreducible adversary of all restraints and of all rules, such is the immutable physiognomy he will present to our eyes. And that hate for the pedagogue is so alive, Pío Baroja takes advantage of every occasion to emit it with such intimate pleasure, that we would almost be tempted to take him seriously.[57]

In *Paradox, Rey,* a strangely philosophical cyclops, watching the explosion that will flood the valley of Uganga, says that destruction is the first step of creation, that it is, in essence, creation itself. "Destruir es crear."[58] This statement of the anarchist's creed, which seems to be Baroja's creed in many facets of life and especially in regard to novelistic technique, is reiterated many times. The following comes from *La caverna del humorismo*: "Man is like a beaver, like an ant, like a swallow; an animal who builds. He is also destructive. He cannot build without destroying."[59] (C)

Many critics consider rejection to be the essence of Baroja's style. Linking Baroja's lack of stylistic formation to those gentlemen from the provinces, noted for their lack of affectation and superficial elegance, Rafael Sánchez Mazas says, "They have achieved a great style, as one always should, by renouncing the superficial."[60] Morales San Martín, in an article that appeared in *El Mercantil Valenciano,* cursorily mentions the lack of three elements in Baroja's prose: high rhetoric, flowered speech, and musical cadence.[61] Ignacio de Areilza comments on the harsh, brusque, and silenced effect of Baroja's prose.

In regard to external dress — style, Pío Baroja has achieved, except for exceptions of unpleasant brusqueness, his ideal of writing with carefully ground and silent words that do not shine or make a noise when pronounced. He has almost arrived at that admirable impossibility of an unexpected style that can't be imitated because of the force of its personality. He finds himself on the difficult peaks of the natural; he makes his thought flow in common words.[62] (D)

Baroja himself speaks of the process as one of economy of literary artifices. In an interview that appeared in the *Comoedia* of Paris he makes the following statement:

Yes, I have always tried for a rapid expression without adornments and practiced an economy of devices that borders on poverty. This has brought me all kinds of reproaches; I have the reputation of writing badly. Since you have insisted on preserving scrupulously the tone of my style, or of my lack of style, they will accuse you of having translated me poorly, of writing as badly in French as I do in Spanish.[63] (E)

(A) Y la desliza así, suavemente, en un estilo transparente, claro, sencillo, fresco, natural, espontáneo. Escribe como si hubiera nacido escribiendo. El estilo no es en Baroja hábito, sino naturaleza. Un teólogo diría que era gracia.[55]

(B) ¿Defectos de forma? . . . Sí, los tiene la obra, y en gran número. Pero son defectos conscientes en algún modo, rasgos de un estilista que se permite demasiadas libertades con el lenguaje, por conocerlo lo bastante para abusar de él, y que empieza por confesar que su manera de escribir no es la clásica o académica, sino la anárquica o romántica, que estriba en imitar la naturaleza sin preocupación de regla alguna e interpretando la vida a capricho.[56]

(C) "El hombre es como el castor, como la hormiga, como la golondrina: animal de instintos constructores. También es destructor. No se puede construir sin destruir."[59]

(D) En cuanto a la vestidura externa, el estilo, Pío Baroja ha llegado, salvo excepciones de una brusquedad ingrata, a su ideal: a escribir con palabras esmeriladas y silenciosas que no brillasen ni metiesen ruido al pronunciarlas. Casi ha llegado al admirable imposible de un estilo inesperado que no se puede imitar en fuerza de su personalidad. Se encuentra en las difíciles cumbres de lo natural, hace fluir su pensamiento en palabras vulgares, . . .[62]

(E) — Sí, siempre he buscado la expresión rápida y sin adornos y practicado una economía de medios que va hasta la pobreza. Eso me ha valido toda clase de reproches; tengo la reputación de escribir mal. Como usted ha puesto empeño en conservar escrupulosamente el tono de mi estilo, o de mi falta de estilo, le acusarán de haberme traducido mal, de escribir tan mal el francés como yo el español.[63]

In the prologue to *La dama errante* he gives the genesis of his hate for the adornments he rejects.

From this little sympathy for the past, complicated by my lack of idiomatic sense — because of being Basque and my ancestors not having spoken Castilian — the repugnance that rhetorical frills inspire in me comes. Rhetorical frills strike me as adornments of a cemetery, rancid things which smell of death.[64] (A)

SIMILES

Much caution should be used in accepting the creed of destruction as the totality of Baroja's belief and practice in regard to his prose. The fact that Baroja does employ stylistic devices is evidenced in his use of the simile. This means of joining or comparing two objects, or certain qualities of two objects, is probably the most common device found in the Spanish vernacular. This is probably why Baroja finds it inoffensive in his own stylistic designs. The linking words *parece* and *como,* because of the frequency of the simile, become a literary constant in all of Baroja's prose. Two principal types of similes are found throughout Baroja's novels. The first type links that which moves to that which doesn't move, that which is unstable to that which is stable. The second type links human beings to members of the animal kingdom. Here is a list of samples of the first type, selected at random from the first decade of his novelistic production.

They are the first hours of the afternoon. Bright sunshine is coming in through the window. In the sky, a pale blue, clouds go swimming along like chunks of marble.[65] (B)

The atmosphere that fills the room is somewhat opaque; it resembles a tenuous liquid, in which objects are swimming, like the fallen leaves in the tranquil and cold waters of a pool in autumn.[66] (C)

And the old woman and the child talk and talk, without tiring, of unimportant things, and affection floats upon their words, like in autumn the rose petal on tranquil pools . . . and they talk and talk about life and about death.[67] (D)

Suddenly, a wooden bridge, long and narrow, appeared before the eyes of the travelers; it looked like the white bones of some fabulous animal.[68] (E)

Now and then a leafy orchard bordered the river, and the royal road stretched out like a white ribbon scaling red and yellowish peaks, shaded by darkish elms and green-topped acacias.[69] (F)

The trees, already stripped of their leaves by autumn, seemed like mist floating upon the ground; from the chimneys of the houses came tenuous and whitish clouds of smoke.[70] (G)

The afternoon, sad and unpleasant, seemed wrapped in tears; drops of rain splashed against the windows of the carriage.[71] (H)

The list clearly shows that many times a moving, dynamic landscape enters into the comparison. In the first simile the clouds, which seem pieces of marble, are swimming in the pale blue sky.[72] The verb *nadar* and the verb *flotar* appear in all the comparisons. These verbs lend a sense of instability and movement to the similes, making of the landscape and the other ingredient of the comparison, a living, moving object.

In some cases the author has been careful to offer an esthetic justification for the simile. In the last example, for instance, it might be somewhat crude to say that an afternoon was soaked in tears. Baroja has the justification in the sentence. The afternoon can be soaked in tears because it is a sad and depressed afternoon, and the drops of rain are splashing on the carriage windows. Thus the comparison stands and seems reasonable.

In the following list, Baroja displays the use of similes to compare human beings to members of the animal kingdom. First is a general comment made by the Englishman Bothwell:

(A) De esta poca simpatía por el pasado, complicada con mi falta de sentido idiomático — por ser vasco y no haber hablado mis ascendientes el castellano —, procede la repugnancia que me inspiran las galas retóricas, que me parecen adornos de cementerio, cosas rancias, que huelen a muerto.[64]

(B) Son las primeras horas de la tarde. Entra un sol brillante por la ventana. En el cielo, azul pálido, van nadando nubes blancas como trozos de mármol.[65]

(C) El ambiente que llena la estancia es algo opaco; parece un líquido tenue, en el cual nadan los objetos, como en otoño las hojas caídas en las aguas tranquilas y frías de un estanque.[66]

(D) Y hablan, hablan la vieja y la niña, sin cansarse, de cosas sin importancia, y el cariño flota sobre sus palabras, como en otoño la hoja de rosa en los tranquilos estanques . . . , y hablan, hablan de la vida y de la muerte.[67]

(E) De pronto, un puente de tablas, largo y estrecho, se presentó ante los ojos de los viajeros; parecía la blanca osamenta de algún animal fabuloso.[68]

(F) Alguno que otro huerto frondoso bordeaba el río, y el camino real se tendía como una cinta blanca escalando lomas amarillentas y rojas, sombreado por olmos negruzcos y acacias de copa verde.[69]

(G) Los árboles, ya desnudos de hojas por el otoño, parecían brumas flotando sobre el suelo; por las chimeneas de las casas salían humaredas tenues blanquecinas.[70]

(H) La tarde, triste y desapacible, parecía empapada en lágrimas; en el cristal del coche salpicaban las gotas de agua.[71]

In Labraz there is no one but you worthy of having his portrait painted . . . replied the Englishman —. Many times I have thought about whom I could paint, and I have reviewed the men of the town: some remind me of a horse; others, a monkey or a dog; there are some who move like an ox, like the notary; others resemble owls or parrots.

— "And the women?" the Mayorazgo asked smiling.

— The same thing happens to me with women. Some resemble lap dogs; many others have the face of a cat; but what I dislike most is seeing how many of them have the face of a pig. Among those that I know, I make only one exception, and she is Blanca, the daughter of the Goya woman; as among the men I make one exception, that is you. She has the face of a woman, and you of a man.[73] (A)

— And all that pile of beggers, scrambled, agitated, palpitating, swarmed like a bed of worms.[74](B)

He wasn't hunchbacked, like his father, but well-built, thin with bright eyes and quick and wild movements. He resembled, as the expression goes, a mouse under a bowl.[75] (C)

The bride and groom showed up, surrounded by a cloud of kids, who were shouting; he looked like a store clerk; she, run-down and ugly, resembled a monkey.[76] (D)

His brother was dozing in an armchair, and one of their cousins, who looked like a fish because of his face, was walking from one side to the other, supporting himself on the backs of the chairs.[77] (E)

To Fernando she seemed like a serpent of fire that had enveloped him within its rings, and that each time squeezed him tighter and tighter, and he was suffocating and he couldn't get any air.[78] (F)

Although many of these similes seem rather arbitrary and perhaps unjustified, some are logical and apropos. A simple comparison of a man to a mouse, in the physical sense, may lack esthetic justification. In Baroja's comparison the justification of the simile is found in the previous elements of the description. After speaking of Perico's sharp features, his shining eyes, his lively and somewhat irregular movements, it seems quite justifiable to compare him to a mouse under a bowl.

The purpose of these similes, however, does not seem to be artistic. By comparing man to an animal or insect, Baroja denies him many of the qualities attributed to human beings. The comparison lowers man, reduces him, more or less, to the animal stage. It takes away from him the moral attributes that he prizes so highly. The comparison is especially efficacious in stripping man of false values, of vital illusions he may have created about his own person.

Another type of lowering or stripping of false qualities is seen in the attribution of these same qualities to animals. In *Camino de perfección* Fernando Ossorio attributes human gestures and attitudes to the animals he sees in a barnyard.

In the pen, that I can see from my balcony, the chickens pick at mounds of manure; the stupid hogs grunt and walk back and forth with suspicious little eyes and attitudes of a misanthrope; the hens cackle, and a rooster, a big insolent bluff, with his round eyes like metal buttons and his crest and gill of red flesh, struts with donjuanesque gestures.[79] (G)

There are, of course, other types of similes: César Moncada in *César o nada* in a sarcastic comparison speaks of Catholicism as a plate of Jewish meat with Roman sauce.[80]

In general the same two types of similes continue throughout. The first continues to hold its relationship to the landscape and maintains its

---

(A) — En Labraz no hay nadie digno de que se le haga un retrato más que usted . . . — replicó el inglés —. Muchas veces he pensado a quién podía retratar, y he pasado revista a los hombres del pueblo: unos me recuerdan un caballo; otros, un mono o un perro; hay algunos que tienen movimientos de buey, como el notario; y otros parecen buhos o papagayos.

— ¿Y las mujeres? — preguntó, sonriendo, el Mayorazgo.

— Con las mujeres me sucede lo mismo. Hay unas que parecen perrillos falderos; otras muchas tiene cara de gato; pero lo que más me desagrada es ver lo que abunda en ellas: el recuerdo de la cara de un cerdo. Entre las que conozco, sólo hago una excepción, y es Blanca, la hija de la Goya; como entre los hombres hago una excepción, que es usted. Ella tiene cara de mujer, como usted de hombre.[73]

(B) . . . Y todo aquel montón de mendigos, revuelto, agitado, palpitante, bullía como una gusanera.[74]

(C) No era contrahecho, como el padre, sino esbelto, delgado, con los ojos brillantes y los movimientos vivos y desordenados. Parecía como suele decirse, un ratón debajo de una escudilla.[75]

(D) Se presentaron los novios rodeados de una nube de chiquillos, que gritaban; él tenía facha de hortera; ella, esmirriada y fea, parecía una mona.[76]

(E) Su hermano dormitaba en una butaca, y un primo de ambos, que parecía un pez por su cara, se paseaba de un lado a otro, apoyándose en el respaldo de las sillas.[77]

(F) A Fernando le parecía una serpiente de fuego que le había envuelto entre sus anillos, y que cada vez le estrujaba más y más, y él iba ahogándose y sentía que le faltaba el aire para respirar.[78]

(G) En el corral, que veo desde mi balcón, los polluelos pican en montones de estiércol; gruñen los estúpidos cerdos y andan de acá para allá con ojillos suspicaces y actitudes de misántropo; cacarean las gallinas, y un gallo, farsantón y petulante, con sus ojos redondos como botones de metal y su cresta y su barba de carnosidad roja, se pasea con ademanes tenoriescos.[79]

dynamic and unstable quality as in the next examples, from the second, third, and fourth periods of Baroja's novelistic production.

Second decade:

Look at Saint Peter, he looks like a piece of cloud.[81] (A)

The snow, compact, pure, had just thickened. The grapevines symmetrically broke this white blanket like bands of crows resting on the land; the pine trees lifted their rounded branches, and the cypresses, dry and narrow stood out very black against so much whiteness.[82] (B)

Mount Izarra is a slate promontory, formed by tilted slabs, eaten away by the waves. The schists of the mountain stand apart like the leaves of an open book and advance into the sea, forming reefs, huge black rocks, lashed by the restless tide and end up in a high black cliff, with an air of mystery, called Frayburu.[83] (C)

In that special light of dusk, the town didn't seem to be real; one would have thought that a gust of wind would carry it away and destroy it like a cloud of dust upon the dry inflamed land.[84]

The dynamic sensation communicated by this simile and others like it comes of course, from the transitional time of day. At dawn and at dusk the quick movements of clouds, mists, shadows, of light and darkness, are more perceptible.

Third decade:

The sunset was admirable. The pearl gray of the ocean darkened and turned into a mica color; the horizon, lighter, changed from a pale yellow to a pink, and just when the sun went down the waves glowed for a moment with bloody reflections, like the scales of a fabulous dragon.[85] (D)

. . . on a nearby hill you could see two rows of cypresses that seemed to march to the graveyard like friars in a procession.[86] (E)

Fourth decade:

This mountain looked like a huge crouching animal.[87] (F)

Juan Pedro's father-in-law was a Dutchman called Courtizux, with very thick eyebrows that gave the impression of ivy on a wall.[88] (G)

In all these examples the landscape is something animate, has life and movement. In most of the aspects of Baroja's style examined so far, there has been a negative element, a rejection or lowering of something. This doesn't seem to be the case with the landscape to which he frequently gives an animated touch. A good example of this is the comparison of a mountain to a crouching cat.

The following list of similes comparing man to an animal, definitely evinces a negative or limiting aspect. The similes tend, in most cases, to reduce man to some essence of the animal kingdom.[89]

Second decade:

To Pello he seemed like a big ugly bird, a real bird of prey.[90] (H)

Among the spectators there was a man who looked like an ape.[91] (I)

Life without purpose, without a goal, without principles or morals, like a panther in the heart of the jungle.[92] (J)

From considering her as a spiritual and delicate lady, he came to look at her as a powerful mare, meriting only whip and spurs.[93] (K)

(A) Mira San Pedro; parece un trozo de nube.[81]

(B) La nieve, compacta, pura, acababa de cuajar. Las vides rompían simétricamente este manto blanco como bandadas de cuervos posadas en la tierra; los pinos levantaban su ramaje redondo, y los cipreses, secos y estrechos, se destacaban negrísimos entre tanta blancura.[82]

(C) El monte Izarra es un promontorio pizarroso, formado por lajas inclinadas, roídas por las olas. Estos esquistos de la montaña se apartan como las hojas de un libro abierto, y avanzan en el mar, dejando arrecifes, rocas negras azotadas por un inquieto oleaje, y terminan en una peña alta, negra, de aire misterioso, que se llama Frayburu.[83]

(D) El crepúsculo fué admirable. El gris perla del mar se oscureció y se convirtió en un color de mica; el horizonte, más claro, pasó del amarillo pálido al rosa, y en el momento de ponerse el sol brillaron un momento las olas con reflejos sangrientos, como las escamas de un dragón fabuloso.[85]

(E) ... en un cerro próximo se veían dos filas de cipreses, que parecían marchar como frailes en procesión al camposanto.[86]

(F) Este monte gris parecía un gran animal agazapado.[87]

(G) El suegro de Juan Pedro era un holandés que se llamaba Courtizux, hombre bonachón, con unas cejas muy frondosas que hacían el efecto de una hiedra sobre una tapia.[88]

(H) A Pello le pareció un pajarraco, una verdadera ave de rapiña.[90]

(I) Había entre los espectadores un hombre que parecía un antropoide.[91]

(J) ... la vida sin finalidad, sin objeto, sin principios y sin moral, como una pantera en medio de la selva.[92]

(K) De considerarla como a una señora espiritual y delicada pasó a mirarla como una yegua poderosa, que no merecía más que el látigo y las espuelas.[93]

Third decade:

The two of them had gray hair and a certain air of old people about them, something always desirable for dwarfs of a fair because then no one can suspect that they are children. One looked like a bad-humored and severe poodle.[94] (A)

The *Inglés* was a small, red snub-nosed man, with a short mustache and a big head. He must have been blond in his youth, but now he was gray. He had the air of a bulldog, frequent among Englishmen.[95] (B)

Fortunatito resembled a cat because of his independence and daring. You couldn't tell from which breed he came.[96] (C)

He compared himself to an owl that they had put in the sun.[97]

Fourth decade:

At times she had an air of a small girl; at times, although the comparison may seem brutal, something of a young and playful heifer.[98] (D)

In his type there wasn't the slightest aristocratic shade. He seemed like a hack driver or a French barkeep. Nothing of the squalid and elegant stamp of El Greco, like Mr. Cuéllar, nor of the air of a fish so characteristic of Spanish aristocrats.[99] (E)

At times he seemed like a very brave and daring rat that wasn't afraid of anything or anybody.[100]

At times also, Baroja makes sweeping comparisons of many different nationalities of men to different animals. Thus César Moncada, in the quotation from *César o nada,* runs the gamut of nationalities and their corresponding members of the animal kingdom while making observations about different guests in a hotel in Rome.

In *Los cínifes,* the second part of *Locuras de carnaval,* Baroja makes a rather complete statement about man's relationship to animals:

Since ancient times, writers, especially moralists and physiognomists, have assigned man conditions similar to those of animals and have compared man to them. There is nothing strange in this because animals are more limited and more specialized. Animals are frequently one line, an arrow with only one direction; man is almost always a circle with several directions. When the circle is deformed, elongated or swollen, then it takes on a more definite character and approaches the unique specialization of animals. Thus, men have been compared with lions, with hyenas, with cows, with tigers, and with asses. In the book called *Concerning the Physiognomy of Man* by Porta, there is a chapter called "Of the parts of the animal, and their habits through which we may know the habits of man."

The comparison not only has been made with vertebrate animals, but also with others of inferior zoological orders, like the ant, the cricket, the bee and the flesh fly.

Just as there are men who somewhat resemble a lion and a tiger, a lamb or an ant, because of their physical and spiritual characteristics, I believe that there are also types who most closely resemble mosquitos.

. . . .

The mosquito men, of whom I wish to speak, have both specialties: they feed on plants and other materials, and they bite their own kind, male or female and inoculate them with harmful fevers. Sometimes the harm is not great, and in some cases the bite produces gills which are useful.

Having made this clarification, we will begin our theoramatic tale.[101] (F)

(A) Tenían los dos aire de viejos y el pelo gris, lo que entre enanos de feria es siempre recomendable, porque así nadie puede sospechar que sean niños. El parecía un perrillo malhumorado y displicente.[94]

(B) El *Inglés* era un hombre pequeño, rojo, chato, de bigote corto, con la cabeza grande. Debía haber sido rubio en su juventud; pero ya estaba cano. Tenía un aire de *bulldog,* frecuente entre los ingleses.[95]

(C) Fortunatito parecía un gato, por lo independiente y atrevido. No se sabía de qué casta venía.[96]

(D) A veces tenía un aire de niña; a veces, aunque la comparación pareciese brutal, algo de ternera joven y juguetona.[98]

(E) No había en su tipo ni el más ligero matiz aristocrático. Parecía un cochero de punto o un tabernero francés. Nada de la estampa escuálida y elegante del *Greco,* como el señor Cuéllar, ni el aire de pez tan característico de los aristócratas españoles.[99]

(F) Desde antiguo, los escritores, sobre todo los moralistas y los fisiognomistas, han asignado a los hombres condiciones parecidas a las de los animales y los han comparado con ellos. No tiene esto nada de extraño, porque el animal es más limitado y más especialista. El animal es con frecuencia una línea, una flecha con una sola dirección; el hombre es casi siempre un círculo con varias direcciones. Cuando el círculo humano se deforma, se alarga o se ensancha, toma entonces un carácter más definido y se acerca a la especialización única del animal. Así, a los hombres se los ha comparado con los leones, con las hienas, con los monos, con las vacas, con los tigres y con los asnos. En el libro titulado *Della fisonomía dell uomo,* de Porta, hay un capítulo titulado «Delle parti degli animali, e loro costumi per li quali possioamo conghietturare li costumi deglo uomini.»

No sólo la comparación se ha verificado con animales vertebrados, sino también con otros de organización zoológica más inferior, como la hormiga, la cigarra, la abeja y el moscón.

Como hay hombres que se parecen en algo, por su carácter físico y espiritual, al león y al tigre, al cordero y a la hormiga, yo creo que hay tipos que a quienes más se asemejan es a los cínifes.

. . . .

Los hombres cínifes, de quienes quiero hablar, tienen las dos especialidades: se alimentan de plantas y de otras materias, y pican a sus semejantes, varones o hembras, y les inoculan fiebres malignas. A veces el daño no es grande, y en algunos casos la picadura del cínife produce la agalla, que tiene su utilidad.

Hecha esta aclaración, comenzaremos nuestro relato teoremático.[101]

From the similes examined in Baroja's works it seems that most of them are not stimulated by literary patterns. They spring from a concrete relationship that Baroja sees between two elements, and as such they seem to play an important part in the total creation of his novelistic world.

SYMBOLS

The second most important stylistic device used by Baroja is the symbol. Unlike the simile, the symbol shows no concrete relationship between two elements. It uses one object, or a series of objects, to evoke a diffuse emotional or spiritual reaction. Carlos Bousoño in his *La teoría de la expresión poética* considers this diffuse spiritual reaction to be the most salient characteristic of the symbol.

For us, then, that fact (continuity) is not the essential characteristic of symbolic figurations, but another more intimately linked to the nature of the symbol that the aforementioned authors did not consider, how diffusely we glimpse the real territory hidden behind it. Actually, the real plane upon which we find the symbol installed is never a material object, as always happens in the traditional and visionary image, but an object of a spiritual nature, and consequently, the limits of the latter will be hazy, not determinable with absolute clarity; or better, only determinable in a generic sense, not in a specific manner; the reader knows the genus to which this reality corresponds, but he doesn't know the species to which it belongs. Before the reality that the symbol hides, the reader acts like an astigmatic before a forest; he sees trees, but he cannot tell exactly whether they are ash or oak.[102] (A)

In 1910 in the *Revue Hispanique,* Peseux-Richard speaks of Mamertín in *El mayorazgo de Labraz* as a symbol of depravity.[103] This interpretation is left strictly up to the reader, and the feelings which the presence of Mamertín elicits may differ from one reader to another. They will always tend to be unpleasant. Mamertín does exist as a person within the novel, and he is therefore both a depraved entity as well as a symbol of all depravity. He is a bimodal symbol, *símbolo bisémico.*[104]

In *La ciudad de la niebla* there is a barber who has his show window decorated with all sorts of monsters — symbols of the life witnessed by María in London.

As more worthy of note, one could point out: a Chinaman with three legs; a woman with a long beard, dressed with a certain coquettishness, a bow around her neck and a fan in her hand, a child savage covered with hair; a giant dressed as a soldier with a very small head; two recently born babies united by their hips; two fat monsters united by matrimony; a pinhead with an ape-like jaw, and a man-skeleton with twisted legs and an impertinent air. (B)

Underneath the window the barber has placed a little philosophical touch. "Man marches towards his grave, leaving behind him his deceitful delusions."[105]

In *La ciudad de la niebla,* Maldonado, before hanging himself with an old strap, sketches the symbol of his life on the wall of his cell in the Central Prison of London.

We have seen these sketches, that, if not a great domination of the art of Apeles, don't fail to indicate a sagacious wit. In one of these scenes an anarchist skeleton is throwing a bomb into the multitude, and arms, heads, and legs of skeleton-like persons go flying through the air. In the other drawing there is a row of skeletons which have been hanged, and in front of them a skeleton sitting at a table, with toga, wig, and other attributes of a judge.[106] (C)

Baroja discusses the sketch and its possible meaning, but he does not interpret it. Although the symbol may be abstruse, it seems surely related to Maldonado's own existence.

In *Camino de perfección* the dead and rotting grandfather makes a perfect symbol of the rotten society of Madrid.

(A) Para nosotros no es, pues, ese hecho (la continuidad) la característica esencial de las figuraciones simbólicas, sino otro más entrañablemente ligado a la naturaleza del símbolo que no consideraron los autores antes aludidos: lo difusamente que divisamos el territorio real guarecido tras él. En efecto: el plano real sobre el que se halla el símbolo instalado no es nunca un objeto material, como ocurre siempre en la imagen tradicional y en la visionaria, sino un objeto de índole espiritual, y en consecuencia, los límites de éste serán borrosos, no determinables con absoluta nitidez; o mejor, sólo determinables de un modo genérico, no de un modo específico; el lector sabe el género a que esa realidad corresponde, pero desconoce la especie a que pertenece. Frente a la realidad que el símbolo encubre, el lector se comporta como un astigmático frente a un bosque: ve árboles, mas no puede precisar si se trata de fresnos o de robles.[102]

(B) Como más notables, podían señalarse: un chino de tres piernas; una mujer de largas barbas, vestida con cierta coquetería, lazo en el cuello y abanico en la mano; un niño salvaje cubierto de pelo; un gigante vestido de soldado con la cabeza muy pequeña; dos recién nacidos unidos por la cadera; dos monstruos de gordura unidos por el matrimonio, un cretino de mandíbula simiesca, y un hombre-esqueleto con las piernas torcidas y el aire impertinente.[105]

(C) Hemos visto estos dibujos, que, si no un gran dominio en el arte de Apeles, no dejan de indicar un ingenio sagaz. En una de estas escenas un esqueleto anarquista lanza una bomba que estalla entre la multitud, y van por el aire brazos, cabezas y piernas de personas esqueléticas. En el otro dibujo hay una serie de esqueletos ahorcados, y enfrente de ellos un esqueleto sentado en una mesa, con toga, peluca y además atributos de juez.[106]

In the study they kept talking about the question of oil; in the living room they were talking about Nini's scandals in a low voice; the servants were all worried over whether or not they would be dismissed from the household staff, and, in the meantime the great-uncle alone, quite alone, without anybody bothering him with cries and lamentations, nor other foolish things of that nature, was rotting tranquilly in his coffin, and one couldn't see more of his thick, fleshy, swollen face through the crystal than a mixture of reddish and black blood, and in his nostrils and in his mouth a few white spots of pus.[107] (A)

The *nacimiento* built by Paradox and his friend Avediz de la Iglesia in *Silvestre Paradox* is a symbol of Paradox and of his inherent goodness. This goodness is unappreciated and, like the rest of Silvestre's traits, rather nonfunctional.

Since he needed money, he went to the house of Policarpo Bardés, the administrator, and told him what was happening to him. Don Policarpo loaned him five hundred pesetas and so they continued the work on the nativity scene which was darling.[108] (B)

Another symbol of Silvestre's nonfunctional genius is the model submarine. Silvestre and his friend have made a valiant attempt to invent a submarine which has been outmoded and forgotten for years. Their efforts are unsuccessful; their procedure is rather blundering, the affair ludicrous, but there is something essentially worthwhile and praiseworthy in their audacious trial. The submarine is a symbol, nonetheless forceful because implied, of Silvestre's existence. Silvestre's invention — like Don Quijote's helmet — did not stand the test of reality, but the aspiring, ingenious, yet ingenuous attempt transcends the hard and unsympathetic reality of Silvestre's unfortunate life.

Again, Silvestre who is a sensitive and scientifically inclined individual interested in the interrelationships of things, sees but does not state a symbolic relationship between the cemetery called *El Este* with its dead — now mere numbers — and the nameless masses of Madrid. At that moment the *Este* and Madrid are joined poetically because they both elicit the same emotional sadness.

Alone he accompanied the bohemian to the East Cemetery, a very beautiful afternoon, with bright sunshine.
After the corpse had been buried, Silvestre walked among the tombs, thinking about how horrible it was to die in a big city, where they catalogued one like a document in an archive, and he contemplated with sharp sadness Madrid in the distance, amidst arid and desolate fields, underneath a reddened sky . . .[109] (C)

Baroja's prose has a great many comparisons that link the obviously ludicrous and grotesque to the apparently formal and serious. Baroja mentions this in *El mundo es ansí*.

Handwerck was truly a pedagogical and philosophical edifice, because the bringing together of the soldiers' mess and the dynamite, the comic and the terrible, made one think against his will, about the seriousness of grotesque things and the grotesqueness of serious things.[110] (D)

The relationship between these two seemingly disparate elements usually receives some comment from the narrator. In his *Prólogo*, which is *casi una fantasía antropológica*, to *El laberinto de las sirenas*, Baroja goes to some trouble to describe certain fish in an aquarium. One of them he describes thus, "Another fish, that showed up suddenly, made us laugh because of his round face and his bulging and stupid eyes."[111] (E) Later in the day, he sees a violinist, supposedly a serious one, and describes him in much the same way. "The violinist was tall, fat, blonde, clean-shaven, with a round face, completely brachycephalic, with eyes bulging like eggs."[112] (F) The relationship between the two is mentioned in the dialogue which follows. "You know who he looks like?" I said to Recalde.

(A) En el despacho se seguía hablando de la cuestión del aceite; en la sala se comentaban en voz baja los escándalos de la Nini; los criados andaban alborotados por si los despedían o no de la casa, y, mientras tanto, el tío-abuelo solo, bien solo, sin que nadie le molestara con gritos ni lamentos, ni otras tonterías por el estilo, se pudría tranquilamente en su ataúd, y de su cara gruesa, carnosa, abultada, no se veía a través del cristal más que una mezcla de sangre rojiza y negra, y en las narices y en la boca algunos puntos blancos de pus.[107]

(B) Como necesitaba dinero, fué a casa de don Policarpo Bardés, el administrador, y le contó lo que le sucedía. Don Policarpo le prestó quinientas pesetas y se continuaron las obras del nacimiento, que era una monada.[108]

(C) Acompañó solo al bohemio al Este, una tarde muy hermosa, con un sol espléndido.
Después de enterrado el cadáver, Silvestre paseó por entre aquellas tumbas, pensando en lo horrible de morir en una gran ciudad, en donde a uno lo catalogan como a un documento en un archivo, y contempló con punzante tristeza Madrid a lo lejos, en medio de campos áridos y desolados, bajo un cielo enrojecido.[109]

(D) Realmente, la sala Handwerck era un edificio pedagógico y filosófico, porque al acercar el rancho a la dinamita y lo cómico a lo terrible, hacía pensar sin querer en la seriedad de las cosas grotescas y en lo grotesco de las cosas serias.[110]

(E) "Otro pez, que se presentó de pronto, nos hizo reír por su cara redonda y sus ojos abultados y estúpidos."[111]

(F) "El violinista era alto, gordo, rubio, afeitado, con la cara redonda, completamente braquicéfalo, con unos ojos abultados como huevos ..."[112]

"Who?"

"That fish with the round face and the bulging eyes we saw this morning."[113] (A)

In spite of the superficial disparity of all these symbols, they are bound together by the similarity of the emotion which they produce, although each one, by the very nature of a symbol as described by Carlos Bousoño, is capable of producing a large variety of emotional reactions. More than anything else each symbol adds its note of sadness to Baroja's novelistic world. The cemetery called *El Este* makes Madrid a rather cold, sad place for Paradox to live in. The nonfunctioning submarine saddens us with the realization that Paradox's adventurous spirit and his ingenuity are confined to this sort of activity. The nativity scene reminds the reader of the absence of the very thing it symbolizes. All three symbols serve to limit the small, cold world in which the indomitable Paradox is forced to live. They are symbols of sadness, of disillusionment, of the wretchedness of life as found in Baroja's novelistic world.[114]

Many of Baroja's symbols of disillusionment are quite poetic and literary. These comparisons are used to underline an already existing emotion or to point in its direction. In *Los amores tardíos* Baroja presents the following treadmill as symbolic of Larrañaga's life.

> Pablo Jovio relates, in his *Dialogue of Military Undertakings,* that Don Diego de Guzmán, having once tried to ford a river in the company of his lady, and having suffered many setbacks and much rough going, invented an emblem that consisted of a treadmill, with buckets that pick up water and spill it out, and since at each moment about half of them were full and the other half empty, he put this nickname on his standard: Those full of sorrow and those empty of hope.[115] (B)

Larrañaga realizes that the buckets of this treadmill are symbolic of the days of his life. "To him life seemed gloomy; the passing of days dull, monotonous, and black, without gusts of light. As in the emblem cited by Pablo Jovio, he could repeat: Those full of sorrow and those empty of hope."[116] (C)

Clocks, as symbols of life, are a literary constant in Baroja's novels. An example is the clock with the inscription "Vulnerant omnes, ultima necat," which appears in *Silvestre Paradox*.[117] It elicits a certain compassion for the trials, sufferings, and disillusionments of the personages of his novels.

The titles of Baroja's works are sometimes literary and contrived symbols of the events which are to happen within the novel. Worthy of mention are the windvane of *La veleta de Gaztizar,* and the shield with the three bleeding hearts of *El mundo es ansí.* Titles such as *Aventuras, inventos y mixtificaciones de Silvestre Paradox* and *Paradox, Rey* are obviously symbolic of what is to take place within the novel. *La nave de los locos,* and *Las figuras de cera* are also symbolic of the hodgepodge of characters found in the stories. *El gran torbellino del mundo* is a symbolic whirlwind. Baroja hasn't been disdainful of the use of one of the oldest literary devices — use of a concrete object to represent the complex whole.

Another constant and rather literary embellishment in Pío Baroja's prose is the *refranes.* These axioms of popular philosophy justify the adventurer Chimista's good fortune in *Los pilotos de altura* and its sequel, *La estrella del capitán Chimista.* These popular expressions escape in part the purely traditional use of *refranes* because of their Basque origin. They are usually *a posteriori* comments, explaining that which has no explanation — that which should be attributed to chance. Rather than serving purely as embellishment, *refranes* such as the following explain and underline the Captain's character and philosophy. *"Campoan uso, echean otso* (Outside a dove and a wolf at home)." [118] *"Alaco tonela, alaco ardoa* (From such a keg, such wine)." [119] *"Barrica charretic ardo on guschi* (From a bad keg, very little good wine)." [120] *"Ontzia galdu esquero gustioc pillotu* (Everybody's a pilot after the ship is lost)." [121] *"Naguia bada astoa, emayoc astazagari eroa* (A lazy burro takes a crazy muleteer)." [122]

WORD DEFLATORS

Baroja, then, is willing to employ certain traditional devices in order to achieve his highly personalized prose style. We have seen that he uses these devices with restraint, but does accept them. With words, however, Baroja is intransigent, having no faith in their efficacy. They interest him only as signs or symbols. "For me, at least, a word is interesting prin-

---

(A) "¿Sabes a quién se parece?" le dije yo a Recalde.
"¿A quién?"
"Al pez aquel de la cara redonda y de los ojos abultados que hemos visto esta mañana." [113]

(B) Cuenta Pablo Jovio, en su *Diálogo de las empresas militares,* que don Diego de Guzmán, habiendo intentado una vez pasar el vado de un río en compañía de su dama, y habiendo sufrido grandes tropiezos y malos pasos, inventó un emblema, que consistía en una noria, con los arcaduces que sacan agua y la vierten, y porque en cada momento casi la mitad de ellos estaba llena y la otra mitad vacía, puso a su enseña este mote: Los llenos de dolor y los vacíos de esperanza. [115]

(C) La vida le parecía tenebrosa; el correr de los días, pesado, monótono y negro, sin ráfagas de luz. Como en el emblema citado por Pablo Jovio, podía repetir: Los llenos de dolor y los vacíos de esperanza. [116]

cipally as a sign."[123] (A) He has no faith in individual words. "The single word says very little; only a group of them, a phrase, and that in a relative manner, can express an idea or a sensorial impression."[124] (B)

Certain words, for Baroja, sometimes tend to be more than mere signs. They tend to connote too much. They overshadow reality. When this is the case, Baroja is faced with the chore of deflating and softening them so they will only point to — or be a sign of — reality, so they will not or cannot possibly be taken for reality itself. Baroja's prose is filled with devices that serve just this purpose — to deflate and soften the potential of words.

One of the most common of these devices is a series of flamboyant and highly rhetorical words representing the concept *nothingness* in life. Baroja seems to be impressed with the number of words in Spanish that indicate the somewhat exotic and poetic idea of being nothing. Through the constant and exaggerated use of such words as the following: *badaluque* (worthless boob), *imbécil, idiota, farsante* (windbag), *cretino marasmo* (mess), *mojigatería* (sanctimoniousness), *granuja* (rascal), *bestia* (beast), *canalla* (scoundrel), etc., he is constantly reminding his reader and himself that many words, although beautiful, euphonic, polysyllabic, and even exotic, have perhaps originated for and serve a very definite purpose, that of pointing to insignificance.[125]

The most common and effective word-deflating device found in Baroja's prose is a group of words or phrases that precede or follow the principal statement or assertion. These make up a worthy percentage of his prose. Sometimes they are just sad, negative words grouped together. In the following examples from *El hotel del cisne,* they deflate and sadden the whole passage, making it seem that every term therein is negative, and depressing.

> I have been living here for some time now in the Swan Hotel in the street of the *Solitary Ones.* The *rain* has blackened the *walls* of the house. The *years* have *wrinkled* the skin of its inhabitants, and *disillusionments* have wilted their spirits. . . . Now, in complete *isolation* and in full *old age,* this is *impossible. Solitude envelops* me and *isolates* me. I would accept it gladly if I could *sleep,* but I cannot *sleep.*[126] (C)

At other times, the deflating words merely cast doubt on the statement made. Baroja has summed up his stylistic creed in his speech of acceptance as a member of the Royal Spanish Academy. "My anarchism was Schopenhaurian and agnostic, which could have been summed up in two phrases: believe not, affirm not."[127] (D) The following passage, with the non-affirmative words and phrases underlined, illustrates the consistency with which he carries out this creed.

> Rosa Vinay is an ancient ballerina who achieved *some* fame in her youth. *I don't know* whether she danced in the Opera, or in the Comic Opera. The

old ex-ballerina is *just a little bit* lame. *I suppose* that in her time she *probably* wasn't, given her profession. *It could be* that now she has rheumatism.

Madame Latour *heard* that the Vinay woman was *somewhat* famous and made money, a lot of money. *I don't know* how she had fallen so low as to live on the fifth floor of a hotel in a poor neighborhood. *Some* people assure us, *according to the manager,* that some time ago they used to call Vinay *Vol-au-vent à la financière. It was thought* that she had gone broke playing the stockmarket.

Vinay *apparently* led a bohemian-type existence until very late in life, entertained by gigolos, by young men, if she wasn't the one who entertained these gigolos, as they called them in peace time. Now, during the war, this word is used *very little.*

They say of Rosa Vinay that during her youth she was a woman without scruples, that she sold herself to the highest bidder. *Apparently,* her concern had always been to become rich in any way possible.[128] (E)

(A) "A mí, al menos, la palabra me ha interesado principalmente como signo." [123]

(B) "La palabra suelta dice poco; sólo un conjunto de ellas, una frase, y eso de una manera relativa, puede expresar una idea o una impresión sensorial." [124]

(C) Desde hace *tiempo* vivo aquí en el Hotel del Cisne de la calle de los *Solitarios.* La *lluvia* ha *ennegrecido* las paredes de la casa. Los *años* han *arrugado* la piel de sus habitantes, y las *desilusiones* han *marchitado* su *espíritu.* . . . Ahora, en pleno *aislamiento* y en plena *vejez,* esto es *imposible.* La *soledad* me *envuelve* y me *aisla.* La aceptaría con gusto si pudiera *dormir,* pero no puedo *dormir.*[126]

(D) "Mi anarquismo era un anarquismo schopenhaueriano y agnóstico, que se hubiera podido resumir en dos frases: no creer, no afirmar." [127]

(E) Rosa Vinay es una antigua bailarina, que tuvo *cierta* fama en su juventud. *No sé* si bailaba en la Opera, o en la Opera Cómica. La vieja ex bailarina es *un poco* coja. *Supongo* que en su tiempo no lo sería, dada su profesión. *Puede ser* que ahora esté reumática.

Madame Latour *ha oído* que la Vinay tenía alguna fama, y que ganaba dinero, mucho dinero. *No sé* cómo habrá caído tan bajo para vivir en el quinto piso de un hotel de un barrio pobre. *Algunos aseguran, según la administradora,* que tiempo atrás llamaban a la Vinay *Vol-au-vent á la financiére. Se creía* que se había arruinado en la Bolsa.

La Vinay llevó, *al parecer,* una vida bohemia hasta muy tarde, entretenida por *gigolos,* por jovencitos, si es que ella no era la que entretenía a estos *gigolos,* como *se decía* en tiempo de paz. Ahora, en tiempo de guerra, esta palabra se emplea *poco.*

De Rosa Vinay *se dice* que en su juventud era una mujer sin escrúpulos, y *que* se vendía al mejor postor. *Al parecer,* su preocupación fué siempre hacerse rica de cualquier manera.[128]

Although the use of phrases to soften and deflate seems exaggerated in the above passage, it abounds throughout Baroja's prose. Gregorio Marañón has mentioned this usage and its importance in an article written for *La Prensa* of Buenos Aires in 1935.

The word "enthusiasm" and the words "farce" and "fake" and the expression "a little," that he puts before almost all his adjectives, always afraid of compromising himself — "a little ridiculous," a "little exact," etc., will be the ones that the future scholars who may write and comment on his vocabulary will most often find written in his works; and in them is summed up, as it could be demonstrated, the most genuine aspect of the author's psychology.[129] (A)

In keeping with Baroja's intent, these word deflators seem to have little effect on reality. They lessen the strength of his affirmations and his presentations of reality, but they do not seem to distort reality or lessen its emotional effect on the reader in any way. Baroja feels that when a person sees a dead man he can say that he thinks the man must be dead, or he may say that he knows the man to be irrevocably and everlastingly banished from the kingdom of the living. In either case, the state of the man has not been altered.

Baroja would go on to lament the fact that most people would be more emotionally impressed by the last statement of the man's condition than with the first. Reference to the tragedy of death itself does not impress people; it must be distorted and falsified by the form in which it is expressed in order to produce an impression on most people. Baroja does not write for these people, but in one of the anecdotes in *El tablado de Arlequín* he illustrates their type admirably. It is the story of a difficult heart case. The death of the man left him and his friend indifferent, but they were moved by some of Victor Hugo's romantic verse. "Form is everything, as my friend was saying; what we need to move us is artistic sorrow, the transparent tear that runs down the smooth cheek. We are a bunch of miserable men."[130] (B)

All these examples illustrate that negation is an important factor in the formation of Baroja's style. It leads Baroja away from many aspects of that prose and even poetry which has been termed *castizo*. It causes him to avoid certain groups of words, rhetorical devices, sentences, and intonation patterns. In Baroja's prose, there is a constant desire to evade what he calls the commonplace in literature, the tailor-made style, the literary style handed down by Spanish tradition. However, he deems a complete sidestepping of the commonplace impossible. "In spite of everything, one mustn't think that the commonplace can be banished, because it keeps on ruling life and literature and probably will continue to do so forever."[131] (C)

Most of Baroja's comments about style are negative; they frequently begin with *no creo*. These comments, along with his obvious rejection of many stylistic devices in his prose, show his personal attitude toward style, his general disbelief, his mistrust, his feeling about the limitations and impotence of stylistic devices.

Baroja's stylistic creed might be summed up as follows: For Baroja, to destroy is to create. "Destruir es crear." This pithy phrase of destruction evokes another of his sententious axioms. "It seems to me that to stylize is to falsify."[132] (D) Furthermore, Baroja feels that to stylize is essentially anti-vital, anti-biological. Therefore, "One writes as one walks se escribe como se anda)," and this phrase must perforce form part of his stylistic creed. These combined ideas probably form the best personal statement of Baroja's stylistic creed. He is seeking the essential and rejecting many of the superficial aspects of form and rhetoric which distort reality.

The stylization and the arbitrariness of ideas and of political systems are like concave or convex mirrors that deform the image of reality. Apparently, the deformation is necessary. Man doesn't want to live face to face with truth; he prefers lies. Perhaps he finds the latter more attractive and more vital.[133] (E)

Critics have seized upon the threefold statement of Baroja's stylistic creed "Destruir es crear; estilizar es falsificar; se escribe como se anda,"

(A) Esta palabra «entusiasmo», con la de farsa y farsante y con la expresión un tanto que antepone a casi todos sus adjetivos, temiendo siempre comprometerse — un tanto ridículo, un tanto exacto, etc., serán las que más veces se encuentren escritas en su obra los eruditos futuros que escriban y comenten su vocabulario; y en ellas se resume, como podría demostrarse, lo más genuino de la psicología de su autor.[129]

(B) La forma es todo, como decía mi amigo; necesitamos para conmovernos el dolor artístico, la lágrima transparente que corre por la tersa mejilla. Somos unos miserables.[130]

(C) "A pesar de todo, no hay que pensar que se puede proscribir el lugar común, porque éste sigue rigiendo la vida y la literatura y, probablemente lo seguirá siempre."[131]

(D) "Me parece que estilizar es falsificar."[132]

(E) La estilización y la arbitrariedad de las ideas y de los sistemas políticos son como espejos cóncavos o convexos, que deforman la imagen de la realidad. Al parecer, la deformación es necesaria. El hombre no quiere vivir de cara a la verdad; prefiere la mentira. Quizá a ésta la encuentra más atractiva y más vital.[133]

as the essence of his stylistic ideal, and some have considered as the whole truth and explanation that Baroja has rejected all stylistic devices and that therefore his style is pure, perfectly natural, and biological.

This is not the case. Baroja's attitude and his creed have led him into the use of certain stylistic devices just as they have led him away from others. Those he uses are categorized as similes, symbols and word deflators, as well as an anti-rhetorical treatment of sentences — short and choppy rather than long and flowing.

Baroja's library and his reading habits further corroborate an essentially negative attitude toward style. Although Baroja marked, underlined, and wrote in the margins of many books — on philosophy and other serious subjects — he must have read novels for content only, as these without exception have no markings. Had Baroja been interested in learning something about style from these authors — many authors have confessed this kind of a stylistic debt — he might well have marked significant passages and stylistic procedures.[134]

Baroja, in his particular prose style, strives to express the essence of a unique reality. He achieves this expression largely through rejection or destruction of crystallized stylistic devices of a dead past, creating a style which points toward the future. Baroja firmly believes that this style will produce its fruits in the years to come. "This period has to produce its flower. It may take a long time; perhaps a hundred years, like the century plant, but it will produce it."[135] (A) This conviction is shared by Azorín. "Is it that you believe that within one or two centuries, or as many as it takes, Baroja will not be read with more pleasure, with more assurance, than those followers of a tradition which is not a tradition?"[136] (B)

The level or tone of Baroja's words, phraseology, and syntax must always be that of the reality they are used to elicit. Baroja fully realizes that if an excessive amount of thought and effort is expended in the communication of certain states of emotion or suggestions, or if this thought and effort become too visible, the emotional states and sensations will be overshadowed or lost, and all that the reader will be able to perceive is the vehicle of communication. The substance of Baroja's novelistic world is nonpretentious; heavy rhetoric would crush it, and light flowery speech would distort it. The writer's style must therefore be unpretentious, yet delicate enough to portray the fragile flickerings and shades of emotion for which it was designed. Baroja's style tends toward understatement when it cannot convey the exact and delicate measure of emotion and sensation the situation demands.

A good example of the type of prose where emotional potential is high but the prose that conveys it is almost colorless is found at the end of a story called *Dos hermanos*. One of the brothers has to leave Cádiz because of ill feeling toward him in the town. He has killed a man, and although legally exonerated of the crime, he is looked upon with mistrust.

In a few days, Juan went to Cadiz and arranged his affairs for leaving. A week later it was learned that he had secretly married María Dolores. The two of them left the town for embarkation.

In Latin America Juan began to get along quite well and to prosper. He put in a small store, which later expanded. Then he bought land and sheep and became rich.

When he was ready to return to Spain the civil war broke out, and he put off the trip . . .

Thanks to that, Juan was saved from the revolution, which in his town was long and violent. His brother, Francisco, was shot, and left his family in dire circumstances.

Destiny, in spite of being blind, has its calls and its chosen.[137] (C)

Since what happens in the selection is essentially tragic, it has the potential to elicit intense emotional reaction, but it may not; for, as Baroja states, it is the form one gives to the occurrence that stimulates, rather than the occurrence per se.

(A) "Este período tiene que dar su flor. Tardará mucho en darla; quizá cien años, como el cactus secular; pero la dará."[135]

(B) "¿Es que creéis que dentro de un siglo, de dos, de los que sean, no será leído Baroja con más gusto, con más seguridad, que los seguidores de una tradición que no es tradición?"[136]

(C) A los pocos días, Juan se marchó a Cádiz y arregló sus asuntos para marcharse.

Una semana después se supo que se había casado en secreto con María Dolores. Los dos salieron del pueblo para embarcarse.

En América, Juan comenzó a marchar viento en popa y a prosperar. Puso una tienda pequeña, que después agrandó. Luego compró terrenos y rebaños y se hizo muy rico. Cuando estaba dispuesto para volver a España estalló la guerra civil, y aplazó el viaje . . .

Gracias a ello, Juan se salvó de la revolución, que en el pueblo fué larga y violenta. Su hermano Francisco fué fusilado, y dejó a su familia en mala posición.

El Destino, a pesar de ser ciego, tiene sus llamadas y sus elegidos.[137]

3. *Dialogue*

D<small>WIGHT</small> B<small>OLINGER</small> has claimed that a good half of any novel by Baroja is devoted to dialogue.[1] Although Bolinger's estimate may be hyperbolic, Baroja does indeed devote a great deal of space to dialogue. Nevertheless this author has commented but little on the nature and importance of dialogue. In his prologue to *Las figuras de cera* Baroja does have Leguía say that one of the greatest faults a novel can have is a lack of dialogue. He goes on to say that the spoken word is what gives the literary work an animation, analogous to the life that color gives to painting.

This clarification made in respect to the historical part — Leguía went on saying — I have to warn, in regard to the novelistic aspect, that the work doesn't satisfy me. The author describes too much, defines too much, traces the outlines of the characters, but he moves them very little, and, above all, he doesn't make them talk. He has a strange lack of affection for words. His men and his elfs speak the minimum. Undoubtedly, in literature, the spoken word is what gives a work something like color in painting.[2] (A)

In spite of the abundance of dialogue, such comments are indeed hard to find in Baroja's writing — a lack that may indicate a negation of the importance of dialogue or a denial of the basic difference between it and prose in general.

A comparison between the following dialogues will serve more or less as an objective starting point.

In the ensuing example, from *Fortunata y Jacinta* by Galdós, Mauricia is talking to Fortunata in the convent. This dialogue from Galdós shows a marked contrast to Baroja's. Both dialogues record the speech of humble people.

"And why was that man looking for me? . . . Why? To make me sin again. Once is enough."

"Men are very capricious," — Mauricia La Dura said in a philosophical tone — "and when they have you at their disposal, they don't pay any more

[44]

attention to you than to an old rag; but if you talk to someone else, then the one before wants to snuggle up, like that business of the sweet bit that someone else is tasting. Well I tell you . . . if you decide to be, for example, virtuous, the sly guys won't stand for that; and if you begin to pray a lot and to go often to confession and to communion, their desires are kindled even more, and they long for us from the moment we accept the ecclesiastical life . . . Well then, do you think that Juanito won't come and prowl around this convent since he knows you are here? *One'd* take you for a fool. (*Paices boba*) You better believe it, and one of those coaches we hear out there, believe you me is his."

"Don't be silly . . ., don't say asinine things," the other one replied turning pale. "It can't be . . . Because, look, he came down with pneumonia in February . . ."

"You are well informed."

"I know through Feliciana, a few days back, a gentleman who is a friend of Villalonga told it to her. Well, you will see: he came down with pneumonia in February, and in that interim I met the young man that I talk to now. . . . The other one was very sick for two months . . . it was touch and go. Finally he came out of it, and in March he went to Valencia with his wife."

"So what?"

"So he probably hasn't returned yet."

"Silly girl . . . That is just a phrase. And if he hasn't returned, he will. . . . That means that he will keep after you when he comes and finds out that you are going for sainthood."

"You are really the silly one . . . leave me alone. And supposing that he does come and hang around me. What does that matter to me?"

. . . .

"You have to keep this crazy dame happy, she is a good person, and as long as you shine her furniture to a T, you have her eating out of your hand."[3] (B)

(A) Hecha esta aclaración con respecto a la parte histórica — sigue diciendo Leguía —, tengo que advertir, con relación a lo novelesco, que la obra no me llena. El autor describe demasiado, define demasiado, traza los contornos de los personajes, pero los mueve poco, y, sobre todo, no los hace hablar. Tiene por la palabra una falta de cariño extraña. Sus hombres y sus homúnculos hablan el mínimo. Indudablemente, en la literatura, la palabra hablada es la que da a la obra una animación algo parecida al color en la pintura.[2]

(B) — ¿Y para qué me buscaba a mí ese hombre? . . . ¿Para qué? Para perderme otra vez. Con una basta.

— Los hombres son muy caprichosos — dijo en tono de filosofía Mauricia la Dura —, y cuando la tienen a una a su disposición, no le hacen más caso que a un trasto viejo; pero si una habla con otro, ya el de antes quiere arrimarse, por el aquel de la golosina que otro se lleva. Pues digo . . ., si una se pone a ser, verbigracia, honrada, los muy peines no pasan por eso; y si una se mete mucho a rezar y a confesar y comulgar, se les encienden más a ellos las querencias, y se pirran por nosotras desde que nos convertimos por lo eclesiástico . . . Pues qué, ¿crees tú que Juanito no viene a rondar este convento

The following dialogue comes from Baroja's *Mala Hierba*.

"Eh! Eh!" Manuel shouted at him.

Don Alonso looked back, stopped and approached Jesús and Manuel, "Where were you going?" they asked him.

"Following that coach to see if I could carry that gentleman's trunk up to his house; but I am tired, my legs are shot."

"And what do you do?" they asked him.

"Psch! . . . die of hunger."

"The lucky break never comes?"

"It is going to come? Napoleon gave up in Waterloo, right? Well my life is a continual Waterloo."

"What are you engaged in right now"

"I have been selling risqué books. I must have one here," he added, showing Manuel a pamphlet whose title was: *Mischievious Tricks by Women on Their Wedding Night.*

"Is this any good?" Manuel asked.

"So, so. I warn you that you have to read every other line. Me! mixed up in these things . . . when I have been the director of a circus in *Niu Yoc!*"

"Your day will come."

"A few nights ago, I went out staggering, dying of starvation, and I went to the Charity Mission, because I couldn't stand it any longer. 'What's wrong with you?' one of them asked. 'Hunger? That is not a disease,' he told me. Then I started out to beg, and now at nightfall I am going to the Salamanca neighborhood; there, I tell the women who are out alone that my son has died, that I need two bits to buy candles. They are horrified, and usually they give me something. I have also found a little place to sleep. It's over there, towards the river."[4] (A)

The reader's immediate impression is that the dialogue of Baroja when compared to that of Galdós is flat and almost colorless. Mauricia's speech is garnished with adornments, with popular rhetoric, rhetoric of the street — simile, *más caso que a un trasto viejo;* adage, *por el áquel de la golosina que otro se lleva;* the rather pedantic *verbigracia;* the euphemistic use of the word *peines;* the use of the substandard form *paices* for *pareces;* popular expressions such as *tía chiflada, la tienes partiendo un piñón.* All of these adornments, coupled with Mauricia's witty use of the good sister's expression of *al hilo,* and the constant circumlocution, make her speech stand out in sharp and colorful relief. The reader, although interested in what Mauricia has to say and, in a certain way, in her philosophical observations, is more impressed with her way of speaking. Her rhetoric of the street, with all its color and vitality, is delightful. She seems to be building her world — her own reality — with these words and seems quite content with it.

In comparison, Baroja's dialogue is purged of all adornments. While Mauricia La Dura seemed to glory in words, expressions, and circumlocutions, Baroja's vagabonds have a distinct distaste for them. There is little joy in their speech, no feeling of wisdom or deep philosophical insight. Rather there seems to be a sort of reticence to speak, a feeling that there is so little that is worthy of putting into a fixed phrase that it is hardly worth the effort. Here again Baroja has rejected in dialogue, as in narrative, the four constellations of words: those dealing with patriotism, those

---

desde que sabe que estás aquí? *Paices* boba. Tenlo por cierto, y alguno de los coches que se sienten por ahí, créete que es el suyo.

— No seas tonta . . ., no digas burradas — replicó la otra, palideciendo —. No puede ser . . . Porque, mira tú, el cayó con la pulmonía en febrero . . .

— Bien enterada estás.

— Lo sé por Feliciana, a quien se lo contó, *días atrás,* un señor que es amigo de Villalonga. Pues verás: él cayó con la pulmonía en febrero, y en este *entremedio* conocí yo al chico con quien hablo . . . El otro estuvo dos meses muy malito . . ., si se va, si no se va. Por fin salió, y en marzo se fué con su mujer a Valencia.

— ¿Y qué?

— Que todavía no habrá vuelto.

— *Paices* boba . . . Esto es un decir. Y si no ha vuelto, volverá . . . Quiere decirse que te hará la rueda cuando venga y se entere de que ahora vas para santa.

— Tú sí que eres boba . . ., déjame en paz. Y suponiendo que venga y me ronde . . . ¿A mí qué?

.   .   .   .   .   .

— Hay que tener contenta a esta *tía chiflada,* que es buena persona, y como le froten los muebles *al hilo,* la tienes partiendo un piñón.[3]

(A) — ¡Eh! ¡Eh! — le gritó Manuel.

Don Alonso miró hacia atrás, se detuvo y se acercó a Jesús y Manuel.

— ¿Adónde iba usted? — le preguntaron.

— Detrás de ese coche para subirle el baúl a casa a ese caballero; pero estoy cansado, ya no tengo piernas.

— ¿Y qué hace usted? — le preguntaron.

— ¡Psch! . . . Morirme de hambre.

— ¿No viene la buena?

— ¿Qué ha de venir? Napoleón se hizo la pascua en *Uaterlú,* ¿verdad? Pues mi vida es un *Uaterlú* continuo.

— ¿A qué se dedica usted ahora?

— He estado vendiendo libros verdes. Aquí debo de tener uno — añadió, mostrando a Manuel una cartilla cuyo título era: *Las picardías de las mujeres la primera noche de novios.*

— ¿Es bueno esto? — preguntó Manuel.

— Así, así. Te advierto que hay que leer un renglón sí y el otro no. ¡Yo, dedicado a estas cosas! ¡Yo, que he sido director de un circo en *Niu Yoc!*

— Ya vendrá la buena.

— Hace unas noches salí tambaleándome, muerto de necesidad, y me fuí a una Casa de Socorro, porque ya no podía más. «¿Qué tiene usted?,» me preguntó uno. «Hambre.» «Eso no es una enfermedad,» me dijo. Entonces me eché a pedir limosna, y ahora voy al anochecer al barrio de Salamanca; allá, a las señoras que van solas les digo que se me ha muerto un hijo, que necesito un par de reales para comprar velas. Ellas se horrorizan y me suelen dar algo. He encontrado también un rincón donde dormir. Está por allá, hacia el río.[4]

that are names of literary figures and places, those lifted from Spain's literary tradition, and those that connote aristocracy.

In fact, his attitude and opinions about dialogue coincide closely with his thoughts on style in general.

The critics agree on the essential differences between the dialogues of Galdós and Baroja. Gregorio Marañón, according to an article in the *Prensa* of Buenos Aires in 1935, believes that Galdós lends a theatrical artifice to his dialogue, while Baroja's is anti-theatrical.

But it is evident that Galdós' characters, also from the humble strata of society, whose soul, whose physical appearance and whose environment he described with infinite care and knowledge — when they talk they don't do it with a similar exactness, but with a notorious artifice; the artifice, undoubtedly, of the theatre, where conventionalism is inevitable.[5] (A)

Marañón goes on to praise the reality, the exactness, and the anti-theatrical quality of Baroja's dialogue.

Baroja, on the other hand, is essentially antitheatrical, and the genuine version of humanity that he gives us in his books is rightly found in his dialogue where he achieves his greatest precision and exactness.[6] (B)

In fact in the same article Marañón sets Baroja's dialogue up as a paragon of that speech which comes from the man on the street and is appreciated by that man.

And precisely the supreme achievement of Don Pío Baroja has been the referral of that inner substance of Spanish vitality, diffused in the anonymous subsoil of the street, with its own expressive norm and not with an invented, literary, and if you like, academic language. The critic, the scholar, the pedant, can find faults with their grammar book in their hand, in the marvelous dialogues always marvelous in their exactness, with which Baroja's characters speak; but the man of the street reads them with fruition because he knows that it is this way, and not any other, that he himself speaks; with the same spontaneous force and also with the same incorrections, blessed incorrections, signs of vitality.[7] (C)

Baroja himself has pointed out this theatrical quality of Galdós's dialogue, thus defending the flatness of his own.

Now some years have gone by, and Galdós comes along with his bourgoise Madrileñian homes, their informal gatherings, the living rooms with their heavy bureaus, with a Christ Child and paintings done with human hair above them. It is love for mediocre and trivial life, enthusiasm for the turns of speech of kilometric conversations, the genuflections of the palace employees or of the Pósitos, the donjuans of the yard goods stores, the discourse of the little friar who is a friend of the family and the gift of a jar of candy from the family's little nun . . .[8] (D)

Comparison of the quoted passages, reveals that the essential difference between Baroja's dialogue and that of Galdós is that one is flat and rather dull, and that the other is colorful and tending toward the theatrical. The causes of this difference will be investigated later.

Among the possible causes of the flatness of Baroja's dialogue is lack of the word and phrase constellations mentioned above — poetic words, words dealing with aristocracy and patriotism, and literary figures of speech. In the most tender of Baroja's scenes, poetic words of love are conspicuously absent. The following fragments of conversation come from a tender love scene between Lulú and the doctor in *El árbol de la ciencia.*

"I have a little theory about love" he told her one day.

"You should have a very big theory about love," she answered teasingly.

"Well I don't. I have discovered that in love, as in medicine eighty years ago, there are two practices: allopathia and homeopathy."

"Explain yourself clearly, Mr. Andrés," she replied with severity.

. . . .

"So that love, in the deepest sense, is a deceit?"

"Yes, it is a deceit like life itself; therefore someone has said, truthfully:

(A) Pero es evidente que los personajes de Galdós, también de los estratos humildes de la vida, cuya alma, cuyo pergeño físico y cuyo ambiente describió con infinito escrúpulo y conocimiento, cuando hablan no lo hacen con una exactitud semejante, sino con notorio artificio: el artificio, sin duda, del teatro, donde es inevitable el convencionalismo.[5]

(B) Baroja, en cambio, es esencialmente antiteatral, y la versión humana genuina que nos da en sus libros, es justamente en el diálogo donde alcanza su mayor precisión y realidad.[6]

(C) Y precisamente el acierto supremo de don Pío Baroja ha sido el referir esa entraña de la vitalidad española, difundida en el subsuelo anónimo de la calle, con su propio módulo expresivo y no con un lenguage inventado, literario y, si se quiere, académico. El crítico, el erudito, el pedante, podrán hacer reparos, con la gramática en la mano, a los diálogos maravillosos — siempre maravillosos de exactitud — con que hablan los personajes de Baroja; pero el hombre de la calle los lee con fruición porque sabe que es así, y no de otro modo, como habla él mismo; con la misma fuerza espontánea y también con las mismas incorrecciones; benditas incorrecciones, signo de vitalidad. . . .[7]

(D) Ahora han pasado unos años, y viene Galdós con sus hogares madrileños burgueses, sus tertulias, las salas con cómodas pesadas, con un Niño Jesús encima y cuadros dibujados con pelo. Es el amor por la vida un poco mediocre y trivial, el entusiasmo por los giros de las conversaciones kilométricas, las genuflexiones de los empleados de palacio o de los Pósitos, los donjuanes de las tiendas de telas, el discurso del frailicito [sic] amigo de la casa y el regalo del tarro de dulce de la monjita de la familia. . . .[8]

one woman is as good as another, and sometimes better; the same can be said
of man: one man is as good as another, and sometimes better."

.   .   .   .   , ...

"Do you hate me, Lulú?" Andrés asked.
"Yes, because you say silly things."
"Give me your hand."
"My hand?"
"Yes."
"Now sit down beside me."
"Beside you?"
"Yes."
"Now look me in the eyes. Loyally."

.   .   .   .

"Lulú, Lulú," Andrés said, "Have I offended you?"
Lulú got up and walked around in the shop for a minute, smiling.
"You see, Andrés; that love, that lie, that you say is love, I have felt it
for you since I first saw you."
"Really?"
"Yes, really."[9] (A)

This dialogue, obviously, includes none of the commonplace rhetoric
of love.

In the preceding chapter, Baroja states that he finds no particular
merit in a long train of synonyms words or phrases all meaning more or
less the same thing. The speech of Baroja's characters reflects the same
disdain for synonyms.[10] They use the same words and phrases over and
over. This repetitive tendency helps to create the flat quality.

Another flattening device is the use of negations and word deflators.[11]

"Look, Mr. Eugenio, I wouldn't go that far." (B)
"I don't believe," Stratford said, "in the amatory conditions of poets and
artists." [13] (C)
"It is strange; it doesn't seem that people taken one by one are so
savage." [14] (D)

The sheer banality of the conversation selected for recording contributes to the same effect. Baroja chose the very dregs and lowest possible
manifestations of the famed Spanish wit. If the jokes, pessimistic wise-
cracks, and other witticisms add any color to his dialogue, it is certainly
drab and opaque color. Here are some examples.

"What you could all do is go see the Bishop, nude, and there he, with that
little piece of soap that tailors use, could mark your bodies showing exactly
how much of them you could reveal." [15] (E)

"I don't know what you see in your father to have all this affection for
him." [16] (F)

"He is a Baron."
"A Baron with a 'b' or a varón (a man) with a 'v'?" they usually ask her.
"Varón (a man) with everything," she always replied.[17] (G)

"Kill him with bayonet thrusts," he said to his soldiers, showing them the officer; and, turning to the young girl, he added ironically: "Now you see that I have kept my promise not to shoot him."[18] (H)

(A) — Tengo una pequeña teoría acerca del amor — le dijo un día él.

— Acerca del amor debía usted tener una teoría grande — repuso burlonamente Lulú.

— Pues no la tengo. He encontrado que en el amor, como en la Medicina de hace ochenta años, hay dos procedimientos: la alopatía y la homeopatía.

— Explíquese usted claro, don Andrés — replicó ella con severidad.

— ¿De manera que el amor, en el fondo, es un engaño?

— Sí, es un engaño como la misma vida; por eso alguno ha dicho, con razón: una mujer es tan buena como otra, y a veces más; lo mismo se puede decir del hombre: un hombre es tan bueno como otro, y a veces más.

— ¿Me tiene usted odio, Lulú? — dijo Hurtado.

— Sí, porque dice tonterías.

— Deme usted la mano.

— ¿La mano?

— Sí.

— Ahora siéntese usted a mi lado.

— ¿A su lado de usted?

— Sí.

— Ahora míreme usted a los ojos. Lealmente.

— Lulú, Lulú — dijo Andrés —. ¿Es que la he ofendido a usted?

Lulú se levantó, y paseó un momento por la tienda, sonriendo.

— Ya ve usted, Andrés; esa locura, ese engaño que dice usted que es el amor, lo he sentido yo por usted desde que le vi.

— ¿De verdad?

— Sí, de verdad.[9]

(B) — Hombre, don Eugenio, yo no tanto.[12]

(C) — Yo no creo — dijo Stratford — en las condiciones amatorias de los poetas y los artistas.[13]

(D) — Es extraño; no parece que la gente sea uno a uno tan salvaje.[14]

(E) — Lo que podíais hacer vosotras es ir adonde el obispo, desnudas, y allí él, con ese jaboncillo que emplean los sastres, os marcaría con exactitud en el cuerpo hasta dónde podíais enseñar.[15]

(F) — No sé qué le encuentra a su padre para tenerle ese cariño.[16]

(G) — Este es barón.

— ¿Barón con b o varón con v? — le suelen preguntar.

— Varón con todo — replicaba ella.[17]

(H) — Matadlo a bayonetazos — dijo a sus soldados, mostrándoles el oficial; y, volviéndose a la muchacha, añadió irónicamente —: Ya ve usted que he cumplido mi promesa de no fusilarlo.[18]

One day Talleyrand was saying to the Duchess of Laval:
"Do you know, Duchess, why I like *monsieur* de Montrond? Because he has few prejudices."
To this, Montrond replied immediately:
"Do you know, Duchess, why I like *monsieur* de Talleyrand? Because he doesn't have any." [19] (A)

There is still another element which tends to flatten and dull the conversation found in Baroja's novels. The colorful bits of speech, the idiosyncratic habits of certain types are not included as something living and vital. Baroja, when he finds some interesting phenomenon in speech, prefers to comment on it first and include it later as mere documentation of his commentary. By this procedure Baroja destroys an essential characteristic of dialogue. Dialogue gives the characters a chance to express themselves in their own words and phraseology. These dialogues, in Baroja's novels, reach the reader only after Baroja has told him just about what the speakers are going to say and just about how they usually say it. As Bolinger states, Baroja sometimes gives rather long lists of these peculiar expressions and sayings instead of letting the characters speak.[20] This procedure constitutes a basic negative treatment in the creation of Baroja's dialogues.

In *Las noches del Buen Retiro,* as in most of his novels, Baroja shows himself an apt and serious student of the language of the street, carefully in tune with the little words in current usage and the commonplace adornments.

Makeup was something for prostitutes, for the horizontalettes — that was the word used at that time, and it was looked upon as something shocking and not very distinguished.[21] (B)

He also seems to worry about the lack of imagination in most of the speech of the epoch.

People enjoy so little imagination that they have to gather up anxiously from each other those little conversational adornments. They are like ragmen or cigarette butt-pickers of tailor-made phrases.[22] (C)

Apparently Baroja thinks most conversation extremely listless, but when he does find some that is lively, he is careful to deaden it by documenting it merely rather than including it as dialogue. Thierry, the protagonist of the same novel, goes to live with a carpenter and his wife. The carpenter is gifted in the ingenious and rather fantastic use of words and phrases. But the carpenter never really speaks — Baroja simply makes a list of his use of imaginative words.

A man with a rich lexicon, quite an observer, Beltrán spoke with great precision and with a great deal of circumlocution; he told about his stay in the hospital, where they operated on him, with as many details as a surgeon. He seemed to find a lot of pleasure in explaining his disease and the surgical treatment to which he was subjected. In this conversation he mixed words from his native land, Castilla la Vieja, with others from Madrid, words from the outskirts and terms used by illegal hunters. He might call a fool "teched," an onion, a stew pot, or he affirmed disdainfully that "one can't even see a gold-finch." About an insolent and presumptuous type he stated assuredly: "This stuckup is more common than a cabbage with a bow tie." Of an inopportune and crude woman he would say, "She's a cheese broad." He knew many gypsy and underworld slang words and liked to use them.

Beltrán was the son of the town's sacristan and had begun to study for the priesthood, but he had given it up because he lacked dedication. He still remembered a few Latin phrases, especially macaronic ones with a pedantic air, but he liked popular slang more than Latin phrases. He called the police force the lung; one hundred peseta bills, papyruses; twenty-five peseta bills, crabs. He always said that he could sweet talk for making love or deceiving; saw logs for sleeping; harpoon for stealing. The bed was the soft one; the jail the chessboard; the tavern the dive; the meal the bucolic; the pocketbook the rage; and the cape the cloud. He called chick peas gabriels, a five-peseta coin a sergeant's aid; a girl, honeycakes; and a little boy a little angelette. He said of pickpockets that they went through the neighborhood bringing in the sheaves. He liked to shorten words and the militia was the *mili;* the delegation was the *Delega;* and the Police Station was the *Polista.*

In tavernesque matters he had a strangely rich vocabulary. A glass might be a bucket or a snub nose, a number fifteen or a flowerpot; drinking a few glasses of wine in a group was to throw down a round or to take a few red ones. Wine was at times morapium, scuffle juice, redpoll, mostagin, etc., and for drunkenness he had fifteen or twenty terms: phylloxera, curdled, poled, plastered, troupial, chestnut, melopoeia, sunbonnet, etc., etc. and he even brought in the Basque language to use the word *moscorra.* He liked to sum up his conversations with some little phrase, half slang and half gypsy. "You've

---

(A) Un día Talleyrand le decía a la duquesa de Laval:
— ¿Sabe usted, duquesa, por qué me gusta *monsieur* de Montrond? Por-que tiene pocos prejuicios.
A esto, Montrand replicó inmediatamente:
— ¿Sabe usted, duquesa, por qué me gusta *monsieur* de Talleyrand? Por-que no tiene ninguno.[19]

(B) El maquillaje se consideraba sólo para las hetairas, para las horizon-tales, era la palabra del tiempo, y se miraba como algo chocante y de poca distinción.[21]

(C) La gente goza de tan poca fantasía, que tiene que recoger con ansia unos de otros estos pequeños adornos de la conversación. Son como traperos y colilleros de frases hechas.[22]

got to wait for 'em in the bushes." "You've got to come on where the money is." "Keep it (your tongue) flat and in your mouth." "Put a tail on the kite!" He said all these phrases pointing his index finger at the lower lid of his right eye.[23] (A)

Baroja continues this documentation of the popular lexicon throughout the novel. "But those guys, according to Beltrán, were nothing more than some miserable *sausages* and *mule herders,* that is to say, petty thieves."[24] This gentleman was simply a house thief, one of those that in the policeman's language they call a second story man."[25] (B) In *Las figuras de cera* Baroja tells how the misanthropic Frechón speaks and what he says, and then he gives an example.

He considered himself old, and one of his manias was talking about his old age.
"You don't fool an old man like me," he would say frequently. "Old men like myself know what they are doing."[26] (C)

At times the documentation shows the philosophical side of the person rather than his manner of talking. But in these cases and others the system seems inflexible. Baroja tells what the person is going to say and how he is going to say it. The actual conversation is merely documentation to back up his affirmations. In the same work Manón, the daughter of the prosperous junk man, discusses love.

Manón and Rosa weren't very much in agreement in their ideas either, and they discussed their different opinions: Manón with authority, and Rosa, in her own timid, vacillating but tenacious manner. Manón thought that love should be something gay and diverting and always new.
"No, no; nothing serious; just laughter, singing and flirting."[27] (D).

As is to be expected, Baroja shows a certain partiality toward the person who exercises a great deal of prudence in his speech.[28] Doctor Guezurtegui, Baroja's spokesman in *La caverna del humorismo,* tells of the extreme prudence exercised by a certain *gallego* with whom he worked. This prudence apparently pleased and amused Baroja.

One day, he was talking to a man from his part of the country about the latter's son, who had become somewhat of a hell-raiser, and he said to him in a very closed accent:
"Because your son acts as if he were from Madrith, and the sons of Madrith tend to be just a little bit like bums, if you please."[29] (E)

(A) Hombre muy rico de léxico, muy observador, Beltrán hablaba con mucha precisión y con muchos requilorios; contaba su estancia en el hospital, donde le habían operado, con tantos detalles como un cirujano.

Parecía tener un gran placer en explicar su enfermedad y el tratamiento quirúrgico a que se le sometieron.

Mezclaba en su conversación palabras de su tierra de Castilla la Vieja con otras de Madrid, de las afueras, y términos de cazador furtivo. A un tonto le llamaba lo mismo atontado, pasmado, cebollo o cazuelo, o afirmaba con desdén: «Ese no ve ni jilgueros.» De un tipo petulante y presumido aseguraba: «Es más cursi que un repollo con lazo.» De una mujer inoportuna y zafia decía «Es una tía queso.» Sabía muchas palabras de caló y de germanía y le gustaba emplearlas.

Beltrán era hijo del sacristán del pueblo y había comenzado a estudiar para cura, pero lo había dejado por falta de vocación. Todavía recordaba algunos latines, sobre todo macarrónicos y de aire pedantesco, pero más que los latines le gustaba el argot popular.

Llamaba a la Policía la bofia; a los billetes de cien pesetas, los pápiros, y a los de veinticinco los cangrejos. Decía siempre que podía camelar, por enamorar o engañar; sornar, por dormir, y apandar a garfiñar, por robar. La cama era la blanda; la cárcel, la trena; la taberna, la tasca; la comida, la bucólica; la bolsa, la zaña, y la capa, la nube. Llamaba a los garbanzos los gabrieles; a un duro, un machacante; a una muchacha, una gachí, y a un chico pequeño, un churumbelillo. Decía de los randas que andaban garbeando por el barrio. Le gustaba cortar las palabras, y la milicia, era la *mili;* la Delegación, la *Delega* y la Comisaría, la *Comi.* En cuestiones tabernarias tenía una riqueza de términos extraña. Tan pronto el vaso era un colodro como un chato, un quince o un tiesto; tomar unas copas entre varios era echar una ronda o tomar unas tintas. El vino era unas veces el morapio, el peleón, el pardillo, el mostagán, etc., y para la borrachera tenía quince o veinte términos: filoxera, cogorza, tranca, pítima, trúpita, castaña, melopea, papalina, etc., etc., y hasta necesitaba echar mano al vascuence para emplear la palabra moscorra. Le gustaba hacer el resumen de una conversación con alguna frasecilla medio argótica o medio gitana: «Hay que estar file.» «Hay que abiyelar parné.» «Hay que achantarse la mui,» «¡Echele usted hilo a la cometa!» Estas frases las decía llevándose el dedo índice al párpado inferior del ojo derecho.[23]

(B) "Pero éstos, según Beltrán, no eran más que unos miserables *chorizos* y *burreros*, es decir, ladronzuelos." [24] "Este señor era sencillamente un ladrón de casas, de esos a los que, en lenguage policíaco, llaman *topistas.*" [25]

(C) El se consideraba viejo, y una de sus manías era hablar de su vejez.
— A un hombre viejo como yo no se le engaña — decía con frecuencia —. Los viejos como yo saben lo que se hacen.[26]

(D) Manón y Rosa no estaban tampoco muy conformes en sus ideas y discutían sus respectivas opiniones: Manón, con imperio, y Rosa, con su manera tímida y apocada, aunque tenaz. Manón consideraba que el amor debía ser una cosa alegre y divertida y siempre nueva.
— No, no; nada de cosas serias, sino reír, cantar y coquetear.[27]

(E) Un día le estaba hablando a un paisano suyo del hijo de éste, que había resultado un tanto calavera, y le decía, con su acento cerrado:
— Porque tu hiju is comu si fuera de Madriz, y lus hijus de Madriz son un tantu a modu de golfus, si bien se quiere.[29]

This reserve in speech, coupled with disgust for the heavy, circumlocutious, and highly adorned speech of the Andalusian,[30] suggests that there may be more than a small note of Baroja's own speech, and especially of his peculiarities of speech, recorded in his novels.

Many critics are of this opinion. Gaziel, in an article called "El error de Pío Baroja," says we so easily forget the characters who appear in Baroja's novels because they are too closely related to the author.

All of Baroja's characters speak the same way: like Baroja speaks. All of them think the same way: like Baroja thinks. All of them act according to Baroja's whims. The author is constantly behind them. Therefore when we want to evoke them it is impossible for us to remember them and, on the other hand, we remember their author perfectly.[31] (A)

Bits of Baroja's conversation recorded by relatives and friends corroborate this relationship.

"Yesterday you woke me up," he told me.
"Yes," he answered, "but I still hadn't entered the room," he lied.
"I wonder if it was late?" he replied.
"Quite," I said.
"O. K., now you know, next time go sleep in the next bedroom." This is the way those incidents usually ended.[32] (B)

"I am not completely sure, but I seem to notice that literature, music and plastic arts are going downhill through the entire world."[33] (C)
"You have a room like Silvestre Paradox might have."
"Could be. My nephew Julio's is just a bit on the luxurious side. Me, those things have never attracted me. I prefer mud to stucco and marble."[34] (D)
"What are you going to do?" he said to me one day commenting on the problem. "You can't change people. It is boring and not very interesting; but solitude is much worse."[35] (E)

Considering his distaste for all that has to do with rhetoric or other forms of adornments, his liking for prudence and discretion in speech, his opposition to the pedantic and dogmatic, his creed of "no afirmar," most of Baroja's recorded dialogue can be seen as quite akin to his own speech. At times it seems that the character is completely set aside or forgotten and that Baroja cannot restrain himself from speaking. The somewhat annoyed phrase of "¿Qué quiere usted?" seems to belong to no one but Baroja. In *La nave de los locos* the weaver of Albarracín called El Epístola gives his impression of the Carlist wars. Not only are the ideas and opinions from Baroja, but the very turn of speech is his.

"They have killed all they could," El Epístola went on saying; "they have burned with the same profusion; now Spain doesn't have any inclination to work nor any ideal. What do you expect those guerrilla fighters to do? If they could they would invent another war for the slightest reason, and the son of the Carlists would appear as a Republican or as any old thing; the idea, naturally, would be to fight, not stay in the same place, go from one place to another and try your luck." [36] (F)

Paco Maluenda, the narrator of *Las mascaradas sangrientas,* explains his choice of military service with this phrase:

I would have gone with the liberals; but there were people among them who knew me, and I preferred to go off with the Carlists. I am not one of those who is convinced, what do you expect? To me one bunch is as good as another. [37] (G)

(A) Todos los personajes de Baroja hablan de la misma manera: como habla Baroja. Todos piensan del mismo modo: como piensa Baroja. Todos obran como se le antoja a Baroja. El autor está constantemente detrás de ellos. Por eso cuando queremos evocarlos nos es imposible recordarles a ellos y, en cambio, recordamos perfectamente a su autor. [31]

(B) — Ayer me despertaste — me decía.
— Sí — contestaba — pero aún no había entrado en el cuarto — mentía.
— ¿Sería tarde? — replicaba.
— Bastante — decía yo.
— Bueno, otra vez ya sabes, vete a dormir al cuarto de adelante — así solían terminar estos incidentes. [32]

(C) — Yo no tengo una seguridad completa, pero me parece notar que la literatura, la música y las artes plásticas van decayendo en el mundo entero. [33]

(D) — Tiene usted un cuarto como podría tenerlo Silvestre Paradox.
— Puede ser. El de mi sobrino Julio es algo así como lujoso. A mí esas cosas no me han seducido nunca. Prefiero el barro a la escayola y al mármol. [34]

(E) — ¿Qué se le va a hacer? — me dijo un día comentando esto —. A la gente no se le puede hacer cambiar. Es aburrida y tiene poco interés; pero es mucho peor la soledad. [35]

(F) — Se ha matado lo que se ha podido — siguió diciendo [sic] *el Epístola* —; se ha quemado igualmente con profusión; ahora España no tiene ganas de trabajar, ni ideal ninguno. ¿Qué quiere usted que hagan estos guerrilleros? Si pudieran, inventarían otra guerra por un quítame allá esas pajas, y el hijo del carlista aparecería como republicano o como cualquier cosa; la cuestión, naturalmente, sería pelear, no quedarse en un sitio, andar de una parte a otra y probar la suerte. [36]

(G) Yo me hubiera ido con los liberales; pero entre ellos había gente que me conocía, y preferí marcharme con los carlistas. No soy un convencido, ¿qué quiere usted? A mí lo mismo me dan los unos que los otros. [37]

Like the indirect presentation of the conversations, this procedure contributes greatly to the negative impression of the novels, making the dialogues monotonous, colorless, and without animation.

Bolinger says that almost half of Baroja's dialogue expresses opinions about something.[38] Many times these dialogues are more like monologues in which Baroja runs through many subjects and ideas with alacrity, expressing his own opinions. This tendency toward a monologue is evidenced in *El cura de Monleón*. Javier, the local curate, merely sets up the conversation of the doctor with such statements as the following: "I don't understand you, that is, that you are an opportunist, that is what one calls agnosticism, that means that you are a sceptic, what do you think?"

"They are just as egotistical and just as much beasts as the rest; but they are more pedantic and have a ridiculous opinion of themselves. They believe in those mystifications of socialism and democracy in the same way that Catholics believe in the Virgin."

"I don't understand you."

"My thought may be good or bad, but I don't believe there is anything obscure or difficult to understand about it. I think that the scientific and spiritual culture of the world is neither terminated nor propagated. To take it as definitive and to strive to create a closed, dogmatic and immutable system and impose it on everyone else, is to do on a smaller scale, badly and coldly, what the Christians did grandly and ardently. I believe that you shouldn't close anything, but leave all the doors open to the fresh air. In short, it doesn't seem to me that my thought is so obscure and so sybiline that it cannot be understood."

"That is to say that you are an opportunist?"

"That's it; a opportunist, or if it pleases you more, a relativist. You priests think that your Saint Thomas defined everything: time, space, ultimate cause, God, miracles. Communists believe that Karl Marx gave the norm of life. Between the silent ox of Sicily and the bearded Jew of Tréveris lies all human knowledge. That is what we do not believe."

"That is what we call agnosticism."

"Yes, that's possible. With opinions everything responds to an initial concept. If you suppose that life and History is governed by economy, like the socialists and Jews believe, you will find economy in every event. You can defend the thesis that religious laws are nothing more than economic principals. Religion would be an economy based on apparently economic dogmas. And if you wanted to, you could look at the maxims of the ten commandments as economic maxims. There is no sentence in religions that commends waste. Perhaps the only one might be the Christian maxim par excellence: 'Love thy neighbor as thyself.' This would be a great waste; but it is such a rare waste that one can almost say that it doesn't happen. If instead of looking for economy in History, you look for religion, myth, pleasure, you will find them also."

"That means that you are a sceptic."

"Half and half, nothing more."

"But in this practical, immediate question of the Socialists, who believe they are exploited. What do you think?"[39] (A)

In *La nave de los locos* when Captain Barrientos wants to escape the war he expresses his opinions about it in much the same language that Baroja uses. Alvarito, the other partner in the dialogue, furnishes the echoes of opinion and the questions that allow the monologue to continue.

"In the Basque Provinces and Navarra," the Captain said, "the war has been barbaric; in Castilla la Vieja, Merino and Balmaseda have given it a more fierce character; in Cataluña, still more cruel, and approaching Valencia and la Mancha it has been the worst of the worst. Here a man's word is no longer respected; everything is done with a repugnant cruelty. This is a Moorish war; they undress prisoners to kill them with bayonets; they undress women

---

(A) — Son tan egoístas y tan bestias como los demás; pero son mucho más pedantes y tiene una idea ridícula de sí mismos. Creen en estas mistificaciones del socialismo y de la democracia como los católicos en la Virgen.
— No te entiendo.
— Mi pensamiento será bueno o malo, pero no creo que tenga nada de oscuro ni de comprensión difícil. Yo pienso que la cultura científica y espiritual del mundo ni está terminada, ni está propagada. Tomarla como definitiva y pretender crear un sistema cerrado, dogmático e inmutable e imponerlo a los demás, es hacer en pequeño, en malo y en frío, lo que hicieron los cristianos en grande y en ardiente. Yo creo que no se debe cerrar nada, sino dejar todas las puertas abiertas al aire. En fin, no me parece que mi pensamiento sea tan oscuro y tan sibilino para que no se comprenda.
— Es decir, ¿que eres un oportunista?
— Eso es: un oportunista, o si se quiere mejor, un relativista. Los curas creéis que vuestro Santo Tomás ha definido todo: el tiempo, el espacio, la causa, Dios, los milagros. Los comunistas creen que Karl Marx ya ha dado la norma de la vida. Entre el buey silencioso de Sicilia y el judío barbudo de Tréveris está todo el saber humano. Eso es lo que no creemos nosotros.
— Eso es lo que se llama el agnosticismo.
— Sí; es posible. En las opiniones todo responde a un concepto inicial. Si se supone que la vida y la Historia, como lo creen los socialistas y los judíos, está regida por la economía, se encuentra la economía en cualquier acontecimiento. Se puede defender que las reglas de las religiones no son más que principios económicos. La religión sería una economía basada en dogmas aparentemente económicos. Si se quisiera, se verían las máximas del decálogo como económicas. No hay ninguna sentencia en las religiones que preconice el despilfarro. Quizá la única sería la máxima cristiana por excelencia: «Ama a tu prójimo como a ti mismo.» Este sería el gran despilfarro; pero es un despilfarro tan raro, que casi se puede decir que no se da. Si en vez de buscar la economía en la Historia, se busca la religión, el mito, el placer, se los encuentra también.
— Eso quiere decir que eres un escéptico.
— A medias nada más.
— Pero en esta cuestión práctica, inmediata, de los socialistas, que se creen explotados, ¿tú qué crees? [39]

to club them and to rape them; they shoot children. This is, in simple terms, a filthy mess."

"It is the Cabrera school."

"Yes, Cabrera, with his Catalan, Valencian, and Manchegan lieutenants, has dishonored the war and the country. Here it is common to vent your rage on corpses, mutilating them and yanking out their eyes."

"How horrible!"

"It is nauseating! Like I say, it is a Moorish war."

"But it seems that war is more or less the same everywhere," Alvarito said.

"No, there in the North, the war has been a war of fanaticism, inspired by the priests, this is a war of ignorance, of cruelty, and of bounty."[40] (A)

At times the monologue is a defensive one, much like Baroja's essays in which he defends himself against criticism. El Lince in *El cantor vagabundo* responds to a series of accusations.

"You are a fascist?"

"No, I am not a fascist."

"You have sold books about saints and miracles."

"So what, what does that have to do with fascism?"

"They say that you fraudulently practiced medicine."

"That is false, it isn't true. If I have given some advice now and then it has been to recommend hygienic measures."[41] (B)

This refutation in a rather annoyed tone of a series of accusations is like the many essays in which Baroja defends himself against a myriad of accusations and criticisms of his work.

. . . somebody else considers me, because I have written historical novels, a follower and imitator of Pérez Galdós.

There is no such thing. I, although I met Galdós, was never very enthusiastic about the writer or the person.[42] (C)

In the last analysis, it seems reasonable to conclude that Baroja's dialogue — so similar to his narrative — neither stands out in sharp relief nor is intended to do so.[43] Many moments in Baroja's novels give the impression that he is merely telling a story over a cup of coffee, that there is hardly any difference between his dialogue and the rest of his narrative, that the *guiones* are placed arbitrarily around some conversation and excluded from other conversation.[44]

This assumed, almost every observation applied to his prose in general can be applied to his dialogue. All the facets of his stylistic creed: *destruir es crear, no afirmar, no estilizar,* and *se escribe como se anda* are much in evidence in all his dialogues. His dialogue, then, like his prose in general, is in minor tones. It is deflated and dulled; it rejects rhetoric and adornment: it has the quick, uneven rhythm of the narrative and it bears the inequivocal stamp of Baroja's personality.

Besides reaffirming all the negative aspects of his prose in general, Baroja's dialogue shares another important negative aspect of his novelistic technique. It stresses the limitation — sometimes the futility — of communication through conversation. There is almost indicated a negative correlation between the amount and the complexity of words exchanged and the amount of actual communication. Greater length and complexity may well indicate less communication, while a few unordered words may convey a wealth of meaning. An example is the final exchange of words between El Cura Merino and Aviraneta.

(A) — En las provincias Vascongadas y Navarra — dijo el capitán —, la guerra ha sido bárbara; en Castilla la Vieja, Merino y Balmaseda le han dado un carácter más fiero; en Cataluña, más cruel aún, y al acercarse a Valencia y a la Mancha, ha sido lo peor de lo peor. Aquí ya no se respeta la palabra, todo se hace con una saña repugnante. Esta es una guerra de moros; se desnuda a los prisioneros para matarlos a lanzadas, se desnuda a las mujeres para apalearlas y violarlas, se fusila a los chicos. Esto es, sencillamente, una porquería.

— Es la escuela de Cabrera.

— Sí, Cabrera, con sus lugartenientes catalanes, valencianos y manchegos, han deshonrado la guerra y el país. Aquí es corriente cebarse en los cadáveres, mutilándolos y sacándoles los ojos.

— ¡Qué horror!

— ¡Es un asco! Como le digo a usted, es una guerra de moros.

— Pero parece que en todas partes la guerra es poco más o menos lo mismo — dijo Alvarito.

— No; allá, en el Norte, la guerra ha sido una guerra de fanatismo, inspirada por los curas; esta es una guerra de ignorancia, de crueldad y de botín.[40]

(B) — ¿Usted es fascista?

— Yo no soy fascista.

— Usted ha vendido libros de santos y de milagros.

— Y eso ¿qué tiene que ver con el fascismo?

— Dicen que usted ejercía fraudulentamente la Medicina.

— Eso es falso, no es cierto. Si he dado alguna vez algún consejo, ha sido recomendar medidas higiénicas.[41]

(C) . . . otro me considera, por haber escrito novelas históricas, como un seguidor e imitador de Pérez Galdós.

No hay tal cosa. Yo, aunque conocí a Pérez Galdós, no tuve gran entusiasmo ni por el escritor ni por la persona.[42]

"It's true. No one remembers the losers."
"Some of them, yes."
"We are irreconcilable enemies, Eugenio, but nevertheless . . ."
"I say that same nevertheless."
"Adios, Eugenio!"
"Adios, don Jerónimo!"[45] (A)

Baroja's dialogue then, in essence, is a strong negation of the importance of dialogues. He feels that far from being a soul-searching investigation of one soul and its innermost workings and thoughts by the intelligent and untiring questioning of another, dialogue is just another vehicle for expressing an attitude or opinion — his own. The opinion can be placed in dialogue for variety or can be included in the narration. There seems to be little difference.

All the negative qualities of Baroja's dialogue, the lack of theatrical speech, certain types of words, affirmation, the paucity of direct presentation, the intrusion of Baroja's peculiar speech and opinions, and the reduction of the dialogue to a monologue make significant contributions to the total negative impression of his novels.

(A) — Es verdad. Nadie se acuerda de los vencidos.
— De algunos, sí.
— Somos enemigos irreconciliables, Eugenio, y sin embargo . . .
— Ese mismo sin embargo digo yo.
— ¡Adiós, Eugenio!
— ¡Adiós, don Jerónimo![45]

4. *Atmosphere*

FOR THOSE who have had the revealing experience of reading Antonio Machado's poetry immediately after finishing one of Baroja's novels, a comparison of the two artists will seem appropriate. The objective starting point for this chapter will be a comparison of selections from these two authors.[1]

The poem is taken from Machado's *Soledades*.

> The coals of a purple dust
> are sinking behind the black cypress trees . . .
> In the square, shaded, stands the fountain
> with its winged and nude Cupid, made of stone,
> which dreams mute. In the marble basin
> the dead water lies.[2] (A)

The following passage is from the prologue to *El mayorazgo de Labraz*. The words having associations useful in the formation of a novelistic climate, are italicized.

One *afternoon in August* I went to visit Labraz, a town of *the ancient* Cantabria. They had told me that it was a town *in its death throes*, a *dying* city, and my spirit, *depressed* at the time by the *bitter sadness* that the *failure* of *romantic dreams* leaves, wanted to refresh itself in the *profound desolation* of an almost *dead* town.

The city appeared in the distance with its houses grouped on the side of a hill, standing *yellow* against the sky, with a *humble* and *sad* look; some tall

---

(A) Las ascuas de un crepúsculo morado detrás del negro cipresal humean . . .
En la glorieta en sombra está la fuente con su alado y desnudo
Amor de piedra, que sueña mudo. En la marmórea taza reposa el agua
muerta.[2]

[63]

and *blackish* towers rose *erectly* from among the *brown mass* of *twisted* and *discolored* roofs.

Labraz was a *terrible* town, a town of the *Middle Ages*. There was no street that wasn't *hunchbacked;* almost all the houses had a stone shield. Almost all of them were *silent* and *grave;* many of them were *collapsed,* completely *sunken.*

Here and there *an old woman* dozed in a doorway, a beggar passed tapping the ground with his white stick, and the *starving* dogs ran along the gutter.

There were four or five *ruined* churches; some converted into hay-lofts.[3] (A)

This passage from *El mayorazgo de Labraz* and the six-line poem from Machado seem to elicit just about the same emotional feeling. Both give the feeling of solitude, loneliness, the hopeless dejected feeling often elicited by something almost immobile, something almost lifeless.

Juan Uribe Echevarría supports the authenticity of these feelings in his comparison of Antonio Machado and Baroja's descriptions of Segovia.

Baroja provides us with a beautiful impressionistic description of Segovia, with psychological interpretations of its inhabitants:

" . . . habitually sullen faces, people with a sinister look and a soft sweet speech.

In those types one could understand the enormous decadence of a race which didn't retain more than the facial expressions and the gestures of its ancient energy, the hollow shell of its gallantry and force."

It is the negative and pessimistic vision that Antonio Machado, the poet of 98, will capture later on in his book, *Fields of Castile* (1907–1917).

" . . . decrepit cities, roads without inns, and astonished country people, without songs or dances . . ."

> Wretched Castile, yesterday the ruler,
> Wrapped in your rags you despise all you don't know.
> Its mother, in other times, fertile with captains
> Today is only a stepmother of humble laborers.[4] (B)

As usual one does not have to rely on just his own feelings or those of critics in order to be sure of his emotional reaction after having read a passage from Baroja. Baroja seldom fails to comment on his own works and his own feelings. In the special edition of *Indice* dedicated to him, he speaks of his solitude and lack of optimism.

My mother, poor soul, when she was very old and we lived in Madrid, on Mendizábal street, and I would come home at dusk an hour later than usual, used to say to me: "I have been alone all afternoon."

I, now that I am as old as my mother was then, have been alone for long periods of time, in the morning, in the afternoon and at night. I have become accustomed to it and solitude no longer oppresses me, and many times it proves enchanting, as long as it doesn't perturb me, like when it goes along with insomnia or lumbago . . .

Disconnected memories, the purely sensual images of the land and of the sea, the impressions of a magnificent night in the South or in the North, with a moon or with stars, a snow-capped mountain or the drawing room of an elegant and cold woman, pass across the gray screen of the unfortunate and melancholy man.

I don't have much capacity for optimism. Any small sorrow gets me down and perturbs me. I have fought as best I could against this depressing and melancholy tendency, and at times I have dominated it, not by reason, but by the imposition of my will. Generally logic is completely useless in these cases.

(A) Una *tarde* de *agosto* fuí a visitar Labraz, pueblo de *la antigua* Cantabria. Me habían dicho que era una ciudad *agonizante,* una ciudad *moribunda,* y mi espíritu, entonces *deprimido* por *la amarga tristeza* que deja el *fracaso* de *los ensueños románticos,* quería recrearse con *la desolación profunda* de un pueblo casi *muerto.*

La ciudad apareció a lo lejos, con su caserío agrupado en la falda de una colina, destacándose en el cielo con *color amarillento,* con traza *humilde* y *triste;* algunas torres altas y *negruzcas* se perfilaban *enhiestas* entre la *masa parda* de sus tejados *torcidos* y *roñosos.*

.   .   .   .   .   .

Era Labraz un pueblo *terrible,* un pueblo de la *Edad Media.* No había calle que no fuese *corcovada;* las casas tenían casi todas escudos de piedra. Casi todas eran *silenciosas* y *graves;* muchas estaban *desplomadas,* completamente *hundidas.*

En alguno que otro portal dormitaba alguna *vieja,* pasaba un mendigo tanteando el suelo con la blanca garrota, y los perros *famélicos* corrían por el arroyo.

Había cuatro o cinco iglesias *arruinadas;* algunas convertidas en pajares.[3]

(B) De Segovia, Baroja nos proporciona una bella descripción impresionista, con interpretaciones sociológicas de la vida de sus habitantes:

" . . . . caras hoscas por costumbre, gente de mirada siniestra y habla dulce.

En aquellos tipos se comprendía la enorme decadencia de una raza que no guardaba de su antigua energía más que gestos y ademanes, el cascarón de la gallardía y de la fuerza."

Es la visión negativa, pesimista, que captará más tarde Antonio Machado, el poeta del 98, en su libro *Campos de Castilla* (1907–1917).

. . . decrépitas ciudades, caminos sin mesones,
y atónitos palurdos, sin danzas ni canciones

.   .   .   .   .

Castilla miserable, ayer dominadora,
envuelta en sus andrajos desprecia cuanto ignora.

.   .   .   .   .

La madre en otro tiempo fecunda en capitanes
Madrastra es hoy apenas de humildes ganapanes.[4]

A day of sunshine or a day of rain, or the clear laughter of a young woman are worth much more.[5] (A)

After establishing the close relationship or affinity of the two atmospheres created by Antonio Machado and Pío Baroja, it is easy to discern the close relationship between the two procedures used in their creation. The italicized words indicate that Baroja lost no opportunity to darken his novelistic climate. Almost every word in the passage contributes to the atmosphere of sadness, loneliness, and depressed hopelessness. Words that ordinarily do not bear this connotation are charged with it in this paragraph. For example, the words *tarde* and *agosto* in the first line do not necessarily connote sadness; however, in this passage, through the re-iteration of other words associated with sadness, they are charged with a feeling of gloom, of hopelessness. Their slight connotation of decadence is further charged by other and stronger signs, such as *antigua, agonizante, moribunda, deprimido, amarga tristeza, fracaso, ensueños románticos, desolación profunda, casi muerto*. The paragraph produces a sensation of depression, and does so with an efficiency of words and devices. This feeling can be attributed mainly to the intensifying reiteration of closely aligned associations or connotations.[6]

Once the prevailing tone of the emotional environment has been set, once the first paragraph has suggested a certain emotional tone, the other words strengthen and accentuate it. Elements in the rest of the passage, which ordinarily might serve as mere picturesque factors in a description, take on that tone. In general, the words *caserío agrupado en la falda de una colina* (a group of houses on the side of a hill) do not necessarily provoke a feeling of sadness or of solitude, but here they do just that. Because of the *signos de sugestión* which precede and those which follow, the group of houses on a hillside become a symbol of solitude and of the past, of something almost dead and forgotten. The same group of houses, found in a novel without the constant reiteration of these dark signs, might have a certain charm.

One of the associations of this passage quite often encountered in writings of the Generation of 98, is the association or connotation of something in a state of disrepair, something on its last legs, something crumbling or rotting.[7] The passage is full of *signos de sugestión* elicited by words such as: "twisted and discolored roofs, many (houses) which had collapsed, completely sunken, an old woman dozed, a beggar passed by, feeling his way along the ground, starving dogs, ruined churches converted into haylofts, a dry river." On all of these objects and persons the tag *casi muerto* of the first paragraph is placed; thus reinforced, they become efficient *signos de sugestión* which create or help create the atmosphere of solitude and hopeless desolation.

As stated before, the sadness of the atmosphere lends a symbolic potential to objects that ordinarily would not have it, or it reinforces their symbolic impact. It has been pointed out that Baroja feels melancholy when he sees a school in Labraz.

> Passing through a little square with trees I stopped to contemplate a school through the open windows.
> I don't know why a school makes me very melancholy; those posters with big letters, the maps, the black desks with their ink wells, remind me of my childhood, a prologue to life which is almost never pleasant.[8] (B)

The school here becomes a bimodal symbol, *símbolo bisémico*. It represents youth never quite lived or enjoyed — what Baroja considers to be the worst outcome of Spanish education, brutal pedantry, and perhaps stupidity.[9] More important than these levels, which the school in part symbolizes and which produce a part of the melancholy, is the fact that the school is *empty*. He sees no life therein, so the school like everything else in Labraz is almost dead, lifeless; this is one of the principal causes of Baroja's sadness upon seeing it. This feeling is suggested to Baroja and intensified by his own sensitivity to loneliness and feelings of solitude, as expressed in the article in *Indice*. It is significant for the atmosphere of the novel that Labraz is an isolated pueblo. Its people, and especially its *capitán de las llaves,* cannot conceive of a pueblo without walls. "The

---

(A) Mi madre, la pobre, cuando ya tenía muchos años y vivíamos en Madrid, en la calle de Mendizábal, y yo llegaba un día a casa al anochecer una hora después que de costumbre, solía decirme: "He estado sola toda la tarde."

Yo, que tengo ahora tantos años como tenía mi madre en esa época, he estado solo durante mucho tiempo, por la mañana, por la tarde y por la noche. Al fin me he habituado y la soledad ya no me pesa y muchas veces me encanta, siempre que no perturbe, como cuando va unida al insomnio o al lumbago . . .

Pasan por la pantalla gris del hombre desafortunado y melancólico, los recuerdos sin ilación, las imágenes puramente sensuales de la tierra y del mar, las impresiones de una noche magnífica en el Mediodía o en el Norte, con luna o con estrellas, el monte nevado o el salón de una mujer elegante y fría.

Yo no tengo mucha capacidad de optimismo. Cualquier dolor pequeño me aploma y me perturba. He luchado como he podido con esa tendencia deprimente y melancólica, y a veces la he dominado, no por razonamiento, sino por imposiciones de la voluntad. Generalmente la lógica no sirve en esos casos para nada. Vale más un día de sol o un día de lluvia o una risa argentina de mujer joven.[5]

(B) Al pasar por una plazoleta con árboles me detuve a contemplar la escuela por sus ventanas abiertas.

No sé por qué una escuela me produce una gran melancolía; aquellos cartelones de letras grandes, los mapas, las mesas negras con sus tinteros, me recuerdan la infancia, un prólogo de la vida casi nunca agradable.[8]

Captain didn't understand, and it was understandable that he didn't understand, that there were towns so crazy and so shortsighted that they would want to tear down their walls." [10] (A) The small plaza where the house of *el mayorazgo* is located is quite isolated and little frequented. Only two very narrow streets lead to it. Human life is little in evidence there, except for the occasional presence of a curate, or of an old religious woman.[11] The *hidalgo's* house itself is for the most part empty, and this emptiness lends its sadness to the atmosphere. The presence of spiders, a lone swallow, and bats in the deserted upper chambers of this old house cannot help but darken the novelistic climate.[12]

One of the most important groups of words that help build this novelistic climate centers around ideologies.[13] In this case the predominant ideology seems to be the Catholic, but in this novel, as in most of Baroja's others, no distinction is made between Catholicism, Judaism, Communism, Fascism, Socialism, and Protestantism. For Baroja, they are all just about one and the same.[14] The shadow of the new and old church dominates all of Labraz. It is, as Baroja states here and in other novels, a levitical town.

When the new church was built, an alligator was hung on the wall of the entrance. The people of Labraz did not know whether someone had placed the alligator there or whether it had arrived under it own power.[15] Baroja merely wishes to indicate with this device that a superstitious ignorance formed an integral part of the overexalted religious faith of these people. Of course, the alligator himself, grinning down at humanity from the walls of a church, is not the most pleasant of sights and adds its morbid touch. When the Mayorazgo and the members of his household go to church, the scene in the chapel lends itself to the darkening of Labraz.[16]

The whole town of Labraz was filled with little niches, each with its corresponding saint, its lantern, and garland of dry flowers.[17]

Perhaps more important than the artifacts of the ideological atmosphere of the town is the cruel, vicious, and unenlightened spirit of the town, caused by its ideology. When one of the women of the lower class slipped, or was supposed to have slipped, morally, the town showed no mercy. When Blanca thought that her sister Marina was in trouble, she feared the terrible wrath of a levitical town.

> Blanca remembered two or three young girls who had committed an error. The conduct of the towns people toward them had been of such a cruel nature, that life for them there became impossible. The other girls avoided them like the plague; the men believed they had a right to their bodies, already lost, and would send them notes by Cañamera and Zenona, the two celestinas of Labraz; the boys insulted them. It was the spirit of all levitical towns.[18] (B)

Weather is an important element which Baroja uses in the novel to strengthen the feeling of darkness and solitude. When Don Ramiro and Doña Cesárea appear in Labraz, it is on a very cold night. The inclement weather, as well as the words that describe it, darkens the atmosphere. While the couple are inside the inn of La Goya, the wind moans outside. "While she waited on the tables for the guests, they talked excitedly in the kitchen. The wind whistled in the fireplace and moaned softly in the distance."[19] (C) The words *mugía sordamente* intrinsically darken the scene. The moments of relative happiness and brightness occur in the summer or in the spring, but when another tragedy approaches, Baroja in the best romantic literary tradition uses autumn to help prepare the scene.[20] We remember that the last hardships of *el mayorazgo* and Marina took place in the worst part of winter, but, as the novel approaches its happy ending, the signs of spring return.

A ray of sunlight entered the woods; the birds came out in bands; among the heather thickets the red bird sang, the turtle dove whistled and the sun began to raise its radiant face over the crests of the snowcapped mountains.
The sky remained blue, pure and splendid; on the slopes of the mountains a golden flower sparkled in the furze thickets.[21] (D)

Death, with all accompanying medieval Catholic pageantry is one of the most important groups of *signos de sugestión* which help to create the total atmosphere of the novel. Every word associated with death becomes an agent of intensification within the novel's atmosphere. Micaela, who soon is to aid in the death of Cesárea who befriended her, contemplates a

---

(A) No comprendía el señor Capitán, y se comprendía que no lo comprendiese, que hubiera pueblos tan locos y tan imprevisores que quisieran derribar sus murallas.[10]

(B) Blanca recordaba dos o tres muchachas que habían cometido algún desliz. La conducta del pueblo para ellas había sido de una crueldad tal, que la vida allí se les hizo imposible. Las demás muchachas se apartaban de ellas como de un apestado; los hombres se creían con derecho a su cuerpo, ya perdido, y les mandaban recados con la Cañamera y la Zenona, las dos celestinas de Labraz; los chicos las insultaban. Era el espíritu de todos los pueblos levíticos.[18]

(C) Mientras servía la mesa a los huéspedes, en la cocina hablaban intrigados. Silbaba el viento en campana de la chimenea y mugía sordamente a lo lejos.[19]

(D) Entró en el bosque un rayo de sol; los pájaros salieron en bandadas; por entre los matorrales del brezo cantó la malviz, silbó el tordo y el sol fué levantando su cabeza radiante sobre las cimas de los montes nevados.
El cielo quedó azul, puro y espléndido; en las faldas de los montes alguna flor de oro brilló entre los matorrales de retama.[21]

cypress tree — always associated with cemeteries in Spanish tradition — and is saddened, just as the whole novel is, by its presence.

> Distracted, she pulled out the seeds of the reeds that were growing in the dry pond and contemplated the musty old cypress that was standing, obscure and rigid, in the orchard.
> How sad that tree was! . . . Always alone, withered. Only at its very top the branches, of a bronze color, showed a little green, a pale sign of life.[22] (A)

This particular cypress seems a little sadder than most because it stands alone, and because of the adjectives that describe it. These adjectives themselves *vetusto* (musty), *oscuro* (obscure), *rígido* (rigid), *triste* (sad), *solo* (alone), *mustio* (withered), *pálida señal de vida* (pale sign of life), as well as the cypress, become *signos de sugestión* and darken considerably the atmosphere of Labraz.

The death and burial of Doña Cesárea lend great possibilities to the author for darkening and saddening the novelistic climate of Labraz. Her death itself is not exactly a pretty one.[23] It has been hastened by an overdose of medicine, but the funeral reveals more completely the essentially medieval darkness of Labraz. Labraz seems especially suited for funerals, and the Mayorazgo has spent more than two-thirds of the year's income from his lands on this one. Chapter three deals exclusively with the description of the funeral, and our sympathy for Doña Cesárea is lost in the complex ritual of burial.[24]

The death of Rosarito is much more serene, and her burial is not described.

> Afterwards, the child began to babble; Marina noticed that she was getting cold and pale; she called to her and she answered in a vague way; then she saw that the child was murmuring something very weakly. Finally, she breathed a gasping sigh, closed her eyes and was dead.[25] (B)

In spite of the delicate way in which her death is handled, it has a deeply saddening effect on the total atmosphere of the novel.

Another element associated with death — an important one for all of Baroja's novels — is the appearance of the gallows. Here the appearance is cursory, but it does appear. During the fair in Labraz, a man with a huge cardboard figure gave a moral lesson to the onlookers. "A man with a huge sign was explaining the life of a man from the time he began to disobey his parents until he ended up on the gallows, to everyone's satisfaction."[26] (C) The little paragraph seems to be inserted by chance. It seems to serve little purpose in the novel, except to further darken it.

Many of the literary quotations that serve as chapter headings prove to be excellent *signos de sugestión* contributing greatly to the peculiar atmosphere of Labraz. It is worthy of note that the literary and artistic taste of the eccentric Englishman, Bothwell, is quite in keeping with the dark and medieval atmosphere of Labraz. Among the painters he first toasts Ribera, who certainly represents a somber note in painting. Dickens is first to be mentioned among the writers, and with the mere mention of the name, we feel oppressed by the damp gloomy atmosphere created in many of his novels and sketches. Berceo, Jorge Manrique, and the author of *La Celestina* are mentioned by the Englishman and add their own medieval note.[27]

The novelistic world created by Dickens seems to be ever present in Baroja's mind and in his writings. In *El mayorazgo de Labraz* Baroja borrows freely from the milieu created by Dickens merely by quoting a few lines from one of his novels. These lines become *signos de sugestión* and serve as atmospherical depressants. The following is from *Martin Chuzzlewit*. "When I left London (I'm a Kentish man by birth, though) and took that situation here, I quite made up my mind that it was the dullest little out-of-the-way corner in England, and that there would be some credit in being jolly under such circumstances."[28] (D)

Following the same procedure Baroja brings to his novel all the tragic ambience of a certain Shakespearean play with just two lines.

Hark I hear horses.
Give us a light here, ho![29] (E)

(A) Distraída, arrancaba la simiente de los juncos que crecían en el seco estanque y contemplaba el vetusto ciprés que se alzaba, oscuro y rígido, en el huerto.

¡Qué triste era aquel árbol! . . . ¡Siempre solo, mustio! Unicamente en lo alto de la copa el ramaje, de color de bronce, verdeaba un poco, una pálida señal de vida.[22]

(B) Después, la niña comenzó a balbucear; Marina notó que se iba poniendo fría y pálida; la llamó y ella contestó de un modo vago; luego vió que la niña murmuraba algo muy débilmente. Por último, lanzó un suspiro anheloso, cerró los ojos y quedó muerta.[25]

(C) Un hombre con un gran cartelón explicaba la vida de un criminal desde que empezó por la desobediencia a sus padres hasta que terminó en el patíbulo, para satisfacción de todos.[26]

(D) Cuando me marché de Londres (he nacido en Kent, aquí donde usted me ve) y me coloqué en este pueblo, pensé que era éste el rincón más triste y más apartado de toda Inglaterra y que tendría algún mérito en seguir siendo jovial en semejante rincón.[28]

(E) Suenan herraduras.
¡Eh!, una luz.[29]

The same device is used in the quotation from Victor Hugo,

La oscuridad es una presión. La noche es una especie de mano puesta sobre nuestra alma.

and in the quotation from Byron,

Un silencio frío reina en las salas desoladas.[30]

The funeral atmosphere that accompanies Doña Cesárea's death is intensified and given serenity by the well-known lines from the *Coplas* of Jorge Manrique.

> Then let no man himself deceive
> And think that there will come a day
>   he hopes will last
> More than the days now gone and past
> For all and everything
>   Must go that way.[31] (A)

Although the literary quotations may serve other functions in the novel,[32] it is quite clear that some of them do function in *El mayorazgo de Labraz* as *signos de sugestión*.

For the creation of the novelistic climate of *El mayorazgo de Labraz*, Baroja has used *signos de sugestión* that fall into the following groups: those indicating *solitude* and *decadence*, those relating to certain *ideologies*, those which deal with the *meteorological atmosphere*, those closely associated with *death*. These different groups tend to blend into one, and that one tends to establish the peculiar atmosphere of the novel. Thus any word associated with any of these groups will become a *signo de sugestión*, and the reiteration of each of these *signos*, which abound in the novel, will help strengthen the character of the environment.

In spite of the superficial disparity of these groups, there is a unifying factor. They all represent a stagnation and immobility of life; they are all oppressive to humanity; they all dwell on death rather than life; they all are, as Baroja would say, antibiological and antivital. They form an ambient that is nonconducive to life. This is evidenced much more clearly when the darker scenes of the work are compared to those which seem to have more life-giving light and energy — those settings which are more conducive to human warmth.

Some brighter scenes in the work shed a ray of hope and life, but usually these are marred by the perversity of participants — such as the priests when they go to visit the old monastery. Perhaps the most forceful of the contrasting ambients is the Christmas scene in the rather poor and humble town in the mountain pass.

In this scene, Baroja seems to have reversed his procedure for establishing a novelistic ambient. The *signos de sugestión* here, contrasting with the majority of those in the novel, all indicate vitality, humanity, life. The literary quote from *The Pickwick Papers,* although surrounded by sorrow, strongly evokes a feeling of friendship and solidarity with other human beings, which is in direct contrast to the many other literary citations that speak of extreme solitude and loneliness.[33]

In the house itself are many *signos de sugestión* indicating vitality and life. The fretting of the mother of the bride about the kettles in the fireplace and the fire itself are all *signos* which indicate life.[34] The kitchen itself is one of these *signos* and, significantly, neither kitchen nor corresponding kettles and artifacts of vitality accompanying it appeared in the dark musty interiors of the house of the Mayorazgo. The fire especially is mentioned several times during the passage.

The calmness and cheerfulness of the country doctor who has come on horseback inspires confidence and a sense of well-being.[35] The animals lend their note of domestic tranquility and of vital existence to the whole scene.[36] These animals do not appear in Labraz.

The snow adds its note of purity to the nativity scene. "It kept on snowing, the snowflakes dancing in the air."[37] Snow does not appear in the physical atmosphere of Labraz because it is white, pure, and soft. In Labraz, although the novel takes place mostly in fall and winter, there is only bitter cold, sleet, and rain.

The preparation for the Christmas Eve supper, *nochebuena,* is replete with *signos de sugestión* which elicit not only a biological hunger, something which did not seem to exist in the meals at Labraz, but also a sense of the kinship of humanity. Just about everything having to do with the complex and lengthy preparations of the meal is a *signo de sugestión* indicating vitality. The big log, the two lambs being roasted on spits, the children waiting to lick the pan, are all signs of this type.[38] The meal itself, the music that follows, and especially the riddles, all indicate and establish firmly an atmosphere of vigorous and unaffected humanity.

If one were to choose just one symbol to best contrast this atmosphere with that of Labraz, this symbol would be that of the newborn child. All of the *signos* seem to point toward this infant, and their presence make of

---

(A) No se engañe nadie, no,
pensando que ha de durar
lo que espera
más que duró lo que vió
porque todo ha de pasar
por tal manera.[31]

him a bimodal symbol. The people of this little village take the birth of the child as a joyous event, but the Mayorazgo, who comes from a different ambient, foresees the ill treatment and perhaps the crucifixion of the Christ-like child. " — ¡Pobrecillo! — murmuró don Juan en voz baja —. ¡Qué mal regalo te han hecho con la vida!"[39] Thus the gloomy sterility of Labraz is contrasted with the joyous vitality of this small village with its living nativity scene symbolic of life or of a new life for Marina and Don Juan.

Another important factor in Baroja's contrast of the vital and anti-vital atmosphere within the novel is the dynamic movement of its protagonist. Throughout the work Don Juan has been steeped in immobility within the walls of Labraz. He has been completely passive. As the novel draws to an end this passive immobility is reversed, and Don Juan becomes a man of action. He burns the cornfields and escapes from Labraz with Marina. Their walk across the countryside of Spain is a strong indicator of vitality, and it stands in bright contrast to the dark, passive immobility of the past.

Thus the atmosphere in *El Mayorazgo de Labraz* impresses the sensibility of the reader in much the same way as the poetry of Antonio Machado. It depresses him. In the same manner the creative procedures of the novelist and poet are similar. Baroja, like Machado, creates the peculiar atmosphere of many of his novels through the association and reiteration of selected verbal signs. This creates an antivital mood, further intensified by a sprinkling of bright vital signs that serve as contrast. The corroboration of the existence of this same atmosphere and creative procedure throughout the four periods of Baroja's novelistic production should reveal a great deal about his creativity. The four works to be studied are *Camino de perfección, Aprendiz de conspirador, Las agonías de nuestro tiempo, El hotel del cisne.*

Camino de perfección was selected from the first period because of the poignancy of its novelistic climate. The essence of this climate is expressed in the author's own words in a description of one of Fernando Ossorio's own paintings. "The painting was called *Silent Hours.* It was painted unevenly; but there was in all of it an atmosphere of contained suffering, an anguish, something so vaguely sorrowful that afflicted one's soul."[40] (A) Those *signos de sugestión* that center around death are found in abundance in the first part of the novel. One of the most significant is the mention of suicide, which Baroja uses in many of his novels.[41] In some novels it is mentioned only in passing; in others it is definitely the climax and serves as a compendium of all the accumulated futility and despair. Suicides, for example, bring to a close *El árbol de la ciencia* and *El cantor vagabundo.*[42] In *Camino de perfección,* suicide receives only a mention.

"Yes; hysterical influence," Ossorio said after a few minutes, when I thought that he had already forgotten the disagreeable theme of his conversation, "Hysterical influence is easily traced in my family. My mother's sister, crazy; a cousin committed suicide; one of my mother's brothers, an imbecile; in an insane asylum, an alcoholic uncle."[43] (B)

The factors in the novel dealing with or centering around death continue to appear. While Fernando Ossorio is in Toledo, at a moment in which the air is charged with gloom, a coffin appears which is intended for a very young girl.[44] This appearance of the coffin allows the author to use a series of lugubrious words in relation to it. The words *locuras* (madness), *visiones, ataud blanco* (white coffin), *siniestra, sombra* (shadow), *silueta confusa y negra* (dim black silhouette), *desesperada, caserones grandes* (huge stone houses), *un ruido a hueco terrible* (a terrifying sound of emptiness), coupled with the fact that a coffin seems to be wandering through the streets, from door to door, looking for a young girl of six or seven years who has passed away, bring the atmosphere of the novel to its highest pitch.[45] Even the reaction of his protagonist to the scene seems more of an excuse to reiterate some of the *signos de sugestión* than anything else.[46] The unreality, the indeterminant quality of the atmosphere here reach a peak.

Closely related to the *signos de sugestión* associated with death are those that center around ideology which, as has been pointed out, quite evidently centers around Catholicism. The various aspects of this Catholic ideology would be its sensual and erotic elements often associated with mysticism, its asceticism, its dogmatism, and especially its ritual and pageantry.

The symbol of all this ideology is Yécora.[47] Its shadow stands over Fernando's life throughout all his wanderings. It is directly responsible for Fernando's first education or lack of same.

My mother, since I undoubtedly got in her way around the house, and who didn't want to have me with her, sent me to Yécora, a big and ugly,

---

(A) El cuadro se llamaba *Horas de silencio*. Estaba pintado con desigualdad; pero había en todo él una atmósfera de sufrimiento contenido, una angustia algo tan vagamente doloroso, que afligía el alma.[40]

(B) — Sí; la influencia histérica — dijo Ossorio al cabo de unos minutos, cuando yo creí que había olvidado ya el tema desagradable de su conversación —; la influencia histérica se marca con facilidad en mi familia. La hermana de mi madre, loca; un primo, suicida; un hermano de mi madre, imbécil, en un manicomio; un tío alcoholizado.[43]

clerical, and unfriendly place in La Mancha, to finish my preparatory schooling. I spent three years in that levitical town, two in a Escolapian boarding school and one in the house of the administrator of some of our farms, and there I became vicious, a knave, and ill disposed; I learned all those graces which adorn people with a cassock and those which deal intimately with them.[48] (A)

This ambient evokes an air of perversion because it renders impossible the satisfaction of basic desires.

"Bah!, that all depends," the most serious one murmured. "I don't think that girl is as lewd as her mother. Undoubtedly she has a perverse instinct, but it is a moral perversity. What is more; it is possible that her way of being may be born from a romanticism which failed since she lived in an atmosphere where it was impossible to satisfy her desires. I don't know, but I don't believe in the evil or the sin of those who smile ironically.[49] (B)

This reaches its peak, as does the total atmosphere of the novel, in Toledo. There amid all the artifacts of Catholicism — the constantly appearing image of Christ set into a wall,[50] the religious paintings of El Greco such as *El entierro del conde de Orgaz* seen at night by candle-light,[51] the old church of Santo Domingo el Antiguo,[52] and the love affair with the nun, La Desamparados[53] Fernando's perverse sexual agitation, stimulated by the ambient, reaches its most acute stage and causes him to enter Adela's room at night.

Along with his religious crisis is a feeling of asceticism that seems to spring principally from his quite perverse relationship with his cousin Laura. These ideas of asceticism are part of the total picture of Christianity, that part of Christianity which is basically antivital and anti-human.[54]

Fernando Ossorio's terrible feeling of solitude is reflected in the gloomy decadence and solitude of his surroundings. Everything that surrounds him seems immobile and stagnant. After the rather unsuccessful and shameful end of his affair with La Desamparados, he wanders through the streets of Toledo one Sunday until he comes to a small plaza.[55] In this plaza and its surroundings, he sees all the signs of his own solitude and depression. It is a sad plaza, solitary, and is reached by two narrow, obscure, and tortuous passageways. The tiles of a nearby church roof are covered with moss, symbol of that which is rotting and nonproductive. On the other sides of the square are high brick walls to keep out the sun. The doors seem unfriendly, and the bars on the oversized windows are rusted. The silence of the countryside reigns in the small square, the shout of a child or the clatter of horses' hoofs are absent, adding to the intensity of the silence. This silence is broken only by the distant murmur of the Tajo or the shrill crowing of some rooster.[56] The small square and everything pertaining to it is quite closely related to the silence and the dark, still solitude felt by Fernando. There is no life in the plaza; and absence of life is suggested by the words just mentioned: *triste, solitario, oscuros, tortuosos, musgos, puertas hurañas, rejas carcomidas, silencio.* The café, which receives the full impact of Ossorio's dark desolation before it leads him to visit Adela's room in the dark of the night, is another of the many symbols of his sadness. Perhaps a café was picked because it was meant to leave us with a last bit of sick loneliness and nausea in the pit of our stomachs.[57]

After leaving Toledo, Fernando goes to Yécora. Yécora has not changed; it is still the symbol of all the sordid, grotesque, antivital aspects of Catholicism, a symbol of all of its dogmatic oppression, its ritual and pageantry. In the chapter dedicated to its description, Yécora is presented as the symbol of the antispiritual, the antihuman, and the antivital. It contains none of the charm of the old, the venerable, no art objects unless they are quite new and without taste.[58] Art has fled from Yécora and left it in the hands of small political leaders, a dry, formalistic religion, petty lawyers, priests, and usurers, and people with all sorts of sordid vices and miserable hypocrisies.[59]

Fernando's horrible impressions of Yécora are intensified by his visit to the school that the Escolapian fathers have there. The school, like the one in Labraz, is a symbol of wasted youth. Fernando remembers the days there as being long, sad, and extremely boring.[60] His description of the school contains the same suggestions of darkness and antivitality used throughout the novel. The place seemed horrible enough to him during the day, but at night it was a veritable prison.[61]

Examining the meteorological elements in *Camino de perfección,* one is surprised at how little overt mention they receive. Nevertheless their presence is keenly felt. Rain and fog are mentioned a few times during the course of the novel — rain, especially, intensifying the emotional tone.

(A) Mi madre, a quien indudablemente estorbaba en su casa, y que no quería tenerme a su lado, me envió a que concluyese el grado de bachiller a Yécora, un lugarón de la Mancha, clerical, triste y antipático. Pasé en aquella ciudad levítica tres años, dos en un colegio de escolapios y uno en casa del administrador de unas fincas nuestras, y allí me hice vicioso, canalla y malintencionado; adquirí todas estas gracias que adornan a la gente de sotana y a la que se trata íntimamente con ella.[48]

(B) — ¡Bah!, según — murmuró el más serio —. Yo no creo que esta chica tenga la lubricidad de su madre. Indudablemente, en ella hay un instinto de perversidad, pero de perversidad moral. Es más: es posible que esta manera de ser nazca de un romanticismo fracasado al vivir en un ambiente imposible para la satisfacción de sus deseos. Yo no sé, pero no creo en la maldad ni en el vicio de los que sonríen con ironía.[49]

In Fernando's first sally, rain drives him into a cathedral. The mobility of the dark, gray rain clouds form a background for the dark, empty, dominical silence found in the church. These rain clouds are a setting for the cathedral scene; they tend to give it a sense of instability and unreality in much the same way the dark clouds lend a similar illusory effect to El Greco's *Vista de Toledo*.[62]

The beautiful poem of the corpse contributes no little bit to the darkened environment of the novel. It tells of the putrefaction of a bishop in his tomb. But it also tells of the purification of this same bishop by the elements of water, flowers, and air.[63] The poem then is symbolic of the purification of all that is corrupt by nature. The bishop, like Yécora, is the symbol of all that is corrupt, ugly, and antivital. Contrasting with this symbol is the purifying nature found in the poem and throughout the novel. Nature is what might be called a secondary theme. It plays an important role in creating the minor or vital novelistic climate. It leads to strong biological life and youthful vitality, as opposed to degenerate old age and corruption.

The minor or vital atmosphere that is closely related to nature in the novels appears many times in *Camino de perfección*. The line, "Me parece que estos montes son Dios," serves as a good example. Some of these minor atmospherical notes deal with dawn and sunrise, something quite logical.[64] "It was a splendid and happy dawn: nature was awakening with a timid smile; the roosters crowed; the swallows shrieked; the air was clean, saturated with the odor of humid earth."[65] (A) This invigorating description of daybreak shows that after having a night's sleep in the little mountain town, the protagonist feels rejuvenated, full of vitality.[66] In the isolated little farm of Marisparza, Fernando recovers from the terrible oppression and desolation he felt in Toledo. He seems to think that his contact with nature is causing him to replace his old cerebrum with a new one, just as lizards replace their tails.

"As the lizards grow a new tail," he said, "I must be growing a new brain."[67] (B)

From this moment, Fernando Ossorio steeps himself in fresh air and sunshine. He stops off at a little town near Alicante and spends a few days as a boarder with some country people. Everything there is filled with life, with signs of nature's color and vitality. Such are the invigorating qualities of this atmosphere that he sings praises of spring, life, and nature.[68] From this small village he goes to live with his uncle Vicente in a small village in the province of Castellón. Nature continues to pour life into his veins and spirit. What once might have been a symbol of the dark atmosphere of Catholicism and superstition of the Middle Ages now elicits a jovial salutation. The windvane on top of the church tower with its rather grotesque adornment elicits an optimistic and felicitous salutation.[69]

We notice in this happy salute that the words *triste, escuálido, pobre,* appear, but they lose all force because of the preponderance of the happy signs such as *cómicamente, jovial, bondadoso.*

Throughout the novel it becomes obvious that Fernando Ossorio's walking, his moving through the countryside of Spain, is a definite part of his cure. Walking through the countryside is part of the brighter more vital atmosphere of the novel, and it stands in direct contrast to the depressed and lethargic immobility felt in Madrid and Toledo.

The novel closes in this vital atmosphere, but three notes detract from an otherwise completely happy ending. First, the new atmosphere, this nature which is so vital and conducive to life and happiness, is not nearly as convincing as the other atmosphere which shrouded everything in darkness and despair. This latter atmosphere seems, for Baroja, more fictional, less realistic. Baroja has lived the darker part of the novelistic atmosphere, and when he utters the words *triste, desoladora,* he feels their meaning. We sense, likewise, that the invigorating vitality of nature belongs to that part of him which was never quite realized. Fernando Ossorio, like Baroja, is not sure that all of this life-giving nature is quite the thing for him. Strangely enough he feels a nostalgia for the sad ideas.

The truth of the matter is that I have been here for two weeks, and I am beginning to grow tired of being happy. I find myself with an agile body and mind, I don't feel the old accumulation of indecisions which choked my will; and something stupid which makes me indignant with myself; at times I miss the sad ideas I had before, the tribulations of my spirit. Isn't that too much stupidity?[70] (C)

The different novelistic environments created in Baroja's novels show a marked predilection for the antivital. The author himself finds his novels gray and somber.

The second detracting note is the realization that this fight between vital and antivital is still in progress. We read the reply of the orchard

---

(A) Era un amanecer espléndido y alegre: despertaba la Naturaleza con una sonrisa tímida; cantaban los gallos, chillaban las golondrinas; el aire estaba limpio, saturado de olor a tierra húmeda.[65]

(B) Como las lagartijas echan cola nueva — se decía —, yo debo de estar echando cerebro nuevo.[67]

(C) Lo cierto es que hace dos semanas que estoy aquí, y empiezo a cansarme de ser dichoso. Como me hallo ágil de cuerpo y de espíritu, no siento el antiguo cúmulo de indecisiones que ahogaban mi voluntad; y una cosa imbécil que me indigna contra mí mismo: experimento a veces nostalgia por las ideas tristes de antes, por las tribulaciones de mi espíritu. ¿No es ya demasiada estupidez? . . .[70]

to the church and the counterreply of the church to the orchard when they are on their vacation in Tarragona.

> Some canons dressed in red began to cross the cloister; the bells rang in the air. The music from the organ began to be heard, arriving softly, followed by the murmur of prayers and canticles. The murmur of the prayers was ceasing. The murmur of the canticles was ceasing. The music from the organ was dying out, and it seemed that the birds were chirping with greater force and the roosters crowed in the distance with a more strident voice. And suddenly those murmurs hid themselves once more among the voices of the somber prayer that the chorus of priests entoned to their vengeful God.
>
> It was the reply that the orchard gave to the church and the terrible answer of the church to the orchard.
>
> The choir, the laments of the organ, the psalms of the priests were hurling a formidable anathema of abomination and of hate against life; in the orchard, life celebrated its placid triumph, its eternal triumph.[71] (A)

The battle is never-ending, and there seems to be no decisive victory for either side.

The third note detracting from the minor atmosphere is the temporal superimposition that occurs at the end of the novel. Fernando, thinking about his newborn child, swears that his son will not be tortured by the same terrible, dark, and Catholic atmosphere that he was tortured by in his earlier years. "No, no, she would not torture his son with useless studies, nor with sad ideas; she would not teach him a mysterious symbol of any religion."[72] (B) But while Fernando makes these solemn promises himself, the grandmother sews a symbol of all these things into the clothes which the child is to wear. The future with its symbol of the antivital atmosphere is thus superimposed upon the present represented by the young child — as yet free from these corrupting and crippling elements. "And as Fernando was thinking thus, Dolores' mother was sewing a folded leaf of the New Testament into the sash the child was to wear."[73] (C) Thus, with these three detracting elements, the novel remains in the antivital atmosphere — shrouded in its somber Catholicism. As in many of Baroja's novels, the control of light and darkness seems to be such that any light and happy moments which may appear are always framed by dark, despairing hours.

In the second decade of Baroja's novelistic production, the nine novels from his *Memorias de un hombre de acción, El árbol de la ciencia* and *El mundo es ansí,* the reader's sensibilities are affected in much the same way as they were affected by the novels of the first decade. These novels depress him. They make him feel the futility of life, the omnipresence of death. They sadden him, make him feel alone in the world. These novels without exception seem to be impregnated with a dark and devitalized atmosphere. An examination of the atmosphere and its creation in the first of the novels about Aviraneta called *El aprendiz de conspirador* will corroborate this general impression.

The effects of the physical atmosphere on the total novelistic atmosphere are much in evidence as the novel opens. Pello Leguía, apprentice conspirator and narrator of the story, is on his way to La Guardia in a small berlin with broken windows, drawn by three squalid nags. It is raining.[74] When the carriage breaks down, Pello Leguía and his fellow travelers, two women, seek hospitality in a nearby town. They find the place to be ugly, full of mud and filth.[75] The mud and filth reach the belly of the horse that Pello rides into town.[76]

The opening scene of the novel then is darkened by the rain and the ugliness and filth of the nearby town. The final scene of the novel is also shrouded in rain.[77] Aviraneta and Leguía are on the highway to Bayona in a tilbury. It is a gray, rainy afternoon.[78] Just before they get settled down for the night and Aviraneta prepares to tell Pello his story, it begins to rain again.[79]

The meteorological atmosphere of *El aprendiz de conspirador* centers around rain. The rain which darkens the first moments of the novel and which is falling as Aviraneta tells the story of his childhood makes its total impression on the novel. The reiteration of the word "rain" with all its concomitant phenomena serves to darken and devitalize the atmosphere.

Rain, so essential to the life of all plants and animals, is used as a conductor of a depressed mood because of Baroja's personal, subjective reaction to it. Baroja had arthritis, and rain must have caused him considerable physical discomfort.[80] Besides, Baroja was keenly sympathetic to vagabonds who are the most unprotected of earth's creatures. Rain or any inclement weather, to them, was most unwelcome and

---

(A) Comenzaron a cruzar por el claustro algunos canónigos vestidos de rojo; sonaron las campanas en el aire. Se comenzó a oír la música del órgano, que llegaba blandamente, seguida del rumor de los rezos y de los cánticos. Cesaba el rumor de los rezos. Cesaba el rumor de los cánticos. Cesaba la música del órgano, y parecía que los pájaros piaban más fuerte y que los gallos cantaban a lo lejos con voz más chillona. Y al momento estos murmullos tornaban a ocultarse entre las voces de la sombría plegaria que los sacerdotes en el coro entonaban al Dios vengador.

Era una réplica que el huerto dirigía a la iglesia y una contestación terrible de la iglesia al huerto.

En el coro, los lamentos del órgano, los salmos de los sacerdotes lanzaban un formidable anatema de execración y de odio contra la vida; en el huerto, la vida celebraba su plácido triunfo, su eterno triunfo.[71]

(B) No; no le torturaría a su hijo con estudios inútiles, ni con ideas tristes; no le enseñaría símbolo misterioso de religión alguna.[72]

(C) Y mientras Fernando pensaba así, la madre de Dolores cosía en la faja que había de poner al niño una hoja doblada del Evangelio.[73]

absurd. They envied the snail with its generous protection from the elements.

A MISANTHROPHIC VAGABOND

Absurd! Absurd! It is already Springtime. What a lack of seriousness in the weather! What a lack of consideration for us who don't have a good wardrobe! One doesn't know what to do. It rains, hails, thunders, the sun comes out, the sun goes down, it gets cloudy, a rainbow appears . . . Why so much phantasmagoria? Absurd! Absurd!

.   .   .   .

Who wouldn't like to be a snail so that he would have his boarding house assured![81] (A)

Baroja recalls having to study huddled over a brazier in order to keep warm.[82] Rain, like most inclement weather, is depressing; it inflames his arthritis, makes his daily walks impossible, confines the restless student to the monotony of a shut-in, and drenches the homeless. Although the part played by rain in *El aprendiz de conspirador* is minor, it is the most important element in the creation of that dark and depressed mood of *Las mascaradas sangrientas* and *La casa de Aizgorri*.

Rain, in *El aprendiz de conspirador,* is linked to and reinforces the feeling of solitude. The puddles of water and the humidity contribute to the sadness and desolation of the little plaza which Pello Leguía encounters when the coach breaks down.[83] The fact that this plaza is empty, and that the only living sign is a completely desolate cat, increases the feeling of loneliness.

The character of the city of La Guardia intensifies these feelings. The same signs that made Labraz the paragon of the devitalized towns, that made it the symbol of emptiness, unproductivity, hopelessness, and immobile solitude are all reiterated in Baroja's description of La Guardia. Like Labraz, it was a walled city. The beautiful poplar trees that surrounded it have all been chopped down in order to avoid a surprise attack.[84] The fields were seldom cultivated, and fire and cannon shot had added to the desolation and the barrenness. Winter added also to this solitude and desolation.

During the winter, with the snowfalls, the countryside became even more sad than it ordinarily was; the sierra appeared like a gray wall, with white stripes, and upon the white and solitary extension of the country estates and of the grapevines the flame of the fires glowed and the blasts of the cannon resounded.[85] (B)

It seems that many of the towns in Baroja's novels are much the same, because the same signs of desolation, solitude and sadness are used in describing them.[86] Yécora in *Camino de perfección,* Monleón and the nameless town in Alava which appear in *El cura de Monleón,* Arbea of

Las mascaradas sangrientas, Castro Duro in *César o nada,* Herrera in *El mundo es ansí* furnish excellent examples of such cities. The dark hues with which these cities are painted almost destroy their individuality, reducing them to a dark and amorphous mass.

Death contributes its share to the antivital elements. The shadow of death is ever-present because of the Carlist wars. The mysterious Carlist spy brings this shadow nearer to the reader by telling of the murder of his ex-master Don Luis and how it was avenged.

Don Luis started out in a lamentable condition. We didn't have to walk very far; eight days after leaving, upon arriving at Lerma, he couldn't take the weariness any longer, and he fell exhausted, without strength.
He was left in the city jail, where they declared that he had typhus, and he died in two weeks.
At that moment, just when the dance was at the height of its animation and uproar, a heartrending cry was heard, so penetrating that it reached the street. A woman fell to the floor.[87] (C)

Other scenes of death darken the atmosphere of the novel. When Aviraneta and Pello are attacked in the inn outside the walls of La Guardia, their attackers kill one of the guests. There is no indication that the man was involved in any way in the intrigues and struggles taking place between

---

(A)   UN VAGABUNDO MISÁNTROPO
¡Absurdo! ¡Absurdo! Ya estamos en primavera. ¡Qué falta de seriedad en el tiempo. ¡Qué falta de consideración para los que no tenemos un buen guardarropa! No sabe uno a qué atenerse. Llueve, graniza, truena, sale el sol, se pone el sol, se nubla, aparece el arco iris . . . ¿Para qué tanta fantasmagoría? ¡Absurdo, absurdo! . . .
.   .   .   .
¡Quién fuera un caracol para tener segura la casa de huéspedes![81]

(B) Durante el invierno, con las nevadas, la campiña quedaba aún más triste que de ordinario; la sierra aparecía como un paredón gris, veteado de blanco, y sobre la alba y solitaria extensión de las heredades y de los viñedos brillaba el resplandor de los incendios y resonaba el estampido del cañón.[85]

(C) Don Luis se puso en camino en un estado lastimoso. No tuvimos que andar mucho tiempo; ocho días después de la marcha, al llegar a Lerma, ya no pudo más con el cansancio, y cayó agobiado, sin fuerzas.
Se le dejó en la cárcel del pueblo, donde se le declaró el tifus, y murió a las dos semanas.
En esto, en el momento en que el baile estaba en su mayor animación y algaraza, se oyó un grito desgarrador tan penetrante, que llegó hasta la calle. Una mujer cayó al suelo.[87]

Aviraneta and his enemies. More than anything else the incident seems to be a sign of the violence of the times, which further darkens the novel.

> They went to the room of the two guests and found themselves facing a horrible spectacle: one of the men was dead, stabbed repeatedly with a knife, in the bed; the other one, on the floor, nude, bound, and gagged. They untied him and he managed to tell them what had happened. He had awakened and encountered five strange men who tied and gagged him. When he looked towards his companion's bed he saw him dead and bathed in blood.[88] (A)

The Carlist spy is captured and shot a few days later. His execution by the firing squad contributes to the total emotional impact of the novel.

Of all the devitalizing signs used, the ideological ones are probably the most effective. The sinister shadow of the Carlist wars hovers over the whole novel. These wars, as depicted by Baroja, are exceptional in that they are almost completely devoid of any altruistic motives, any true loyalty to a cause, any mass heroism. [89]

To bolster the effects of these Carlist wars on the background of the novel as a whole, Baroja brings another sinister element into focus. This element is the Inquisition, still a powerful force and still active during Aviraneta's childhood. Aviraneta recalls some of the acts of this tribunal that occurred in Madrid around 1800. He remembered the exile of Pablo Antonio de Olavide whose intelligence and desire for reform put him in a bad light with the *Santo Oficio*.[90] The completely unjust and inhuman encarceration of the crippled mathematics teacher, Don Benito Bails, brings some of the sinister darkness of the grandiose auto de fe with its witch burnings to the novel. The Holy Office also had to struggle with the popular superstitions of the day. During this period there seemed to be many unofficial saints and mystics.[91] All this, then, forms part of the lifelessness and despair contributing to the atmospherical cloak of *El aprendiz de conspirador*.

Although the signs of despair and desolation dominate the novel, there are moments in which the scene brightens and one feels the surge of vital humanity. In Aviraneta's little country house in Ithurbide, there is the same sense of warmth given off by a fire, the same sense of human solidarity, and the same sense of the well-being caused by good food and shelter experienced in the nativity scene from *El mayorazgo de Labraz*.[92] These things contribute to human life, while the other signs destroy it.

As in the two preceding novels, movement here indicates vital human life and activity. As soon as the three passengers of the berlin mount their horses and start to move across the countryside, the spirit of the novel brightens. The fact that the three passengers participate actively in the crossing of the countryside makes them more alive and hence revitalizes the reader's spirits. The countryside becomes a thing of beauty, color appears in Corito's cheeks, their appetites are whetted and their spirits lifted.[93]

Las agonías de nuestro tiempo, a trilogy composed of *El gran torbe-llino del mundo, Las veleidades del tiempo,* and *Los amores tardíos* written in the third period of Baroja's creative activity furnishes an excellent example of a powerful and consistent novelistic atmosphere. The trilogy seems permeated with an extra touch of sadness and disillusionment. After reading the three novels, one feels the penetration of a silent but powerful despair and grief. Nothing has really happened in the novels — nothing meaningful, that is. They represent a chain of monotonous days that have passed sadly and quietly. These days are all the same. Some are full of sorrow and some without hope. The symbol of the treadmill with its buckets full of sorrow one moment and empty of hope the next, "Los llenos de dolor y los vacíos de esperanza,"[94] seems to describe perfectly the days which have passed darkly before our eyes.

The atmosphere of the novel makes a strong impression on the reader because as in *El mayorazgo de Labraz* its elaboration is literary. However, in this trilogy, the literature comes directly from the author-protagonist, Joe Larrañaga. Throughout, the author has given free rein to the poetic emotions which happenings and landscapes have elicited. Upon witnessing a certain landscape in the northern countries, in Holland, or in France, for example, the author-protagonist felt compelled to record in an unrestricted lyrical manner this impression. Also when some trivial incident occurs, and most of the events tend toward a monotonous triviality, he reflects philosophically upon this matter in a subjective and uninhibited way. His emotions are recorded in much the same manner. In his own literary genres called *Evocaciones, Fantasías de la época, Las sorpresas de Joe, En voz baja, Estampas iluminadas, Croquis sentimentales,* he creates the greater part of the emotional tone of the trilogy.

There are exceptions, but the majority of these poetic impressions lend to Joe's surroundings an air of instability, an air of unreality and indeterminism.[95]

In one of the poetic impressions interpolated in the trilogy Baroja speaks of this tendency toward fantasy, toward unreality, toward indeterminism.

Between Hugo de Vries, Mendel and the applications of their discoveries to Philosophy, again they have made the amateurs think that, if there isn't a

---

(A) Fueron al cuarto de los dos huéspedes, y se encontraron con un espectáculo horrible: uno de los hombres estaba muerto, cosido a navajadas, en la cama; el otro, en el suelo, desnudo, atado y amordazado. Le quitaron las ligaduras y pudo contar lo ocurrido. Se había despertado y encontrado con cinco hombres desconocidos, que le ataron y amordazaron. Al mirar hacia la cama de su compañero le vió muerto y bañado en sangre.[88]

great liberty, absolute and theoretical, there is a small practical liberty, a certain spiritual spontaneity that they call indeterminism.[96] (A)

The system of signs that create the background of the novel can be divided into four groups, as with the works from the three previous decades. The groups tend to blend imperceptibly into one another.

For the physical atmospherical side of the quadrangle, the poetic impressions caused by the scenes from the North are of great importance — especially in setting the tone. In the passage below, the words lending themselves to the creation of an environment which is indeterminant, unreal, and nonconducive to human life are italicized.

Fields of Jutland, a blue sky, *an immense horizon, a land without a tree,* with a few slight *undulations in the distance.*
The great *thickets of purple heather* cover the *enormous expanses of sad, savage looking, stony ground.*
"This plain of Jutland, *deserted, level,* and *rocky,* has its charm, Joe murmurs: "it is a land *for going* and *coming,* a land for *wanderers* and *vagabonds.*"
Here and there, among the *blackish rocks* the big *pools* sparkled, sometimes like little lakes.
It is an *uninhabited land, something like the sea, without obstacles.* The roads, *narrow and full of puddles,* are *rock-filled sand gullets.* At times small hills appear, perhaps dolmens, with their tumulus; *at times a shepherd, knitting, shows up with his flock and his dog.*[97] (B)

There is little light in the picture. The signs indicating darkness abound: *brezo morado* (purple heather), *enorme pedregal* (enormous beds of rock), *pedregosa* (rocky), *rocas negruzcas* (black boulders), *charcos* (puddles). The word *triste* appears here, as it does in almost all the poetic impressions. The idea of desert-like barrenness is reinforced by the mention of roads full of ruts, chuckholes, sand, and rocks.

In *Las veleidades de la fortuna,* a pond elicits the poetic impression. In this *Croquis sentimental,* the pond is a symbol of a thing of beauty which becomes stagnant and corrupted, a symbol of that which no longer lives. It becomes plugged up, the flowers die, the water becomes stagnant and evil-smelling, and the dead goldfish rise to the top.[98]

The gardens of the Luxembourg in August give the impression of something sad, languid, and immobile. The signs *triste, lánguido, pesado* (heavy), *hojas amarillas* (yellow leaves), *desiertas* (deserted), *letargo, tejados grises de pizarra* (gray roofs of slate), *solitario,* are repeated here. Repeating some of the same words used throughout the impression, Joe sums up in the last paragraph. "Nightfall is quite oppressive, and one goes unwillingly towards his hotel to shut himself in his room, with an immobile and suffocating air."[99] (C) The impressions of the Rhine at night [100] and of Montmartre [101] are of the same shades of darkness, irreality, and antivitality. These shades correspond to Joe's inner spirits and are projected throughout the novel.

Ideology produces its signs of suggestion in this trilogy, just as it does in most of Baroja's works. Protestantism here elicits just about the same signs of sadness, of dark antivitality, as Catholicism and Judaism. "A little bit of sunshine seems to touch the objects weakly, and then the bells ring, slow, protestant, heavy bells, promising a long and boring sermon in a sad and cold church."[102] (D) Many of the atmospherical suggestions elicited by Protestantism are the same as those elicited by the scenes from the North. Thus the words *triste, largo, pesado, aburrido, lentas, fría,* etc., are repeated in most of the impressions, and through this repetition they gain greater potentiality for creating atmosphere.

Another common denominator of all of the ideological ambience in Baroja's novels is an air of dogmatic, pedantic, and farcical charlatanism. It seems to invade the ranks of all religions, of all ideologies. In *Las veleidades de la fortuna,* Joe dedicates one of his *Fantasías de la época* to *Los charlatanes.*[103] One of his *Estampas iluminadas* is dedicated to *La conversación alemana,* which excels, according to Baroja or Joe, in pedantry.[104]

(A) Entre Hugo de Vries, Mendel y las aplicaciones de sus descubrimientos a la Filosofía, han hecho pensar otra vez a los aficionados, que, si no la gran libertad teórica y absoluta, hay una pequeña libertad práctica, una cierta espontaneidad espiritual que llaman indeterminismo.[96]

(B) Campos de Jutlandia, cielo azul, *un horizonte inmenso, tierra sin un árbol,* con algunas ligeras *ondulaciones en lo lejano.*

Los grandes *matorrales de brezo* morado cubren el *enorme pedregal, triste,* de *aire salvaje.*

— Esta llanura jutlándica, *desierta, plana* y *pedregosa,* tiene su encanto — murmura Joe —: *es país para ir y venir,* país para *andariegos,* para *vagabundos.*

Aquí y allá, entre las *rocas negruzcas,* brillan los *charcos* grandes, a veces como pequeños lagos.

Es una *tierra deshabitada, algo como el mar, sin obstáculos.* Los caminos, *estrechos* y *encharcados,* son *regueros* de *arena llenos de piedras.* A veces aparecen pequeños cerrillos, quizá dólmenes, con su túmulo; *a veces se presenta, con su rebaño y su perro, algún pastor haciendo media.*[97]

(C) El anochecer es algo pesado, y se va uno acercando sin ganas al hotel, a encerrarse en el cuarto, de aire inmóvil y sofocante.[99]

(D) Un poco de sol parece tocar débilmente los objetos, y luego suenan campanas, campanas lentas, protestantes, pesadas, prometedoras de un sermón aburrido y largo en una iglesia fría y triste.[102]

That side of the quadrangle which runs the gamut from decadence to death is also included in the poetic impressions. In one of the *Estampas iluminadas* in which he describes the left bank along the Seine, he makes the comment that everything is old.

> Nearby, everything is old; Saint-Pères street, Seine street, Bonaparte street and the intermediate alleys are replete with shops, antique stores, stamp and print dealers, second-hand book dealers, art shops selling porcelain objects and paintings.[105] (A)

Terms indicating oldness appear explicitly twelve times in the *Estampa*. The words *triste, seria, negro, pesado, grises,* make their appearance and reappearance as in almost all the impressions.

Perhaps the most poignant atmospherical impression from the trilogy is that of solitude and disillusionment. Joe was alone on a train at the beginning of the trilogy; he has lost two rather close but temporary friends and is much alone and thoroughly disillusioned at the end of the novel. One of *Las sorpresas de Joe* tells the story of a young Englishman who went off to distant and exotic lands in order to lead a more interesting and meaningful life. Soon he found out that the life he led in the distant land was no different from the one which he probably would have followed in his native England. The surprise ends with these words. "And in the letters that he wrote to a friend were contained his disillusionments."[106]

In a sense, all the poetic impressions interpolated into the novel are statements of the disillusions brought on by the monotonous days of his life. Each new impression is another reiteration of solitude and disillusionment, an atmospherical stimulant that steadily and surely creates that atmosphere of sadness, penetrating depression, and hopelessness which the reader feels as he finishes the trilogy. One of the most powerful symbols of this disillusionment is the sea gull with the clipped wings. The sea gull, accustomed to the freedom of the open seas, never accepts his fate and never becomes domesticated. The wings become the symbol of man's illusions, which are promptly truncated.[107]

Even at the end of the first novel, what seemed to Joe in the beginning to be the great whirlwind of the world, now seems quite diminutive. The impression and the novel end with these following words, which make their final contribution to its atmosphere.

> His Great Whirlwind of the World had been diminished in his imagination and now it seemed a little twister.
> The cabin at the fair, which before had impressed him as being spacious, full of figures, of mirrors and of landscapes, now seemed little, empty and deserted. In the silent night he heard a sob.
> It was the sound of a streetcar, that seemed to sigh in the distance.[108] (B)

In one of his *Fantasías de la época* he speaks of the man who loses enthusiasm for himself because he loses his illusions. "When he begins to see himself without enthusiasm, like a common example, it isn't the result of having better and clearer vision, but of having lost his illusions and his youth." [109] (C) In another one of his fantasies the disillusionment of a complete generation or age is linked with the practices of the Jewish merchants. "Our age has lived on illusions, on mad illusions, placed in the future. The material from which illusions and hopes are created has finally run out and the liquidation of dreams and hopes has come, and for that liquidation, as for all commercial liquidations, the Jews have appeared." [110] (D) All of this disillusionment is summed up in the last symbol of the treadmill, *los llenos de dolor y los vacíos de esperanza,* "those full of sorrow and those empty of hope."

After this brief survey of some of the poetic impressions of the trilogy of *Las agonías de nuestro tiempo,* it seems quite safe to assume that one of their principal functions as well as one of their artistic raisóns d'être is the creation of an atmosphere. Each one of them paints, with about the same lugubrious colors, the ever-darkening atmosphere of a nonrhetorical but quite hopeless disillusionment. The darkness of this disillusion is deepened and considerably augmented by the few contrasting bright spots of the trilogy which make up the minor atmosphere. This atmosphere, following the same pattern found in works of earlier periods, points toward life, hope, vitality. Some prime examples of this minor atmosphere — they don't appear with great frequency in the trilogy — are the praises of the fertile fields of Fyn and the Sunday parade of bicycles in Holland. [111] The only sad note found in the latter is the fact that Joe does not belong

---

(A) Cerca, todo es viejo; la calle Saint-Pères, la calle de Sena, la de Bonaparte y los callejones intermedios están repletos de tiendas, anticuarios, estamperos, libreros de ocasión, comerciantes de porcelanas y cuadros. [105]

(B) Su Gran torbellino del Mundo se le había achicado en la imaginación y le parecía un diminuto torbellino.
La barraca de feria, que antes se le antojaba amplia, llena de figuras, de espejos y de paisajes, la veía ahora pequeña, vacía y desierta. En la noche silenciosa se oía un sollozo.
Era el ruido de un tranvía, que parecía suspirar a lo lejos. [108]

(C) Cuando empieza a verse sin entusiasmo como un ejemplar corriente, no es a consecuencia de tener la vista mejor y más clara, sino de haber perdido las ilusiones y la juventud. [109]

(D) Nuestra época ha vivido de ilusiones, de locas ilusiones, puestas en el porvenir. La materia con que se crean las ilusiones y las esperanzas se ha agotado al fin y ha venido la liquidación de los sueños y de las esperanzas, y para esta liquidación, como para todas las liquidaciones comerciales, han aparecido los judíos. [110]

to this happy group of people. "We anticyclists are not Aryan, Joe affirmed happily."[112]

Like many works in his fourth period of production, *El hotel del cisne* is a bleak, gloomy, and often lugubrious novel. It is the study of the quimerical and onirical wanderings of a lonely, sensitive old man through an indifferent sea of hopelessness and disillusionment. The old man is known by the name of Procopio Pagani; he has had other names, which have been forgotten. He is seventy-two years old and is in Paris during the early stages of World War II.

Reading the rather long novel, it is hard to find a clear optimistic note, a bright ray of hope that is not immediately swallowed up in the sea of gloom forming the total background of the novel. *El hotel del cisne* is almost completely a novel of atmosphere, and this atmosphere is one of the most consistently gloomy of all those painted by Baroja.

Without the quadrangle of factors that proved so important in the creation of the atmosphere in most of Baroja's novels so far, the novel would be unbearably gloomy. However, these factors are much in evidence throughout the work and serve to reintensify the feeling of total darkness and disillusionment. Weather receives little overt mention. But, because of Procopio Pagani's delicate health and slight resistance, the omnipresence of those inclement Parisian winters is keenly felt. His room on the fifth floor of the hotel is cold; he would indeed have suffered during the cold winter nights if someone had not given him an electric footwarmer.[113]

This feeling of the cold, bleak weather heightens the feeling of emptiness and loneliness completely surrounding and engulfing Procopio Pagani. Life to him is a weary, stupid, monotonous thing. "I feel tired; my life seems stupid and monotonous."[114] He feels himself near death, has insomnia, dizzy spells, is extremely nervous. For him, life's most simple tasks are treacherous and terrifying hurdles that become more and more difficult to overcome.[115] The street on which he lives is called "street of the solitary ones"; the hotel in which he stays is shabby and offers few signs of comfort or cheer.[116]

With death lingering so near to Procopio Pagani, it does not seem necessary at all to bring in extraneous material to strengthen and intensify this part of the atmosphere.[117] Nevertheless, this is exactly what Baroja has done. Chapters 12 and 13 at the end of the first part of the novel deal exclusively with notable crimes and executions of the past. Some of these crimes and executions are related by the ex-policeman, Barbier; others, such as the stories by Edgar Allen Poe and Arthur Conan Doyle, come from newspapers and literature. The first three chapters of the second part are a continuation of the same macabre theses with Deibler, *Monsieur de Paris* the hangman, getting the usual recognition that Baroja's novels always seem to bestow upon this character.

All these factors which seem to darken and depress the world which surrounds Procopio — the bleak coldness, the empty solitude, the grotesque death — can scarcely be separated from the foreboding clouds of World War II hovering over the city. The war is one of the most important ideological factors in the formation of the novel's depressing atmosphere.[118] Procopio Pagani seems to be completely indifferent to all the conflicting ideologies and values involved in this war. He is merely their victim.[119] The blackouts that accompany the war serve to further darken the atmosphere.

All these atmospheric factors are greatly intensified by the form of narration. The body of the narration is made up of a series of dreams which Procopio Pagani wrote down. This form allows Baroja to distort and disfigure reality in such a way that it will seem much more depressing. These dreams add a terrifying sense of irreality and insecurity, spreading to all other parts of the narrative.

There seems to be little vital atmosphere in *El hotel del cisne*. Those things which contribute to life are the very things Procopio Pagani cannot find in the dark and depressing atmosphere surrrounding him. His needs are simple. Most of all he needs a few hours of sound sleep. "What bothers me most is insomnia; it produces in me a physical depression, dark ideas, useless and bothersome. Although it were only for two days out of the week, I would like to have a strong hypnotic available in order to sleep seven or eight hours in a row." [120] (A) The one thing that seems to sustain Procopio Pagani is the electric foot-warmer. This, then, becomes a symbol of friendship — it was a gift from a thoughtful friend — and a symbol of the vital things that sustain life.

In *El hotel del cisne,* as in many other novels, Baroja shows a concern for the individual's fight for life and existence in a dark and negative novelistic world. This concern links his novels to the contemporary novels of Spain. Many of the novelists who followed Baroja — some of whom have confessed their debt to him — show a tremendous preoccupation with the physical aspects of day-to-day existence in a bleak and sterile novelistic world. Like Baroja, they seem to be more interested in the basic problems of man than in abstractions; they deal with the individual's biological existence rather than with ideas. No clearer statement of this direction in the contemporary Spanish novelists can be found than in the third prologue to Camilo José Cela's *La colmena*.

(A) Lo que más me molesta es el insomnio; me produce una depresión física, ideas negras, inútiles y enojosas.

Aunque fuera un par de días a la semana, quisiera tener a mano un hipnótico fuerte para dormir siete u ocho horas seguidas.[120]

I would like to develop the idea that a healthy man doesn't have any ideas. At times I think that religious, moral, social, and political ideas are nothing more than manifestations of a disequilibrium of the nervous system. The time is still distant in which it will be known that the apostle and the *enlightened* man are both flesh of the insane asylum, sleepless and trembling flowers of weakness. History, indefectible history, goes against the grain of ideas. Or apart from them. In order to make history it is necessary to have no ideas, just as it is necessary to have no scruples in order to make money. Ideas and scruples — for the harrassed man; the one who manages to smile with the bitter convulsive grin of one who triumphs — are hindrances. History is like the circulation of the blood or the digestion of food. The arteries and the stomach where the historical substance runs and where it ferments are of hard and cold flint. Ideas are something atavistic — some day this will be recognized — never a culture and still less a tradition. The culture and the tradition of a man, like the culture and the tradition of a hyena or of an ant, could orient itself on a compass of only three points: eating, reproduction, and destruction. Culture and tradition are never ideological, but they are, always, instinctive. The law of heredity — which is the most frightening law in biology — is not foreign to all of this I have been saying. In this sense, perhaps I would admit that there is a culture and a tradition of the blood. Biologists, sagaciously, call it instinct. Those who deny it, or, at least relegate it to instinct — the ideologists — construct their scheme upon the problematic existence of what they call the *interior man,* forgetting Goethe's luminous prophecy: everything that is inside is outside.

Some day I will return to the idea that ideas are a sickness.

I think the same as I did two years ago. From my house you can see, anchored in the bay, the gray, powerful, sinister boats of the American fleet. A rooster crows, in just any chicken yard, and a child with a sweet little voice sings — oh! instinct! — the old lines from the widow of the Court of Oré.

It isn't worth it to let ourselves be invaded by sadness. Sadness is also an atavism.[121] (A)

It is easy to trace the same preoccupations with the basic things of life in Carmen Laforet's *Nada.* Andrea, the protagonist, comes in darkness to the darkest house on a dark street in Barcelona. She finds there a vortex of ideological madness, a sort of compendium of all of Spain's past ideologies, such as the traditional Spanish honor and Catholicism. Against this background, Andrea becomes highly sensitive to and appreciative of the basic things of life — such as sunshine, good food, and the pleasure of a walk. In José Suárez Carreño's *Las últimas horas,* Manolo finds the meaning of life in his own physical assurance, in the physical things surrounding him and concludes, "You have to live, something inside him kept saying, be like you are this very instant." [122] *La noria* by Luis Romero shows the same concern about daily lives and struggles of a series of individuals. It traces the vicious but vital circle of life, the heroic struggle for existence.

In these examples not only is the positive answer of the basic things much like that given by Baroja, but also this positive factor depends on the negative background, the nothingness surrounding it, for its emotional and esthetic impact. In these cases, as in Baroja, the negative forms the background and outlines the positive.

The reiteration of negative signs and symbols appears to be the principal creative process in forming this novelistic background. These negative signs and symbols can be divided into the four groups already mentioned: those centering around decadence and solitude, those which create and suggest the meteorological atmosphere, those which center around death, and those which create the ideological atmosphere. The darkness and antivitality of this atmosphere are further intensified by contrast with a few bright and vitally human atmospherical touches within the novel.

The negative qualities in Baroja's novels are by no means a natural consequence of the particular time, place, and setting chosen for it. All the towns which serve as a background for Baroja's novels seem to be alike in that they are all gloomy, lonely, isolated, and barren, towns on which Baroja's antivital atmosphere has been superimposed. Baroja has not rejected any device that might make them seem more morbid and

---

(A) Quisiera desarrollar la idea de que el hombre sano no tiene ideas. A veces pienso que las ideas religiosas, morales, sociales, políticas, no son sino manifestaciones de un desequilibrio del sistema nervioso. Está todavía lejano el tiempo en que se sepa que el apóstol y el iluminado son carne de manicomio, insomne y temblorosa flor de debilidad. La historia, la indefectible historia, va a contrapelo de las ideas. O al margen de ellas. Para hacer la historia se precisa no tener ideas, como para hacer dinero es necesario no tener escrúpulos. Las ideas y los escrúpulos — para el hombre acosado: aquel que llega a sonreír con el amargo rictus del triunfador — son una rémora. La historia es como la circulación de la sangre o como la digestión de los alimentos. Las arterias y el estómago por donde corre y en el que se cuece la substancia histórica, son de duro y frío pedernal. Las ideas son un atavismo — algún día se reconocerá —, jamás una cultura y menos aún una tradición. La cultura y la tradición del hombre, como la cultura y la tradición de la hiena o de la hormiga, pudiera orientarse sobre una rosa de tres solos vientos: comer, reproducirse y destruirse. La cultura y la tradición no son jamás ideológicas y sí, siempre, instintivas. La ley de la herencia — que es la más pasmosa ley de la biología — no está ajena a esto que aquí vengo diciendo. En este sentido, quizás admitiese que hay una cultura y una tradición de la sangre. Los biólogos, sagazmente, le llaman instinto. Quienes niegan o, al menos, relegan al instinto — los ideólogos —, construyen su artilugio sobre la problemática existencia de lo que llaman el «hombre interior,» olvidando la luminosa adivinación de Goethe: está fuera todo lo que está dentro.

Algún día volveré sobre la idea de que las ideas son una enfermedad.

Pienso lo mismo que dos años atrás. Desde mi casa se ven, anclados en la bahía, los grises, poderosos, siniestros buques de la escuadra americana. Un gallo cacarea, en cualquier corral, y una niña de dulcecita voz canta — ¡oh, el instinto! — los viejos versos de la viudita del conde de Oré.

No merece la pena que nos dejemos invadir por la tristeza. La tristeza también es un atavismo.[121]

depressing. The same can be said of his novels as a whole. He always seems to bring in additions to reinforce the atmosphere, even though these are entirely unrelated to the main body of the novel. The literary quotes and the many tales of famous hangings and assassinations provide excellent examples.

The conclusion emerging from this adding of unrelated material to strengthen the total atmospherical impression is that the consistent dark and depression serve a vital artistic purpose in Baroja's novels. It is not simply an atmosphere which any sensitive person might feel upon exposure to the multifarious aspects of Spain and the universe reflected in Baroja's novels. Neither is it, necessarily, the atmosphere which Baroja senses when he encounters the same aspects in real life. It is rather the atmosphere which Baroja feels he must create and intensify to establish his novelistic world. Evidently he considers blacking-out of large areas of the novelistic world a most important and completely necessary step in its creation, "Destruir es crear."

Once it becomes clear that the atmosphere which floods Baroja's novels with darkness has a purely creative raisón d'être, insight is gained into the nature and essence of this creation. The darkened atmosphere evidently does not form a part of the essential creation; it serves only as background. Although it forms the bulk of the novelistic world, it fails to cause the most intense impact on the emotional and esthetic sensibilities of the reader. It is not the vital atmosphere of the novel, but rather the antivital part of it. There is a sharp division between the two atmospheres.

This division gives firm indications of some of the things which are to be part of Baroja's essential creation. By elimination it becomes obvious that this essence will contain nothing of the ideological — all ideologies are relegated to the antivital. The same can be applied to the decadent and the lifeless, the solitary, and the dismal rainy side of the weather.

This elimination suggests that the essential in his novels will bear no tag. It will of necessity be nameless and without affiliation. Part of this essence will be composed of human solidarity, human solidarity achieved without ideologies. This peculiar human solidarity will generally be achieved through the mutual seeking of those things, like food and shelter, which support life. The bright clear day and morning sunshine will play an important part in this essential creation and will be intimately connected to it. Most of those things that basically contribute to human life will form part of this creation — the warmth of a fire; the pleasure of food when one is hungry; the pure physical love of a healthy woman unadulterated by religious, social or mystic concepts; procreation of children; and sheer physical activity.

All these matters seem to be carefully set aside from the antivital. Within Baroja's novelistic orb, they are tangible realities that stand in bright and sharp relief against the dark, unreal, and indeterminate background.

5. *Character Revelation*

"It is strange — Ossorio was thinking — how man is unmasked on some occasions; taking him out of his place, out of his center, places his inclinations, his way of being, clearly in evidence. A railroad car is a school of egoism."[1] (A) These words by Fernando Ossorio in *Camino de perfección* indicate a fundamental direction followed by Baroja in the revelation of his major characters. (The term character revelation is used in place of character development to stress the static and nonchanging essentials of a character as opposed to its growth or change.) Fernando Ossorio observes that taking a person from his accustomed surroundings reveals his inclinations and his essential being. The veracity of this observation can be tested by tracing the protagonist of one of Baroja's earlier novels, Manuel of *La busca,* from the time he is taken from his middle-class circumstances until he is left alone in Madrid at the end of the novel.

Until Manuel Alcázar's father died, his mother had owned a boardinghouse. Because of foolish management and a change of locale she lost everything and became a servant. "De ama pasó a criada, sin quejarse."[2] (She went from owner to servant, without complaint.) She still had hopes that her two sons would study and become priests,[3] but Manuel's first step in life leads him away from the middle class and its values. He, much as his mother did, goes from a more or less privileged class to that of a servant in a rather short time. He had been staying with relatives in Almazán, but because he was not inclined to study and to

---

(A) «Es extraño — pensaba Ossorio — cómo se desenmascara el hombre en algunas ocasiones; el sacarlo de su lugar, de su centro, pone claramente en evidencia sus inclinaciones, su modo de ser. Un vagón de un tren es una escuela de egoísmo.»[1]

accept the formality imposed on him by the ambient, he was sent to Madrid, to work as a servant in the boardinghouse with his mother.[4] There Manuel was not treated with much respect,[5] and he received a lot of abuse, some unmerited, from the boarders.

Manuel's situation in the boardinghouse became unbearable, and he had a fight with one of the boarders. As a result Manuel was sent to the slums of Madrid as an apprentice shoemaker. There he lived with an old shoemaker and his son Leandro. Thus Manuel was taken from a fairly respectable environment and the corresponding contact with socially respected people and placed in a more socially degraded one with its corresponding lower class. Baroja seems to attach a great deal of importance to this new environment.

The man from Madrid who sometimes, by chance, finds himself in the poor districts near the Manzanares River, will be surprised by the spectacle of misery and sordidness, of sadness and ignorance that the outskirts of Madrid offer with their miserable roads full of dust in the summer and mud in the winter. The capital is a city of contrasts; it presents a strong light alongside a dark shadow; a refined life, almost European, in the center; an African life, an Arab camp, in the suburbs. A few years ago, not many, near Segovia and Campillo de Gil Imón roads, there was a house of suspicious aspect and not of very good reputation, if one can judge from public gossip.[6] (A)

He also is careful to describe Manuel's new associates. Vidal, his cousin, takes him in tow and places him in contact with some even less respectable elements of society who inhabit the neighborhood.

"Come on, you, let's go," Vidal said to Manuel.
"Where?"
"With the Pirates. Today we have a date; they are waiting for us."
"But, what pirates?"
"Crosseyes and those guys."
"And why do they call them that?"
"Because they are like pirates."[7] (B)

Once this negative direction is started, it seems to be followed relentlessly. Manuel's surroundings and his friends become progressively worse. Most of those ideas, ideals, or spiritual inclinations he might have retained from his middle-class experience are stripped away. He is placed in an environment in which the middle-class protocol of lovemaking and courtship is not in the least respected.

Manuel's first night in the Corrala, he saw, not without a certain amount of surprise, the truth of what Vidal was saying. The latter and almost all those of his age had sweethearts among the little girls of the house, and it wasn't rare, when one passed near a corner, to see a couple jump up and start to run.[8] (C)

Manuel is surrounded by types such as the pirates and by young dreamers such as Roberto.

Listen to me, because it is the truth. If you want to be something in life, don't believe in the word impossible. Nothing is impossible for an energetic will. If you shoot an arrow, aim very high, as high as you can; the higher you aim, the farther it will go.
Manuel looked at Robert with surprise, and lapsed into silence.[9] (D)

Leandro commits suicide, and his father the shoemaker soon dies of heartbreak. This takes away from Manuel two supports holding him partially within the world of respectability, and moves him deeper into the world of those who live apart from society. The direction of Manuel's life is becoming more and more apparent. Step by step he is being isolated from friends and family and placed in the world of outcasts. Petra, his mother, gets him a place in a bread and vegetable store in the *plaza del Carmen*. Because his new masters are stingy and refuse to give him any

---

(A) El madrileño que alguna vez, por casualidad, se encuentra en los barrios pobres próximos al Manzanares, hállase sorprendido ante el espectáculo de miseria y sordidez, de tristeza e incultura que ofrecen las afueras de Madrid con sus rondas miserables, llenas de polvo en verano y de lodo en invierno. La corte es ciudad de contrastes; presenta luz fuerte al lado de sombra oscura; vida refinada, casi europea, en el centro; vida africana, de aduar, en los suburbios. Hace unos años, no muchos, cerca de la ronda de Segovia y del Campillo de Gil Imón, existía una casa de sospechoso aspecto y de no muy buena fama, a juzgar por el rumor público.[6]

(B) — Anda, tú, vamos — dijo Vidal a Manuel.
— ¿Adónde?
— Con los Piratas. Hoy tenemos cita; nos estarán esperando.
— Pero ¿qué piratas?
— El *Bizco* y ésos.
— ¿Y por qué los llaman así?
— Porque son como los piratas.[7]

(C) La primera noche de Manuel en la Corrala, vió, no sin cierto asombro, la verdad de lo que decía Vidal. Este y casi todos los de su edad tenían sus novias entre las chiquillas de la casa, y no era raro, al pasar junto a un rincón, ver a una pareja que se levantaba y echaba a correr.[8]

(D) — Hazme caso, porque es la verdad. Si quieres hacer algo en la vida, no creas en la palabra imposible. Nada hay imposible para una voluntad enérgica. Si tratas de disparar una flecha, apunta muy alto, lo más alto que puedas; cuanto más alto apuntes, más lejos irá.
Manuel miró a Roberto con extrañeza, y se encogió de hombros.[9]

salary for his labor, she finds him a place in a bakery. The work is hard in the bakery, and there Manuel is stripped of something which highly respected societies greatly esteem, his name.

Then, nobody paid any attention to him; the rest of the bakers, a bunch of pretty stupid Galicians, treated him like a mule; not one of them even bothered to learn Manuel's name, and some of them called him: "Hey, you, kid"; others shouted at him, "Get going, Big Belly"; when they talked about him they called him "the bum of Madrid," or just "the bum." He answered to whatever name or nickname they called him.[10] (A)

Manuel's mother still tries to look out for him, but she soon dies and leaves him alone. Significantly enough his next friend is called *el expósito.* He has never known his parents or had a home.[11]

Manuel spends a great deal of time running with Vidal and *el bizco.* These two make him a member of their crew, and they manage to get along quite well by robbing a few rather insignificant articles of clothing when they are hung out to dry. Thus he breaks another precept of conventional social ethics. Manuel is even abandoned by these two when they go into the center of town and find themselves some more sophisticated women of the street to exploit.

After his mother dies Manuel experiences one touch of friendliness in a Madrid which otherwise seems to have abandoned him to hunger and cold. He is taken into the home of a ragman. Suddenly, and from outside the confines of respected society, Manuel finds all the things he seems to need: affection, a home, food, and useful work to do. The house of el señor Custodia, the ragman, and his wife, seemed to please Manuel. He thought that a house built out of the detritus of society of Madrid should be very apropos for him who was also a part of the detritus, who has also been rejected by the big city. " . . . le parecía a Manuel un lugar a propósito para él, residuo también desechado de la vida urbana."[12]

Manuel found all the *signos de sugestión*[13] there which indicate a vital atmosphere, all that which shows the presence of life and humanity. The combination of such various *signos de sugestión* of the vital, human atmosphere — the hand of a well-organized person, an earthen pot was boiling with a soft *gurgle,* a village-like silence, the hens, burros, *Reverte,* the dog, etc. — makes el señor Custodia's home, as far as Manuel is concerned, a symbol of asylum for the lost.[14]

Manuel soon lost that home. In love with Justa, the daughter of the ragman, he became extremely jealous when she became engaged to a young, worthless dandy called Carnicerín. Carnicerín, being the son of a meatpacker, was above the daughter of a ragman socially, and for this reason Manuel did not really think him serious in his engagement to Justa. He got into a fight with Carnicerín, and a friend of the latter hit him over the head with a club. In anger, and swearing vengeance against the young dandy, Manuel decided to leave the house of el señor Custodia and never return. Thus he again joined the ranks of the outsiders.

The last episode of the book finds him protecting a helpless young orphan from a bully. The fracas is over, and the gang of curious ones has drifted away when he hears two men, one an old man and the other a municipal guard, talking about the vagabonds.

The gentleman lamented the abandonment in which these young boys were left, and he said that in other countries they created schools, homes, and a thousand things. The municipal policeman shook his head signifying doubt. Finally he summed up the conversation, saying in the tranquil tone of a Galacian:

"Believe me, sir: these boys are no longer good."

Manuel, upon hearing that, shivered; he got up from the ground where he was, left the Puerta del Sol and started to walk without direction or destination.

"These boys are no longer good." The sentence had produced a profound impression on him. Why wasn't he good? Why? He examined his life. He wasn't bad, he hadn't harmed anybody. He hated Butcher because he was taking away his happiness. He made it impossible for him to live in the only corner where he had found some affection and some protection. Afterwards, contradicting himself, he thought that perhaps he was bad and, in that case, there was nothing else to do but correct himself and become better.[15] (B)

The last paragraph of the novel shows Manuel's comprehension of the fact that he is one of those who like to work in the daytime.

(A) Luego, nadie le hacía caso; los demás panaderos, una colección de gallegos bastante brutos, le trataban como a una mula; ni siquiera se ocupó alguno de ellos en saber el nombre de Manuel, y unos le llamaban: «¡He, tú, *Choto!*»; otros le gritaban: «¡Hala, *Barriga!*»; cuando hablaban de él, decían «o golfo de Madrid,» o solamente «o golfo.» El contestaba a los nombres y motes que le daban.[10]

(B) El señor se lamentaba del abandono en que se los dejaba a los chicos, y decía que en otros países se creaban escuelas y asilos y mil cosas. El municipal movía la cabeza en señal de duda. Al último resumió la conversación, diciendo con un tono tranquilo de gallego:

— Créame usted a mí: éstos ya no son buenos.

Manuel, al oír aquello, se estremeció; se levantó del suelo en donde estaba, salió de la Puerta del Sol y se puso a andar sin dirección ni rumbo.

«¡Estos ya no son buenos!» La frase le había producido una impresión profunda. ¿Por qué no era bueno él? ¿Por qué? Examinó su vida. El no era malo, no había hecho daño a nadie. Odiaba al Carnicerín porque le arrebataba su dicha, le imposibilitaba vivir en el rincón donde únicamente encontró algún cariño y alguna protección. Después, contradiciéndose, pensó que quizá era malo y, en ese caso, no tenía más remedio que corregirse y hacerse mejor.[15]

He understood that the lives of the night owls and the lives of the workers ran parallel, that they would never come together not even for a moment. For the first ones, pleasure, vice, the night; for the others, work, fatigue, sun. And he also thought that he must be one of the latter — those who work under the sun, not those who seek pleasure in the shadows.[16] (A)

The thing that strikes the reader most forcibly about this series of events and their impact upon the character of Manuel is that they apparently have caused no change. When the novel ends Manuel accepts none of the precepts of the vagabond society to which he has been exposed for a rather long period of time. In fact, Manuel holds few precepts. He has few or no illusions about life. Manuel, placed in a different class by the words of the two strangers, *ya no son buenos,* shudders at the thought of his being one of the vagabonds. He finally denies this to himself. As the light of the new day breaks, he decides he belongs to the class that works honestly by day, and not to that which seeks sustenance and pleasure at night.

Baroja places his protagonist in a certain environment, but he is careful to point out, through Manuel's reflections at the end of the novel, that no change has taken place. Manuel's character at the beginning and at the end is about the same. The rather adverse environment in which he was placed seems to have produced little if any alteration in his character.[17] Bolinger believes that environment reflects on but seldom changes the characters in Baroja's novels.[18] Delgado Olivares, in an article in *Gaceta literaria* of May 1, 1931, expresses this same opinion.

The various episodes of the novel reveal Manuel's need for love and affection, for a home and the basic, vital things of life. They reveal his essential goodness and his keen sensibility for social justice. In short, Manuel has been taken away from his natural ambient so that the reader can see him more clearly.

As the novel ends, Manuel is seen as a simple young man. He seems to know few of the great truths of life, seems to be puzzled by most of the things that happen before his eyes and to him. He is reduced to a human, likable, sensitive, little boy who seeks something basic and essential in life.

The critics have sensed this type of character revelation in Baroja's novels. Juan Uribe Echevarría speaks of the procedure as novelistic displacement.

If Zola knows how to manipulate multitudes, Baroja is insuperable in the novelistic displacement of individualities. There is no selection in his art of narration. Everyone who with more or less luck avoids, surpasses, or despises the human herd, manages to squeeze into some page of the Basque novelist.[19] (B)

Ortega has called Baroja's novels a kind of flophouse.[20] Uribe tells how Baroja fails to defend his heroes, and leaves them abandoned in the cruel world.

This autobiographic substratum of his novels could be fatal for any author with less talent, but Baroja doesn't defend his heroes much. The latter have nothing of D'Annunzio or of Valle-Inclán. Life tramples them; women flee from them; the world shows itself hostile towards them and, finally, they succumb or vegetate. Adventure, momentarily, swells the sails of their absurd destinies. Baroja leaves them to their fate like an animal sheds its skin. Thanks to this they acquire more versimilitude and elicit more sympathy from the reader.[21] (C)

The last sentence of the passage from Uribe indicates that he attributes the human sympathy elicited by Baroja's heroes to the fact that they have been displaced and abandoned by the world.

The novelistic procedure mentioned by Ortega, Uribe and by Baroja's characters themselves is clearly in evidence in two novels of Baroja's first decade. In *Los últimos románticos* and *Las tragedias grotescas* Don Fausto Bengoa seems to undergo the same process of revelation. As a young man in Madrid he suffers many of the common disillusionments of his generation. Going through a period in which he read only novels of a certain type, such as those written by Eugène Sue, romantic love in fiction leads him to the romantic love of an actress. He is so conditioned by reading these novels that he has difficulty seeing his new love as she really is. Although his friends advise him that her reputa-

---

(A) Comprendía que eran las de los noctámbulos y las de los trabajadores vidas paralelas que no llegaban ni un momento a encontrarse. Para los unos, el placer, el vicio, la noche; para los otros, el trabajo, la fatiga, el sol. Y pensaba también que él debía ser de éstos, de los que trabajan al sol, no de los que buscan el placer en la sombra.[16]

(B) Si Zola sabe manejar multitudes, Baroja es insuperable en el desplazamiento novelesco de individualidades. No hay selección humana en su arte de narrar. Todo aquel que con mayor o menor suerte evita, supera, o desprecia al rebaño humano, logra colarse por alguna página del novelista vasco.[19]

(C) Este substrato autobiográfico de sus novelas podría resultar fatal para cualquier escritor menos dotado, pero Baroja no defiende mucho a sus héroes. Estos no tiene nada de dannunzianos o valleinclanescos. La vida los atropella; las mujeres les huyen; el mundo se les muestra hostil y, al final, sucumben o vegetan. La aventura hincha, momentáneamente, las velas de sus destinos disparatados. Baroja los abandona a su suerte, como quien bota la piel. Gracias a ello adquieren más verosimilitud y suscitan las simpatías del lector.[21]

tion is more than questionable, he is sure of her purity. A young soldier tried to shake him free from this illusion, through an open love affair with the actress and by calling him a fool. Only when she marries is he forced to forget her, although still believing in her purity.[22]

His next illusion is political. He becomes an ardent republican and considers the rhetoric of this political party as something more than sacred. He is to lose this illusion later in Paris, but his last disillusionment while he is still in Madrid comes after he is married to the daughter of a hatmaker. He soon finds out that he is not exactly the man of the house and that he is expected to exercise little authority therein.[23]

As the novel opens Baroja takes Don Fausto to Paris for a more complete revelation of his character through this same process of disillusionment. As a first step in this direction Fausto lets his young friend write articles for him. Taking credit for them, he realizes that this is to be slightly untrue to himself, but he shrugs this twinge of conscience off without much difficulty.

Later on, the traditional horns of a cuckold are placed squarely upon his head when he finds out that Gálvez, a rich American, has been sleeping with his wife in his own house. This awakening upsets him much less than he thought possible.

> He arrived home. It occurred to Clementina, who hadn't been eating with him for a long time, that they should have lunch together. She was polite, respectful, and friendly with him. Don Fausto understood that metaphysical ideas about honor are harmful and they damage the stomach, and as a hygenic measure, without lowering himself in any way, he decided in just one moment to forget everything.[24] (A)

Like this sense of honor, his political faith is changed without too much difficulty. Before, he had bitterly denounced Queen Isabel, but later he accepts a decoration from her.[25]

These incidents indicate that the process of revelation in *Los últimos románticos* and *Las tragedias grotescas* is the same as in *La busca*. It is the same negative direction in which the protagonist is stripped of many things. The things that are taken away from Don Fausto here are not essential to his well-being. He comes to realize, at a certain stage of the novel, that these things he at one time thought important are really quite superficial, that they are in essence a vital fiction some men need in order to exist and try to be happy. Such superficial things as true love, personal honor lying in the fidelity of one's wife, political beliefs, even personal integrity and honesty, seem more fictional than real. Moral values become confused between seeming and being and therefore lose their vital importance.[26]

Without all these false values, Don Fausto has found the wisdom of life. He is not an important man, but he seems to be a happy and very human one. He is completely aware of what has happened to himself and is completely resigned.

Don Fausto went into his room and lit the lamp.

Niní served him his supper; afterwards he read the paper beside the fire. He poked at the fire from time to time, and many times he remained enchanted contemplating the flames. As he was going to bed, closing the shutters, he took a look at the street, and saw in the fog a poor gaslamp lighter buffeted by the wind . . .

From his bed he heard the murmur of the rain and the howling of the wind in the chimneys.

"It is the voice of Autumn," he thought, "the voice of good sense and the wisdom which spoke and said softly: 'Unfortunate are those who have no home! Blessed are those who sleep between sheets! Worry not about what your wife or your friend may do. What does this matter in the presence of all the centuries which pass? All your constructions, great or small, will be swept away by the mighty winds of time, that blow frenetically. Savor the present moment. Take advantage of life! Each day is a gain over the abyss which surrounds us. Squeeze it! Abandon the impossible! Reduce your projects to the narrow limits of existence, and since life is brief don't try to carry your plans too far.'"

And Don Fausto listened to this voice of good sense and of wisdom and went to sleep.[27] (B)

(A) Llegó a casa. A Clementina, que desde hacía mucho tiempo no comía con él, se le ocurrió que almorzaran juntos. Estuvo con él atenta, respetuosa y amable. Don Fausto comprendió que las ideas metafísicas sobre la honra son perjudiciales y dañan el estómago, y como higiene, sin rebajarse en nada, se decidió en un momento a olvidarlo todo.[24]

(B) Don Fausto se metía en su cuarto y encendía la lámpara.

Le servía la cena Niní; después leía los periódicos al lado del fuego. Atizaba de cuando en cuando la lumbre, y muchas veces quedaba embebecido contemplando las llamas. Al irse a acostar, al cerrar las maderas, echaba una mirada a la calle, y veía entre la niebla un pobre mechero de gas azotado por el viento . . .

Oía desde la cama el murmullo de la lluvia y el gemido del aire en las chimeneas.

«Es la voz del otoño — pensaba —, la voz del buen sentido y la sabiduría que hablaba y decía suavemente: «¡Desdichados los que no tiene hogar! ¡Felices los que ahora duermen entre sábanas! No os preocupéis por lo que hagan vuestra mujer o vuestro amigo. ¿Qué importa eso ante los siglos que pasan? Todas vuestras construcciones, grandes o pequeñas, serán barridas por el vendaval de las horas, que corren frenéticas. Saboread el minuto presente. ¡Aprovechad la vida! Cada día es una ganancia sobre el abismo que nos rodea. ¡Exprimidla! ¡Abandonad lo imposible! Reducir vuestros proyectos a los estrechos límites de la existencia, y puesto que la vida es breve no intentéis llevar demasiado lejos vuestros planes.»

Y don Fausto escuchaba esta voz del buen sentido y de la sabiduría, y quedaba dormido.[27]

Here again there seems to be no organic change. Don Fausto has been stripped of some rather bothersome ideals and morals that seemed to him more fictional than real. His happiness comes from within, and as Baroja explains in the first part of the two novels, has little or nothing to do with exterior circumstances.[28]

> Blanca, with conditions for being happy, found herself wretched, and Pilar, in the same situation or similar, felt happy.
> In the depths of our being, all the spring of happiness or of misfortune comes from the organic life, the ultimate result sent to the consciousness from the senses, not from adverse or happy events, shadows without reality, nor from ideas, which are skeleton-like images of things. This interior function of the organs gives the happy or sad tone to our consciousness.[29] (A)

Just what it is that makes Don Fausto Bengoa so human might be difficult to explain. Baroja feels that many times words that seem to categorize and catalog humanity are useless. One thing, however, adds greatly to Don Fausto's humanity. Don Fausto, having denied many illusions, clings the more tenaciously to one — the cross of the Legion of Honor given him by his former political enemy. It contributes a great deal to his happiness. It gives him prestige among his friends, most of them rather humble people.[30] He ceases to have anything to do with his old friend Pipot because the latter thinks little of the cross. Because of the latter's rather disparaging remarks about it, Don Fausto dismisses him as a man who has no sense of reality.[31]

Baroja seems quite aware of the fact that men need vital illusions in large or small quantities, in order to survive. Roberto, in *Aurora roja,* makes the statement, "Who is going to live without affirming anything because of the fear of deceiving himself, waiting for the ultimate synthesis? It isn't possible. One needs some lie in order to live. The republic, anarchy, socialism, religion, love . . . anything, the idea is to deceive oneself."[32] (B) Yarza, the young friend who wrote the articles for Don Fausto, not only sees the necessity for this vital fiction but prefers to live enmeshed in it.[33] Yarza also lends support to the displacement theory of character revelation when he speaks of Paris as something solid for the French and as a dissolvent for the Spaniard. Hans Jeschke, in his aforementioned work, shows how Baroja, a man who likes the scientific materialism that rejects fantasy and caprice, is quite aware of the need for some vital fiction.[34] Aviraneta, a man considered and lauded throughout twenty-two volumes as being a clear-sighted realist, does not escape this human affliction. He, like Don Fausto and many others, clings to a particle of vital fiction. He wears a wig. This contributes greatly to making him human. Aviraneta has just finished stating that he does not like imaginative literature, that he prefers the truth in everything. "That way, no. The truth, the truth in everything that has always been my ideal. Upon saying this, Aviraneta smoothed down his red hairpiece which had a tendency to bulge and to come loose from his head."[35] (C) Baroja feels that this vital fiction is necessary and propitious for his novels. In *La caverna del humorismo* he tells us how admirable a school for his type of humor — a humor usually expressed in his novels and seemingly germane only to Baroja — are such things as artificiality, injustice. "Artificiality! Injustice! What an admirable school of humor! Give me a country with wigs, with robes . . ." In the same essay he tells how humor tends to undermine certain truths and values.

"To the quality of being an art of violent contrasts one can add that it is an art subversive of human values."[36] (D) The variations of this fiction, so propitious for Baroja's novelistic art, seem to be endless. Few, perhaps none, of the characters are exempt from dependence on it. Some of the characters are guided by literature, which shapes their lives. An example of this type is Micaela, in *El mayorazgo de Labraz,* who reads romantic literature and is not quite capable of distinguishing where this romantic literature ends and real life begins. Don Fausto, for a short time, was affected in much the same way by romantic novels. Subliterature, in the form of superstitions, tall tales, proverbs, etc., forms an important section of this vital illusion. Baroja's characters reject huge proportions of this vital illusion, but they always seem left with a vestige, a small particle of fiction to which they cling.

(A) Blanca, en condiciones de ser feliz, se encontraba desgraciada, y Pilar, en situación igual o parecida, se sentía feliz.

En lo hondo de nuestro ser, todo el manantial de la felicidad o de la desgracia proviene de la vida orgánica, del último resultado enviado a la conciencia por los sentidos, no de los acontecimientos adversos, o felices, sombras sin realidad, ni tampoco de las ideas, que son imágenes esqueléticas de las cosas. Ese rodaje interior de los órganos da el tono alegre o triste a nuestra conciencia.[29]

(B) — ¿Quién va a vivir sin afirmar nada por el temor de engañarse esperando la síntesis última? No es posible. Se necesita alguna mentira para vivir. La república, la anarquía, el socialismo, la religión, el amor . . . cualquier cosa, la cuestión es engañarse.[32]

(C) — De esa manera, no. La verdad, la verdad en todo: ése ha sido siempre mi ideal.

Al decir esto, Aviraneta se planchaba su peluca roja, que tenía la tendencia a abombarse y a separarse de su cabeza.[35]

(D) — ¡Lo artificial! ¡Lo injusto! ¡Qué admirable escuela de humor! Dadme un pueblo con pelucas, con togas . . .

A la cualidad de ser un arte de contrastes violentos se puede añadir que es un arte subversivo de los valores humanos.[36]

Another example of what Baroja considers vital illusion is the idea that life has a purpose and that our actions must have a meaning. María Aracil in *La dama errante* is looking at the universe and asks if it has meaning. The answer is negative.

María felt something like dizziness as she submerged her glance into that strange ether, full of worlds unknown. . . . The young girls had gone to sleep; Venancio kept on talking and María listened and looked at the sky.
"And that, what's it for?" María asked suddenly.
Venancio smiled.
"Even if it had a reason, the universe an object," he said, "we men wouldn't be able to understand it."
"And if it had one?" María asked anxiously.
"If it had one, we would also have one. We would be within a divine intention."
"And if it doesn't have one?"
Venancio shrugged his shoulders.
"If it doesn't have," María added brightly, "we are forsaken."[37] (A)

In the second decade Luis Murguía, in *La sensualidad pervertida* becomes the epitome of displacement, disillusionment, and denial of vital illusion. These words, "Man marches toward the grave, leaving behind him his deceitful illusions,"[38] found on a sign which hung over *la tienda de los tres peces* in *La ciudad de la niebla* could well describe his own life.

This denial is overtly stated and often reiterated throughout the pages of *La sensualidad pervertida* by its protagonist.

It surprises me a great deal, thinking about my life, the few illusions I have made about my own self, about other people, about society, etc.; it surprises me, and I don't think that it is flippancy, how clearly I have seen some political, social, and family events; nevertheless, how little I have consciously achieved.[39] (B)

The problem of illusions is continually being turned over in Luis Murguía's mind. At one point he reaches the conclusion that such vital illusions as traditions are harmful in life but that they are a necessary something that gives life energy and direction.[40] Again, in a chapter called "Limitation," he speaks of the vitality, of the necessity of certain illusions. "I haven't fallen into that trap of believing that the age of my youth was worth more than the present one. I am convinced that this idea is an illusion of old age, but a vital illusion." Fully cognizant of the vitality and even of the practicality of this illusion, Luis Murguía is confronted with the problem of what to do about it. "I believed that I should take a new attitude toward life. I had to limit myself even more, and not let myself get carried away by illusions or dreams."[41] (C) The novel traces his denial of illusions. At times they are denied by choice, at other times circumstances force him to give up this or that illusion, but in almost every case the direction is away from illusions and toward a limited reality. As in *La busca* and *Los últimos románticos* and its sequel *Las tragedias grotescas,* the direction is a negative one, one which strips the character of almost all that is not absolutely vital.

As befits the title of the novel, one of the principal things rejected or denied by Luis Murguía is romantic love and the various illusions that accompany it. Luis Murguía is denied a proper outlet for his sensuality. "The constant excitations, the preoccupations, the readings, the lone walks, were perverting my sensuality and making it pathological."[42] (D) He seeks the answer to his problem in authorities who had written on the question.[43] After his studies and cavilings on the subject he comes to the following conclusion. "For me, the solution in the future would be something like the de-poetization of physical love, without dressing it up, without lying about it, without giving it an air of adventure or lending it false proportions."[44] (E) This quotation shows that Luis Murguía has

---

(A) María experimentaba como un vértigo al sumergir la mirada en aquel éter desconocido, lleno de mundos ignotos . . . Las niñas se habían dormido; Venancio seguía hablando y María escuchaba y miraba al cielo.

— Y eso, ¿para qué? — preguntó, de pronto, María.

Venancio sonrió.

— Aunque tuviera una razón, un objeto el universo — dijo —, los hombres no lo podríamos comprender.

— ¿Y si lo tuviera? — preguntó María, con ansiedad.

— Si lo tuviera, lo tendríamos también nosotros. Estaríamos dentro de una intención divina.

— ¿Y si no lo tiene?

Venancio se encogió de hombros.

— Si no lo tiene — agregó María, con viveza —, estamos desamparados.[37]

(B) A mí me asombra mucho, al pensar en mi vida, las pocas ilusiones que me he hecho acerca de mí mismo, acerca de los demás, de la sociedad, etc.; me asombra, y no creo que es petulancia, lo claramente que he visto algunos acontecimientos políticos, sociales y familiares; sin embargo, lo poco que he conseguido conscientemente.[39]

(C) No he caído en ese lazo de creer que la época de mi juventud tenga más valor que la actual. Estoy convencido de que esta idea es una ilusión de la vejez, pero una ilusión vital.

Creí que debía tomar una actitud nueva ante la vida. Tenía que limitarme más aún, y no dejarme llevar por ilusiones ni por sueños.[41]

(D) Las excitaciones constantes, las preocupaciones, las lecturas, los paseos solitarios iban pervirtiendo mi sensualidad y haciéndola patológica.[42]

(E) Para mí la solución en el porvenir será algo así como la despoetización del amor físico, sin vestirlo, sin mentirlo, sin darle aire de aventura ni prestarle proporciones falsas.[44]

discarded a vital illusion that serves as the mainspring of existence and happiness for the greater part of humanity. With the totality of this vital illusion goes one of its important manifestations, that illusion which makes of every Spaniard — for that matter, of every man — a Don Juan Tenorio.[45] At first he is impressed with the love scenes from *Don Juan Tenorio,* but he soon regards them with antipathy.[46]

As a symbol of all this vital illusion which he cannot assimilate, Luis Murguía chooses the Spanish cape. The shedding of this artifact of dress makes it more difficult to maintain the romantic fictions concerning love.

> I find that the use of a cloak foments different ideas in man than wearing a topcoat. Covering one's face with a cloak seems to hide and defend and be propitious for complications and adventure. Perhaps, in reality, it isn't, but it gives this impression. In Spain one notices that as long as they used the cloak there were adventures, love affairs, and revolutions. When the cloak disappeared all of the romantic apparatus of life disappeared with it.[47] (A)

Such is the importance of this cape that he finds it boring and disagreeable to pursue young ladies in Madrid without it. "Además, hacer el amor a la madrileña, sin capa, me parecía una cosa aburrida y enojosa."[48] At the end of the novel Luis Murguía attributes his lack of success to his denial of a vital illusion summed up in just two things: studied indifference and a black beard. "And why should they have shown this indifference for you?" "What do you expect, mam? I believe that all I lacked, in order to be like your neighbor, was disdain and a black beard."[49] (B) He repeats these words as the novel ends. "Yes. I have not been too successful with the feminine syndicate . . . Like I was saying, I lacked the disdain . . . and a black beard."[50] (C) Luis Murguía is quite aware that the studied indifference and the black beard are fictional assets. They have no value in his real world. They do, on the other hand, serve a vital function in the world of the masses. For those who are permitted to partake of this illusion, for those who are permitted to beguile themselves into thinking that the indifference and black beard are more than a fiction, these fictional assets seem to be quite advantageous; they seem to function with amazing efficaciousness. Baroja does not allow Luis Murguía to participate, and this nonparticipation further reduces and concentrates the human entity which the reader beholds as the novel ends.

The denial of the fiction of romantic love is just one of the many denials Luis Murguía is made to suffer during his novelistic existence. There existed, in his time, a political fiction that might be termed invincible Spain. True, a large portion of this political fiction, which proved so vital and functional to the Spaniards when they ruled the world, had been whittled away. Nevertheless it seems to exist for Luis Murguía in 1898, and when its last vertiges are stripped away, his physical and spiritual being are affected.

One day, on Alcalá street, I spit up blood.
"Fine," I said to myself. "This is the beginning of the end."
I went shaking to the *Casa de Socorro* of a doctor friend of mine. He examined me. There was nothing in my lungs, according to him. The uneasiness that believing myself sick produced mixed with the news of the disaster of our small fleet, and I was sad, weak and nervous for several days.[51] (D)

The complete lack of illusions with which Luis Murguía is made to face the world can be seen more clearly perhaps by contrasting him with his cousin Joshé Mari. Joshé Mari, who plays the role of a Don Juan when he is away from his wife and has no consideration for the welfare of his victims, finds a complete justification of his action in the all-forgivingness of the Christian religion. Belief and adherence to this religion settles all the problems confronting Joshé Mari. This faith not only settles the problems in this life but also offers the added attraction of a reward in the life to follow.[52] At first, Luis Murguía thought Joshé Mari a hypocrite, but as their conversation progressed he came to realize that this faith was a vital part of his life and that it functioned as if it were a reality.[53]

To Joshé Mari's ideal of Christian conduct, Luis opposes his own ideal of ethical conduct. He soon realizes that this ideal has no universal acceptance or practice, that it is, in reality, a vital illusion created by himself. "Of course, life isn't going to give each one what he deserves," I thought as I left the house. "Looking for the idea of justice outside of man's mind is an illusion."[54] (E) He is not able to maintain this vital

---

(A) Yo encuentro que el uso de la capa fomenta en el hombre ideas distintas que el empleo del gabán. El embozo parece ocultar y defender y ser propicio al enredo y a la aventura. Quizá, en realidad, no lo sea, pero da esta impresión. En España se nota que mientras se ha usado capa ha habido aventuras, lances de amor y revoluciones. Al desaparecer la capa ha desaparecido todo el aparato romántico de la vida.[47]

(B) — ¿Y por qué habrán tenido ese desvío con usted?
— ¿Qué quiere usted, señora? Yo creo que me faltaba, para ser como su vecino de usted, el desdén y la barba negra.[49]

(C) — Sí. No me ha ido completamente bien con el gremio femenino . . . Como decía antes, me ha faltado el desdén . . . y la barba negra.[50]

(D) Un día, en la calle de Alcalá, escupí sangre.
— Bien — me dije —. Este es el principio del fin.
Fuí temblando a la Casa de Socorro de un médico amigo mío. Me reconoció. No había nada en el pulmón, según él. La intranquilidad que me produjo el creerme enfermo se mezcló a las noticias del desastre de nuestra pequeña escuadra, y anduve varios días triste, decaído y nervioso.[51]

(E) — Claro, la vida no ha de dar a cada uno lo que merece — pensaba yo al salir de su casa —. Buscar la idea de la justicia fuera de la cabeza del hombre es una ilusión.[54]

fiction even in his personal life. When the moment arrives, he improperly invests in stock money entrusted to him. The shares he buys with the money go up quickly, and he is soon able to repay the money entrusted to him. For the moment he disregards his personal ethical code and appeals to legality. "I remembered Don Bernabé's money. Why not invest those fifteen thousand *pesetas?* It was robbery, of course, but one for which the law would have no penalty."[55] (A)

As already seen in many novels, the theory of displacement and disillusionment receives its most eloquent expression and substantiation in the trilogy, *Las agonías de nuestro tiempo.* This trilogy belongs to the third decade of Baroja's production. In the prologue to *Las veleidades de nuestro tiempo* Joe expresses his disbelief in many of the vital illusions of life. He realizes that these are popular instincts born of a desire for justice, but he cannot believe in them.[56] Joe also realizes that men attach more seriousness to myths than they do to the hard facts of reality.[57] He is also aware of the unhappiness which dreams bring to young ladies who seem to lose contact with harsh reality. Nelly, José Larrañaga's friend, seems to live in such a dream world.

Nelly lived half dreaming. She was very thin, and her chest seemed to have shrunken.

She didn't attach any importance to her disease, and the idea of death didn't present itself in her imagination or, if it did, to her it seemed sweet and poetic.

Joe speaks of these young ladies in one of his *Evocaciones:*

"These young girls die peaceful and satisfied. If I were to die, it wouldn't matter to me, one used to say, because I know what life is."

What life could she know? She believed it, and that was enough. In those weakened brains the disease itself forges a dream that produces a great sense of well being, a complete euphoria, and thus they go from life to death facing those mirages which accompany them along the way.

"Should we feel sorry for them or envy them?" Joe asks himself. It is hard to know.

While the old man clings to his miserable life, and Madam Dubarry, with her gray hair, pleads with the executioner at the foot of the guillotine for one more moment of life, the young girl releases the cord that binds her to existence with her small hand, with a serenity which induces terror.[58] (B)

The trilogy is, in essence, the story of José's disillusionment in a world which admits no illusion. Joe, in one of *Las estampas iluminadas,* comments on this process of daily disillusionment. He speaks of the monotony of the days in which past, present, and future hold no illusion or hope.

The triumphant Autumn; the countryside turns yellow, the leaves of gold sleep in the dead water of the canals. The air is charged with humidity. The sky is gray and of a pinkish color. There are flocks of birds in the air. One feels something like a weight in his heart as he notices this "we must die" of Autumn, and upon thinking that it was that way yesterday, it is that way today and it will be that way tomorrow.[59] (C)

The chapter on atmosphere mentioned Baroja's belief that our age has lived on illusions.[60] Also mentioned in the same chapter was the loss of the illusions of youth. "When one begins to look at himself without enthusiasm, like an ordinary example, it isn't the result of having a better and clearer vision, but from having lost his illusions and his youth."[61] (D) This disillusionment is due in part to an exaggerated sensibility.

There are strange men, over-sensitive travelers who go through life leaving behind them, torn to shreds, their illusions and their hopes. Thus for some, passing from cold to heat, from the torrid zone to the hyperborean, invigorates and fortifies them, but for others it softens them and makes them miserable.[62] (E)

(A) Me acordé del dinero de don Bernabé. ¿Por qué no negociar con aquellas quince mil pesetas? Era un robo, claro es, pero para el que no podía tener sanción la ley.[55]

(B) Nelly vivía medio soñando. Estaba muy flaca, y su pecho parecía haberse estrechado.

No le daba ninguna importancia a su mal, y la idea de la muerte no se le presentaba en la imaginación o, si se le presentaba, le parecía dulce y poética.

Estas muchachitas mueren tranquilas y satisfechas. Si me muriera no me importaría, decía una, porque conozco lo que es la vida.

¿Qué vida podía conocer? Lo creía, y eso basta. En esos cerebros débiles la misma enfermedad fragua un sueño que produce un gran bienestar, una completa euforia, y así pasan de la vida a la muerte por delante de esos espejismos que les acompañan en el camino.

— ¿Compadecerlas o envidiarlas? — se pregunta Joe —. Difícil es saberlo.

Mientras el viejo se agarra al vivir miserable, y la Dubarry, con sus canas, suplica al verdugo, al pie de la guillotina, un minuto más de la vida, la muchacha joven suelta la amarra que le une a la existencia con su mano pequeña, con una serenidad que infunde pavor.[58]

(C) El otoño triunfa; el campo se torna amarillo, las hojas de oro duermen en el agua muerta de los canales. El aire está cargado de humedad. El cielo es gris y de color de rosa. Hay bandadas de pájaros en el aire. Se siente como un peso en el corazón al notar este «morir tenemos» del otoño, y al pensar que así era ayer, así es hoy y así será mañana.[59]

(D) Cuando empieza a verse sin entusiasmo como un ejemplar corriente, no es a consecuencia de tener la vista mejor y más clara, sino de haber perdido las ilusiones y la juventud.[61]

(E) Hay hombres curiosos, viajeros demasiado sensibles que han ido dejando sus ilusiones y sus esperanzas hechas jirones por la vida.

Así como a otros, el pasar del frío al calor, de la zona tórrida a la hiperbórea, los tonifica y los fortalece, a éstos los ablanda y los hace miserables.[62]

Among characters in the novels of the fourth decade, the priest in *El cura de Monleón* makes an excellent subject for this stripping process. Step by step Baroja strips him of all the training, of all the teachings, by which he has been strongly influenced in the Jesuit seminary at Victoria. Without doubt Baroja chose a priest for this novel to better illustrate the importance of the vital illusion called faith. This faith is taken away step by step, and the priest is aware of the process.

> The crumbling of his faith and the beginning of his irreligion wasn't an improvised phenomenon in his soul, as it seemed to him at first. It had been developing little by little; several things collaborated in this: the teachings of the confessionary, the conversations with Bastereche and with the socialists, the trip to Lourdes and to Aralar mountain, the attitude of the priests of the village and even speaking with Shagua. Skepticism and incredulity had come to him from everywhere.[63] (A)

When this faith is stripped away, there remains little of Javier. What does remain is a very tender appreciation for his housekeeper, love for his sister Pepita, and a desire and love for one of his maids, la Eustaqui. The last love is considered by Baroja to be more real, less fictional, than his strong relationship with the church. As usual, Baroja is rather noncommittal in these matters of love, but la Eustaqui is mentioned by the priest, Javier, as the novel ends.

> The Eustaqui girl was prettier than ever; tall, smiling, well dressed.
> Doctor Basterreche and Javier ate, served by her.
> "Did you bring the Eustaqui girl?"
> "Yes; she is a very good girl, very intelligent. She is like one of the family."
> Javier didn't say anything.[64] (B)

A more complete understanding of vital illusion and its relationship to life and to Baroja's novel can be gained by reading the fourth part of *El árbol de la ciencia* called "Inquisiciones." Here the direction in which the denial of this illusion must lead is also pointed out. In its exterior form this part represents a discussion between Doctor Iturrioz and the protagonist, Andrés Hurtado. Little insight, however, is required to perceive that the discussion is actually a monologue in which Baroja expresses some of his own ideas and preoccupations about the utility and the pros and cons of vital illusion.[65]

Both Iturrioz and Andrés Hurtado recognize the existence of the fiction. But Doctor Iturrioz, while completely aware of the falsity of it, thinks it is vital to humanity. He rejects all philosophy that takes one away from life. Therefore he prefers the English philosophers to the German philosophers Kant and Schopenhauer. "Yes, perhaps they may be less agile in their thinking than the Germans, but, on the other hand, they don't take you away from life."[66] (C) Iturrioz sees clearly the utility of a vital lie, and for this reason defends it. "O.K.; but I was talking about a practical, immediate use. I, basically, am convinced that truth in wholesale lots is bad for life. The anomaly of nature they call life needs to be based on caprice, perhaps on a lie."[67] (D) Andrés Hurtado, strangely enough, is in complete agreement with the doctor. He sees that there must be some fiction in order to satisfy the vital instincts of man, but he thinks that the amount should be determined by science.

"I agree with that," Andrés said. The will, the desire to live is as strong in animals as it is in man. Comprehension is greater in man. The more one understands the less one desires. This is logical, and besides it is proven in reality. The appetite for knowledge awakens in those individuals who appear at the end of an evolution, when the instinct for life languishes. Man, whose necessity is to know, is like the butterfly who breaks chrysalis in order to die. The healthy, live, strong individual doesn't see things as they are, because it is not good for him. He is inside an hallucination. Don Quijote, to whom Cervantes tried to give a negative meaning, is a symbol of the affirmation of life. Don Quijote lives more than all the sane persons who surround him, he lives more and with more intensity than the others. The individual or the nation that wants to live envelops itself in clouds like the ancient gods when they appeared before mortals. The vital instinct needs fiction to affirm itself.

(A) El desmoronamiento de su fe y el comienzo de su irreligión no era un fenómeno improvisado en su alma, como le pareció al principio. Se había ido preparando poco a poco; habían colaborado en él las enseñanzas del confesionario, las conversaciones con Basterreche y con los socialistas, el viaje a Lourdes y al monte Aralar, la actitud de los curas del pueblo y hasta el hablar con Shagua. Por todas partes le había llegado la incredulidad y el escepticismo.[63]

(B) *La Eustaqui* estaba más guapa que nunca; alta, sonriente, bien vestida.
Comieron el doctor Basterreche y Javier, servidos por ella.
— ¿Habéis traído a *la Eustaqui?*
— Sí; es una chica muy buena, muy inteligente. La tenemos como de la familia.
Javier nada dijo.[64]

(C) — Sí, quizá sean menos ágiles de pensamiento que los alemanes; pero, en cambio, no te alejan de la vida.[66]

(D) — Está bien; pero yo hablaba de un aprovechamiento práctico, inmediato. Yo, en el fondo, estoy convencido de que la verdad en bloque es mala para la vida. Esa anomalía de la Naturaleza que se llama la vida necesita estar basada en el capricho, quizá en la mentira.[67]

Science then, the critical instinct, the instinct of investigation, should find one truth: the quantity of lies one needs for life. You are laughing?"[68] (A)

Although both agree that this fiction which denies science, which denies the tree of knowledge and recognizes only the tree of life with all of its imperfections, has ruled the earth down to the present, Andrés, nevertheless, thinks the supremacy of the myth has ended, and that the day of reason is beginning to appear.

"Ah, of course! Semitism, with its impostors, has dominated the world, it has had the opportunity and the force; in the age of wars it gave man a God of battle; to women and to the weak, a motive for laments, for complaints and for cheap sentimentality. Today, after centuries of semitic domination, truth appears like a pale aurora from the terrors of the night."[69] (B)

Andrés, furthermore, scorns the materialistic utility of vital fiction. He thinks of it as just another reason for the bishops and generals to draw their salary and for the merchants to sell rotten codfish.[70] He insists that it all has to come to an end; he believes that science will triumph. "One has to laugh when they say that science fails. Foolishness; what fails is lies; science marches ahead, sweeping everything before it."[71] (C) Iturrioz chooses the tree of life in preference to the tree of knowledge. Andrés agrees, and the fact that he does not laugh at the idea shows us that he is aware of his own fate. He is condemned because he cannot partake of the tree of life, and because he finds that the fruits of the tree of knowledge, the tree that denies vital illusion, bring death.

"On the other hand, closing that door and not leaving any other norm except life, life languishes, becomes pale, anemic, sad. I don't know who said: legality kills us; like him we could say: reason and science crush us. The more one insists on this point the more one understands the wisdom of the Jews; on one side, the tree of knowledge, on the other, the tree of life."
"One will be forced to believe that the tree of knowledge is like the classical manchineel tree, that kills whomever seeks shelter beneath its shade," Andrés said mockingly.
"Yes, laugh."
"No, I am not laughing."[72] (D)

One's attitude toward this vital illusion leads, then, in a direction quite obvious, a negative direction which tends to reduce life, and finally, if carried to extremes, as in the case of Andrés Hurtado, destroys it. Andrés commits suicide as the novel ends.

María Aracil goes through the same process of disillusionment in *La ciudad de la niebla*. In England she discovers that her father is not a very strong character, and she is forced to make her own way. She is revealed as a strong personality and becomes quite independent. This independence does not bring happiness, and as the novel ends she resolves

to return to the domination of Spain. "I don't know whether or not you
think it's bad, Iturrioz; but I think that I am going to submit" and then she
added charmingly: "I don't have the strength to be immoral."[73] (E) The
happy epilogue of the novel ends on a pathetic note. "Epílogo feliz, casi
triste." María Aracil, whose personality stood out in such sharp relief in
London, now seems lost in the dreams and tranquility of the illusions of
the numberless masses. "And María went for walks along Rosales street
with her nephews, who now called her *mamá,* and with her son. She has

---

(A) — En eso estoy conforme — dijo Andrés —. La voluntad, el deseo
de vivir, es tan fuerte en el animal como en el hombre. En el hombre es mayor
la comprensión. A más comprender, corresponde menos desear. Esto es lógico,
y además se comprueba en la realidad. La apetencia por conocer se despierta
en los individuos que aparecen al final de una evolución, cuando el instinto de
vivir languidece. El hombre, cuya necesidad es conocer, es como la mariposa
que rompe la crisálida para morir. El individuo sano, vivo, fuerte, no ve las
cosas como son, porque no le conviene. Está dentro de una alucinación. Don
Quijote, a quien Cervantes quiso dar un sentido negativo, es un símbolo de la
afirmación de la vida. Don Quijote vive más que todas las personas cuerdas
que le rodean, vive más y con más intensidad que los otros. El individuo o el
pueblo que quiere vivir se envuelve en nubes como los antiguos dioses cuando
se aparecían a los mortales. El instinto vital necesita de la ficción para afir-
marse. La ciencia entonces, el instinto de crítica, el instinto de averiguación,
debe encontrar una verdad: la cantidad de mentira que se necesita para la vida.
¿Se ríe usted?[68]

(B) — ¡Ah, claro! El semitismo, con sus impostores, ha dominado al
mundo, ha tenido la oportunidad y la fuerza; en una época de guerras dió a
los hombres un dios de las batallas; a las mujeres y a los débiles, un motivo de
lamentos, de quejas y de sensiblerías. Hoy, después de siglos de dominación
semítica, el mundo vuelve a la cordura, y la verdad aparece como una aurora
pálida de los terrores de la noche.[69]

(C) Hay que reírse cuando dicen que la ciencia fracasa. Tontería; lo que
fracasa es la mentira; la ciencia marcha adelante, arrollándolo todo.[71]

(D) — En cambio, cerrando esa puerta y no dejando más norma que la
verdad, la vida languidece, se hace pálida, anémica, triste. Yo no sé quién
decía: la legalidad nos mata; como él podemos decir [*sic*]: la razón y la ciencia
nos apabullan. La sabiduría del judío se comprende cada vez más que se insiste
en este punto: a un lado, el árbol de la ciencia; al otro, el árbol de la vida.
— Habrá que creer que el árbol de la ciencia es como el clásico manza-
nillo, que mata a quien se acoge a su sombra — dijo Andrés burlonamente.
— Sí, ríete.
— No, no me río.[72]

(E) — No sé si a usted le parecerá mal, Iturrioz; pero creo que me voy
a someter — y después añadió graciosamente —: No tengo fuerza para ser
inmoral.[73]

gotten a little heavier and is a sedentary and tranquil lady."[74] (A) Few of Baroja's protagonists escape this process of revelation through the loss of vital fiction. Some are allowed to enter the game freely and with success, but in the final analysis they too come to realize that their success was fictional and not real.

This happens to Quintín in *La feria de los discretos*. He outwitted the crooks and the politicians at their own game and thought his successes to be of real value. In the eyes of the world he was looked upon with respect, but his girl friend, Remedios, reduced these false values, these illusions, to ashes when she said that she would consider him only when he became good.

"Ah poor Quintín!" he murmured. "Here your deceits and tricks haven't worked. You are not good? You can't enter paradise. Here you don't have to fight with stockbrokers and politicians, with people of bad faith. The one who has beaten you, Quintín, is a little girl who knows nothing more of the world than what her heart tells her. Poor man, you are not good? You can't enter paradise."
The horse started to move slowly. Quintín looked back. A huge dark cloud covered the moon; all the countryside was left in darkness.
Quintín felt his heart oppressed and sighed deeply.Then, to his amazement, he found he was crying.
And he kept on going.
And the nightingales kept on singing in the darkness, while the moon, high in the sky, bathed the fields with its silver light.[75] (B)

Other protagonists, much like José Larrañaga, end their days in complete disillusionment. El Lince, in *El cantor vagabundo* dies because he no longer has the ability to invent illusions.

One night in May, Don Luis spent long hours in bed without being able to go to sleep, he got up when dawn was breaking. He was incapable of feeling that least bit of optimism. There was nothing left for him: only the light of the sun, the breeze and the color of the sea, but this no longer gave him any illusion, but rather tended to tire him. He had nothing to cling to in life, couldn't invent something for himself that would produce a small illusion. He dressed and went out into the country. He went to the little landing, where the boat was; he untied it, took up the anchor, let out the sail and began to pull away from the coast.
At noon he hadn't returned. There was a storm in the afternoon and, probably, Don Luis, the vagabond singer, disappeared in the sea.[76] (C)

A significant number of Baroja's protagonists are unmasked in foreign lands. Baroja proves to be much aware of and concerned about the strange things that happen to the character of people placed in foreign lands. José Larrañaga, in *Las veleidades de la fortuna,* discusses and comments on the strange rift that has come between his friend Pepita and her husband the moment they find themselves in a foreign land.

After we left Paris, Fernando and Pepita began to quarrel. I made efforts to fix things up, but it wasn't possible. Fernando criticized Pepita for having a bad temper, for being capricious, and Pepita criticized Fernando for the same thing.

"And they hadn't realized that until then?"

"No."

"One recognizes that upon finding themselves in a foreign country, in each one of them an unknown character came forth, which hadn't yet manifested itself." [77] (D)

José Larrañaga is never seen in his native Spain and among old friends and loved ones of his home town. Although there are few glimpses of Don Fausto Bengoa in Madrid, he scarcely becomes interesting until he arrives in Paris. The strange character of Paradox is revealed in the fantastic kingdom of Uganga. The reader gets to know María Aracil, the

---

(A) Y María pasea por la calle de Rosales con sus sobrinas, que ahora la llaman mamá, y con su hijo. Ha engrosado un poco y es una señora sedentaria y tranquila. [74]

(B) «¡Ah, pobre Quintín! — murmuró —. Aquí no te han valido tus argucias y tus tretas. ¿No eres bueno? No puedes entrar en el paraíso. Aquí no tienes que luchar con bolsistas, ni con políticos, ni con gente de mala fe. Es una chiquilla que no sabe del mundo más que lo que le dice su corazón la que te ha vencido, Quintín. ¿No eres bueno, pobre hombre? No puedes entrar en el paraíso.

El caballo echó a andar lentamente. Quintín miró hacia atrás. Un nubarrón se interpuso delante de la luna; todo el campo quedó en las tinieblas.

Quintín sintió el corazón oprimido y suspiró fuertemente. Luego quedó extrañado. Estaba llorando.

Y siguió adelante.

Y los ruiseñores siguieron cantando en la oscuridad, mientras la luna, muy alta, bañaba el campo con su luz de plata. [75]

(C) Una noche de mayo, don Luis pasó largas horas en la cama sin poder conciliar el sueño, y se levantó cuando amanecía. No era capaz de sentir el menor optimismo. Ya no quedaba nada para él: únicamente la luz del sol y la brisa y el color del mar, pero esto ya no le ilusionaba y más bien le cansaba. No tenía agarradero ninguno en la vida, no podía inventarse algo para sí mismo que le produjera una pequeña ilusión. Se vistió y salió al campo. Fué al pequeño desembarcadero, donde estaba la barca; la desamarró, la desancló, desplegó la vela y comenzó a alejarse de la costa.

Al mediodía no había vuelto. Por la tarde hubo una borrasca, y, probablemente, don Luis, el cantor vagabundo, desapareció en el mar. [76]

(D) Desde que salimos de París, Fernando y Pepita comenzaron a reñir. Yo terciaba para arreglarlos, pero no era posible. Fernando reprochaba a Pepita que tenía mal genio, que era caprichosa, y Pepita reprochaba de lo mismo a Fernando.

— ¿Y hasta entonces no se habían dado cuenta de eso?

— No.

— Se conoce que al encontrarse en el extranjero, en el uno y en el otro brotó un carácter inédito, que aún no se había manifestado. [77]

heroine of two of the novels in the trilogy called *La raza,* on her trip from Madrid to Lisbon and in London. César Moncada, in the novel *César o nada,* is partly revealed in Italy, although he returns to Spain for his work of regeneration of a small town. Sacha, the heroine of *El mundo es ansí,* travels extensively throughout Europe. She spends little time in her native Russia. *El laberinto de las sirenas* takes place in Italy, and the rest of the novels of the trilogy called *El mar* take place, for the most part, on the high seas or in foreign countries. The same can be said for *La estrella del Capitán Chimista,* whose protagonist, Chimista, is seen in all sorts of foreign lands and on foreign seas but never in his native Basque province.

Although Aviraneta spends a good deal of time in Spain, he is also seen in many parts of the globe such as Mexico, Africa, England, and especially France. Miguel Salazar, the protagonist of *Susana o las cazadoras de moscas,* is revealed to the reader and to himself in Paris. *Laura o la soledad sin remedio,* is the story of a young girl's trial and sorrows in Paris and other foreign lands. Procopio Pagani of *El hotel del cisne* and Luis Carvajal of *El cantor vagabundo* complete the list of protagonists whom Baroja has chosen to take from their native lands and place in a foreign land in order that the reader might see them more clearly.

Baroja has taken many of his characters from their homes or preferred corner of Spain and placed them in a less natural setting. Javier, the priest in *El cura de Monleón,* suffered this fate. He is taken from his house and its beloved gardens in Monleón and sent to a nameless little village in Alava. "Compared with Monleón the town seemed like a skeleton to Javier. He saw it as something completely dry, primitive, and gloomy, like the people and the countryside." [78] (A) Often the displacement is temporal rather than geographic. Aviraneta seems to appeal to Baroja because of his temporal displacement. He seems to belong either to the past or the future, not to the present. "Aviraneta was a man from another time: he had been born too early or too late, probably too late. In an age of absolutism he would have been something greater." [79] (B) *El mayorazgo de Labraz* is essentially a temporally displaced person. His nobility and virtue seemed to have no place or recognition in Labraz. Baroja, in his desire to show more clearly just what sort of man this was, stripped him of his material wealth, his prestige, his home, and finally of his native city Labraz.

Given Baroja's method of revelation of his characters in which he consistently strives to rid his protagonist of all that might be superficial in the way of illusions or material surroundings, it is easy to understand how his characters never quite achieve greatness. At this point one might well ask just why Baroja went to all of this trouble to reveal his protagonists if they are in his own words *poca cosa.* Certainly Silvestre Paradox will never be a paragon of virtue and success to be emulated by future generations. Few would want their children to grow up to be like Paradox Rey, Luis Murguía, or Don Fausto.

The answer to the question of greatness is not a direct one, nor is it easy to formulate. Baroja, however, tends to defend these poor creatures whom he has gone to considerable trouble and ingenuity to reveal by saying that they are real, sincere, and most human. This very lack of greatness, this lack of any great occidentally recognized virtue, is probably their most human attribute.

Baroja gives this answer in an article called *El héroe, el señor y yo.*

"So that, according to you, here everything is small and only the trouble makers, the bloodthirsty, the turbulent ones, the Aviranetas are the great ones?"

"That's it."

"So that, for you, thought is nothing?"

"Yes, *hombre,* when it is thought."

"So that for you democracy is a farce?"

"Yes; something like that."

"And social justice a lie?"

"For the present, I think so."

"And morality a mystification?"

"Something like that."

"And what is left then?"

"Man is left, man, who is above religion, democracy, morality, electric light and typists, the poetry of Nuñez de Arcex and the hallelujahs of Campoamor . . .; man is left, that is to say, the hero, who, in the midst of storms, of hates, of the resources of mediocrity, of the envy of sallow men with their calculating bladders, imposes a norm on the rest; yes, man remains, the hero . . ."[80] (C)

(A) El pueblo le parecía a Javier esquelético al lado de Monleón. Le veía completamente seco, primitivo y adusto, como las personas y el paisaje.[78]

(B) Avinareta [*sic*] era hombre de otro tiempo: había nacido demasiado temprano o demasiado tarde, probablemente demasiado tarde. En una época de absolutismo hubiera sido algo más.[79]

(C) — ¿Así que, según usted, aquí todo es pequeño, y únicamente los alborotadores, los sanguinarios, los turbulentos, los Aviranetas son los grandes?

— Eso es.

— ¿De manera que el pensamiento para usted no es nada?

— Sí, hombre, mucho; cuando es pensamiento.

— ¿De manera que la democracia para usted es una farsa?

— Sí; algo de eso.

— ¿Y la justicia social una mentira?

— Por hoy, creo que sí.

— ¿Y la moral una mistificación?

— Algo por el estilo.

— ¿Y qué queda entonces?

— Queda el hombre, el hombre, que está por encima de la religión, de la democracia, de la moral, de la luz y taquígrafos, de los versos de Núñez de Arce y de las aleluyas de Campoamor . . .; queda el hombre, es decir, el héroe, que, en medio de las tempestades, de los odios, de los recursos de la mediocridad, de la envidia de los hombres cetrinos con las vejigas calculosas, impone una norma difícil a los demás; sí, queda el hombre, el héroe . . .[80]

This same answer is given in an article which also compares Ortega y Gasset's esthetic and artistic ideas with those of Baroja.

> For Baroja on the other hand art can never be an end in itself. Such so-called "Art" is for him mere *palabrería* and mixtification. It is a means, not of escape from reality (for Baroja there can be no escape from reality whether through action, as he at first thought, or through abstention, his final attitude) but of exploration of it. Reality presents him not merely with an artistic problem, but, from the moment he declares "no sé lo que es la realidad," with an aspect of the general metaphysical problem which the novel can analyze and try to solve. Instead of looking out from art towards life, as Ortega tends to do, he looks from life, from the center of the human problem, towards art. For this reason his attitude is as inclusive as Ortega's is exclusive; everything that is human and part of life is part of the problem and perhaps part of the answer. It might be said, therefore, that his conception of art is as closely centered on the novel as Ortega's is on the other art-forms. At any rate Baroja stuck to it. In his last broadside against Ortega, in *Rapsodias,* he leaves no doubt as to his final standpoint: "Cuando el arte es humano, auténticamente humano, es cuando vale."[81]

Baroja, then, uses a single technique in revealing almost all of his major characters. The characters do not grow through the process of gradual accruement. They are not the sum total of many ideas and things. They tend to shrink and become smaller and smaller. They are taken away from family and friends and stripped of material possessions and basic ideas and beliefs. They are revealed and not developed.

Examples from four decades of Baroja's novelistic production demonstrate a patent consistency and thoroughness in the use of this singular method of character revelation. Baroja has stated this method overtly; other critics have corroborated it, and Baroja has used it in most of his novels.

From the consistency and thoroughness with which this method of character revelation is carried out, one must conclude that the end product, the revealed protagonist, is most important to Baroja. However, this revealed character does not impress one, at first, as a vehicle capable of tremendous emotional and intellectual appeal. At the end of the novel, Baroja's protagonist is best defined as *poca cosa,* as a man who is not much, hardly anything, a very little thing.

As the reader encounters more and more of Baroja's protagonists, his sensibilities become more finely attuned to the little bit of humanity revealed in each novel. This increased sensibility helps him to perceive more instantaneously and more tangibly the physical minutiae of sensation which surround him. Almost without exception Baroja's insignificant protagonists have a hypersensitivity and appreciativeness of the most vital, physical sensations: sunshine, warmth, color, movement, air, etc. These were the last things to be taken away from Don Luis in *El cantor vagabundo.* "There was nothing left for him: only the light of the sun and the breeze and the color of the sea, but this no longer gave him any illusion, but rather tired him."[82] (A) Besides this refinement of the reader's sensitivity to selected minutiae of physical sensations, strong emotional and intellectual undertones begin to emanate from the little derelict bits of humanity. These "little" men come to represent a quasi affirmation of man's littleness and insignificance or a quasi denial of his greatness. In them is an ever-increasing suggestion that this is all man is, that there is nothing more — that man is, after all, in unadorned essence, *poca cosa*. The poignant suggestion is reiterated at the end of almost every novel. This is the end of *El caballero de Erláiz,* "¡Qué pobre miseria! ¡Qué cínico resto sin valor del sueño de la vida!"[83]

Running parallel to the idea "This is all there is to man," is the suggestion that, if there is something more, man's sensibility must be too awkward and too obscured to perceive it. One of the strongest hindrances to finding anything more in this little man, in this little thing, is the obfuscation caused by traditional vital illusions, many of which presuppose a completely false and antiquated means for measuring man. Protesting against all this, Baroja quotes Protagoras in saying that man is the measure of all things. "There are two apothegms which strike me as some of the most profound of primitive philosophy. One is the one from Protagoras, which says: "Man is the measure of all things, of things possible as possible and of things impossible as impossible."[84] (B) Baroja implies that things are a poor yardstick for man. Thus man for Baroja cannot be the sum total of circumstances and things, even if these are computed with the precision of an I.B.M. machine. This preoccupation with the inexactitude and limitations of the means for knowing things and man runs throughout his work called *La intuición y el estilo*.[85]

When man's vital illusions become universalized and standardized they become clumsy tools for the understanding and measuring of man. It is only when individual man, with little assistance or guidance, welds into a highly personal illusion a personal handful of ideas and things which surround him that this fiction becomes revealing. Even then, it tends to reveal an essential need of the individual rather than an essential part of his being. Thus Baroja takes great pains with many or most of his novels to show the difference between the suggestive and illuminating

---

(A) Ya no quedaba nada para él: únicamente la luz del sol y la brisa y el color del mar, pero esto ya no le ilusionaba y más bien le cansaba.[82]

(B) Hay dos apotegmas que me parecen de los más profundos de la filosofía primitiva. Uno es el de Protágoras, que dice: «El hombre es la medida de todas las cosas, de las posibles como posibles y de las imposibles como imposibles.»[84]

potential of a personal vital fiction and the dark and antivital sameness of those fabricated by time and what he might call many generations of *farsantes*. The basic difference seems to be that the traditional vital illusions, the official dogma of things and ideas, come from outside the individual, not forming an integral part of his being, while the personal ones come from within, expressing — or suggesting, at least — one of his vital needs.

Thus Baroja's stripped and misplaced men stand alone in their human littleness at the end of the novel. They seem to represent, not the result and final conclusion of the investigation into the essential nature of humanity, but rather its beginning. They seem to mark the first step, point out its fundamental direction. This direction, which so carefully reveals these little men, seems to be a living negation of the efficaciousness of all the literary and intellectual apparatus intended to plumb the depths of their being and reveal their most essential humanity.

When fully cognizant of the method and purpose of Baroja's character revelation, it is easy to see the necessity for extreme care in creating an antivital atmosphere. Baroja seems to feel that this is the only atmosphere in which he can hope to get a glimpse of undistorted humanity. Man, in an atmosphere charged and turbulent with emotions, ideas, truths, philosophies (Baroja would say) may be greater, more powerful, perhaps even a superman, but he will be deformed, false. This is the atmosphere which creates *mixtificadores* and *farsantes,* as Baroja calls them.

This protagonist, then, is the beginning of Baroja's positive answer to a sad, negative, chaotic world. He is one of the few values retained by Baroja and perhaps a key or guide to other values. And the continual use of negation is essential for the creation of the world in which the protagonist was placed and revealed. Almost every negative aspect of Baroja's novels discussed up to this point — the non-rhetorical prose, the uneven syntax, the listless dialogue, and the dark antivital atmosphere — helps to show this protagonist more clearly and sharpens the emphatic response to his human frailty.

6. *Minor Characters*

BAROJA HAS FOLLOWED a definite procedure for revealing to the reader the essential self of his protagonists. To follow the same procedure in revealing secondary characters would be quite impractical. In the first place they are too numerous. The first impression critics receive from Baroja's novels is that of the exaggerated number of secondary characters. An article in the *Saturday Review of Literature* in 1925 made this comment:

> Queer extravagant characters were introduced, as from a conjuror's hat, only to disappear again as inexplicably; while they lasted many of them were highly diverting, but within the concept of the ordered novel, they had no role.[1]

Francisco Pina speaks of the legions of characters who march through Baroja's novels, considering them to be the novels' greatest drawing force.[2] According to Ballesteros de Martos, Baroja's concept of the novel has been that of a heterogeneous parade of characters and their respective environments.[3] He finds Baroja superior to Galdós, Dickens, and Balzac in this respect.[4] Bolinger too has been impressed by the great number of people who appear in Baroja's novels. He quotes Luis Bello in saying that the census of Baroja's novelistic world is probably greater than that of Galdós.[5] Counting only those named and excluding those only described, he found that *Las noches del Buen Retiro* had 116, that a short dialogued novelette, *El hermano Beltrán,* had forty-three, and *El Mayorazgo de Labraz* thirty-five.[6]

A step-by-step unmasking of the multitude of characters in Baroja's novels would be impossible. Given the mere physical limits of the novel, Baroja could not possibly take each one from his home and loved ones, from his native Spain, and from all those beliefs that support the lives of most of his human compeers in order to show his human essence.

Another important factor apparently prohibits the use of this system of revelation for the secondary characters. It has been generally supposed that Baroja has taken these characters from real life, merely transposing them into his novelistic world. Bolinger thinks the secondary characters more convincing because they are copied from reality.[7] Baroja himself goes to great lengths to illustrate and document the genesis of his secondary characters. For someone interested in looking into the genesis and background of some of Baroja's earlier secondary characters, a series of introductions the novelist wrote for an edition of *Páginas escogidas* is quite useful. Here are some of the comments he makes about the genesis of his characters:

The landscapes of *La casa de Aizgorri* are formed with memories of Cestona; the characters, some seen, others invented. The father, Don Lucio de Aizgorri, is the counterpart of an old friend of mine; the crazy people of the town have something of reality.[8] (A)

There are quite a few personages in the book taken from real life. All of those who appear in the first part, which takes place in an inn in the town, come from life. Many years ago, in a town of the province of Alava, I was at a similar inn.[9] (B)

The rest of the book, almost all of it is based on reality. The majority of the characters are also real. Doctor Aracil, although altered by me, is still living; the one that served as a model for painting Iturrioz, died; in the mornings María Aracil takes walks along Alcalá street. Some supposed, I don't know why, that in María Aracil I had tried to picture Soledad Villafranca, an absurdity, which has no appearance of reality.
When I wrote *La dama errante,* I didn't know Soledad Villafranca; I met her afterwards, in Paris, in the house of a professor where I was invited for supper. Since she is from Pamplona, and I went to school there, we talked for a long time, and in the course of the conversation, she told me that she had read *La dama errante.* As is logical, she hadn't encountered any allusion to herself in the book, but, on the other hand, she had thought she saw the counterpart of Ferrer.
The rest of the characters were also taken from real life, and my brother and I made the trip through Vera de Plasencia, carrying provisions on a burro, and an army tent.
The wretched little roadhouses and the inns along the way are, more or less, like those described by me, with the same names and the same kind of people. It is possible that el Musiú, el Ninchi, and el Grillos still are found in those villages, leading their life of wandering along the roads and deceiving fools.[10] (C)

In *Las inquietudes* there are autobiographical notes and memories of San Sebastian from when I was a child. My Aunt Cesárea, who in the novel is called Aunt Ursula, lived on a street next to the docks, and from the balconies of her house I used to contemplate the movement of the port.[11] (D)

Those characters which are historical figures have obviously been taken from real life. George Borrow appears in two or more of Baroja's novels as a secondary figure. In *El Mayorazgo de Labraz,* he is the man who brings Bothwell, the Englishman, to Labraz.

"A year; but I didn't discover Labraz; it was a friend and fellow country-man who brought me here. My friend was one of the strangest men that could ever have existed. He had insisted on making Spain a Protestant country, just see what barbarity, and had spent a goodly number of years traveling through the country with his Bibles."[12] (E)

In *El sabor de la venganza* he teaches Aviraneta to speak *caló* (jargon used by gypsies). In the same novel the popular bandit, Luis Candelas, makes an appearance. Important literary figures such as Lord Byron,[13] as well as Juan Valera,[14] appear in his novels. The character Max Schulze, whom Fernando Ossorio met in Paular, is taken straight from reality.[15]

(A) Los paisajes de *La casa de Aizgorri* están formados con recuerdos de Cestona; los tipos, unos están vistos, otros están inventados. El padre, don Lucio de Aizgorri, es la contra-figura de un viejo amigo mío; los locos del pueblo tienen algo de realidad.[8]

(B) Hay bastantes personajes en el libro tomados del natural. Todos los que aparecen en la primera parte, que ocurre en una posada de un pueblo, lo son. En una posada semejante, estuve hace muchos años en un pueblo de la provincia de Alava.[9]

(C) Lo demás del libro, casi todo está hecho a base de realidad. La mayoría de los personajes son también reales. El doctor Aracil, aunque desfigurado por mí, vive; el que me sirvió de modelo para pintar a Iturrioz, murió; María Aracil pasea por las mañanas por la calle de Alcalá. Algunos supusieron, no sé por qué, que en María Aracil había querido yo pintar a Soledad Villafranca, la amiga de Ferrer, cosa absurda, que no tiene apariencia de verdad.
Yo, cuando escribí *La dama errante*, no conocía a Soledad Villafranca; la conocí después, en París, en casa de un profesor, donde estuve convidado a cenar. Como ella es de Pamplona y yo me eduqué también allí, hablamos largo rato, y en el curso de la conversación me dijo que había leído *La dama errante*. Como es lógico, no había encontrado ninguna alusión a ella en el libro, y, en cambio, sí había creído ver la contrafigura de Ferrer.
Los demás tipos de la novela fueron también tomados del natural, y el viaje por la Vera de Plasencia lo hicimos mi hermano y yo y un amigo, llevando en un burro provisiones y una tienda de campaña.
Los ventorros y paradores del camino son, poco más o menos, como los descritos por mí, con los mismos nombres y la misma clase de gente. El Musiú, el Ninchi y el Grillo es posible que anden todavía por esas aldeas, siguiendo su vida de trotar caminos y engañar a los bobos.[10]

(D) Hay en *Las inquietudes* notas autobiográficas y recuerdos de San Sebastián de cuando yo era chico. Mi tía Cesárea, que en la novela se llama la tía Ursula, vivía en una calle que da al muelle, y desde los balcones de su casa solía yo contemplar el movimiento del puerto.[11]

(E) — Un año; pero yo no descubrí a Labraz; fué un amigo mío y compatriota el que me trajo aquí. Mi amigo era uno de los hombres más curiosos que han podido existir. Se había empeñado en hacer protestante a España, ya ve usted qué barbaridad, y llevaba una porción de años recorriendo el país con sus biblias.[12]

Thus evidence indicates that a goodly number of Baroja's secondary characters are taken from reality. This is not to say, however, that he has not retouched them or transformed them as he pleased. What does seem to be present nearly always is the contact with reality. Baroja has called this "el trampolín de la realidad" in his prologue to *La nave de los locos*.[16]

Counterbalancing this evidence and these opinions are the affirmations that he is a great inventor of characters. Francisco Pina praises his ability to create living creatures. He devotes a chapter to this point; the heading reads, "El creador de personajes."

> Baroja is a strange chiromancer who, in order to add just a little seasoning to his life, creates worlds plethoric with living creatures, which are his novels. And they are so populated, so dropsical that they have the "full up" sign out.
>
> His facility for creating characters is so resolved that the least perceptive of readers understands quickly the little effort the author needs to animate his multiple creatures. One senses, in fact, without need of great intuition, this amazing creative faculty, which is one of Pío Baroja's preeminent novelistic qualities.[17]

Ortega y Gasset is also amazed at the amount of talent Baroja shows in the invention of personages.

> It is impossible to calculate the talent Baroja expends in the invention of characters, each one of which encloses condensed allusions to an essential element of life and of the times. The wise Canon Chirino who hides his favorite readings about skeptical and rationalistic man in a wall; the Confessor Sansirgue, a *heavy, hairy spider,* capable of anything a spider is capable of; Damián Diente, who beneath his clock with carved figures, where Caronet in his boat presides over the hours, makes caskets and philosophies, etc., etc.[18]

This opinion is not to be taken lightly, and it certainly is not uncomplimentary to Baroja's genius. The characters who parade through his novelistic world, in spite of their numbers, live and breathe. They achieve a flicker of undeniable life even in the few short moments in which they appear and disappear. Furthermore, they have a close kinship to the protagonists, whose essential humanity has been revealed with care and patience. Benjamín Jarnés, commenting on the novel *Las noches del Buen Retiro,* speaks of the great family of Baroja's characters: " . . . Admiramos la gran familia barojiana, no el gran personaje barojiano."[19] The embryonic relationship of these secondary characters to the principals of the novels should be a helpful clue in answering the question. Given the numerousness of Baroja's secondary types, one might be surprised to find a close resemblance between all, as well as a close relationship to the protagonists. The point merits clarification.

There can be little doubt that Baroja shows a predilection for certain types and a great disdain for others. That the good burgher is not the object of this search seems more than evident. The character who is fully caught up in the cogs of society and tradition is usually excluded from his novels. When he is included, he is treated with anything but enthusiasm.

Many years ago I was a doctor in a little Basque town, in Cestona. Sometimes, during the summer, while making calls to the huge country homes I used to encounter along the highway and on the roads walkers with a poor physical appearance, hepatic sick people who were taking the waters in a nearby health resort.

These people with their leather-like color didn't make me feel any curiosity or sympathy. The bourgeois businessman or employee of the big cities, healthy or sick, is repugnant to me. I would exchange an ill-humored greeting with those hepatic types and go on my way mounted on my old nag.[20] (A)

Baroja's greatest aversion to the middle-class subjects is that they are victims of routine and tradition. "Don Matías was the good burgher type: stupid, set in his routine, crude, and at heart, immoral. All routines seemed holy to him; precedent, the best reason."[21] (B) Vagabonds do abound in the novels of Baroja. The relationship these vagabonds have to the protagonists explains why there are so many. A young vagabond found in *La nave de los locos* could be the prototype of these wanderers.

Ollarra had no social sense. Take money away from the one who has it. Why not? Take this man or that man's daughter if you can, he used to say. In the final analysis, robbing your neighbor or cutting out his guts also seemed O.K. to him. He lived apart from any social idea and from any consideration for his fellow man, like a perfect savage.[22] (C)

The sentence clearly makes him a blood brother of most of Baroja's protagonists, a blood brother not only of the gypsy Ramiro but also of *el mayorazgo,* who at the end of the novel of this name makes a complete breakaway from all environmental and sociological moorings.

(A) Hace ya muchos años estaba yo de médico en un pueblecillo vasco, en Cestona. Algunas veces, los veranos, al ir a mis visitas a los caseríos solía encontrarme en la carretera y en los caminos paseantes de mal aspecto, enfermos hepáticos que tomaban las aguas en un balneario próximo.

Estas gentes de color de cuero no me producían ninguna curiosidad ni simpatía. El burgués comerciante o empleado de las grandes poblaciones, sano o enfermo, me repugna. Cambiaba con aquellos tipos hepáticos un saludo displicente y me alejaba montado en mi viejo rocín.[20]

(B) Don Matías era el tipo del buen burgués: bruto, rutinario, indelicado, y en el fondo, inmoral. Toda rutina le parecía santa; el precedente, la mejor razón.[21]

(C) *Ollarra* no tenía ningún sentido social. Quitar el dinero al que lo posee. ¿Por qué no? Llevarse la hija de éste o del otro. ¿Si se puede?, decía él. En último término, robar al vecino o destriparle le parecía también lícito. Vivía fuera de toda idea social y de consideración al prójimo, como un perfecto salvaje.[22]

Ragmen hold a high place in the census of Baroja's fictional characters. Enlarging the category to include junkmen, second-hand booksellers, and other out-of-the-way merchants and peddlers, one can safely say that such a character appears in almost every novel. Although most of them do not make such repeated appearances in the novel as does Chipiteguy, he may serve as an example because more is known about him.

> It was thought that the ragman was still a Jacobin. They knew that more than once he defended Danton and Anacarsis Clootz with great ardor. Some strange rumors were circulating about him; it was rumored that he had run contraband, and even indulged in counterfeiting; they added that he had distributed leaflets and papers for the Carbonari and that he belonged to a secret republican organization, called The Seasons, with which such dangerous men as Blanqui and Barbés were affiliated. In spite of his republicanism and his volterianism, *Chipiteguy* celebrated with big fiestas in his home the two patron saints of junkmen: San Roque and San Sebastian; but it was because it seemed to him that any pretext was good reason for a party.[23] (A)

Chipiteguy is presented as living apart from the society of his day. Later in the novel he smuggles jewels and valuable religious artifacts into France without the least scruple. He, along with most of Baroja's rag pickers and secondhand dealers, has his own, self-created philosophy toward life. In this he is a brother of Ollara and the other vagabonds.

Hangmen abound in Baroja's novels. From the following quotation it is easy to discern the virtue by which they become a part of Baroja's family.

> As a matter of fact, Master Juan, when I asked him if he was an executioner, answered me smiling that he was, and he spoke to me about the men he had dispatched to the other world like a doctor about his patients or a priest about his parishioners. Undoubtedly to him, the thing seemed quite natural and not very important.
>
> He also told me that he had been a sheepherder in a small village and that he had come to Madrid as a guard. When the executioner's position became vacant, he had asked for it, because you earned more; but his decision had seemed so horrible to his wife and his son that they no longer wanted to live with him.
>
> Master Juan didn't understand this, and he shrugged his shoulders, like someone who can't explain an absurd preoccupation.
>
> "Your Excellency wasn't aware that I was the executioner?" he asked me right away, smiling.
>
> "No."
>
> "But Don Eugenio, he knew it,"
>
> "Yes, Don Eugenio did."
>
> "When you have a trade like Your Excellency has, you have to be on good terms with the executioner," Master Juan said philosophically.
>
> I shuddered.
>
> "It is true," Eugenio said, "because on any given day one is exposed to turning his neck over to one of you."
>
> "Fortunately," he said, "there are executioners and executioners, sir."

"Certainly. In that profession, like in all of them, there will be some good and some bad."

"And Your Excellency can say that again, sir, because part of the trade depends on the materials. And no other executioner has the good straps that I have; but part of it, and excuse me for telling Your Excellency this, depends on the hands."

"And you have good hands, Master Juan?"

"It isn't because I wish to brag, sir; but I believe that for sending a Christian cleanly to the other world, there are not many who stand ahead of me." [24] (B)

(A) Se creía que el trapero seguía siendo jacobino. Se sabía que más de una vez defendió a Danton y a Anacarsis Clootz con mucho calor. Algunos rumores extraños corrían acerca de él; se murmuraba que había hecho contrabando, y hasta moneda falsa; se añadía que había repartido hojas y papeles carbonarios y que pertenecía a una sociedad secreta republicana, titulada Las Estaciones, en la que estaban afiliados hombres tan peligrosos como Blanqui y Barbés. A pesar de su republicanismo y de su volterianismo, *Chipiteguy* celebraba con grandes fiestas en su casa los dos patronos de los chatarreros: San Roque y San Sebastián; pero era porque cualquier pretexto le parecía bueno para un festín.[23]

(B) Efectivamente; maese Juan, al preguntarle si era verdugo, me contestó, sonriendo que sí, y me habló de los hombres que había echado al otro mundo como un médico de sus enfermos o un párroco de sus feligreses. La cosa sin duda, le parecía natural y sin gran importancia.

Me contó también que había sido pastor en el pueblo y que había venido a Madrid de guarda. Al quedar vacante la plaza de verdugo, él la había solicitado, porque se ganaba más; pero a su mujer y a su hijo les había parecido tan horrible su decisión, que no querían vivir con él.

Maese Juan no comprendía esto, y se encogió de hombros, como quien no se explica una preocupación absurda.

— ¿Usía no estaba enterado de que yo era el verdugo? — me preguntó luego, sonriendo.

— No.

— Don Eugenio sí lo sabía.

— Sí; don Eugenio, sí.

— Cuando se tiene el oficio de usía, hay que estar bien con el verdugo — dijo filosóficamente maese Juan.

Yo me estremecí.

— Es verdad — dijo —, porque el mejor día se está expuesto a entregar a uno de ustedes el cuello.

— Por fortuna — dijo él —, no todos los verdugos son iguales; hay verdugos y verdugos, caballero.

— Cierto. En esa profesión, como en todas, habrá sus más y sus menos.

— Y que lo puede usía decir muy alto, señor, porque parte del oficio depende del material. Y buenas cuerdas como yo, no hay verdugo que las tenga; pero parte, y perdone que se lo diga a usía, depende de la mano.

— ¿Y usted la tiene buena, maese Juan?

— No es por alabarme, caballero; pero creo que para enviar con limpieza a un cristiano al otro mundo no hay muchos que se me puedan poner delante.[24]

Maese Juan's attitude and profession, far from being accepted by the general run of moral people, is rejected even by his family. The very thing that makes Maese Juan part of the Baroja family is isolation from his own family and from society in general. He has his own social and moral code, of which he is duly proud. He even expects to gain the rewards of heaven by it.

"And do you think that with this profession you will go to heaven?"

"I hope so, sir; I will have to pass through purgatory; but I suppose that it won't be for very long." [25] (A)

Judging from the three types of character seen in these prototypes, standard moral values — or at least what Baroja would deem the standard moral values of his day — have no place nor do they command respect in Baroja's family of characters. According to the dictates of his time, imposed by the church, the laws, and general public opinion, these men may be good or bad indifferently. The important thing is that their code of conduct, their philosophy, and their way of life are determined by themselves, from within, and not superimposed by the dictates of society.

Ramón Sender in his book on *Unamuno, Valle-Inclán, Baroja y Santagora* accuses Baroja of an unrealistic distribution of virtues.

> Baroja's realism fails in the structure of his novels and in the sense of social values. For example, in a splendid novel entitled *El laberinto de las sirenas* the degrees of natural goodness and virtue are awarded according to the economic level of the characters. The richest man — the millionaire — is a perfect man. His rich friends are no less virtuous. The Marchioness' Basque administrator is a rustic and honest man. But he has one trait which lessens him — his rustic side. The doormen, guards, fishermen, laborers represent different aspects of evil, some of crime. The same thing happens in other novels by Don Pío. His realism, then, isn't in the structure or in his way of reflecting society.[26] (B)

This accusation of stacking the deck in favor of the aristocracy is refuted, indirectly, in *La caverna del humorismo*. Here Baroja is discussing Ortega y Gasset's *Observaciones de un lector,* which appeared in *La lectura* in 1915. Ortega's praise of aristocratic art finds a rebuttal in Baroja's defense of plebeian art.

> "I find that all this smacks of a rabid and puerile aristocrat," Guezurtegui said. "We gracefully admit that there has been a literature of nobles and plebeians; but we don't admit that the literature of the nobles (as a social class) is noble also in the ethical sense or that the literature of the plebes is plebeian in the sense of abjection and lowliness."
>
> "You are a romantic, Guezurtegui," Luna said.
>
> "No. It's that, if this were so, the Gotha almanac would be the index of the world's spiritual qualities. It doesn't seem to me that one can state that the division of servants and masters, of nobles and plebeians, can be the norm for literature, and, above all, for morality. Do you think so?"[27] (C)

Two characters in *Las inquietudes de Shanti Andía* add to Baroja's defense against this accusation. Machín recognizes that in the human breast there is a little of the good and a little of the bad.[28] The narrator recognizes him as a violent man capable of both good and bad things.[29] Wilkins, in the same novel, points out the mutual dependence of these two virtues. "Evil, meaness, envy, he forgave everything. For Wilkins, evil was no more than the amount of shadow necessary to make goodness shine forth."[30] (D)

This mixture of the good and bad seems to be what interests Baroja, as Joe expresses it in one of his *Fantasías de la época.* "In a restricted sense, the human side is not only the sublime; but neither is it just the ignoble. It is the compensated mixture of good and bad which can come out of our heads."[31] (E) Although the important person of *El laberinto de las sirenas* called *el Inglés* may be virtuous, he has other salient features

---

(A) — ¿Y cree usted que con esta profesión ganará usted el cielo?
— Así lo espero, señor; habré de pasar por el purgatorio; pero supongo no será por mucho tiempo.[25]

(B) El realismo de Baroja falla en la estructura de sus novelas y en el sentido de los valores sociales. Por ejemplo, en una espléndida novela que titula *El laberinto de las sirenas* los grados de bondad natural y de virtud están adjudicados según el nivel económico de sus personajes. El más rico — el millonario — es un hombre perfecto. Sus amigos ricos no le ceden en virtud. El vasco administrador de la marquesa es un hombre rudo y honesto. Pero ya tiene un rasgo que lo disminuye, la rudeza. Los porteros, guardas, pescadores, obreros, representan diferentes aspectos de la maldad, algunos del crimen. Eso mismo sucede en otras novelas de don Pío. Su realismo, pues, no lo es en la estructura ni en la manera de reflejar la sociedad.[26]

(C) — Encuentro todo eso de un aristocratismo rabioso y pueril — ha dicho Guezurtegui —. Aceptamos graciosamente que haya habido una literatura de nobles y plebeyos; pero no aceptamos que la literatura de los nobles (como clase social) sea noble también en el sentido ético ni que la de los plebeyos sea plebeya en el sentido de abyección y bajeza.
— Es usted un romántico, Guezurtegui — ha dicho Luna.
— No. Es que, si esto fuera así, el almanaque de Gotha sería el índice de las calidades espirituales del mundo. No me parece que se puede afirmar que la división de criados y señores, de nobles y plebeyos, sea la norma para la literatura, y, sobre todo, para la moral. ¿Usted cree que sí?[27]

(D) La maldad, la ruindad, la envidia, todo lo disculpaba. Para Wilkins, el mal no era más que la cantidad de sombra necesaria para que brille el bien.[30]

(E) En un sentido restringido, lo humano no es sólo lo sublime; pero tampoco es sólo lo innoble. Es la mezcla compensada de lo bueno y de lo malo que puede salir de nuestras cabezas.[31]

that give him entrance into Baroja's novelistic family and even make him an important member thereof. The first and most important of these qualifications is that he is English. He is called *el Inglés* by antonomasia. Englishmen hold a high place in Baroja's family of characters because they belong to a different world, the Anglo-Saxon world as opposed to the Latin world, and are products of a culture that stands apart from the vital illusions of Spain. It is hard to find a novel written by Baroja in which an Englishman does not appear. These Englishmen are almost always eccentric, love Spain because of its idiosyncrasies and paradoxes, and have a philosophy all their own. They come to Spain seeking solitude.

Samuel Bothwell Crawford could well serve as the prototype of all the Englishmen who appear in Baroja's novels. He is slightly mad, and this quality helps him to fit into Baroja's novelistic family.

"Besides, they all must be mad," Marina added.
"No, not all of them . . . , unfortunately," Bothwell answered. "Only some. Here you are, sir," he added, "in one of the most cultured cities of Spain."[32] (A)

He thinks Labraz one of the most artistic towns and praises it because it has nothing of the false and artificial qualities of science and progress.

"Oh! Yes? Labraz is one of the most artistic towns. Here they don't permit factories, nor smokestacks, nor modern constructions."
"What are you saying?"
"Nothing of this false and stupid progress; nothing artificial."[33] (B)

It is easy to see that Bothwell has exchanged the vital illusion of England with its belief in progress and science for the vital illusion of Labraz with its medieval Catholicism. At first it seems strange that Bothwell should like the town of Labraz, but one soon discovers that he is completely liberated, that he is aware of all the illusion of Labraz. In fact, this seems to be the very thing which attracts him to the town. The fact that Labraz has long since stopped searching for the truth and is living in the dreams and superstitions of the Middle Ages is most appealing to the Englishman. Truth, he feels, leads to unhappiness and destruction, while a continual dream is a pleasant thing. He does not know how to paint, but he imagines that he paints well, and this illusion brings life. He finds no better place for this continual dream than Labraz.[34]

El inglés has other qualifications which allow him to become a member of Baroja's family. He is a lover of solitude, of contemplation, and as such, is an exception to the general run of humanity. He stands apart from the world, and this admits him into Baroja's created world.

"This is not worth anything," Toscanelli said; "the construction is poor and the lot is small. Here you couldn't make a medium size garden."

"Why?"

"Because there is no room. From another point of view, the wind will hit this in a terrible manner; the place, besides, is gloomy and solitary."

"Well, me, I like the place," the Englishman said; "the solitude enchants me, looking at the sea, not having indiscreet neighbors."

"Yes, this I like for a while."

"Me, I always like it."

"Nevertheless, solitude is boring, in the long run."

"For me, it isn't."

"It is possible that you are an exception."[35] (C)

Many other types, because of their very nature, fit into the *familia barojiana*. Men with just a touch of insanity certainly have their place. By definition, they have lost contact with the world and its vital illusion and are therefore admitted. They display varying degrees of madness; some are mere fools, while others tend to be mystics and prophets. Bertrand was of the latter type.

I had been in Paris for two months; I was ready to go back to Spain, when a French adventurer got me the job of copying some documents for a Central American politician. Since there was a lot of work, I divided it with Más y Gómez; but Más didn't like to work. He had become friends with a half-mad Frenchman who believed that it wasn't even necessary to eat and that you had diseases because you wanted to and that they could be cured with a prayer.

This man, Bertrand the Prophet, didn't have a home and slept in churches, on benches, anyplace, sometimes standing up. Más, with his insubstantiality,

---

(A) — Además, todos deben estar locos — añadió Marina.

— No, todos, no . . ., desgraciadamente — contestó Bothwell —. Sólo algunos. Aquí está usted, señor — agregó —, en uno de los pueblos más cultos de España.[32]

(B) — ¡Aoh! [*sic*] Sí. Labraz es uno de los pueblos más artísticos. Aquí no se permiten fábricas, ni chimeneas, ni construcciones modernas.

— ¿Qué me dice usted?

— Nada de ese falso y estúpido progreso; nada artificial.[33]

(C) — Esto no vale nada — dijo Toscanelli —; la construcción es pobre y el terreno pequeño. Aquí no se podría hacer un jardín mediano.

— ¿Por qué?

— Porque no hay espacio. Por otra parte, el viento atacará esto de una manera terrible; el sitio, además, es sombrío y solitario.

— Pues a mí el sitio me gusta — dijo el Inglés; me encanta la soledad, el mirar el mar, el no tener vecinos indiscretos.

— Sí, eso me gusta un momento.

— A mí, me gusta siempre.

— Sin embargo, la soledad es aburrida, a la larga.

— Para mí, no.

— Es posible que usted sea una excepción.[35]

accepted the doctrines of the Prophet and after four of five days of copying told me that he was fed up with working and that he didn't want to continue. "O.K., O.K. It's all right."

A couple of years later I ran into Más in Madrid, already very sick, and I asked him what had become of his friend, and he told me a story that to him seemed very serious and which struck me as grotesque. One day in the church of the Sacred Heart of Jesus, they found the prophet Bertrand who was washing the hemorrhoides from which he suffered in the font of holy water. They looked upon the act as a profanation, and they took the Prophet to jail, and there he died.[36] (A)

The anarchists fit into the *familia barojiana* quite easily. They not only stand apart from society, they are also aggressive toward all its institutions. The destructive tendency of Yann, who appears briefly in *La casa de Aizgorri,* seems to be his most outstanding quality.

"Yann." (*Who seems dazzled from listening to the music.*) If you intend to set fire to the factories, you can count on me."[37] (B)

Environmental factors produce some of the characters who enter almost automatically into *la familia barojiana.* "Urbistondo was an extraordinary type, an old sea wolf, . . . Only the sea can produce types like him."[38] (C) Although the list of types forming part of Baroja's novelistic family is too extensive to catalogue fully, one other group should be mentioned. Youth, by its very nature, stands apart from society. Youth is autonomous and therefore freely accepted in Baroja's novelistic world. When Fernando Ossorio goes to stay a few days with his Uncle Vicente in *Camino de perfección,* he feels that he is an outsider. They think of him as an aristocrat and treat him with respectful coldness. Blanca, because of her youth, is exempt from such social preoccupations.

In this house they treat me with great consideration but with absolute indifference. The little esteem that his dead wife's relatives had for him still burns my uncle, and, rejected, he can't see me either. His wife thinks that I am an aristocrat; you can tell that she has heard her husband talk about my aunts as if they were princesses, and she imagines that, although everything seems bad to me, I don't say anything because I am a master at dissimulation.

I am afraid that I have come to upset the customs of the house. The most accessible one of all is Blanca, the little girl, who usually comes to my room and the two of us chat.[39] (D)

Baroja's minor characters are interesting and seem the product of an inventive genius because they have undergone the same process of revelation outside of the novel as his protagonists did within it. Life has stripped them of much of the exterior and revealed their true human essence. Baroja has been criticized for not developing more fully the novelistic potentiality of these individuals. He seems to limit himself to finding them, introducing them into novels, and then letting them disappear. Ortega y Gasset has commented at length on the possibility of inventing types and of achieving a greater profundity in their development. Most of his comments seem to have been prompted by discussions with his friend Baroja on the subject.

"These are the thoughts about the novel that an allusion from Baroja has incited me to formulate."[40] (E) Here are some of Ortega's comments on the subject.

(A) Llevaba dos meses en París; estaba dispuesto a volver a España, cuando un aventurero francés me proporcionó una copia de unos documentos para un político centroamericano. Como había mucho trabajo, lo repartí con Más y Gómez; pero a Más no le gustaba trabajar. Se había hecho amigo de un francés medio loco, místico, que opinaba que no había apenas necesidad de comer, y que las enfermedades se tenían porque se querían, y se curaban por la oración.

Este hombre, Bertrand *el Profeta,* no tenía casa, y dormía en las iglesias, en los bancos, en cualquier parte, a veces en pie. Más, con su insubstancialidad, aceptó las doctrinas del Profeta, y a los cuatro o cinco días de copia me dijo que estaba harto de trabajar y que no quería seguir.

— Bueno, bueno. Está bien.

Un par de años después encontré a Más en Madrid, ya muy enfermo, y le pregunté qué había sido de su amigo, y me contó una historia que a él le parecía muy seria y que a mí se me antojó muy grotesca. Un día, en la iglesia del Sagrado Corazón de Jesús, le encontraron al profeta Bertrand que se estaba lavando las hemorroides que padecía en el agua de una pila de agua bendita. Miraron el acto como una profanación, y llevaron al *Profeta* a la cárcel, y allí murió.[36]

(B) Yann. — (*Que parece alucinado oyendo la música.*) Si piensan ustedes pegar fuego a las fábricas, pueden contar conmigo.[37]

(C) Urbistondo era un tipo extraordinario, un viejo lobo de mar.... Sólo el mar puede producir tipos semejantes.[38]

(D) En esta casa me tratan con gran consideración, pero con un despego absoluto. A mi tío le escuece aún el poco aprecio que hicieron de él los parientes de su difunta esposa, y, de rechazo, no me puede ver a mí tampoco. Su mujer cree que soy un aristócrata; se conoce que le ha oído hablar a su marido de mis tías, como si fueran princesas, y se figura que, aunque todo me parece mal, no lo digo porque soy maestro en el disimulo.

Temo haber venido a perturbar las costumbres de la casa. La más asequible de todos es Blanca, la chica, que suele venir a mi cuarto y charlamos los dos.[39]

(E) Estos son los pensamientos sobre la novela que una alusión de Baroja me ha incitado a formular.[40]

The souls of the novel have no reason for being like the real ones. And this psychology of possible spirits which I have called imaginary is the only one that is important for this literary genre.[41] (A)

This possibility of constructing spiritual fauna is, perhaps, the major creative means that the future novel can manipulate. Interest peculiar to the external mechanism of the plot remains today, necessarily, reduced to a minimum. So much the better for centering the novel on a superior interest which can emanate from the internal mechanism of the characters. I see the best future for the novelesque genre not in the invention of actions but in the invention of interesting souls.[42] (B)

What constitutes the true talent of the artist, contrary to what might have seemed possible at first, is not the creation of the individual — something quite problematic — but the creation of more profound generic types.[43] (C)

Here is Baroja's answer.

Our friend, and in many fields teacher, supposes that it is easy to amplify, to invent details in order to give more body to a novel. I don't see any such ease. That is to say, it seems easy for the uninitiated, who can't very easily distinguish the stone from the mortar; but for one who has sharpened his sensibility on this point through the practice of the trade, it is very difficult.

A character we have seen or talked to isn't like an ideological concept, which one can amplify at will if he wishes. A concept has a philological, spiritual, and anecdotal history and a goodly number of derivations. You can write a whole library about coquetry, about the vanity of modesty or self love.

Neither is a character like a town, that a traveler can see from an "auto" in its vague silhouette, and an employee who may live in and know it with all its streets and little squares, with its stories, its gossip and its tales. No.

There are characters that don't have more than a silhouette and there is no way to fill it out. About some of them at times you can't write more than a few lines, and what is added always seems vain and superfluous.[44] (D)

The reverse side of the same question comes up in *Las figuras de cera* when Ochoa and Aviraneta are discussing the cause of the macabre sensations which the wax figures elicit. They decide that their size, which is precisely that of a human being, is one of the great contributing factors.[45]

Baroja makes fun of the ideal character by having Aviraneta invent an ideal business partner:

He didn't complain if they opened his letters, nor if they signed his name, nor if they blamed him for forgetting something or a mistake; he didn't ask for an accounting of money spent, nor did he get angry, nor did he gossip or scheme.

He was the ideal man and the ideal partner. All that he lacked was to exist; but, surely, if he had existed, he wouldn't have been so ideal.[46] (E)

There is another reason causing Baroja's characters to appear as if they were products of a highly imaginative, inventive, and artistically creative genius. Obviously the strange creatures we see wandering through Baroja's novels are not the same beings who exist in the extra-novelistic world. These are, as Baroja has already told us, mere springboards of reality. The strange vagabonds and mystics who flit through the pages are the poetic essence of what Baroja wanted to find. They are what his eyes have been seeking, what he expected and hoped for. The creation, then, has taken place in Baroja's own mind before he discovers these outcasts and vagabonds who serve only to authenticate his rather poetic image of them. Baroja does not look for complex characters; consequently he does not find them. Instead he finds a rather poetic simplicity that stands isolated in the world.

(A) Las almas de la novela no tienen para que ser como las reales, basta con que sean posibles. Y esta psicología de espíritus posibles que he llamado imaginaria es la única que importa a este género literario.[41]

(B) Esta posibilidad de construir fauna espiritual es, acaso, el resorte mayor que puede manejar la novela futura. Todo conduce a ello. El interés propio al mecanismo externo de la trama queda hoy, por fuerza, reducido al mínimo. Tanto mejor para centrar la novela en el interés superior que puede emanar de la mecánica interna de los personajes. No en la invención de acciones, sino en la invención de almas interesantes veo yo el mejor porvenir del género novelesco.[42]

(C) Contra lo que al principio pudo parecer, no es tanto la creación de lo individual — cosa muy problemática — como la creación de tipos genéricos más profundos lo que constituye el verdadero talento de novelista.[43]

(D) Nuestro amigo, y en muchas materias maestro, supone que es fácil amplificar, inventar detalles para dar más cuerpo a una novela. No veo yo tal facilidad. Es decir, es fácil eso ante el profano, que no distingue muy bien la piedra del cemento armado; pero para el que ha aguzado la sensibilidad sobre este punto con la práctica del oficio, es muy difícil.

Un personaje, visto o entrevisto, no es como un concepto ideológico, que se amplía si se quiere voluntariamente. Un concepto tiene una historia filológica, espiritual y anecdótica, y una porción de derivaciones. De la coquetería, de la vanidad del pudor o del amor propio, se puede escribir toda una biblioteca.

Tampoco un personaje es como un pueblo, que un viajero puede ver desde un «auto» en su vaga silueta, y un empleado que viva en él conocerlo con todas sus calles y plazuelas, con sus historias, sus chismes y sus cuentos. No.

Hay personajes que no tiene más que silueta y no hay manera de llenarla. De alguno a veces no se pueden escribir más que muy pocas líneas, y lo que se añade parece siempre vano y superfluo.[44]

(E) No se quejaba si se le abrían las cartas, ni si se firmaba con su firma, ni si se le echaba la culpa de un olvido o de una falta; no pedía cuentas del dinero gastado, ni se enfurruñaba, ni murmuraba, ni intrigaba.

Era el ideal del hombre y el ideal del socio. No le faltaba mas que existir; pero, seguramente, si hubiera existido, no hubiera sido tan ideal.[46]

Baroja's characters must fit into a greatly reduced and deflated novelistic orb. Much of the material that would amplify and enrich their lives has been removed or negated.

Given the profusion of the secondary characters and the reduced simplicity of their human essence, Baroja is confronted with the problem of revealing them with a minimum of words and devices. He is faced with the necessity of transplanting the character he sees or feels, neatly and precisely into his novelistic world. He has to reveal him with a minimum of words and a simple technique. Baroja is not interested in the standard classifications. He would like to disregard them completely, destroy them, and start anew.

The fauna of evolutionary "humorismo" will accept all the samples from biology — the characteristic ones and the common ones, from the tiger and the camel to the protozoan, without forgetting those absurd animals, like the ornithorhyncuss (duckbill) and the echidna, which are mammiferous and oviparous, and those rare creatures that lived, like the pterodactyls and the archaeopteryx, big ugly birds that had a beak and teeth, feathers and the tail of a lizard at the same time. "Humorismo" will throw all the old tags to the wind and look at its creatures anew.[47] (A)

Baroja has dedicated the first chapter of the prologue to *César o nada* to the defense of the individual versus the species. The first two paragraphs give the tenor of the whole discussion:

The individual is the only reality in Nature and in life.

The species, the genus, the race, basically, don't exist; they are abstractions, methods for designating, scientific artifices, useful synthesis, but not absolutely exact. We reason and compare with these artifices; they constitute a norm within our own selves, but they have no exterior reality.[48] (B)

Francisco Pina praises the economy of words used by Baroja in the presentation of his characters and the originality he employs in their presentation.

Baroja isn't like anybody, he doesn't remind us of anybody, in the way he presents his characters; he employs original formulas, most peculiar, completely his, and no one has bested him in that art of infusing an extraordinary vigor into his creatures, always using a minimum of words in the process.[49] (C)

In order to achieve this verbal economy and avoid the traditional appellations for his secondary characters, Baroja uses a series of character devices which seem to function efficaciously. The most important of these devices of characterization is the accessory. Baroja firmly believes that certain little accessories are of paramount importance in the rapid scrutiny and understanding of a character. This belief is expressed in *Las figuras de cera.*

"My dear uncle," Marcelo said: "this is more difficult than it seems at first sight, because there are types, of course, that can be identified just by the face; but for many others, for the majority, you know them by their accessories, by the way they comb their hair, by their uniforms or by their clothing.

It is so certain that men, in general, have such little character, that if from the most illustrious and best depicted you take away their historical accessories, the mustaches and the sideburns, their braids and their plumes, a pair of sentences and another pair of anecdotes, not even their own father would know them."[50] (D)

The first insight into the character of Silvestre Paradox is afforded by a rather detailed look at his luggage as he is moving into his attic. The bustard and the little snake quickly set Silvestre Paradox apart from the common herd.

The curiosity of the doorman, as one could suppose, wasn't satisfied. The man opened the little door of the cage and stuck his hand through the hole. At first he noticed something that slipped through his fingers; then he felt that it was biting him. He yelled and withdraw his arm rapidly, and as he took it out, he saw with consternation a snake which seemed to him monstrous, curled up in his hand.

(A) La fauna del humorismo evolucionista aceptará todos los ejemplares de la Biología, los característicos y los vulgares, desde el tigre y el camello hasta el protozoario, sin olvidar esos animales absurdos, como el ornitorrinco y los equidnas, que son mamíferos y ovíparos, y los bichos raros que vivieron, como los pterodáctilos y los arqueopterix, pajarracos que tenían al mismo tiempo pico y dientes, plumas y cola de lagarto. El humorismo tirará al viento las antiguas etiquetas y mirará de nuevo a sus bichos.[47]

(B) Lo individual es la única realidad en la Naturaleza y en la vida.
La especie, el género, la raza, en el fondo no existen; son abstracciones, modos de designar, artificios de la ciencia, síntesis útiles, pero no absolutamente exactas. Con estos artificios discurrimos y comparamos; estos artificios constituyen una norma dentro de nosotros mismos, pero no tiene realidad exterior.[48]

(C) Baroja no se parece a nadie, no recuerda a nadie, en la manera de presentar sus tipos; emplea fórmulas originales, peculiarísimas, completamente suyas, y nadie le ha ganado ciertamente en esto de infundir un vigor extraordinario a sus criaturas, empleando en todo caso para ello el mínimo de palabras.[49]

(D) — Querido tío — dijo Marcelo —: esto es más difícil de lo que parece a primera vista, porque hay tipos, claro está, a quienes se puede identificar sólo por la cara; pero a otros muchos, a la mayoría, se les conoce por los accesorios, por el peinado, por el uniforme o por la indumentaria.

Tan cierto es que los hombres, en general, tienen tan poco carácter, que si a los más ilustres y mejor dibujados se les quitan los accesorios históricos, los bigotes y las patillas, los galones y los penachos, un par de frases y otro par de anécdotas, no les conocería ni su padre.[50]

He was so scared he couldn't even yell; livid, with the energy of terror, he uncoiled the ugly animal from around his arm, and possessed by the greatest panic, he fled up the stairs without daring to look back.

Meanwhile the snake, one of those little snakes called Aesculapius, annoyed by the bad treatment so unjustly received, had asked the great bustard for protection and coiled on the floor next to it and raised its head hissing, its little bifid tongue outside its mouth.[51] (A)

The fact that a character wears a wig and a few other details about his personal accoutrements can add a great deal to the understanding and insight into his personality. Many times these seemingly exterior accessories become an integral part of the personality; they become a substitute for the character himself. This seems to be the case with the Frenchman, Bazin.

The physician of the French town, Monsieur Bazin, was brilliant. All his thoughts wouldn't fit inside of his skull, and he used to take walks with his hat in one hand and in the other a reed cane that had a beautiful white knob on the handle. He would brandish the cane in the air, make thrusts at trees, hit it against his pants, beat dogs, caress children, because the cane constituted an integral part of the interesting personality of Monsieur Bazin, physician of the French town.[52] (B)

Ollarra, the prototype of the vagabond, is better understood after the reader gets a glimpse of his dog, Chorua. Without the dog, one might tend to think of Ollarra as a rather animal-like brute. The dog reveals some of the human kindness within the man's breast as well as some of his playful, boyish innocence, because the dog senses these qualities more keenly and accurately — at least according to tradition — than humans do.

Ollarra partook of the fruits of his new position with delight. He swaggered, dedicated himself to making mortifying comments, cracked the whip in the air and the old hack went flying.

The same day that they left Vera, the first stop was in Yanci's inn. During lunch, Manón and Alvarito laughed, watching the dog, Chorua, who was pouncing upon his master, playing with him and licking his face. The boy and the dog lived in complete communion: a look from *Ollarra* or a whistle were enough for the dog to understand him.[53] (C)

Animals seem to play an important role in rapid characterization. It almost seems to add a more human touch when the animal is a cat or dog, and a touch of inhumanity when the animal is ugly or unacceptable. Cats are quite highly esteemed by Baroja; they usually point to a certain kind of domestic tranquility and unconcern for the trivialities of the world. The cat which Andre Mari continually holds in her lap is probably the most significant detail of her presentation.

"Andre Mari, a widow without children, skinny woman, sour, with a sharp and pale face, had a figure that seemed like you were always seeing her in profile. She was constantly knitting with a cat on her lap."[54] (D)

The evidence presented in this chapter points to the conclusion that Baroja did not use the same technique of revelation with his minor characters as he did with his protagonists. This technique was made impossible by the number of minor characters and by their having been taken from real life.

A comparison of these minor characters to Baroja's protagonists has shown that they have many traits in common. Both tend to be isolated from society and from its ideologies, to formulate their personal philosophy, and to fabricate their own vital illusion.

The comparison has also shown that Baroja has not tried to give these characters any great profundity or depth, that he prefers them

---

(A) La curiosidad del portero, como podrá suponerse, no estaba satisfecha. El hombre abrió la puertecilla de la jaula y metió la mano por el agujero. Notó al principio una cosa que se deslizaba entre sus dedos; luego sintió que le mordían. Dió un grito y retiró el brazo velozmente, y al sacarlo vió con espanto arrollada en la mano una culebra que le pareció monstruosa.

De miedo ni aun pudo gritar siquiera; lívido, con la energía del terror, desenroscó el animalucho de su brazo, y poseído del mayor pánico, con los pocos pelos de su cabeza en punta, huyó escaleras arriba sin atreverse a mirar hacia atrás.

Mientras tanto, la culebra, una culebrilla de esas pequeñas llamadas de Esculapio, incomodada con los malos tratos recibidos tan inmerecidamente, había pedido protección a la avutarda y junto a ella se enroscaba en el suelo y levantaba la cabeza bufando, con su lengüecilla bífida fuera de la boca.[51]

(B) El físico del pueblo francés, *monsieur* Bazin, era genial. Los pensamientos no le cabían en el cráneo, y solía pasear con el sombrero en una mano y en la otra un bastón de junco, que tenía una hermosa bola blanca en el puño. Con este bastón hacía molinetes en el aire, daba estocadas a los árboles, se sacudía los pantalones, pegaba a los perros, acariciaba a los niños, porque el bastón constituía una parte integrante de la interesante personalidad de *monsieur* Bazin, físico del pueblo francés.[52]

(C) *Ollarra* disfrutaba de su nueva posición con delicia. Se pavoneaba, se dedicaba a comentarios mortificantes, hacía restallar el látigo en el aire y el carricoche iba al vuelo.

El día mismo que salieron de Vera, la primera parada fué en la venta de Yanci. Durante el almuerzo, *Manón y* Alvarito se rieron viendo al perro, a *Chorua,* que se echaba sobre su amo, jugaba con él y le lamía la cara. El muchacho y el perro vivían identificados: una mirada de *Ollarra* o un silbido bastaban para que el perro le entendiera.[53]

(D) La Andre Mari, viuda sin hijos, mujer flaca, agria, con cara afilada y pálida, tenía una figura que parecía que se la veía sólo de perfil. Solía estar haciendo media constantemente con un gato en la falda.[54]

life-size, that he is interested in human essence even though it is seen in a person of insignificance.

This chapter indicated that Baroja's job as a novelist was not to imagine or invent minor characters but rather to search out in real life that particular person who would naturally form part of his own novelistic family. This person, once found, acts as the springboard of reality from which Baroja briefly sketches the character, emphasizing what he considers the most essential human qualities, as predetermined by his own sensibility.

Again, negation as the *modus operandi* of the novelist has been most efficient in building a world in which these isolated bits of humanity can be most sincerely and authentically presented. A world where literary or conversational rhetoric play no part, where the biological elements which sustain life do not abound, where all the commonplace vital illusions are negated, is especially appropriate for capturing during the moment of their novelistic appearance the essence of their humanity. This negative world makes their little accessories and their affection for animals highly significant.

In regard to the minor characters themselves, negation, the work of displacing and stripping them, is done in real life. Baroja merely exploits the product of this negation by including the vagabond, the hangman, the adventurer, and the errant Englishman in his novelistic family and introducing them into his negative novelistic world.

Baroja's minor characters, so different one from another, are united by their consistent negation of almost all systematic value systems, philosophical truths, and social mores. For them, life's highest value may well be a plot of ground in the cemetery for the cultivation of cabbage.[55] Their only philosophical truth may well be a self-deception, the illusion that they can paint when they cannot. Their social relations may be reduced to the company of their favorite dog. These little creatures, shunned and pushed aside by a hard and sometimes hostile world, stand as living negations of man's greatness.

7. Landscape

BAROJA'S DESCRIPTIVE PASSAGES give us a sensation of something dynamic, something living and vital, something that moves. These sensations are especially evident in the following passage. It is taken from *La ciudad de la niebla*.

I *was contemplating* the awakening of the day from the gunwale. My father *dozed* after many hours of seasickness.

The ship *was leaving* a great white wake in the sea, the engine *hummed* in the depths of the steamer, and clouds of sparks *came* from the stacks.

It *was* at dawn; the haze lifted from the waters *formed* a gray cover a few yards high. At times on the coast, long lines of electric lights *were shining*, reflected in the colored sea. The sea gulls and the petrels *launched* their strident cries in the midst of the fog, *played* above the foamy waves and *ascended* in flight until *losing* themselves from sight.

After an hour of breathing the fresh air, I went down to the cabin to see how my father *was getting* along.

"Come on, cheer up," I said to him, *seeing* that he was awake. "We *are* already near the mouth of the Thames."

.   .   .   .

It *was already getting* light when *we began* to go up the Thames; the river, a lead color, *was opening* up and *showing* its broad surface under an opaque and gray sky. On the distant banks, enveloped in the haze, you still *couldn't distinguish* either trees or houses. Every moment large black ships *went passing* one after another, *sounding* their hoarse sirens.

As we *advanced* the rows of ships were fuller, the banks *were narrowing*, you *could begin to see* houses, buildings, parks with huge trees; you *could glimpse* little gray towns, rectangular pastures divided by light fences and with billboards indicating the sporting places. A sinuous, violet-colored road, in the midst of the green of the country estates, *ran* until it became lost in the distance.

We passed some river towns. The curves in the river *produced* a strange illusion, that of *seeing* a row of ships that *were advancing, belching* smoke, through the houses and the trees.

The river *was narrowing,* the day *clearing,* the precise outlines of the two banks *could* now *be seen,* and ships *kept passing* by in a continuous stream.[1] (A)

The dynamic, cinematic sensations in the passage are quite vivid. Francisco Pina, along with many others, has pointed out this quality in Baroja's descriptive passages.

Besides, his retina is powerful, capable of capturing, indelibly, like in a vertiginous film, the most varied perspectives. That is why we say that his lyricism is dynamic, that is to say, that it develops cinematographically, as his retina receives the external suggestions from nature.[2] (B)

An examination of the passage should reveal various procedures and devices that produce these sensations. These sensations stand out in sharp relief when the passage is compared to one from Azorín. Some of the observations to be made about Baroja's descriptive passages are the result of just such a comparison. The description from *La ciudad de la niebla* was compared with a short impression from *Castilla* called *El mar.* Reading *El mar* produces a static sensation. Azorín attempts to arrest the march of time, to blend past, present, and future into an artistic time, which is both fleeting and eternal. *El mar* shows clearly some of the ways in which he achieves this sensation. Repetition, the use of the present tense, of verbs which indicate only being or location, or the total absence of verbs, the lengthy series without conjunctions which weigh down and deactivate the verbs, are important factors.

It is easy to see that the impression is related to another work of literature and makes use of other works of art as well as history. Moreover, the fact that the viewer of the scene is fixed and immobile seems important. Marguerite Rand, in a recent and comprehensive study called *Castilla en Azorín,* studies this description at length. She mentions most of these points, placing special emphasis on the fact that the sea is evoked, not seen directly, and the emotional response its description elicits.[3] The following short selection will suggest many of them.

A poet who lived by the Mediterranean has grieved over Castilla because he can't see the sea. Centuries ago, another poet — the author of *The Poem of the Cid* — took his wife and the daughters of Rodrigo Díaz from the heart of Castilla to Valencia; there, from a tower, he made them contemplate, surely for the first time, the sea.

> Look at Valencia how the city lies,
> And the other way your eyes can reach the sea

The solitary and melancholy Castilla cannot see the sea. The sea is very far from these level, smooth, barren, dusty fields; from these rocky gullies; from these rugged reddish lands in which the torrential rains have opened deep marks, from these hard and abrupt breaks of the mountains, from these gentle hills and earthy mounds from which one can glimpse a little road that goes zigzagging up to a little brook. The gentle sea breezes don't reach these brown villages of crumbling shacks, that have their little wood of black poplars next to the commons. From the little window of this attic, in the highest part of the house, you cannot see the blue and flitting expanse; there

---

(A) *Estaba contemplando* desde la borda el despertar del día. Mi padre *dormitaba* después de muchas horas de mareo.

El barco *iba dejando* una gran estela blanca en el mar, la máquina *zumbaba* en las entrañas del vapor, y *salían* de las chimeneas nubes de chispas.

Era el amanecer; la bruma despegada de las aguas *formaba* una cubierta gris a pocos metros de altura. *Brillaban* a veces en la costa largas filas de focos eléctricos reflejados en el mar de color de acero. Las gaviotas y los petreles *lanzaban* su grito estridente entre las niebla, *jugueteaban* sobre las olas espumosas y *levantaban* el vuelo *hasta perderse* de vista.

Tras de una hora de respirar el aire libre, *bajé* a la cámara a ver cómo seguía mi padre.

— Vamos, anímate — le dije, *viéndole* despierto —. Ya *estamos* cerca de la desembocadura del Támesis.

.   .   .   .   .

Clareaba ya cuando *comenzamos* a remontar el Támesis; el río, de color de plomo, *se iba abriendo y mostrando* su ancha superficie bajo un cielo opaco y gris. En las orillas lejanas, envueltas en bruma, no *se distinguían* aún ni árboles ni casas. A cada momento *pasaban haciendo sonar* sus roncas sirenas grandes barcos negros, uno tras otro.

A medida que *avanzábamos,* las filas de barcos eran más nutridas, las orillas *iban estrechándose,* se *comenzaba* a ver casas, edificios, parques con grandes árboles; *se divisaban* pueblecillos grises, praderas rectangulares divididas con ligeras vallas y con carteles indicando los sitios de *sport*. Un camino sinuoso, violáceo, en medio del verde de las heredades, *corría* hasta perderse en lo lejano.

Pasamos por delante de algunos pueblos ribereños. Las vueltas del río *producían* una extraña ilusión, la *de ver* una fila de barcos que *avanzaban echando* humo por entre las casas y los árboles.

El río *se estrechaba* más, el día *clareaba, se veían* ya con precisión las dos orillas, y *seguían* pasando barcos continuamente.[1]

(B) Además, su retina es poderosa, capaz de aprehender, indeleblemente, como en una vertiginosa película, las más variadas perspectivas. Por eso decimos que su lirismo es dinámico, es decir, que se va desenrollando cinemáticamente, a medida que su retina recibe las sugestiones externas de la naturaleza.[2]

on the hill you can make out a hermitage with its rigid black cypresses on both sides, standing out against the limpid sky.[4] (A)

As all of the verbs in the short paragraphs taken from Baroja have been italicized, it should be easy to see that every one of them contributes to the dynamic sensation the passage produces. Only two of the verbs — *eran,*[5] and *estamos* — merely indicate existence or location. Baroja has made copious use of the progressive tense in this passage. Such verbs as *estaba contemplando, iba dejando, hasta perderse, de respirar, viéndole, se iba abriendo, pasaban haciendo sonar, iban estrechándose, de ver, avanzaban echando, seguían pasando,* add a great deal to the graphic intensity of the description and contribute more than a little to its dynamic quality.

As can be seen by glancing at the italicized verbs, the imperfect tense is predominant throughout. The predominance of the imperfect and its reiteration give just the opposite impression from that given by the present tense in Azorín. The imperfect tense in Baroja indicates a momentary perception, something that was and is no more. The use of the two tenses, the past progressive and the imperfect, both in combination and separately, gives the impression of something that was passing and becoming history, of something that was appearing and disappearing before our eyes even while being perceived. The selection of the verbs themselves increases this sensation. Words such as *levantaban, comenzaban, se iba abriendo,* give the impression of something appearing at a given moment in the past, and words like *pasaban, hasta perderse, corría hasta perderse, seguían pasando* give the impression of something disappearing almost as rapidly. Another factor which contributes to this same impression is the use of the preterite. The three or four times that it occurs in the quoted passage help to fix the passage in the past and give it a vital temporality. "Come on, look alive, I told him; the day was already clearing when we began to go up the Thames; we went by some small towns along the banks."

A comparison of the verbal content of the passages to the other component parts provides another interesting insight into the descriptive passages.

The verbs in Baroja's passages do not carry the weight of inordinate enumerations. There are, in fact, no enumerations in this particular passage. The only series consists of groups of clauses completely activated by their corresponding verbs. The following example is only one of many found therein. "The sea gulls and the petrels launched their strident cries in the midst of the fog, played upon the foamy waves, and ascended in flight until losing themselves from sight."[5] (B)

Verbal usage and the relationships of the verbs to the other parts of speech in the description have a great deal to do with the production of the two sensations. However, the verbs are probably not the most important item in the creation of these two distinct sensations. Baroja's descriptive passage gives the impression that the landscape was experienced or perceived by only one person and that this perception occurred at only one moment of time. It gives the sensation, in fact, of something unique.

His description seems to have no ties to anchor it in time and space; therefore it must move through both of these elements. It must appear and disappear, and this appearance and disappearance are a considerable factor in the dynamic sensation the description elicits. The perception of this scene is momentary, and this passing quality is one of its activating forces, one of the forces lending it great rapidity of movement, making it dynamic rather than static.

Furthermore, Baroja's descriptive passage is independent; it is free at least from any obvious dependence on any other artistic creations. Thus his description seems to be autonomous. This autonomy, if it persists throughout his works, could be important in the investigation of the author's descriptive procedure and purpose.[6]

Baroja's description is void of perceptive fixation.[7] The eyes move from the water to the mist, which is separated from it by a few yards, from the long lines of electric lights reflected in the water to the sea gulls, from the foamy waves to the flight of the gulls as they drift out of sight. Throughout the passage Baroja never focuses on one single object, his gaze constantly shifting in order to take in new objects, most of these

---

(A) Un poeta que vivía junto al Mediterráneo ha plañido a Castilla porque *no puede ver el mar*. Hace siglos, otro poeta — el autor del *Poema del Cid* — llevaba a la mujer y a las hijas de Rodrigo Díaz desde el corazón de Castilla a Valencia; allí, desde una torre, las hacía contemplar — seguramente por primera vez — el mar.

Miran Valencia como iaze la cibdad,
E del otra parte a oio han el mar.

No puede ver el mar la solitaria y melancólica Castilla. Está muy lejos el mar de estas campiñas llanas, rasas, yermas, polvorientadas; de estos barrancales pedregosos; de estos terrazgos rojizos, en que los aluviones torrenciales han abierto hondas mellas; de estas quiebras aceradas y abruptas de las montañas; de estos mansos alcores y terreros, desde donde se divisa un caminito que va en zigzag hasta un riachuelo. Las auras marinas no llegan hasta estos poblados pardos, de casuchas deleznables, que tienen un bosquecillo de chopos junto al ejido. Desde la ventanita de este sobrado, en lo alto de la casa, no se ve la extensión azul y vagorosa: se columbra allá en una colina una ermita con los cipreses rígidos, negros a los lados, que destacan sobre el cielo límpido.[4]

(B) Las gaviotas y los petreles lanzaban su grito estridente entre la niebla, jugueteaban sobre las olas espumosas y levantaban el vuelo hasta perderse de vista.[5]

objects themselves in motion. The objects described in this passage are given no symbolic value. They may and do carry certain emotional potentialities, but the determination of these is left to the sensitivity of the reader. Again Baroja's description retains its artistic autonomy.[8]

The most obvious device used by Baroja to make this passage dynamic is the moving perceiver. The camera, the perceiver in this case, is on a boat entering the Thames; thus everything perceived, even the most stationary objects, will appear to move. The perceiver suffers from a common illusion in this case; he attributes motion to stationary objects. Without effort, the reader partakes of this illusion and the resulting dynamic sensation. But, in order to reassure himself of the reader's awareness and perhaps to intensify the illusion, Baroja points out a similar effect: "The curves of the river produced a strange illusion, that of seeing a row of ships which advanced, belching smoke, through the trees."[9] (A) Where do the critics, and Baroja himself, stand in regard to these two salient features of his descriptive writing; dynamism and a tendency toward esthetic autonomy?

Baroja accepts the dynamic as an essential part of his ideal of style. He feels that he must strive toward rapidity in order to keep the attention of his readers. He also feels that to do something slowly when it can be done rapidly is antivital and antibiological. In nearly all his discussions of style, the word rapidity appears. Speaking of literary tastes in his significant essay, *La intuición y el estilo,* rapidity is one of the four qualities he likes in other writers. "I always like the author who expresses himself with the most clarity, the most precision, the most rapidity and at the same time, with the most nuances." The word appears again in the same essay. "For me the stylistic ideal is neither pure Spanish, nor decoration, nor eloquence; it is, on the other hand, clarity, precision, and rapidity."[10] (B)

Juan B. González, in an article published in *Nosotros,* mentions the rapidity with which Baroja's descriptive passages move. He, as well as many other critics, compares Baroja's descriptive technique to a cinematographic process. Francisco Pina made a similar comparison — "as in a vertiginous film."

A cinematographic rhythm dominates the development of this book. And it is that succession, that mobility, that urgent actuation of the dynamic elements that give vigor and color to his sentence. Thus, that lean sentence becomes incisive, rapid, nervous. It jumps over objects with lively mobility. It adapts itself to the exchange of dialogue, or sketches a landscape in four strokes.[11] (C)

Ramón Sender thinks this frenetic movement a detriment or imperfection of style.

Prolixity in Baroja, when it exists, is not in the accumulation of trivial details but rather in the nonessential frenetic movements, that is to say, with an unmotivated *frenesí*. In Baroja there is no fear of formal prolixity. On the contrary, we would like him more prolix in detail because in Baroja's works, words are always animated and lively.[12] (D)

So many critics have insisted upon this one quality of Baroja's prose that its rapidity in his descriptions can be taken as a matter of fact.

In the passage cited, the rapidity seemed to be produced by these four factors: the use of the verb and its relationship to the other parts of the sentence; the ephemeral quality of the landscape itself; the mobility of the perceiver; and the autonomy of the landscape. The latter factor, while aiding the dynamic sensation, becomes important in itself.

It is difficult to find critics who mention Baroja's use of the verb as such to produce the dynamic sensation in his prose descriptions. Nevertheless if this verbal usage exists throughout the four decades, and if the sensation produced is still the same, it should be safe to conclude that it forms an integral and necessary part of his descriptive passage and helps produce the dynamic sensation.

Baroja himself points to the fleeting quality of his work. "This ephemeral character of my work doesn't displease me. We the men of today are people enamored of the passing moment, of the fleeting, of the transitory,[13] and whether or not our work endures worries us very little,

---

(A) "Las vueltas del río producían una extraña ilusión, la de ver una fila de barcos que avanzaban echando humo por entre las casas y árboles."[9]

(B) Me gusta siempre el autor que se expresa con mayor claridad, con mayor precisión, con *más rapidez* y al mismo tiempo, con los mayores matices. Para mí no es el ideal del estilo, ni el casticismo, ni el adorno, ni la elocuencia; lo es, en cambio, la claridad, la precisión, y la rapidez.[10]

(C) Un ritmo cinematográfico preside el desenvolvimiento de sus libros. Y son esa sucesión, esa movilidad, ese urgente actuar los elementos dinámicos que dan vigor y colorido a la frase. Así, ésta de descarnada se torna incisiva, rápida, nerviosa. Salta sobre los objetos con viva movilidad. Se adopta a las alternativas del diálogo o en cuatro trazos diseña un paisaje.[11]

(D) La prolijidad de Baroja, cuando la hay, no está en la acumulación de detalles triviales sino de movimientos frenéticos sin esencialidad, es decir, con un frenesí no motivado. En Baroja no hay miedo de prolijidad formal, al contrario. Lo querríamos más prolijo en el detalle porque en Baroja la palabra es siempre animada y viva.[12]

so little, that it almost doesn't worry us at all."[14] (A) Dwight Bolinger, quoting Baroja's statement about directness, continues with the following:

This sort of impressionism makes him overlook *most of the details in a description* of nature . . . this is necessary, also, for the sake of the sentimental effect he often wishes to produce when painting a large canvas; on a smaller scale, in descriptions of characters and artifacts, he appears to be more detailed, but is relatively about the same; where objects have been particularized by human use he particularizes them in his descriptions, but *never is minute or prolix.*[15]

The ephemeral sensation is probably due, in part, to the intrinsic qualities of the thing described. Many of the objects in the entrance into the Thames river were mobile. Baroja seems to prefer this kind of object. Bolinger has pointed out that Baroja prefers such scenes as sunsets, fog, or distant mountain ranges, and that the reason for this preference is probably that sunsets give the illusion of mobility.[16]

However, this dynamic quality, this sensation of something appearing and disappearing before our eyes, seems to be due principally to the mobility of the perceiver. It was pointed out in the passage taken from *La ciudad de la niebla* that the person perceiving the landscape with all of this activity was herself moving. María Aracil was on a boat entering the Thames. Moreover, the perceptive impulse was restless and insatiable. The eyes shifted rapidly from one object to another; they never dwelled long on any one object. Baroja himself is not in favor of dwelling too long on any aspect or object. "Chip . . . You shouldn't look too long at landscapes. They lose twenty-five per cent."[17] (B) Laín Entralgo contrasts the two different types of perceivers found in *La voluntad* and in *Camino de perfección,* two works published in the same year, with a great similarity of theme and setting.

The difference between Fernando Ossorio and Antonio Azorín is only modal, adjectival. Antonio Azorín stands still, enchanted by the landscapes that he contemplates. Fernando Ossorio, on the other hand, journeys without rest, like a spiritual quicksilver, through landscapes and landscapes; he is an insatiable drinker, a threader of impressions and landscapes in search of an impossible serenity.[18] (C)

The third quality, autonomy of the descriptive passage as well as autonomy of the described objects — that is to say, their lack of mutual interdependence — finds an echo in many of the critics. Baroja sees clearly the possibility of a description's standing alone as an esthetic entity: "Description by itself, achieving a certain degree of perfection is something artistic which interests and attracts us. Some of the pages of Pierre Loti, of Azorín, are like that."[19] (D) Azorín considers this artistic independence of the description of a landscape as an innovation. He calls

Baroja's *Camino de perfección* a magnificent collection of landscapes. "What really is an innovation is landscape for landscape's sake, landscape in itself, as the only protagonist of the novel, the story or the poem. . . . Baroja's *Camino de perfección* is a collection, a magnificent collection, of landscapes."[20] (E) Bolinger seems to have trouble accepting the idea of the autonomy of the description. He thinks Baroja uses it for a parting gesture or as a means to end a chapter.[21] This usage is found throughout Baroja's works, but it doesn't seem to detract from the tendency toward autonomization of the descriptive passage.

With these comments from Baroja and from the critics, a descriptive passage from each of the decades of Baroja's work can be examined. First the examination should determine whether the same dynamic sensation is produced in all of them, and if it is produced with the same degree of intensity. Secondly it will also examine the tendency toward and the possibility of autonomization of the descriptive passage. It will examine the autonomy of the parts described and the tendency toward autonomy of the description as a whole, and also, how this autonomy, if it exists, adds to the dynamic sensation. The third phase of the scrutiny will show whether the same three factors contribute to the dynamic and autonomous sensation of the passages. This phase would also reveal any other factors involved in producing these sensations.

The description taken from the first decade of Baroja's works is from the prologue of *El mayorazgo de Labraz*. The words and phrases pertinent to the investigation are italicized:

(A) Este carácter efímero de mi obra no me disgusta. Somos los hombres del día gentes enamoradas del momento que pasa, de lo fugaz, de lo transitorio,[13] y la perdurabilidad o no de nuestra obra nos preocupa poco, tan poco, que casi no nos preocupa nada.[14]

(B) "Chip . . . No hay que mirar demasiado los paisajes. Pierden un veinticinco por ciento."[17]

(C) La diferencia entre Fernando Ossorio y Antonio Azorín es sólo modal, adjetiva. Antonio Azorín se detiene embebecido ante los paisajes que contempla. Fernando Ossorio, en cambio, peregrina sin reposo, como un azogado del espíritu, a través de paisajes y paisajes; es un bebedor hidrópico, un ensartador de impresiones y paisajes en busca del sosiego imposible.[18]

(D) La descripción sola, llegando a cierto grado de perfección es algo artístico que interesa y atrae. Así son algunas páginas de Pierre Loti, de Azorín.[19]

(E) Lo que sí es una innovación es el paisaje por el paisaje, el paisaje en sí, como único protagonista de la novela, el cuento o el poema. . . . *Camino de perfección* de Baroja es una colección, colección magnífica de paisajes.[20]

The city *appeared in the distance* with its houses grouped on the side of a hill, *standing* yellow against the sky, with a humble and sad look; some tall and blackish towers *rose erectly* from among the brown mass of twisted and discolored roofs.

I *went along, approaching* Labraz from a very steep road, full of stones, which *climbed* first and then *circled* the walled area of the town, the remains of the bulwarks that *were still standing,* the ancient and crumbling fortifications which, *climbing* and *descending, crossed* the hills, the crags and the ravines that *surrounded* the city.

From the escarpment of the moat the grass, that *ended* at the palisades, *sprang up,* like a shining dark green carpet.

I *crossed* a stone bridge which spanned a dry river. The barbican *ran* along its left bank and above the slope, *twisting* to the right, *supporting* a steep path that *ended* at the blackish gate, with its drawbridge, that *gave* access to the enclosed portion of the town.

Once across the bridge, you *found* the door, of one solid piece, the wood already worm-eaten. It *slid* up and down between two grooves and *had* iron nails and enormous bolts for reinforcements.

The doorway *ended* in a passage, narrow and full of embrasures, that *opened* up on a square paved with slabs, with some sickly looking weeds *growing* in the cracks. Halfway across the passage *there was* another wooden door.[22] (A)

The dynamic sensation from reading this passage is unmistakable. It gives the feeling that our eyes have traveled a goodly distance in a short time, that a number of things have appeared before our eyes only to disappear again, that Labraz has been sketched in broad outlines, and that many details have been by-passed.

The artistic and esthetic autonomy of the description are quite apparent in this passage. The author does not compare Labraz with any other city famous in art, history, or literature. Labraz, until this moment, does not seem to have any history. None of the objects mentioned — such as the wall, the barbican, the drawbridge — are related in any way to history. They seem to exist momentarily and autonomously. Thus, this failure to dwell on any particular ingredient or object of the description, this failure to relate any object or stretch of landscape to any work of art or history, adds a great deal to the dynamic sensation created by the passage. They are not connected to anything except the visual impression the author has received. This freedom allows the description to move swiftly and dynamically.[23]

It seems that about the same constellation of verbs exists in this passage as in the one quoted from *La ciudad de la niebla.* There is only one verb or phrase denoting pure existence, "Halfway across the passage there was another wooden door," and only one passive voice, "Once across the bridge the door was found." These six examples of the progressive tense add a great deal to the graphic sensation of movement: standing yellow against the sky, I went along, approaching Labraz from a very steep road, climbing and descending, twisting to the right, supporting a steep path. It seems quite logical to suppose that Baroja used the graphic progressive tense in order to activate the description, in order to give it a dynamic vitality.

Of the fourteen verbs of the imperfect tense in the passage, five: *subía, nacía, partía, daba,* and *nacían* indicate a beginning action; four: *terminaba, terminaba, se deslizaba,* and *concluía* indicate an act of conclusion or ending; and five: *rodeaba, se conservaba, circundaban, sosteniendo* and *torciendo* indicate a circling or continuing action. From this it is easy to see that Baroja has chosen his verbs well. He has been careful to choose verbs that indicate action, verbs that cause objects to appear and disappear, verbs that give a transitory and ephemeral sensation to his descriptions.

No lengthy enumerations occur in this passage to slow down the rapid sequence of the verbs. Never are more than two objects linked to one verb.

Contrary to the passage from *La ciudad de la niebla,* here the objects described do not possess movement — that is, intrinsically. The highway does not move by itself; only the verbs give it movement, the highway climbed first and then circled. The same can be said for the other objects in the passage: the ancient and crumbling fortifications that were climbing and descending the slopes of the hills, *partía la barbacana, que torciendo a la derecha,* etc. These objects do not move by themselves.[24] To attribute to them motion or movement is to use a poetic license or a figure of

---

(A) La ciudad *apareció a lo lejos,* con su caserío agrupado en la falda de una colina, *destacándose* en el cielo con color amarillento, con traza humilde y triste; algunas torres altas y negruzcas *se perfilaban* enhiestas entre la masa parda de sus tejados torcidos y roñosos.

Fuí *acercándome* a Labraz por una carretera empinadísima, llena de pedruscos, que *subía* primero y *rodeaba* después el recinto amurallado de la población, los restos de baluartes que aún *se conservaban* en pie, las antiguas fortificaciones derruídas que *iban subiendo y bajando* por los desniveles de las lomas, por los riscos y barrancos que *circundaban* la ciudad.

Desde la escarpa del foso *nacía* el césped, que *terminaba* en la empalizada, como alfombra de un verde oscuro y brillante.

Atravesé un puente de piedra tendido sobre un río seco. Por la margen izquierda de éste, y por encima de un talud, *partía* la barbacana, que *torciendo* a la derecha, *iba sosteniendo* un camino en cuesta que *terminaba* en un portal negruzco, con su puente levadizo, que *daba* acceso al recinto de la población.

Pasado el puente, *se hallaba* la puerta, de una sola pieza, de madera ya carcomida, que *se deslizaba* de arriba abajo entre dos ranuras y que *tenía* como refuerzo clavos de hierro y enormes cerrojos.

El portal *concluía* en un pasillo estrecho y lleno de aspilleras en las paredes, que *daba* entrada a una plaza empedrada con losas, entre cuyas junturas *nacían* hierbas de aspecto enfermizo. A la mitad del pasillo *había* otra puerta de tablas.[22]

speech or to indicate an illusion. The latter is the case here. The movement of the perceiver produces an illusion of motion in the thing perceived. Because the author is approaching Labraz, *fuí acercándome* (I was approaching), *atravesé* (I crossed), his movement gives the impression or the illusion that the highway, as revealed by his ever-changing perspective, is climbing and circling. The movement or the illusion of movement is produced by the moving lens which describes it. The eyes of the observer here are in constant movement. This by itself should be ample cause for the illusion of movement in the objects perceived.

In the movement of the optical lens in order to give the dynamic and living sensation so often found in Baroja's landscapes, there is considerable artistry — artistry being mostly a matter of timing. The author must find the proper speed, perhaps one not so slow as to produce a static sensation and one not so fast as to produce distortion, and he must maintain this speed. The consistent velocity with which Baroja moves the optical lens seems to be one of his secrets.[25]

Explanation for the success of the art of description in this passage should not omit the obvious. The person who saw the village and recorded the description was possessed of a keen poetical insight. He knew by intuition just how many details he might include without overburdening the description. His poetic intuition told him just how fast to move his lens of description in order not to distort; it told him just how many items a description of a certain length might include. He seemed to possess poetic timing and intuition similar to those of the popular poet who described Labraz in the four lines which serve as a topical heading for the description. This poet uses just four objects in his descriptive sketch, yet it seems poetically complete.

> On one side circles the river,
> And on another, the watch tower;
> On another, fourteen turrets;
> On another, the barbican.[26] (A)

The uniqueness of perspective adds to the autonomy of the description and to its poetic intensity. Others, who live in the universe, were not invited to look at Labraz. One person, the author, sought asylum for his somber mood there on a certain day.

One afternoon in August I went to visit Labraz, a town of ancient Cantabria. They had told me that it was a town in its death throes, a dying city, and my spirit, depressed at that time by the bitter sadness that the failure of romantic dreams leaves, wanted to refresh itself in the profound desolation of an almost dead town.[27] (B)

The passage from the second decade of Baroja's descriptions is taken from *La veleta de Gastizar*. Again, in order to facilitate the scrutiny, the verbs and phrases most meaningful to the investigation have been italicized.

The three riders *were* Spaniards. They drank a little after *leaving* Bayona by the highway that *runs* beside the Nive river and *were chatting* as they *rode*.
The weather *was* beautiful, the afternoon tranquil and peaceful; on both sides of the road the leaves in the trees *were turning* yellow, and the foliage in the oak groves on the sides of the mountain *was beginning to redden*.
In the direction of the coast there were big clouds in the sky.
As the riders passed by Villefranque a *thunderstorm caught* them; the clouds *began to invade* the sky *rapidly* and they *covered* it in a short time; *a few minutes later* big round drops of rain *fell* like coins on the highway.[28] (C)

The dynamic sensation is even more intense here than in the previous passages. It cannot be denied that much of the sensation of movement comes from the inherent characteristics of the atmospheric phenomenon described. The rapidity with which a squall of this nature comes upon one is known by the reader through experience. All Baroja had to do in this case was to mention some of the elements involved in order to recall the complete phenomenon to the reader. Some of the elements here mentioned are the large rain drops, *gruesas gotas redondas como monedas,* which always provide the overture to such squalls, the dark, heavy clouds, *había nubarrones,* and their rapid invasion of the sky, *las nubes comenzaron a invadir rápidamente el cielo.* A bare minimum of these elements of the squall is enough to recall the entirety of the scene to the

---

(A) De un cabo, la cerca el río,
y del otro, la atalaya;
del otro, catorce cubos;
del otro, la barbacana.[26]

(B) Una tarde de agosto, fuí a visitar Labraz, pueblo de la antigua Cantabria. Me habían dicho que era una ciudad agonizante, una ciudad moribunda, y mi espíritu, entonces deprimido por la amarga tristeza que deja el fracaso de los ensueños románticos, quería recrearse con la desolación profunda de un pueblo casi muerto.[27]

(C) Los tres jinetes *eran* españoles. Tomaron poco después *de salir* de Bayona por la carretera que *corre* al lado del río Nive y *fueron charlando*.
El tiempo *estaba* hermoso, la tarde tranquila y apacible; las hojas *iban amarilleando* en los árboles de ambos lados del camino y el follaje de los robledales en la falda de los montes *comenzaba a enrojecer*.
Había nubarrones en el cielo en la dirección de la costa.
Al pasar los jinetes por delante de Villefranque les sorprendió una *turbonada;* las nubes *comenzaron a invadir rápidamente* el cielo y lo encapotaron *en poco tiempo; unos minutos después* gruesas gotas redondas como monedas *cayeron* en la carretera.[28]

reader, and this economy of expression contributes, as always, to the total effect of rapidity.

However, the same verbal elements are still there to activate the description. The progressive tense still abounds and still adds to the dynamic sensation. It is interesting to note the use of the progressive tense with the turning gold of the leaves, *las hojas iban amarilleando.* The phrase merely indicates the season of the year and the fact that the leaves turn during that season, but the use of the progressive tense gives it a certain delicate instantaneousness, gives the landscape life and vitality.

The fact that the three men are on horseback and are moving through the countryside adds to the dynamic quality of the description.

The potentiality of artistic autonomy here is quite strong. It is not at all difficult to enjoy the perception of the atmospheric phenomenon and the landscape for their intrinsic worth. No symbols are attached to the things described, so the description can move freely.[29]

Other descriptions can and do elicit emotional and philosophical responses and comparisons. But these responses are almost completely devoid of direction; they are artistically pure and for the most part do not rise to the level of verbalization in the consciousness of the reader. Torrente Ballester finds this a great virtue in Baroja's descriptions.

One of the things in which Baroja has demonstrated his skill is in the creation of a novelistic climate, understanding the word climate like the movie people understand it. The descriptions, made in an impressionistic manner, that is to say, without reflection intercalated between the experience and the direct emotion and the transcription; without any other selection or deformation than those done unconsciously by the author.[30] (A)

In *El laberinto de las sirenas,* of the third decade, dynamic descriptions of nature abound.

On the following day, when I woke up, my first idea was to contemplate the sea. I jumped out of bed, pulled back the curtains and looked through the window panes.

Dawn had still not broken; it was that intermediate moment between the night that is ending and the aurora which begins its initiation.

The sky, blue, didn't have a single cloud; the sea sparkled with little gray waves, as if it were of mother-of-pearl. Some small dark boats were slipping along like ghosts and were drawing away across the pearl-covered surface and losing themselves in the light fog. You could see the silhouette of the standing crewmen.

The horizon was taking on a opal tone above the promontory of Sorrento.

Suddenly, the sun began to climb into the sky with the rapidity of a theatrical sun. Its luminous body kept appearing like a firey eye above the rocks of the promontory. These golden rays, that broke into clusters, recalled the flaming swords of the huge baroque church altars.[31] (B)

The scene, like the one from *La veleta de Gastizar,* is of transition. It carries within itself a certain amount of vitality and movement. The verbal constellation lends its impetus to this vitality. The progressive tense such as *iban alejando, desvaneciéndose, fué tomando, iba apareciendo;* the verbs that indicate beginning and ending, such as *acaba, comienza, comenzó a subir, partían;* and the indicators of the delicate march of time such as *rapidez, un momento después, momento intermedio,* all add their quota to this dynamic sensation. Although the perceiver here is contemplating the scene from a fixed position, his perception shifts quickly from one object to another, giving more movement to the things perceived.

The description stands as an artistic autonomy.[32] Its only connection with the main body of the novel, which begins later, is that it carries the same tone of pure esthetic appreciation prevalent in the rest of the novel. No symbolic values are attached to it or to any of its parts. It gives the impression that it has never been described before, that a unique relationship exists between the perceiver and that which he perceives. Baroja, in the prologue to this same work, seems to insist on the freshness, on the virginity of the thing perceived or described. He and his friend, Recalde, make fun of Mount Vesuvius because they feel that tourist posters, literature, legend, etc., have disfigured the mountain so that one cannot possibly perceive it as it is.

Recalde and I found several faults with Vesuvius: first it didn't have the shape of a perfect cone, as was its obligation as a classic volcano; then, it

---

(A) Una de las cosas en que Baroja ha demostrado su maestría es en la creación de un *clima* novelesco, entendiendo la palabra clima como entre los cineístas. Las descripciones, hechas al modo impresionista, es decir, sin reflexión intercalada entre la experiencia y la emoción directa y el traslado; sin otra selección o deformación que las realizadas inconscientemente por el espíritu del novelista.[30]

(B) Al día siguiente, al despertarme, mi primera idea *fué contemplar* el mar. *Salté* de la cama, *descorrí* la cortina y *miré* por los cristales.

Aún no *había amanecido;* era el momento intermedio entre la noche que *acaba* y la aurora, que *comienza* su iniciación.

El cielo, azul, no *tenía* ni una nube; el mar *brillaba* con pequeñas olas grises, como si fuera de nácar. Unas barcas negras *se deslizaban* como fantasmas y *se iban alejando* por esta superficie de color de perla y *desvaneciéndose* en la ligera bruma. *Se veía* la silueta de los tripulantes a pie.

El horizonte *fué tomando* un tono de ópalo por encima del promontorio de Sorrento.

De pronto, el sol *comenzó a subir* en el cielo con una rapidez de sol de teatro. Su cuerpo luminoso *iba apareciendo* como un ojo de fuego por encima de las rocas del promontorio. Estos rayos dorados, que *partían* en haces, *recordaban* las espadas flamígeras de los grandes altares barrocos de las iglesias.[31]

didn't smoke in a solemn and majestic manner, as we had always seen in the prints. Instead of going up in an erect and decorative column, it sprawled out over the sides, driven by the currents of air.

It was a common smoke, smoke from the stack of a factory or from the oven of a charcoal-maker.[33] (A)

Later Baroja goes on to say that he does not like any remembrances or souvenir descriptions of famous places or buildings.

The truth is that the same thing happens to me. When in a book of fiction — these and those about travel are the only ones that I have read lately — the Parthenon, the Coliseum, Mount Parnassus, or Pindus show up, I close the book at once because my experience has shown that those memories come wrapped in the most timeworn and trivial of literatures.[34] (B)

His friend, Recalde, adds, "Those memories and evocations are nothing more than used commonplaces, theatrical props that have been knocked around so much they no longer make any impression."[35] (C) The last example is taken from *La familia de Errotacho*. This novel belongs to the trilogy *La selva oscura* and was published in 1931.

One summer night, in the second year of World War II, a young man walked down the highway from France to the village of Alzate, in Vera of Bidasoa.

It was a fresh night. The road was lighted by the glow from the stars. The sky appeared to be framed between the two walls of the gorge. The trees showed themselves full of leaves; on the embankments one could glimpse the thick and heavy underbrush.

The boy was walking down in a hurry. He wore a black shirt, soldier's pants, high boots and carried a stick in his hand.

On his right rose the cliff of the nearby mountain, full of trees and of kermes oak. On his left, in the distance, alternately you could see, the vague glow of the stars, the whitish heap of mount Larrun and the silhouette of Pañaplata and of Mendaur.

Nearby, on the very edge of the highway itself, the gorge plunged downward, populated with huge trees with their massive trunks and robust branches.

The boy whistled softly, as he walked along with a light and rhythmic step. Upon arriving at a watering place, he stopped and took a drink from the pipe. A little later he left the road and took a short cut. This shortcut rushed down to the left like a white ribbon and descended and avoided several turns in the highway. By following it, one could cut off more than a kilometer's distance.

The highway meandered, tracing curves. Looking down on it, one could suppose that three or four roads were crossing.[36] (D)

The relationship of this passage to the others cited is quite obvious. It has the same verbs of beginning and ending; the same verbs of going up and coming down; the same winding road. It also has the movement of the perceiver down the winding road and the movement of his eyes from the sky back to the foliage and the winding road.

The tendency toward artistic autonomy is quite marked in this passage, as it was in the others. The landscape is symbolic of nothing, and nothing slows the consistent movement of the optical lens, nothing distorts the landscape picture. The lack of symbolic meanings attached to the description is no indication, however, that this description does not set

---

(A) Al Vesubio le encontramos, Recalde y yo, varias faltas: primeramente no tenía la forma de un cono perfecto, ni acababa en punta, como era su obligación de volcán clásico; luego, no echaba el humo de una manera solemne y majestuosa, como habíamos visto siempre en las estampas. En vez de subir en una columna recta y decorativa, se desparramaba por los lados, a impulsos de las corrientes de aire.

Era un humo vulgar, un humo de chimenea de fábrica o de horno de carbonero.[33]

(B) — La verdad es que a mí me pasa lo mismo. Cuando en un libro novelesco — éstos y los de viajes son los únicos que últimamente he leído — sale a relucir el Partenón, el Coliseo, el Parnaso o el Pindo, cierro el libro en seguida, porque tengo la experiencia de que todos esos recuerdos vienen envueltos en la más manoseada y trivial de las literaturas.[34]

(C) — Esos recuerdos y evocaciones — dijo Recalde — no son más que lugares comunes usados, bambalinas demasiado traídas y llevadas que ya no hacen efecto.[35]

(D) Una noche de verano, del segundo año de la guerra europea, un joven *bajaba* por la carretera de Francia al barrio de Alzate, de Vera de Bidasoa.

Era la noche fresca. El camino *se alumbraba* por la claridad de las estrellas. El cielo *aparecía* recortado entre las paredes del barranco. Los árboles *se mostraban* llenos de hojas; en los ribazos *se entreveían* los matorrales espesos y tupidos.

El muchacho *bajaba* de prisa. *Llevaba* blusa negra, pantalón de soldado, botas altas y palo en la mano.

A su derecha *se levantaba* el cantil del monte próximo, lleno de árboles y de carrascas. A mano izquierda, a lo lejos, *se veían* alternativamente, al vago resplandor de las estrellas, la mole blanquecina del monte Larrun y la silueta de Pañaplata y de Mendaur.

Cerca, al borde mismo de la carretera, *se hundía* el barranco, poblado de grandes árboles de troncos gruesos y ramas robustas.

El muchacho *silbaba* suavemente, mientras *marchaba* con paso ligero y cadencioso.

Al llegar a un abrevadero, *se detuvo* y *bebió* agua del caño. Poco después *se separó* del camino y *tomó* por un atajo. Este atajo se precipitaba por la izquierda como cinta blanca y *descendía* y *evitaba* varias vueltas de la carretera. *Siguiéndolo, se acortaba* más de un kilómetro de distancia.

La carretera *serpenteaba trazando* curvas. *Mirándola* hacia abajo, *podía* suponerse que *se entrecruzaban* tres o cuatro caminos.[36]

the mood of the story and that it does not give a few interesting indications about the man who perceives the landscape. In this description is a feeling of joy that only someone's home can give; also a feeling of youth and light-heartedness, and a feeling of liberty — liberty that springs from unadorned nature. Contrasting these feelings with those descriptions which preceded the entry into the Thames in *La ciudad de la niebla,* and the entry into Labraz, we can see that the latter descriptions elicited the slightly depressing feeling of the unknown and the unfriendly. Here the young man knows the path well because he takes a shortcut and because he stops for a drink of water. He whistles, a sign of assurance and familiarity with his surroundings, and his gait is light and rhythmic. The link, then, which joins this descriptive passage to the rest of the novel is one of tone and is not overtly indicated but merely sensed.

Landscape seems to be the one thing Baroja cannot deny. For Baroja, it seems to be that phase of life which has suffered the least falsification by man. It is physical, biological, vital. Instead of trying to destroy this landscape or severely reduce it, Baroja tries to convey it to the reader in all its dynamic vitality and life. Negation in the landscape begins at this point. After the landscape has been conveyed to us in all its purity, its movement, and its beauty, Baroja denies it any other qualities. As finely illustrated in *La leyenda de Jaun de Alzate,* Nature with a capital "N" can have no further transcendental meaning. Jaun de Alzate believed in the spirits closely associated with Nature, but as the novel develops, he comes to realize that this belief is just one more vital fiction he will have to reject, and that all that remains is Nature itself.[37]

A brief and incomplete list of many things that Baroja's landscape neither is nor represents should indicate the role negation has played in preserving the landscape's purity. Baroja's landscape is not and does not represent the following: an idyllic and artificial countryside where man can escape from the madness of the city, the natural home of the noble savage, a nature that is completely in tune with and sympathetic to the hero's emotions, a symbol of man's depravity, a howling wilderness, the force of barbarity that civilization must conquer.

Baroja's interpretation of the landscape is pure, simple, and essentially lyrical. This lyrical simplicity recalls the appreciation of the landscape in *Cantar de Mio Cid* which so impresses with its purity and simplicity.[38] Baroja, then, in his negation of the literary and transcendental aspects of the landscape has underlined and reaffirmed the poetical beauty and the vital spring of life that it holds for man, especially for the man who has been able to disassociate and liberate himself from life's non-vital circumstances.

Baroja's personal and poetical interpretation of the countryside definitely forms part of that essential quality he has been striving to communicate. All the negative qualities of Baroja's novels discussed to this point underline, reaffirm, and accentuate the vital reality of this landscape. They form a dark and unstable background from which it projects itself in sharp relief and solid reality. The unstable and dark frame tends to delimit and restrict the landscape; however, it neither defines, classifies, nor names it. Its substance, in the final analysis, remains poetic, and as such has reality within the breast of Pío Baroja, and of the reader who has attuned his poetic sensibilities to Baroja's. The number of poems dedicated to the pure contemplation of the countryside in *Canciones del suburbio* substantiate the essentially lyrical quality of this vital reality.[39]

8. *Yoísmo, Ego-Identification, and Poetic Moments*

THE THREE FACETS of Baroja's creativity point toward a negation of the importance of all other members of the human race except self, a negation of most traditional virtues, and a negation of the form and subject of traditional poetry.

No one can doubt the importance of *yoísmo*[1] in the works of Don Pío Baroja. Critics who have commented on his works have ranked this tendency to project himself into his novels as one of the most important facets of his artistic technique. Gregorio Marañón has summed up his novels with the phrase, "Baroja es así."[2] Salaverría finds his tendency to inject his own opinions into the novel excessive. He feels that many of the novels should have been essays.[3] H. Peseux-Richard, one of Baroja's admirers in France, sees Baroja as the representative of all the restless human souls who, completely disillusioned, wander through his novels.

We enjoy seeing in him — let this be said between us so no one will know — the representative of those troubled and passionate souls for whom the most seductive reality is no more than a grotesque caricature of the lowest reality, of those deceptive beings who are always disappointed and who spend their entire life regretting not having been able to do things they would have been sorry to have done.[4] (A)

Julio Laborde asks if these novels have any other purpose than that of revealing Baroja's soul.[5] Jorge Pillement echoes this thought.[6] One of the phases of Baroja's *yoísmo* most frequently commented on is the projection of his personal desire for action into his novelistic world. This desire to be a man of action, frustrated in his personal life, is carried out in his novels. Juan B. González is counted among the many who make this affirmation.

But the rough living types interest him more — like Elizabide el Vaga-bundo — and when Nordic or Pyrenean hazes make them dreamers or sensitive, in no instance does he achieve the sharp intellectualism of a Roberto Grelou or the Hamlet-like irresolution of an Andrés Cornelis. In this Baroja is consistent with himself, for he has proclaimed action superior to pure speculation. He has said of himself that he is a failure, dedicating himself, therefore, to literature. His failure is in being a man of action. In *César o nada* he has written: "Art is a good thing for those who don't have enough strength to live in reality."[7] (B)

He then goes on to say that all of Baroja's adventurers are just so many manifestations of the different elements, of the different moments of his own *yo*. He lists several of these phases.[8] Baroja substantiates this when he speaks of a list of *yoes* from which we all choose and the possibility of manifesting more than one. "Undoubtedly, all men have a list of I's from which to choose, and we choose one and we cultivate it as a musician can choose one instrument to play."[9] (C)

Baroja's interest in men of action and in adventure stems from his lifelong reading habits. From his early childhood and throughout his life he read adventure stories by such authors as Captain Maine Reyd, Frederick Marryat, Edward Laboulaye, Jules Verne, Edgar Allen Poe. Most of these adventure stories were merely adventure for adventure's sake. The predominance of this type of literature in the fiction section of Baroja's library in Itzea shows predilection in reading which, according to his nephew Don Julio Caro Baroja, continued throughout Baroja's life. It is quite natural, then, for this phase of Baroja's self to be projected into his novels.

If further evidence of the importance of *yoísmo* in Baroja's novels

---

(A) Nous nous plaisons à voir en lui — ceci soit dit entre nous pourque personne ne le sache — le représentant de ces âmes inquiètes et passionnées pour qui la réalité la plus séduisante n'est qu'une grotesque caricature du rêve le plus vulgaire, de ces êtres dêcevants qui sont toujours décus et qui regrettent toute leur vie de n'avoir pu faire ce qu'ils eussent été navrés d'avoir fait.[4]

(B) Pero más le interesan los tipos rudos, vivientes — tal, Elizabide el Vagabundo —, y cuando brumas nórdicas o pirenaicas los hacen soñadores o sensitivos no alcanza en ningún caso el intelectualismo agudo de un Roberto Grelou o la irresolución hamletiana de un Andrés Cornelis. En ello es consecuente consigo mismo, pues ha proclamado la acción superior a la especulación pura. Ha dicho de él que es un hombre fracasado, dedicándose por eso a la literatura. Su fracaso es como hombre de acción. En *César o nada* ha escrito: El arte es una cosa buena para los que no tienen fuerza para vivir en la realidad.[7]

(C) Indudablemente, tenemos todos los hombres una lista de yoes que elegir, y elegimos uno y lo cultivamos como un músico puede elegir un instrumento que tocar.[9]

were needed, Granjel's *Retrato de Pío Baroja* would serve very well. Here, more or less, is the thesis there developed.

The second part of the *Portrait* that I seek to sketch in this work is to lead us to know how Barojan literature offers to his readers not only the life of its creator, transfused into the existence of some characters, for the author also put into it his interior world and the circumstances in which he happened to live; in a word, all that Pío Baroja dreamed and thought in his meditative existence of a contemplative and daydreaming man.[10] (A)

Baroja, in fact, seems to write mostly for himself. In *Las figuras de cera* he justifies putting so many songs in novels by the simple fact that he is the author, and he likes them. "The author understands that putting so many insignificant songs is a little abusive. They say something to him, although for the majority of his readers, of course, they don't say anything. The author is an individualist, and puts them in."[11] (B) Baroja firmly believes that everything is egotism in art. "Is everything egotism in art? I think so. In art and in the better part of science, the base is egotism, individualism."[12] (C) All artists, Baroja exclaims, put something of themselves into their work. None escape this egotism.

Big and small we see nothing more in everything than that which interests us. Egotism! In the final analysis, all art, all philosophy, every drive, even those that seem to us more objective and serene, are egotisms, narcissisms. Botticelli or Velázquez, San Francisco de Asís or Atila, Protagoras or Wundt.[13] (D)

Refuting Ortega's statement that copying is criticism and not creation, Baroja affirms that the copyist must necessarily put something of himself into his copy.[14]

One of Baroja's principal justifications of this *yoísmo* is that today he thinks we seek the man behind the work and not the work itself.

Today what we look for, principally, is the man underneath his work, and the fact the artist with great spirit may not have much discernment, and say mediocre things alongside of admirable things, doesn't stand in our way."[15] (E) As a literary justification of his desire to occupy the center of his creations, he quotes Montaigne.[16]

Nearly every prologue written by Baroja is a means of calling the reader's attention to himself. The prologue is one method of placing himself in the center of the novelistic orb to be created. Unlike many authors who step aside after this personal introduction, Baroja maintains this spotlighted position and seems to remain omnipresent throughout the novel.

By now, the reader has become aware of another aspect of Baroja's *yoísmo*. When Baroja speaks of the novel in general, he is almost exclusively concerned with his own novels. When Baroja speaks of life with a tone and a certain phraseology which would usually refer to life in general, he is speaking about life which is primarily concerned with Don

Pío Baroja. In his speech of acceptance to the Royal Spanish Academy it is difficult to discern whether he is talking about life in general or his own life. He mixes the two concepts constantly. In a chapter in which he talks about his personal character traits, he begins to talk about individuals, about adolescence in general. It is obvious that what he says refers more to himself than to humanity.

In adolescence you are facing life with the anxiety of a spectator who is seeing a theatrical performance for the first time. "What will happen when the curtain is raised?" he asks himself. He is going to contemplate extraordinary things in the glow of the footlights.

After a little time has passed, he suspects that the few combinations he knows will be the only ones; that nothing new will happen. The idea is perfectly sad.[17] (F)

In *La caverna del humorismo* Baroja defines the humorist. The reader needs only to scan a few pages of this rather lengthy essay to perceive that Baroja himself is the *humorista,* and as such admits no paragon. Although

---

(A) La segunda parte del *Retrato* que busco dibujar en esta obra ha de llevarnos a conocer cómo la literatura barojiana ofrece a sus lectores no sólo la vida de su creador, transfundida en la existencia de unos personajes, pues también puso su autor en ella su mundo interior y la circunstancia en que le tocó vivir; en una palabra, cuanto soñó y pensó Pío Baroja en su meditabunda existencia de hombre contemplativo y fantaseador.[10]

(B) El autor comprende que es un poco abusivo el poner tantas canciones insignificantes. A él le dicen algo, aunque a la mayoría de sus lectores, claro es, no le dicen nada. El autor es un individualista y las pone.[11]

(C) ¿Es todo egotismo en el arte? Yo creo que sí. En el arte y en gran parte de la ciencia, la base es el egotismo, el individualismo.[12]

(D) Chicos y grandes no vemos en todo más que lo que nos interesa. ¡Egotismo! En último término, todo arte, toda filosofía, todo impulso, aun los que nos parecen más objetivos y serenos, son egotismos, narcisismos. Botticelli como Velázquez, San Francisco de Asís como Atila, Protágoras como Wundt.[13]

(E) Actualmente lo que buscamos es, principalmente, al hombre debajo de la obra, y el que el artista de gran espíritu no tenga un gran discernimiento y diga cosas mediocres al lado de cosas admirables no nos estorba.[15]

(F) En la adolescencia se está ante la vida con la ansiedad del espectador que asiste por primera vez a una función de teatro. ¿Qué pasará al levantarse el telón? — se pregunta —. Va a contemplar cosas extraordinarias a la luz de las candilejas.

Transcurrido el tiempo, se sospecha si las pocas combinaciones conocidas serán las únicas; si no pasará nada nuevo. La idea es perfectamente triste.[17]

Baroja includes a few of his favorite authors under this category, he is essentially concerned with auto-definition and delimitation throughout the essay. Noting a few of the requirements for a humorist, it becomes evident that Baroja fulfills these requirements quite adequately. The humorist laughs, but with a sad laughter.[18] The humorist should be old. Baroja also fulfills this requirement.[19] He must convert his motives for complaint into laughter.[20] And thus Baroja continues to define himself and his art while he pretends to define a humorist.

With the weight of the evidence already presented, Baroja's own defense of his *yoísmo,* and the comments of the critics — Granjel, Sender, Juan B. González, Gregorio Marañón — it would be hard to deny this general tendency in Baroja's novels. He does project his own personality into the novels, and this forceful projection must negate or at least delimit the personality of his characters. Yet, given the variety and the interest stimulated by the reading of these novels, it seems that this attitude or theory is limited. All of Baroja's characters bear the stamp of a novelistic entity created by Baroja, but all seem to be completely autonomous. In a novelistic lineup of all of Baroja's protagonists, there would be little possibility of confusing Silvestre Paradox with Fausto Bengoa, or Luis Murguía with José Larrañaga, in spite of the many traits they hold in common.

The unequivocable stamp of originality that each character bears should caution against lumping them into one mold and saying categorically that they are all Baroja.

Granjel many times seems to have this limited and partial concept of the characters found in Baroja. He divides them into three types and then shows how the three types are a rather complete manifestation of Baroja, of the flesh-and-blood Baroja he knew.[21]

Granjel has based this integration on his knowledge of extra-novelistic facts of history and politics. Excluding all extra-novelistic information, and viewing the protagonist as he has been carefully revealed throughout the pages of the novel and as he appears at the end of the novel, it can be safely assumed that neither César Moncada nor any of Baroja's protagonists believe in any ideals, whether they be political, philosophical, or religious. At best his characters may still have, as the novel ends, an appreciation for good food and wine, and for pretty, freshly scrubbed young ladies, a sort of sentimental attachment for an old friend or old treasured possessions such as books, a love for children, or a keen sensibility to the beauties of an autumn landscape, but they seem to be devoid of any enthusiasm for or belief in utopias or ideals.

Apart from this obsession, Granjel does point out that Baroja's *yoísmo* takes many forms, that Baroja projects many facets of his personality into his different protagonists. Bolinger also makes a point of the multiplicity of factors from Baroja's extra-novelistic self which are projected into his protagonists.[22]

Pina and the other critics seem to consider Baroja's soul as a somewhat fairly fixed quality. Baroja considers it to be quite the opposite.

Leibniz tried to demonstrate that the soul is a monad, that it is a unity that is always equal and identical to itself. This is contrary to what observation induces us to think. In the same person the soul is different when he is a child and when he is old; it is also different in a man when he is sick and when he is well, when he is an alcoholic and when he is a teetotaler.[23] (A)

Considering Baroja as a dynamic and ever-changing entity, the projection of himself into his novelistic characters becomes even more fractionary. These critics saw him as placing large sections and constellations of himself and his hopes and aspirations into the lives of his protagonists — which is certainly a reality — yet Baroja apparently does not limit the novelistic projection of his *yo* to these greater manifestations.

He seems to have placed a countless number of the lesser idiosyncrasies of his being and existence into the formation of the principal and minor characters of his novels. A complete tabulation and analysis of these lesser manifestations might be very revealing, not as to the tangible facts of his life, although these are also included, but as to his true spiritual, philosophical, ethical, sensitive, and esthetic self. Such a tabulation and analysis, besides being nearly impossible, is probably more appropriate for the field of psychology than for literature.

More important is the enrichment that such a multiplicity of traits affords Baroja as a character within his own novels. With each addition of a trait, idiosyncrasy, opinion, Baroja as an entity of fiction gains reality and novelistic life. Baroja, who is ever present in his own novels as an entity of fiction as well as the author of that fiction, enriches his own novelistic reality by attributing certain qualities to his fictional characters.

When we read of a strongly opinionated character in one of his novels — almost all of his characters are strongly opinionated — we do not necessarily think of this person as being Baroja himself. The opinionated character seems to maintain his autonomy while the presence of Baroja as a fictional entity is accentuated. Many characters in his novels are bibliophiles. All the enthusiasm shown for rare or interesting books merely underlines Baroja's presence in the novel.

Chipiteguy, in *Las figuras de cera*, obeys Baroja's stylistic creed in regard to his personal dress. "Chipiteguy didn't want to become elegant;

(A) Leibniz quiso demostrar que el alma es una mónada, o sea una unidad siempre igual e idéntica a sí misma. Es lo contrario de lo que nos induce a pensar la observación. En la misma persona el alma es distinta cuando es niño y cuando es viejo; también es distinta en el hombre cuando está enfermo y cuando está sano, cuando es alcohólico y cuando es abstemio.[23]

he liked to appear just like he had always been."²⁴ Baroja here does seem to replace Chipiteguy because they both seem to agree about so many things, but this mutual agreement seems to be complimentary to both of them. The statement makes the reader think of Baroja and feel his presence within the novel, but at the same time it adds its bit to the autonomy of Chipiteguy.

These examples show the almost unlimited field Baroja has for self-revelation, as a creature of fiction, within his novels. This unrestrained projection of ego seems to be strangely related to his inclusion of the weird multitudes who parade through his novels. The sympathy which Baroja extends to them seems to manifest a tremendous sensibility and concern for the sorrows, sufferings, and other human manifestations of those who, on the surface, stand quite apart from him. In spite of his all-consuming concern for self-revelation within the novel, he seems able to make of himself a sensitive tool for the understanding of others.

In a sense, this sensitive comprehension of the generally bypassed and forgotten multitudes who appear and disappear in his novels without scheme or pattern can be considered as a further, perhaps more subtle and poetic projection of his own ego. Baroja leads us to consider this possibility while discussing the real interests which a criminal holds for us, and thus for himself.

"I don't believe that there is a man or a woman that can live apart from evil passions, ignoring them," he ended up by saying. The most wicked thoughts, the most perverse intentions can assault anybody. That is why we are interested in crimes and the worst outrages, because we are capable of feeling them and even carrying them out.²⁵ (A)

In *Susana,* Fernando is motivated by the same reason to feel sorrow and commiseration at the sight of an old beggar.

The life of that man must have been terrible. Alone, old and abandoned in a big city.
I compared his poor existence with that of some beggars of the town where I had lived in the Mancha, and I thought that theirs was much better.
When I saw the old man leaning against the wall of the tavern, his overcoat buttoned up to his neck, his hat soft and shapeless, his look vague, smoking a short clay pipe, terror seized me.
"Perhaps I may end up the same way he is I would say to myself."²⁶ (B)

EGO-IDENTIFICATION

Baroja's extreme sensibility comes from an almost complete ego-identification with these characters who are cut adrift from the norms of life. This ego-identification tends to be momentary. One is reminded of Baroja's statement that one cannot add to a character, one cannot dwell upon the complexities of his life, if these complexities of life do not exist. This seems to be another way of saying that one's ego-identification with a certain character cannot be sustained. It seems to be a rather poetical flickering of humanity that for a moment reaches a full comprehension of the character through the realization that a very fine line of circumstance separates the observer and his mode of life from that of the observed.

This ego-identification cannot exceed the potential human understanding of the observer, and, in a sense, there is a moment when the observer completely negates his own importance and reduces himself to the level of the vagabond he is observing. The author, for a fleeting moment, places himself in the shoes of the ragman, the anarchist, the prostitute, the adventurer — all types, that, in a sense, real life has rejected. During this moment there seems to be a complete identification. This identification does not deny the ego of the author-observer, but it molds the ego to fit the exact size of the subject observed.

This molding usually involves a considerable reduction of the ego of the author. It usually signifies a negation of his own importance, a denial of many of his moral values, and a breaking of the ties which bind him to society.

These same negations are many times suffered by the reader, who somehow feels that his momentary identification with a certain character has reduced his own importance to almost nothing, that his most deeply ingrained moral values are shaken, and that he stands in social nudity and isolation. After all, the observed subject has already undergone a very rigid process of negation in real life.

This negation of the commonplace values of the author and the reader sharply underline the essence of the identification. In these instances

---

(A) — No creo que haya ni mujer ni hombre que pueda vivir al margen de las malas pasiones ignorándolas — concluí diciendo —. Los pensamientos más atravesados, las intenciones más aviesas, pueden asaltar a cualquiera. Por eso nos interesan los crímenes y los mayores atropellos, porque somos capaces de sentirlos y hasta de realizarlos.[25]

(B) Debía de ser terrible la vida de aquel hombre. Solo, viejo y abandonado en una gran ciudad.

Comparaba su pobre existencia con la de algunos mendigos del pueblo donde había vivido yo en la Mancha, y pensaba que era mucho mejor la de éstos.

Cuando veía al viejo recostado en la pared de la taberna, el gabán abrochado hasta el cuello, el sombrero blando y sin forma, la mirada vaga, fumando una pipa corta de barro, me entraba el terror.

«Quizá acabe yo lo mismo que él,» me decía.[26]

the author, reader, and vagabond seem to be joined by an ineffable human bond. The particle of humanity which has no label and is divorced from all the standard human values could best be called poetic — in the most pure and least formalized sense of the word poetry.

Baroja illustrates this ego-identification in a brief sketch called *Dulce egoísmo*. In this short sketch, which covers less than one page, two men come to a complete understanding with each other. They are both, for the moment, reduced to an essential and sweet egotism as they both think of their comfortable homes, fireplaces, food, and clothing, while others must face the inclement winter without these comforts.

"Well to think that there are people who are cold when I am between blankets; that there are people who don't eat when I am at the table. It's foolish, right?" the friendly gentleman added, smiling.

"No it's not foolish."

"Doesn't it really seem foolish to you?"

"So it is supposed to seem foolish to me! It seems quite all right, quite all right indeed."

And the friendly man and I said goodby to one another amiably, exchanging the most affectionate of smiles.[27] (A)

At this moment there is a complete identification of the two egos. Baroja's reader, if he merits the appellation, will for an unguarded moment, suffer this same ego-identification.

Baroja appears to be striving for just this type of momentary identification or fusion of human sympathies. In the severely reduced and darkened ambient of his novels he sees, momentarily sympathizes with, and with great sensibility reflects, the humanity of these characters. Thus when the critics speak of the acutely human qualities of Baroja's characters, part of this human feeling comes from Baroja's own reaction to them. Author and character, for a moment only, are humanely fused into one, within the novelistic orb. The characters themselves are not only limited by the fact that they have been chosen because they were already limited, and by the fact that they are more observed than invented, but they are also limited by Baroja's own wealth of human sympathy, by his store of sentimentalism which gradually exhausts itself.

The writer, especially the novelist, has a sentimental reserve that forms the sediment of his personality. This word sentimental can be used in a pejorative sense of affectation of sensibility, of excessive sentimentality; I am not using it in this sense.

In that sentimental reserve of the writer his good and bad instincts, his memories, his successes and his failures have remained and have fermented. The novelist lives from that reserve; there comes a time in which one notices that the stream, good or bad, starts diminishing, running out. Then he goes to look for something to tell, because he has become accustomed to the trade of a story teller; but this something is no longer within him, and he has to get it from the outside.[28] (B)

POETIC MOMENTS

Baroja's consistent attempts in his novelistic world to strike out and destroy that which does not appeal to his reserve of sentiment or to his human sensibilities are balanced by his poetical effusion before all which sincerely does affect him. Ramón Sender sees Baroja's poetic effusion in the presence of all that strikes his peculiar sensibilities as his greatest virtue.[29] Few critics have failed to find this lyrical vein in his novels.

Baroja has several names for this lyrical quality. At times he refers to it as his sentimentalism; other times he speaks of it as a tendency toward romanticism. On other occasions he refers to it as sensibility. It seems quite obvious that these terms point up Baroja's desire to capture what he considers the fragmentary poetic essence of his novelistic world.[30]

True to Baroja's general theory of literature, these poetic effusions scattered throughout his novels tend to follow no particular poetic form. They tend to be a denial of what Baroja has called *la condenada forma*. They neither treat nor show any tendency to treat the more common subjects of formal poetry. It never occurred to Baroja to write a sonnet in which he would compare the temporal beauty of love to a rose. At least, if it occurred to him, he has never published such a sonnet.[31]

More than the rejection of the traditional form and theme of poetry, rejection of most formal poets seem to have been the philosophy of Baroja. A few verses from Verlaine are about the only formal poetry to be found in the wealth of extraneous elements included in his novels.[32]

(A) — Pues pensar que hay gente que tiene frío cuando yo estoy entre mantas; que hay gente que no come cuando yo estoy en la mesa. Es una tontería, ¿verdad? — ha añadido el señor amable, sonriendo.

— No, no es una tontería.

— ¿De verás no le parece a usted una tontería?

— ¡Qué me ha de parecer una tontería! Me parece muy bien, pero que muy bien.

Y el señor amable y yo nos hemos despedido amablemente, cambiando la más afectuosa de las sonrisas.[27]

(B) El escritor, sobre todo el novelista, tiene un fondo sentimental que forma el sedimento de su personalidad. Esta palabra sentimental se puede emplear en un sentido peyorativo de afectación de sensibilidad, de sensiblería; yo no la empleo aquí en este sentido.

En ese fondo sentimental del escritor ha quedado y han fermentado sus buenos o sus malos instintos, sus recuerdos, sus éxitos, sus fracasos. De ese fondo el novelista vive; llega una época en que se nota cómo ese caudal, bueno o malo, se va mermando, agotando, y el escritor se hace fotográfico y turista. Entonces va a buscar algo que contar, porque se ha acostumbrado al oficio de contador; pero ese algo ya no está en él y lo tiene que coger de fuera.[28]

Baroja's lyrical interpretations have not been limited to the country-side. Some of the more eloquent ones have been interpolated into his novels in the forms of dithyrambs. Critics such as Bolinger have seen in these dithyrambs a possible influence of Nietzche, although it is difficult to find a statement by Baroja to corroborate this influence. The important thing is that in the midst of a reduced and deflated novelistic world Baroja became enthused over something, and this enthusiasm was manifested in spontaneous lyrical outbursts.

Interestingly enough the objects which elicit Baroja's lyrical response, like the characters fill his novels, are all quite liberated. They have been cast aside and forgotten by the progressive march of society. The old merry-go-round no longer exists at the time Baroja sings its virtues. The same can be said for the ceroplastic art and other objects. Most of them are described as old because they have been by-passed by time,[33] as is the case with the old figureheads.

Figureheads; Old figureheads of a prow!
When I contemplate you, figureheads on a prow, eroded by wind and water, I think of your daring adventures, in the abysses you have glimpsed in the depths of the sea, of the clouds of foam you have cut through, of the rocks and shoals you have evaded, of the dangerous reefs, of the tempests and the storms.
Figureheads! Old figureheads of a prow![34] (A)

Dithyrambs of this type are quite frequent in Baroja's complete works. Consider how each of the following sing the praises of the forgotten, of the isolated, of that which is of little value.

In praise of the ceroplastic art:

Ceroplastics! Ceroplastics! Your art not a triumphant art.
Your sons, it is true, have eyes and hands and feet, like the sons of men, and suits and hats and shoes, and no one stops them from wearing drawers and even leggings; but your sons don't reach the appreciation of the intelligent nor of the esthetes. They are not installed in palaces nor in museums, like the dolls of Greek art, in spite of these being pantless and shirtless; they are not admired, they are relegated to the shacks, outside the city, like those attacked by a plague, like miserable beggars.[35] (B)

In praise of the old accordions:

Oh modest accordions! Charming accordions! You don't tell big poetic lies, like the fatuous guitar; you don't invent pastoral legends, like the flute or the bagpipe; you don't fill men's heads with smoke, like the strident bugle or the warlike drums. You are of your own epoch: humble, sincere, sweetly plebeian, perhaps ridiculously plebeian; but you speak of life perhaps as life is in reality: a melody, vulgar, monotonous, coarse, before the unlimited horizon . . .[36] (C)

Some of these dithyrambs are bitterly ironic. Nevertheless, the poetic sentiment is still poignant. For instance, one praises the wisdom and good sense of the cuckolded husband; another, such as the following, is in praise of the good burgher.

"Long live luxury! Long live luxury! Enjoy it, enjoy it, good burghers: Bolshevism still isn't coming for awhile.

"Enjoy it, savor its fruits. May your daughters walk beautiful and elegant, and seem to descend from the knights of the Crusades; may your wives wear furs and jewels; may your sons shine in their automobiles and in the theatre.

"Long live luxury! Long live gaity! Enjoy it, enjoy it; good burghers; Bolshevism still isn't coming for awhile." [37] (D)

These are the types and things that elicit Baroja's poetic effusion — the vagabond, the aristocrats — whether they figure in the Gotha or not, the cuckolded husband, and the old violins. For Baroja all things have a particle of poetic potentiality.[38]

(A) ¡Mascarones! ¡Viejos mascarones de proa!

Cuando os contemplo, mascarones de proa, carcomidos por el viento y la humedad, pienso en vuestras aventuras atrevidas, en los abismos vislumbrados por vosotros en el fondo del mar, en las nubes de espuma atravesadas, en los escollos sorteados, en los arrecifes peligrosos, en las tempestades y en las tormentas . . .

¡Mascarones! ¡Viejos mascarones de proa![34]

(B) — ¡Ceroplastia! ¡Ceroplastia! No eres un arte triunfal.

Tus hijos, es cierto, tienen ojos y manos y pies, como los hijos de los hombres, y trajes y sombreros y zapatos, y nadie les impide llevar calzoncillos y hasta polainas; pero tus hijos no alcanzan el aprecio de los inteligentes ni el de los estetas. No se les instala en palacios ni en museos, como a los muñecos del arte griego, a pesar de hallarse éstos descalzonados y descamisados; no se les admira; se les relega a las barracas, fuera de la ciudad, como a los atacados por una peste, a los mendigos miserables.[35]

(C) ¡Oh modestos acordeones! ¡Simpáticos acordeones! Vosotros no contáis grandes mentiras poéticas, como la fastuosa guitarra; vosotros no inventáis leyendas pastoriles, como la zampoya o la gaita; vosotros no llenáis de humo la cabeza de los hombres, como las estridentes cornetas o los bélicos tambores. Vosotros sois de vuestra época: humildes, sinceros, dulcemente plebeyos, quizá ridículamente plebeyos; pero vosotros decís de la vida lo que quizá la vida es en realidad: una melodía, vulgar, monótona, ramplona, ante el horizonte ilimitado . . .[36]

(D) «¡Viva el lujo! ¡Viva la alegría! Gozad gozad, buenos burgueses; todavía no viene el bolcheviquismo.

«Gozad, disfrutad. Que vuestras hijas vayan bellas y elegantes, y parezcan descender de los caballeros de las Cruzadas; que vuestras mujeres lleven pieles y joyas; que vuestros hijos se luzcan en el automóvil y en el teatro.

«¡Viva el lujo! ¡Viva la alegría! Gozad, gozad, buenos burgueses; todavía no viene el bolcheviquismo.[37]

Sometimes Baroja calls these dithyrambs *arias*. This one sings the glories of limitation, of the good life of raising cabbages and beans, of simplicity:

"Long live Ezcabarte! Long live limitation! Yes. Long live limitation, friend Ezcabarte! Because, although there may be many in the world that make more noise than your hammer, they are not more efficient nor more difinitive because of it. Long live limitation! Because the radiance of the sparks from your forge can compete in brilliance with other radiances. Long live limitation that gives us a country, an environment, a mountain in the distance, and if it closes the road to theatrical aspirations, it doesn't stop us from thinking, nor wanting, nor dreaming . . ."

A reader. "But you are a fake, Señor Baroja! You are contradicting yourself!"

"Me. What are you talking about man? no. It is that I am singing the aria of Limitation." [39] (A)

The most significant of these dithyrambs for the thesis of negation is dedicated to his own failure.

When I go to the edge of the sea, the waves that churn at my feet murmur: "Baroja, you will never be anything." The owl that usually comes to my roof in Itzea every night, knows it and says: "Baroja, you will never be anything." And even the crows that cross the sky usually shout at me, from above: "Baroja, you will never be anything . . ." And I am convinced that I will never be anything. [40] (B)

From this song to himself, to his own nothingness, the restrictions Baroja places on the objects of his poetic moments become quite obvious. He might well be saying here that only he could become enthused, for a moment, over this Baroja who will never be anything, never be a member of any great cause, and never propose any great truth.

Some of the poetic passages found in Baroja might be called symphonies of sound. Some even quite conventional. The following is a good example.

From the window one can hear in the distance confused murmurs of a sweet country symphony, the tinkling of the bells of the flocks as they return to the village, the rippling of the river, that sings its eternal and monotonous complaint to the night, and the melancholy note that a frog modulates in his flute, a crystalline note that crosses the silent air and disappears like a falling star. In the sky, of a dark intense blue, Jupiter glows with its white light. [41] (C)

Others are a more purely poetic rendering of certain sounds that appeal to him.

In the garden the rain resounds as it falls on the leaves of the trees, and only from time to time, breaking the monotonous murmur of the falling rain, the creaking of the wheels of a cart arrives from the outside, the melancholy *aida* of the ox driver, the distant crowing of some rooster or the clear and happy song of the blacksmith's hammers upon the anvil. [42] (D)

Still other passages merely show a childlike poetic enthusiasm for certain sounds, movement, and colors which are not the traditional material of poetry. These two examples are from *La ciudad de la niebla* and are recorded by the keen and eager eyes and ears of a young girl.

Some laborers were working on a viaduct that connected a huge tower on the shore with a reservoir located further inland. The drop hammers resounded like bells and alternated their noise with the deafening sound of the tinner's hammers which came from a shop where they were riveting huge caldrons and big-bellied buoys.[43] (E)

(A) — ¡Viva Ezcabarte! ¡Viva la limitación! Sí. ¡Viva la limitación, amigo Ezcabarte! Porque aunque existan muchas cosas en el mundo que hagan más ruido que tu martillo, no por eso son más eficaces ni más definitivas. ¡Viva la limitación! Porque el resplandor de las chispas de tu fragua puede competir en brillo con otros resplandores. ¡Viva la limitación que nos da un país, un ambiente, una montaña en lo lejano, y que si nos cierra el camino de las aspiraciones teatrales, no nos impide pensar, ni querer, ni soñar . . .
— *Un lector.* — ¡Pero usted es un farsante, señor Baroja! ¡Usted se contradice!
— *Yo.* — Hombre, no. Es que estoy cantando el aria de la Limitación.[39]

(B) Cuando voy a la orilla del mar, las olas que se agitan a mis pies murmuran: «Baroja, tú no serás nunca nada.» La lechuza sabia, que por las noches suele venir al tejado de Itzea, me dice: «Baroja, tú no serás nunca nada.» Y hasta los cuervos que cruzan desde el cielo suelen gritarme, desde arriba: «Baroja, tú no serás nunca nada . . .» Y yo estoy convencido de que no seré nunca nada.[40]

(C) Desde la ventana se perciben a lo lejos rumores confusos de dulce y campesina sinfonía, el tañido de las esquilas de los rebaños que vuelven al pueblo, el murmullo del río, que cuenta a la noche su eterna y monótona queja, y la nota melancólica que modula un sapo en su flauta, nota cristalina que cruza el aire silencioso y desaparece como una estrella errante. En el cielo, de un azul negro intenso, brilla Júpiter con su luz blanca.[41]

(D) En el jardín resuena la lluvia al caer sobre las hojas de los árboles, y sólo de cuando en cuando, rompiendo el murmullo monótono del agua que cae, llega de fuera el chirrido de las ruedas de una carreta, el aida melancólico del boyerizo, el cacareo lejano de algún gallo o la canción clara y alegre de los martillos del herrero sobre el yunque.[42]

(E) Unos obreros trabajaban en un viaducto que unía una gran torre de la orilla con un depósito redondo colocado ya más dentro de tierra. Los martinetes resonaban como campanas y alternaba su ruido con el martilleteo estrepitoso que salía de un taller donde se remachaban grandes calderas y panzudas boyas.[43]

"What a hubbub! What animation!" I exclaimed.

From there the side street gave the impression of a flood in which people and things were dragged along violently. The top decks of the gaily daubed busses were full; men dressed in black and women in light colors passed by without worrying too much about the rain; at the same time automobiles and carriages, big trucks and light bicycles, raced by at dizzying speeds.

"But don't you see all the movement?" I said to my father.

"Yes, but it is a mechanical movement," he answered sternly.

"How can the movement of a town be any other way?" I thought.[44] (A)

Here is another example of unorthodox sights and sounds which sometimes form the material of his poetry.

This is the mysterious voice we hear in the silent, solitary night at the door of the wax figure stands, when the lights of the fair go out, when Jupiter shines brightly upon the chimneys of the houses and the moon stands out like a musical note against the musical staff of the telegraph wires.[45] (B)

Besides making lyrical outbursts of this type, Baroja injects his enthusiasm for many curious little things, things which have largely been forgotten by the world. Principal among these things is his enthusiasm for the odd signs that appear on the fronts of shops. He has made a study of these little signs, which he has called *Epigrafía callejera*. Here are some examples of the discoveries he has made in his deambulations through the streets of Spain.

In the Ventas district, I don't know if they still use the phrase that you could read in a picnic spot some time ago:

YOU ARE BETTER OFF IN THIS ONE (ESTE)
THAN IN THE *ESTE* (THE EAST CEMETERY IN MADRID)

In the roadhouses and inns there used to be mischievous signs. On one side of a wall you could read:

VINO DE BALDE (FREE WINE)

and on the corner wall:

PEÑAS (VALDEPEÑAS IS A WELL KNOWN WINE
GROWING REGION IN SPAIN)[46] (C)

The same type of enthusiasm is shown for proverbs. Proverbs of all kinds occur, but Baroja shows a definite predilection for Basque proverbs. The little bits of philosophy in these appealed to Baroja because they were popular and unpretentious.

Perhaps even more plebeian and more earthy poetic expressions are found in the popular songs strewn throughout his novels. In the popular songs of his day Baroja found a certain crude poetic sentiment and perception which he liked.[47] These songs must have contained for Baroja a certain poetic potential and for this reason are included in his novels without excuses. Baroja simply likes them and includes them.

Some of the reasons for the poetic beauty of the popular songs are given in *Juventud, egolatría.*

Popular songs are just the opposite of universal music, they are the ones that carry the flavor of the land in which they are produced. Of course, they are always intelligible for everyone, for the same reason that music is not an intellectual art; it manipulates rhythms, not ideas, but within this inteligibility, it is distinctly loved by one group and by the other. Popular songs carry something like the smell of the country in which one was born; they recall the air and the temperature one has breathed; it is all of one's ancestors suddenly presented to one. I understand that the predilection is a little barbarous, but if there couldn't be any more than one kind of music or the other, the universal or the local, I would choose the latter; the popular.[48] (D)

(A) — ¡Qué barbaridad! ¡Qué animación! — exclamé.

Desde allí la calle transversal daba la impresión de un torrente en el que fuesen arrastradas con violencia cosas y personas. Las imperiales de los ómnibus pintarrajeados iban llenas; hombres de negro y mujeres vestidas de claro pasaban sin preocuparse gran cosa de la lluvia; al mismo tiempo corrían de una manera vertiginosa automóviles y coches, grandes camiones y ligeras bicicletas.

— ¿Pero no ves qué movimiento? — le dije a mi padre.

— Sí, pero es un movimiento mecánico — replicó papá de una manera displicente.

— ¿Cómo puede ser de otra manera la animación de un pueblo? — pensé yo.[44]

(B) Esta es la voz misteriosa que en la callada noche solitaria se escucha a la puerta de las barracas de las figuras de cera, cuando las luces de la feria se extinguen, cuando Júpiter brilla con fulgor sobre las chimeneas de las casas y la luna se destaca como una nota de música en el pentagrama de los alambres del telégrafo.[45]

(C) En las Ventas, no sé si seguirá la frase cínica que se leía en un merendero hace tiempo:

MEJOR SE ESTÁ EN ESTE
QUE EN EL ESTE

En las posadas y mesones solía haber letreros puestos con malicia. En un ángulo de la pared se leía:

VINO DE BALDE

y en la otra pared de la esquina:

PEÑAS[46]

(D) La canción popular es el polo opuesto de la música universal, es la que lleva más sabor de la tierra en que se produce. Claro, siempre es inteligible para todos, por lo mismo que la música no es un arte intelectual; mueve ritmos, no ideas, pero dentro de ser inteligible, es distintamente amada por los unos y por los otros. La canción popular lleva como el olor del país en que uno ha nacido; recuerda el aire y la temperatura que se ha respirado; es todos los antepasados que se le presentan a uno de pronto. Yo comprendo que la predilección es un poco bárbara, pero si no pudiera haber más música que una u otra, la universal o la local, yo preferiría ésta: la popular.[48]

Included in these nonformal poetic expressions are Baroja's self-created poetic forms which appear in the trilogy *Las agonías de nuestro tiempo*. These — *Evocaciones, Sorpresas, Fantasías* — represent some of his most authentic lyricism.

One book of verse, *Canciones del suburbio,* tells a surprising amount about Baroja's poetic moments. Camilo José Cela considers it of great importance for the understanding of the *novelista*.

If his book of verse, *Canciones del suburbio* was unintelligently poorly received, because his critics forgot — or refused to see — the value that those couplets contained (which wasn't, certainly, a poetic value, but an anecdotal and thematic value and, above all, a value of intense esthetic importance for the better understanding of the novelist, since the book is a repeated sample of the "Baroja alkaloid"), his *Memorias,* in truth, didn't have any better luck with the public.[49] (A)

Azorín considers the same work as a continuity and a condensation of all of Baroja's writings.

No discontinuity exists, therefore, between his novels and these songs; to us everything appears united and compact. In the volume of verse we are surrounded by the same environment that surrounds us in the world of his novels. Baroja couldn't help putting his thoughts about the world and about life down on a few rhymed pages.[50] (B)

The poetic moments do tell the sensitive reader a great deal. They tend to mark clearly that which is of some positive value in life. The most important of these positive elements is the landscape. Novels like *Camino de perfección* and *El laberinto de las sirenas,* and the number of poems in his *Canciones del suburbio* dedicated to the landscape verify this. Baroja's relationship to the multitude of minor characters adrift in his novels seems to be ineffable, momentary, something that could easily be called poetic. Some of the titles in his book of poems, such as *Golfo contemplativo, Los traperos de París, El negro bailarín, Espectros de bohemios, El tonto del pueblo,* corroborate this relationship. Besides these, there is an endless variety of emotions which are deemed worthy of Baroja's unorthodox poetry. For Baroja, as for Joseph Conrad, all that elicits a sincere emotion is deemed worthy of a momentary poetic notice within his works.[51] That which is liberated, isolated, that which has been tossed aside by society or time, seems to be Baroja's most choice poetic theme. To these attributes one might add those of uselessness and misfortune.

Baroja's poetic moments never seem to be prolonged. There is always fear of distortion of true sentiment by exaggeration. Their brevity, their spontaneity, and their sporadic upcroppings from the darkest and most unpoetic pages of his novels, add to their lyrical potential.

These poetic moments are also quite formless. Baroja apologizes for the rough and unpolished appearance of his *Canciones del suburbio,*[52] but this quality is intentional. Thus, breaking the norm of poetry is quite justified by the unorthodox poetic themes and materials about which the poetry is written. More than anything else these poetic moments make the reader more keenly attuned to Baroja's singular but sincere poetic sensibilities.

Thus Baroja's *yoísmo* forces him, or at least allows him, to occupy an inordinate amount of space and importance in his novelistic world, thereby denying this space and importance to his characters. His own character and personality are constantly being projected into his novels, overshadowing and belittling the characters found within, reducing them to a kind of human insignificance. Baroja, considered a great novelist, created only one, if not great, at least complex character, Don Pío Baroja. Undoubtedly, one of the keys to this creation is the systematic negation of the qualities of greatness and complexity in the little human entities that people the nooks and corners of his novels.

Baroja's egotism and his momentary ego-identification with only a limited range of people and objects represent almost total negation of virtue for virtue's sake. For Baroja, virtue operates only when there is ego-involvement or when the individual's sensibility allows him to conceive the possibility of ego-involvement. According to Baroja, one can feel pity for a beggar only if he recognizes the possibility of one day having to beg himself. In any case the ego-identification must be short-lived because the self quickly returns to its own ego-centered moment, to the joy of plenty. Baroja might well say that charity is fine, but who wants to spend three chapters with a beggar. The beggar receives one or two paragraphs before the ego-identification dissolves.

In a sense Baroja's poetic moments are the result of the strong projection of his *yoísmo* and the limitation of his ego-identification.

(A) Si su libro de versos *Canciones del suburbio* fué ininteligentemente mal recibido, porque sus críticos olvidaron — o no quisieron ver — el valor que aquellas coplas encerraban (que no era, de cierto, un valor poético, sino un valor anecdótico y temático y, sobre todo, un valor de intensa importancia estética para el mejor conocimiento del novelista, ya que el libro es una reiterada muestra del «alcaloide Baroja»), sus *Memorias,* realmente, no han corrido una pública suerte mejor.[49]

(B) No existe, por tanto, discontinuidad entre la novela y estas canciones; todo se nos aparece unido y compacto. Nos rodea en el volumen de versos el mismo ambiente que en el del mundo de las novelas. Forzosamente, Pío Baroja había de condensar en unas pocas páginas rimadas su pensamiento sobre el mundo y la vida.[50]

Knowing full well that he could choose and cultivate whatever *yo* or group of *yoes* that he wished, he chose and cultivated the one best suited to the ephemeral identification with special subjects and objects, those which had undergone a process of negation in real life. Thus Baroja's poetic vision may well have been the result of a deliberate limitation. Rejecting the traditional forms and subjects of poetry, he attuned his sensibility to the forms and subjects poetry has rejected or ignored. The negation lies in both the perceiver and the form and subject perceived. His vision may merit the term "lyrical" since it is uniquely Barojian. After all, doesn't negation enter into every lyrical poet's vision of reality? Doesn't he tend to reject even the possibility of any other vision and project only his own?

9. Conclusion

THIS STUDY HAS CONSISTED of an investigation of negation as a principal substance of Baroja's novels and its use as a *modus operandi* in their creation. The topic was, in part, suggested by the works of writers such as James Joyce, Moravia, Silone, Camus, and the writers of the Generation of 98; the study should establish a closer relationship between their creations and Baroja's. The problem was to find out just how consistently negation was used, and its relative importance to the total form and content of Baroja's novels. The hope was expressed that a study of negation would disclose the fundamental purpose of its use, reveal and outline the positive elements in his novels, give a positive answer — although fragmentary — to the sad, nihilistic, and chaotic worlds Baroja created. The study should also reveal some of the creative potential of negation. Finally, such a study should provide a key to just how and why Baroja created his novelistic worlds, helping the reader to appreciate more fully and to become more finely attuned to the essence of humanity reflected in them.

In drawing any conclusions from the study of negation in Baroja's novels, a great deal of caution and care should be used. His writings are complex and diffuse. He is also extremely prolific. Any affirmation that might sum up the totality of his works in a few paragraphs or with a few well-chosen tags might disorient or harm future studies. The summing-up or the conclusions that follow should be considered as topical suggestions offered about one phase of Baroja's writings. A brief reiteration of the principal negative elements in each of the chapters seems an appropriate first step for the formation of the conclusions.

The study of Baroja's style sought to illustrate how important a role negation played, how often Baroja rejected the noble and patriotic terms, the literary names and clichés, the elaborate syntax with its assured and complex patterns of rhythm and intonation so often found in the so-called *prosa castiza*. Baroja's attitude toward this *prosa castiza* is reflected in his comments on style. These comments form a rather negative stylistic creed best exemplified by his three phrases, *destruir es crear* (to destroy is to create), *estilizar es falsificar* (to stylize is to falsify), and *se escribe como se anda* (one writes as one walks).

Most of the critics corroborated this negative attitude of Baroja's style, but some of them exaggerated, describing it as completely natural and devoid of any stylistic device. Baroja used a number of devices, the most common being the simile, the symbol, and the word deflator. Most of these devices seemed to have a negative purpose or direction; one type of simile tends to reduce or limit man by comparing him to an animal; the symbols all seem to elicit a sad, negative, depressing reaction; the word deflators, such as *un tanto, no del todo,* tend to negate or to soften any affirmation or statement. Thus the direction, in regard to style, remains quite consistent.

The study of Baroja's dialogue stressed its extensive use in his novels, its dull and lifeless qualities, its failure to stand out in sharp relief against the narrative background, and its similarity to Baroja's own speech. It was found that the general negative direction followed in Baroja's style is continued in his dialogue and that almost everything said about one applies to the other. Baroja's dialogues point out the near impossibility of an exchange of ideas or opinions through conversation, the tendency of these conversations to become colorless monologues in which only one idea or opinion, usually the author's, is expressed.

Baroja's novelistic atmosphere is principally created through the reiteration of negative signs and symbols. These have been divided into four groups, centering around death, decadence and solitude, ideologies, and meteorology. The totality of this atmosphere is dark, antivital, lifeless. This atmosphere does not necessarily represent Baroja's impressions of objective reality, but it has fulfilled a creative need, a need for darkness and antivitality which he augments with all sorts of unrelated materials.

The term *character revelation* rather than *character development* has been used with reference to Baroja's characters because they show no growth or change, their essential qualities being gradually disclosed — or unmasked — through a special process of revelation. This process is essentially one of negation. Most of Baroja's protagonists have been stripped or denied most of this life's valued things. These persons are taken away from their home, their friends and families, their religion or political beliefs, and exposed to economic and physical adversities. They are left alone, little islands of humanity living apart from the world. The end product is not one of greatness, but littleness — in Baroja's words — *poca cosa.*

Baroja's technique for revealing his protagonist discloses one of his most significant negations. He shows how he denied or strongly questioned most of the traditional values attributed to man, considering these attributes obfuscations of his most essential and real qualities.

Baroja's minor characters were too numerous for the type of revelation used in exposing his protagonists. But these minor characters were related to the protagonists in that they were isolated from the main stream of life, lived apart from society and accepted few of its truths. This relationship showed that life, or objective reality, had done Baroja's work as a novelist and had been the negative force in the revelation of these persons, by stripping them of life's most traditional values, casting them aside from life's main currents.

The investigation of Baroja's work has revealed that the landscape and those strange cast-off elements of life which elicited Baroja's poetic responses were positive values. These values remained essentially poetic and ineffable, being undefined, unnamed, and unrelated — appealing strongly to the reader's guided sensibilities. Negation, and the negative orbs in which the positive values are found, help to keep them unrelated and unnamed, to guard the purity of their poetic essence. This same negation guides and sharpens the reader's sensibilities to these poetic moments.

The reiteration of these negative elements clearly indicates that negativity is used consistently in Baroja's novels and plays a major role in his creative procedure. These negative elements, by themselves, do not reveal their purpose, their *raison d'être,* but their very abundance and consistency strongly suggest that there is such a purpose, that they are fulfilling a creative need.

Baroja felt a need to prune, to whittle away, to take away from the Spanish language, in order to create his novelistic world. He felt obliged to throw out whole constellations of words, to chop and fragment the syntax, to deaden and flatten the flow of the intonation pattern, to weed it of its commonplace and much too violent and overblown images, to deflate it with little nonaffirmative voices. He gave it a certain jerky and sporadic rapidity. This trimmed and deflated instrument seemed best suited for the creation of Baroja's personal novelistic world. Baroja's style appears as a necessary and principal step in his novelistic creativity. It is just as important for what it destroys as for what it creates.

Through this pruning and trimming process Baroja has made a special and personal creative tool of the Spanish language. This tool served him well, having certain destructive potentialities necessary to Baroja's special needs. Its potential for flatness and monotony, its ability to depress and darken, its corrosive action which eats away at values and truths, are indispensable for the creation of an almost completely negative world.

Inasmuch as half of Baroja's novels are made up of dialogue, it was necessary that he used language that could be dull and lifeless in order to achieve the over-all negative impression. A more rhetorical, colorful and scintillating dialogue would have destroyed the total, dark and doomed feeling of the novel, and consequently its novelistic unity.

A major portion of the creation of Baroja's novelistic atmosphere is accomplished through the repetition of negative signs, symbols, and other depressing material. Baroja's major characters seem to be the result of a relentless stripping and displacement, of a novelistic taking-away of all the extraneous elements that surround them. Multitudes of minor characters have undergone this same process before the novel begins. Life, in their case, has done the work of the novelist. It has stripped them of its most highly touted treasures, reduced them to lonely islands of humanity. The rejection found in Baroja's treatment of the landscape, although secondary, is again of surprising importance. He has refused to link it to any other meaning, to any ideology. He has stripped away its long-standing literary dress, ridded it of its ordered rhetoric, captured it directly. Negation plays a surprisingly important role in the lyrical moments found throughout Baroja's novels. The subjects of his lyrical emanations are nearly always sad, lonely, forgotten discards.

It is easy to see the predominance of the negative in all these phases of Baroja's novels is a constant and continuous factor. Moreover, each negative phase complements mutually all the other phases. The dialogue — probably half of the total content of the novel, is one of the most efficacious atmospherical depressants. The dialogue and the atmosphere account for a large percentage of the bulk of the novel and are therefore very important in the revelation of its characters. They also form the background, the frame, for the flickering essences of lyricism and humanity, and for the dynamic landscape.

Besides these negative factors, Baroja's literary doctrine is very iconoclastic.[1] His stylistic creed is negative; most of his discussions of literary doctrine begin with the words, *no creo,* and in his prologue to *La nave de los locos* he systematically denies all of Ortega y Gasset's *Ideas sobre la novela.* He is against all norms of schools, demanding complete liberty of material, procedure, and purpose. When asked what is left after all this negation, Baroja answers that a certain undefined but essentially human quality remains and should be the substance of novels.

Humanity undefined, which Baroja thinks should be the substance and theme of novels, humanity that is left after all other purposes and directions of the novel are rejected, seems a thing quite apart from all these negative factors profusely extended throughout his novels. The antivital factors help to show what this humanity is not. They show that rhetoric or words, conversation, ideologies, are not a vital part of this essential substance of man which Baroja wishes to present. They are, of course, a part of the world in which man lives just as they are a part of Baroja's novelistic world.

A greater part of Baroja's novelistic world is pessimistic and almost lifeless; a consistent use of negative factors plays a major role in its creation. However, the negative factors cannot be the full explanation or even, by themselves, the principal explanation of how Baroja wrote nearly 100 excellent novels. The very consistency of this negation as a builder of novelistic orbs makes the positive values, the unrejected elements, all the more discernible. The sharpness with which this dark side of Baroja's novels brings out the brighter side cannot be overlooked. Baroja cites this process in *La caverna del humorismo.* "In *humorismo* we go from the individual to the general, from the obscure to the clear, from pessimism to optimism."[2] (A)

In Baroja's style the most important positive element seems to be the rapidity, the movement, the idea that one writes as one walks; that style is a biological something. This rapidity, this movement, was usually evidenced in his similes, giving life and animation to his descriptions and especially to the landscape. It is important to note that this same biological rapidity, this same personal manner of speaking so akin to one's manner of walking, is the most salient positive element carried over into Baroja's dialogues. The words therein remain almost lifeless and meaningless — only the author's aggressive tone, his attacks against all things human and divine, his bitterness, seem alive and moving.

The positive aspects of Pío Baroja's novelistic atmosphere are easy to discern and separate from the predominantly negative factors. One of the principal parts of this vital atmosphere is the satisfaction of the physical drives and necessities of the body. Those things which satisfy the need for nourishment, our thirst, fresh air, form an integral part of this atmosphere. Particularly important in this group is physical activity, that which satisfies the need for bodily exercise. There seems to be a close equation in Baroja between that which moves and that which lives. Warmth is also important. Sunshine becomes in Baroja a sort of primitive symbol of life.[3] The fire, preferably in the fireplace or in the Basque kitchens, is part of this vitality.

Sex appears with less frequency than the other vital factors and is presented in its most pure and simplified form. The delicate candor combined with clinical honesty with which Baroja has handled sex is difficult to pin down. It might be helpful and enlightening to state that the inclusion of sex in Baroja's novels has never sold a single copy for him. The difficulty of handling and including sex within a novel without shading it with romantic, moralistic, religious, perverse, or any of the multifarious

---

(A) En el humorismo vamos a lo general por lo individual, a lo claro por lo oscuro, al optimismo por el pesimismo.[2]

overtones to which it lends itself with such great facility, probably accounts for the sparsity of its appearances in Baroja's novels.

We cannot fully separate the fact that Baroja was a doctor and had received medical training — whatever its limitations — from his choice of the vital things of life. After the tragic end of *El árbol de la ciencia,* in which heroic but stumbling and inadequate medical science fails, the attending physician guesses that the vital things of nature — pure air, healthful food, exercise, and the sunshine of the country — might have saved Lulú and her child.[4]

The same basic components of the vital atmosphere become the things to which the stripped, misplaced, and somewhat broken-down protagonists of Baroja's novels cling most tenaciously. When everything has been stripped away, Don Fausto of *Los últimos románticos* and *Las tragedias grotescas* becomes more aware of the lifegiving qualities of shelter, warmth, and food. Procopio Pagani's electric foot-warmer in *El hotel del Cisne* might have been the one touch of vitality that stood between him and complete blackness, desperation, and perhaps suicide. Fresh air and sunshine are the last telluric strings that hold Luis, in *El cantor vagabundo,* to this life before he cuts his boat loose and lets it drift aimlessly into the sea.

Perhaps the most vital and positive aspect of all Baroja's protagonists is their liberty. This liberty is treasured highly by Baroja. For him it seems to be an essential part of humanity. It is principally a freedom from the mores of society, from responsibility except for one's own biological needs, from the fetters of a myriad of ideologies and truths. True, his protagonists all have some little personal philosophy of life, some little vital illusion to which they cling. But this illusion is always a self-elaborated and unique truth; it is never a philosophy elaborated and superimposed upon the individual from the outside. It is never one of those ready-made, store-bought outfits of truth completely adaptable to all those who care to or can be persuaded to don them.

Some of these self-elaborated and personal vital illusions are amazingly biological in nature. Capitán Chimista's philosophy of life seems to be summed up in these words: "¡Eclair! ¡Eclair! ¡Adelante! ¡Adelante! ¡Hurra!"[5] It seems, more than anything else, a philosophy of sheer physical movement, of action and adventure for their intrinsic, biological value. The phrase is reiterated throughout *La estrella del capitán Chimista* and *Los pilotos de altura.* It is the last thing uttered by an adventurer which might have been Chimista himself before the executioner compresses the lever and turns the wheel of the *garrote.*[6] Aviraneta's philosophy does not differ too much from that of Chimista. His principal reason for existence throughout twenty-two adventure novels is adventure and intrigue for their own sake. One of the principals of one of these novels, *La Isabelina,* has a purely biological philosophy of life. He, a priest called Padre Chamizo, believed in his friends and in eating, in satisfying a purely physical hunger. This hunger was the basis for his association with Aviraneta.[7] For Baroja's sense of values, this quality tends to make him more rather than less human.

Some of Baroja's characters are left with no vital fiction as the novel ends. The most extreme of these cases, finding themselves left with no illusions about life, commit suicide. Even in the abundance of suicides in Baroja's works — three occur in the last two pages of *Los enigmáticos* — there is something positive, something vital.[8] These suicides seem to be the ultimate in the denial of all vital illusion. They wrench the physical act of death from the religious will of God, from its social protocol (the expectation that one should die smothered in the tears and sorrows of loved ones), and from the hands of the medical profession. Suicide seems a liberated and independent death. In general, death in Baroja's novels appears somewhat in physical purity, stripped of many of the multifarious fictions built up around it.

As stated before, the minor characters in Baroja's novels suffer no novelistic transformation or stripping process. They are taken into the novel as is, and they are considered as positive human values. They, like the protagonists, appreciate and are finally attuned to biological needs. They are also completely autonomous beings, little hampered or molested by the principal march of society. They too have their own little philosophy of life, their own unique wisdom in the art of living. Baroja insists that this art is unique, that it cannot be communicated from one person to another, and that it most certainly will not fit into any general maxims or doctrines.[9]

The landscape, as it appears in Baroja's novels, stripped of all literary dressing and bucolic falsity, is a completely positive value. Why this is so is not quite clear. Part of the positive value of the landscape springs from Baroja's rendering it as vital, dynamic, and living. This point is well illustrated by the speaking landscape in the novel *La leyenda de Jaun de Alzate*.[10] The study of Baroja's landscape illustrates some of the devices he used to give it movement and animation. Most important of these devices were the moving perceiver and the drifting clouds which gave an illusion of movement to the land, the similes which linked the landscape to something animate or something which moves, and the very rapidity of his prose which described a minimum of details before moving the descriptive lens.

There is also the feeling that man depends on the landscape, that he walks through it and derives his substance from it, that it has the positive and solid value of the biological. The countryside allows the liberated men in Baroja's novels a certain amount of special freedom; it invites them to a free movement of both eye and limb. But the essential attraction and value of the landscape remains poetic and ineffable. It is one of those basic things that endure after all the superficial things, such as ideologies and supposed truths, have been swept away.[11]

The positive values in the poetical moments of Baroja's poetry are inseparable from the mass of negation surrounding them. Both the positive and the negative play a vital role in Baroja's personal lyrical outbursts. The emotional impact that sensitive readers absorb from these poetic moments seems to stem from a basic conflict between that which is vital and that which is antivital, that which is positive and that which is negative. The things which steadily and inexorably destroy life make it momentarily and instantaneously more precious.

First, the negative world reduces, delimits, and beats down the receptor of these poetic moments until he becomes a fine and sensitive tool for recording them. The people who are capable of perceiving these little flickerings of poetry, people like José Larrañaga, Silvestre Paradox, María Aracil, Fernando Ossorio, Luis Murguía — are people who have been reduced to a point where they are just barely clinging to life and existence. From their own reduced status stems their acute sensibility to all the insignificant minutiae around them.

Secondly, this negative world fashions and isolates, clearly outlines, the minutiae which are the objects of these lyrical moments. Only a man neglected by time and isolated in space could feel compassion and sense a certain poetic beauty in the old merry-go-round. Both cling to life precariously; both represent the peripheral or the ephemeral. Both find a sort of heroic pose in this paralytic and undirected movement.

Because of the inexorable march of the negative world which surrounds and crushes them, both the poetic perceiver and the poetically perceived become isolated, fragmented ephemera, these being some of the positive values found in Baroja's poetic moments. Some of the most obvious categories of values are: street epigraphy, popular songs, printed ephemera such as the *literatura de cordel,* the Basque proverbs, some of the jokes and anecdotes of the street. The landscape, because it has to be sensed in this same momentary fashion, could be included in this same category. Vagabonds form an integral part of the ephemeral, and the author, the protagonist, and the reader identify themselves with them for a moment, sense instantaneously the palpitation of their human tragedy.

In a sense, all of Baroja's minor characters are momentary positive values. They are probably the most important found throughout his works. Their main attraction for Baroja appears to be that they are human — human because they have no other qualities. These human derelicts can say of themselves only what one of Gorky's beggars says when asked by the merchant who or what he was. "'A man . . .' he answered in a hoarse voice."[12] This last bit of humanity could hardly be salvaged from a more negative story, significantly called *Creatures That Once Were Men.*

If the most essential thing, the most positive thing, in Baroja's novels is human, then the proportion of inhuman to human is staggeringly in favor of the inhuman. There is human sympathy, this Baroja does not deny, but it is a precious drop of water lost in the nothingness of the sea.[13] According to Baroja, this human sympathy does not emanate from a higher source; it is more basic than this, for it is found in animals as well as men. The proof of this, Baroja feels, is that a war prisoner would rather be tried by a pack of dogs than a human war tribunal.

Those sentiments of sympathy also exist in animals. The dog is one of the most effusive animals toward man. If it were possible, after a war, to allow an accused man to choose between a jury of dogs or a jury of men for his trial, he would choose a jury of dogs, because he would know it would be more benevolent towards him.[14] (A)

It is significant that this ounce of Christian charity is carefully separated from all the standard doctrines that teach the same. Any human sympathy in these doctrines of universal brotherly love is completely obfuscated and its value nullified by its own self-praising ritual, its literature, and its propaganda.

Viewed in retrospect, this clash between the vital and the antivital has been the conflict around which all novels have been fashioned. The title he applies to one of his first trilogies, *La lucha por la vida,* might well be applied to all of his novelistic production. All of Baroja's novelistic entities undergo a savage fight for life and existence. This fight for life seems closely related to the struggle of animals for existence. It is principally the struggle for liberty against social restraint and conformity, the struggle for disorder against order, the struggle for the liberty of physical movement. In fine, it is the struggle of the ego, of the self, for survival.

The odds against the individual who seeks these liberties are overwhelming. For every ray of sunshine, there are a thousand dark moments. A thousand commonplace ideas and mores try to channel his every thought and action. A thousand ready-made tags exist for every emotion within his breast. Then, too, there is the crushing weight of his own lack of will power, his *abulia,* so much a part of his generation. This *abulia* explains, in part, why sheer physical movement is so vital to him. It

---

(A) Esos sentimientos de simpatía existen también en los animales. El perro es uno de los animales más efusivos para el hombre. Si fuera posible, después de una guerra, que a un procesado se le diera a elegir un tribunal de perros o un tribunal de hombres para que lo juzgasen, elegiría un tribunal de perros, porque sabría que sería más benévolo para él. [14]

represents a partial victory over one of his most antivital enemies, his own inertia.

Movement, in Baroja's novels, seems to represent a struggle for a certain spatial liberty. But the struggle for life is also a struggle against time. Baroja's world is extremely sensitive to the inexorable march of time. Clocks seem to be cursedly antivital to him. They are arbitrary, man-made contraptions, which measure out with their monotonous circles, in meaningless minutes and hours, that which is without measure, the human essence which Baroja is trying to portray in his novels. The phrase, linked to clocks — "they all wound, the last one kills" — appears five times in Baroja's complete works.

Baroja's protests here seem feeble but sincere. They are against a man's life, which should be the measure of all things, being cruelly and constantly dissected into little meaningless signs of nothingness by an infernal machine of his own invention. It is T. S. Eliot's protest against our lives being measured out in coffee spoons. But, as Truman Capote says, "The clocks must have their sacrifice," [15] and this fleeting quality so akin to humanity makes it all the more precious. Thus the negative quality of time forces one to attach so much vital importance to egotism and the struggle for life.

Artistically, the advantages of negation seem more than obvious. Principally, it gives Baroja complete artistic freedom. The negation of any canons or precepts concerning the writing or purpose of the novel allows Baroja to construct a completely personal work; it allows him to write a novel in which he can wander around at ease and express his thoughts, angers, sentiments, and, above all, the delicate nuances of sensation, when and how he pleases. They allow him to write a porous novel.

A novel in which everything can be included without any particular reason for the inclusion, must necessarily lack order and continuity. This is certainly true of Baroja's novels. However, the negative tone which plays such an important role in all the facets of his novels does serve as a tremendous unifying force. The myriad things and persons which go into the making of one of Baroja's novels do tend to form an integral whole because of their negative aspects. They are either denied by the surrounding world or deny it.

Negation as an artistic procedure or creed can never be the vehicle of any great truths. It can be, and it certainly is, in Baroja's novels, a vehicle of sincerity. In an age when many feel that too many heads are nodding in the affirmative in too many directions at the same time, Baroja's negative motion before all is at least refreshing. Baroja praises little; when he does single out something as being worthy of attention or praise, he is sincere. Baroja, who has considered everyone to be a *farsante* or a *mixtificador,* and has called them these names repeatedly, has been taken as a most sincere man. This is one of the qualities most often mentioned in works dealing with the author himself. Whether this evaluation of personal sincerity is just is not pertinent to this study. Sometimes it seems that Baroja — he had a hard time believing in anything — would not admit the existence of sincerity in others and in himself. But it is obvious that his denial of most ideals and truths and the devaluation of almost everything lend an air of sincerity to all his novels.

Perhaps the greatest artistic potentiality of negation lies in its ability to fragment, to atomize, to isolate. Affirming the great truths tends to make the surrounding world and all the worlds of the past, present, and future more cohesive, more unified. The great truths tend to unite man, to emphasize his oneness, his universality. The truth of brotherly love makes a fine example of this unifying quality. Negation, on the other hand, tends to destroy this universal unity. It tends to shatter and splinter reality into little particles, into fragments, into small egotistical entities. It often leaves only a moment of an individual, only one aspect. It can never reveal to us a completely noble heart but only at great intervals a somewhat noble gesture or, more often, an inkling of a noble sentiment that fades long before it is translated into an action. Thus, negation as an artistic procedure becomes a vehicle of the fragmentary, of the minute, of the intantaneous.

Another and somewhat surprising artistic potential of negation is its ability to render a dogmatic and general statement, a piece of rhetoric, or a hyperbolic tendency more exact. The negative words, for example, leave just enough of the positive statement to make it plausible and seemingly much more exact. Baroja's word deflators are a fine example of this power of exactness found in negation. Such harmless little phrases as *un poco, no del todo,* and even *no* have the ability to circumscribe and delimit a somewhat commonplace statement with a precision which renders it poetically exact.

This study has tried to show how Baroja can be linked to other writers of this century because of his iconoclastic literary doctrine, his creation of sad, negative worlds, and the positive answer he gave to them. Baroja, with his desire to break most rules and traditions of literary doctrine, and to write as individually as he walked, fits well into the Generation of 98. He, no less than the other members of generation, strove to create a completely autonomous literary doctrine. The independent tenor of these statements of literary doctrine for every member of the generation is manifest. Every member set down his own artistic code. Certainly the ideas about literary art set down in Valle-Inclán's *La lámpara maravillosa* have few points of contact with those outlined by Miguel de Unamuno. All, except Azorín, seemed to deny any vestige of affiliation of their own artistic creed with that of other members of the Generation of 98.

Baroja denies the very existence of any such generation. "I have always stated that I didn't believe that a generation of 98 existed."[16] (A) Antonio Machado expresses his desire for the complete artistic freedom of his poetry in this manner. "Am I classic or romantic? I don't know. I would like to leave my verse, as the captain his sword: famous for the virile hand that blandished it, not appraised for the learned craft of the man who forged it."[17] (B) This same independence of literary doctrine links Baroja to numerous other writers of our century.

Baroja is closely related to the novelists and other writers of his own century, so many of whom created sad, negative worlds. The novelistic worlds of Joyce, Proust, Moravia, Pietro Spina, Camus, Greene, and Faulkner are essentially sad and negative. Baroja's own generation, the Generation of 98, is outstanding in the creation of sad and negative worlds. Some of the best novelistic and literary talents of this century have dedicated themselves to the creation of dark, antivital nihilistic worlds.

Baroja's answer to this nihilistic world links him closely to the writers of this century. R. W. B. Lewis's observation that the answer James Joyce and Proust give — that the artistic experience is to be the only positive value — seems adequate and just. His affirmation that the other writers treated in his study give a human answer is also justified. Both the answers are partial and limited, and they are stated artistically and never overtly and dogmatically. His thesis of the partial human answer to the overpowering nihilism of the novelistic world which is artistically expressed could be applied to any number of the writers of our century. In Azorín, for example, this answer might well take the form of an intensified sensibility to the minutiae of time and space which surround one.

Baroja's answer to the dark and antivital world he created is also a partial one and is expressed artistically and not overtly or as a dogma. It is also a human answer, an answer concerned with that which is most basic and essential to humanity. This positive answer to a negative world is reduced and limited to those things which are available to the senses, to the surroundings that are most essential to the animal or biological existence of man.

Baroja's use of negation in the creation of the sad and negative worlds of his novels, and his fragmentary but positive answer to these worlds, suggest several fields for future study. It seems that an intensive study of the negative elements and the use of negation in other works, especially in those works considered completely negative, might help to disclose more fully the author's creative technique and genius and to outline more clearly their positive values. Such an approach might be rewarding, for example, in certain novels such as *Don Casmurro* and *Memorias póstumas de Brás Cubas* by Machado de Assis. This type of study might also be suitable for some of the more modern poetry and poetic prose of the Spanish-speaking world.

Some of the findings in this study provide more definite avenues for the investigation of Baroja's literary kinship to certain novelists of the nineteenth century. Although Rosalie Wahl states that Dickens, Gorki, Balzac, and Dostoyevsky influenced Baroja's style, she does not say just what the possible influences from each of these writers might be.[18]

In the light of the present study, one of the things that surely would be of interest to Baroja in the writings of Gorki is the latter's tendency to take his characters out of their natural habitat and to strip them of almost everything they once possessed, in order to reveal them. Zunzunegui has clearly recognized that the two authors share this procedure as his answer to the question: "With what foreign author would you associate Baroja?" shows.

With Gorki; both of them write an itinerant literature. In the majority of his novels Baroja needs to get his protagonists out on the highway in the fourth or fifth chapter . . . he constructs his novels to function like a trip, . . . and, as in Gorki, there are no women in his literature.[19] (C)

For one who has read Gorki's short story *Fellow Traveler,* found in his collection of short stories called *Creatures That Once Were Men,* the relationship of the two authors, especially in their technique of character revelation, will need no further proof nor clarification. The porous elements of the novelistic world of Balzac must have interested Baroja considerably. In Dostoyevsky it was probably the ability of the author to double himself into both an actor and observer which intrigued Baroja. Baroja mentions this several times, calling it *el desdoblamiento psicológico.* This *desdoblamiento psicológico* is somehow closely related to Baroja's concern with the author's ability to identity himself, if only for one moment, with the socially displaced character.

The novelistic world of Charles Dickens must have been especially attractive to Baroja because it was essentially a negative world laced with a *soupçon* of true Christian humanity. The temporally and spatially

---

(A) Yo siempre he afirmado que no creía que existiera una generación del 98.[16]

(B) ¿Soy clásico o romántico? No sé. Dejar quisiera mi verso, como deja el capitán su espada: famoso por la mano viril que la blandiera, no por el docto oficio del forjador preciada.[17]

(C) Con Gorki; los dos hacen una literatura itinerante. Baroja necesita en la mayoría de sus novelas sacar al protagonista a la carretera al cuarto o quinto capítulo . . ., construye sus novelas en función de un viaje . . . y, como en Gorki, no hay mujeres en su literatura.[19]

displaced characters of Dickens' world, such as the parish beadle, the shabby genteel, Damon and Pythias, and all the other little isolated and forgotten entities who appear in works like *Sketches by Boz,* must have been very meaningful to Baroja. The character Mark Tapley from Dickens' *Martin Chuzzlewit* must have impressed Baroja — who quoted him at the beginning of a chapter in *El mayorazgo de Labraz* — because of his ability to create his own vital illusion of "jollity" in the face of adversity and sadness. This evidence of specific relationships between these novelists and Baroja suggest that a study might substantiate and enlarge the theme and reveal much more.

Baroja's legacy to younger novelists promises to be the richest field of study.

It is easy to trace the same preoccupations with the basic things of life in Carmen Laforet's *Nada.* Andrea, the protagonist, comes in darkness to the darkest house on a dark street in Barcelona. She finds there a vortex of ideological madness, a sort of compendium of all of Spain's past ideologies, such as the traditional Spanish honor and Catholicism. Against this background, Andrea becomes highly sensitive to and very appreciative of the basic things of life, such as sunshine, good food, and the pleasure of a walk.

In José Suárez Carreño's *Las últimas horas,* Manolo finds the meaning of life in his own physical assurance, in the physical things which surround him and concludes, "'You have to live,' something within him kept saying; 'be what you are this very instant.'"[20] *La noria* by Luis Romero deals with the daily lives and struggles of a series of individuals. It traces the vicious but vital circle of life, the heroic struggle for existence.

These examples demonstrate that not only is the positive answer of the basic things much like that which Baroja gives but also this positive factor depends on the negative background, the nothingness which surrounds it, for its emotional and esthetic impact. In these cases, as in Baroja, the negative forms the background and outlines the positive.

Hemingway, with his emphasis on that which tastes "damn good" and feels "fine" and his use of the concept of nothingness as a framing device for his characters, certainly falls into this group. The Spanish-born Cuban novelist and short-story writer Lino Novás Calvo, who, incidentally, was helped by the Generation of 98, shows the same direction. In his short story called *Cayo canas*[21] he shows a man alone on an island and surrounded by fire slowly creeping up on him, and his struggle for existence. *El negrero,* reminiscent of Baroja's *El capitán Chimista* and *Pilotos de altura* portrays action and adventure without purpose or direction. In this novel, as in the novels of Baroja, action and adventure exist for their own intrinsic and biological value.

A study of Baroja's influence on these young writers would no doubt reveal that Baroja had a direction and a positive answer in his writings, and that it made its imprint on many writers.

Some or many readers may object to the limited and highly restricted answer Baroja has given to the negative world. It does have stringent limitations, but those who seek answers, complete dogmas, and panaceas can find an abundance elsewhere. Baroja's positive values are limited to the individual. They are without significance beyond the pale of the individual ego. They are further limited to the temporal, mortal existence of the individual. The thing you cannot find in Baroja is a promise or hope of immortality or a paradise in a life to come.

Although Baroja's positive values, found scattered throughout the negative world of his novels, are of little scope, they seem values solid and tangible enough, possessing enough vitality to sustain and make interesting the entirety of his prolific novelistic production. These same values must have been the only ones which sustained Baroja during his long writing career. Further, the fresh air, the landscape, the good food, the physical exercise, and the warmth of the morning sun or of a fireplace do leave room for the sublime. They seem to actually carry within themselves the potential of elevating the individual to his highest physical and spiritual point.

Baroja must have intuited that nature's elements have more power spiritually to elevate or depress man than do abstract words or ideas. It is the elements, intensified by a storm at sea, and not the empty literature of revolutions and dogmas, which momentarily tosses Paradox Rey, standing alone amidst the tempest, to the most sublime of physical and spiritual heights.

The wind has taken Paradox's hat, and he ties a handkerchief around his head. The rain, pulverized by gusts of wind, soaks his clothes.

PARADOX (Clinging to the helm) "Who would have ever told you, poor man dedicated to the natural sciences and to philosophical speculation, that you were destined to struggle alone against the immense sea, until you dominated and overcame it, for an instant!"

THE WIND "Hu ... hu ... hu ... I am the whip of these huge and obscure waves that run upon the sea. I lash them, push them toward the sky, sink them into the abyss ... Hu ... hu ... hu ...

THE SEA "I have no freedom of choice; I have no will; I am an inerte mass. I am blind force, fatality which saves and condemns, which creates and destroys.

THE WIND "My angers are your angers; my commands, your furies."

THE SEA "This wave which charges like a furious bull, that strikes like a battering ram, that leaps, that rips, that takes apart, wishes no harm, doesn't seek to destroy; yesterday it sparkled in pearls on the flowers, at dawn, in the fields. Then it ran down the river, was a red cloud in a splendid sunset one afternoon, and today it is a wave, and tomorrow it will once again be what it was, rolling through the eternal circle of eternal substance ...

PARADOX "Yes, everything changes, everything is transformed into the limits of Time and of Space, and everything, nevertheless, keeps on being equal and the same . . . You don't scare me, storm, no matter how much you roar; you are nothing more than one aspect, and an insignificant aspect, of the world of phenomena."

YOCK "There is no other man like my master. Neither the tempestuous sea nor the terrible hurricane frighten him; instead of complaining of this fate, he reasons about the essence of things. Admirable man; you are almost worthy of being a dog! . . ."[22] (A)

(A) *El viento le ha llevado el sombrero a* Paradox, *y se ata el pañuelo a la cabeza. La lluvia, pulverizada por las ráfagas de aire, le cala la ropa.*

PARADOX. — (*Agarrado a la rueda del timón.*) ¡Quién te había de decir a ti, pobre hombre dedicado a las ciencias naturales y a especulación filosófica, que había de luchar tú solo con el mar inmenso, hasta dominarlo y vencerlo, por lo menos, durante un instante!

EL VIENTO. — Hu . . ., hu . . ., hu . . . Yo soy el látigo de estas grandes y oscuras olas que corren sobre el mar. Yo las azoto, las empujo hasta el cielo, las hundo hasta el abismo . . . Hu . . ., hu . . ., hu . . .

EL MAR. — Yo no tengo albedrío; no tengo voluntad; soy masa inerte, soy la fuerza ciega, la fatalidad que salva o condena, que crea o que destruye.

EL VIENTO. — Mis cóleras son sus cóleras; mis mandatos, sus furias.

EL MAR. — Esta ola que embiste como un toro furioso, que golpea como un ariete, que salta, que rompe, que deshace, no ansía el daño, no busca la destrucción; ayer brillaba en perlas en las flores al amanecer, en el campo. Corrió luego por río, fué nube roja en el crepúsculo esplendoroso de una tarde, y hoy es ola, y mañana volverá a ser lo que fué, rodando por el círculo eterno de la eterna sustancia . . .

PARADOX. — Sí, todo cambia, todo se transforma en los límites del Espacio y del Tiempo, y todo, sin embargo, sigue siendo igual y lo mismo . . . No me asustas, tempestad, por más que brames; no eres más que un aspecto, y un aspecto insignificante del mundo de los fenómenos.

YOCK. — No hay otro hombre como mi amo. No le asusta ni el mar tempestuoso, ni el terrible huracán; en vez de quejarse contra el destino, discurre sobre la esencia de las cosas. ¡Hombre admirable; eres casi digno de ser perro! . . .[22]

Notes

NOTES TO CHAPTER 1
pages 1—3

1 Pío Baroja,* *Canciones del suburbio,* VIII, p. 989. All the quotations from Baroja are taken from the edition of *Obras completas* (Madrid: Biblioteca Nueva, 1946–1951). The Roman numerals will indicate the volume, and the Arabic numerals, the page.

2 R. W. B. Lewis, *The Picaresque Saint* (Philadelphia and New York: J. B. Lippincott Company, 1959), p. 17.

3 *Ibid.,* p. 18.

4 "Allow me to pay this small tribute to you who taught so much to those of us who wanted to be writers when we were young." ("Hemingway Visits Baroja in Madrid," *Time,* XLVIII, No. 18 [1956], p. 47.)

5 "There is in all these works a certain atmosphere of universal doom: especially in *Ulysses,* with its mocking *odi-et-amo* hodgepodge of the European tradition, with its blatant and painful cynicism, and its uninterpretable symbolism — for even the most painstaking analysis can hardly emerge with anything more than an appreciation of the multiple enmeshment of the motifs but with nothing of the purpose and meaning of the work itself. And most of the other novels which employ multiple reflection of consciousness also leave the reader with an impression of hopelessness. There is often something confusing, something hazy about them, something hostile to the reality which they represent. We not infrequently find a turning away from the practical will to live, or delight in portraying it under its most brutal forms." (Erich Auerbach, *Mimesis* [Princeton, New Jersey: Princeton University Press, 1953], p. 551.)

6 Lewis, p. 22.

7 The term "Generation of 98" is used here to refer to a group of writers which includes Valle-Inclán, Unamuno, Benavente, Baroja, Maeztu, Machado, and Azorín. Azorín coined the phrase in 1906. Baroja denied the existence of the generation. "Yo siempre he afirmado que no creía que existiera una generación del 98." (Baroja, *Artículos,* V, p. 1240.) Although the term is loose, and one is never sure which writers to include in the generation, it is the name now applied to these writers — Baroja included — and as such is useful for referring to them as a group.

8 Azorín [José Martínez Ruiz], *Clásicos y modernos, Obras completas* (Madrid: Aguilar, 1947–54), II, p. 902.

9 *Ibid.,* p. 912.

10 Pedro Laín Entralgo, *La generación del noventa y ocho* (Buenos Aires: Espasa-Calpe Argentina, 1947), p. 90.

198

Notes to pages 3—9

11 Lewis, p. 9.

12 *Ibid.*

13 Angel Valbuena Prat, *Historia de la literatura española* (Barcelona: Editorial Gustavo Gili, 1957), III, p. 451.

14 "«DE LIMO TERRAE»
«Entonces formó Yahué Dios al hombre del polvo de la tierra» (Gen. II, 7). Polvo de la tierra, polvo del campo de España forma la materia primera de que están hechos estos hombres del 98. Precisaré más: de la tierra más extremada y próxima al mar, límite y peligro de España. Por su nacimiento y por su destino, son hombres de confín, de finisterre. Salvo Benavente, madrileño de nación y de vida, todos los del 98 ven la primera luz en la franja más excéntrica de nuestro suelo. Unamuno, Baroja, Maeztu, Bueno y Zuloaga son vascos; Ganivet, granadino; los Machado, sevillanos; *Azorín,* levantino; Valle-Inclán y Menéndez Pidal, gallegos. Los cantores del paisaje castellano son auténticos *descubridores* de Castilla, y acaso por eso puedan ser *inventores* de una Castilla. «Castilla... ¡Qué profunda, sincera emoción experimentamos al escribir esta palabra!... A Castilla, nuestra Castilla, la ha hecho la literatura», dirá, con innegable verdad, el literato e inventor *Azorín.*" (Laín Entralgo, p. 30.)

15 James Joyce, *Dubliners* (New York: B. W. Huebsch, 1916), p. 132.

16 Carlos Baker, *Hemingway* (Princeton, New Jersey: Princeton University Press, 1956), p. 125.

17 Hans Jeschke, *La Generación de 1898 en España;* translation, introduction and notes by Y. Pino Saavedra (Santiago de Chile: Ediciones de la Universidad de Chile, 1946), p. 142.

18 "Todo lo que es enfermizo, efímero, negativo atrae irresistiblemente a esta generación en una especie de simpatía sinal y llega a ser para ella expresión simbólica de su sentimiento pesimista de la vida." (*Ibid.,* p. 100.)

19 *Ibid.,* p. 117.

20 *Ibid.,* p. 142.

21 "El estilo desesperado es la forma de un existir desesperado." (Américo Castro, *La realidad histórica de España* [México: Editorial Porrúa, 1954], p. 534.) "Bajo esa atmósfera oprimente florecerán la ascética y la picaresca, hijas gemelas de un judaísmo hecho Iglesia, y de un cristianismo sin fe en el hombre, y sin la abierta y piadosa sonrisa de su Fundador." (*Ibid.,* p. 536.)

22 Camilo José Cela, *La colmena* (Barcelona-México: Editorial Noguer, 1957), p. 17.

23 In these last three novels it becomes more and more evident that the mad and negative world serves to artistically underline the slight but intensely felt human values. In *Nada* the year of madness, of degenerate decadence and half existence which surrounded and engulfed Andrea shows clearly her hunger for friends, family, and the vital necessities of life such as food and sunshine. The year she spent in Barcelona begins in darkness and ends with the breaking through of the matutinal sun. Manolo, in *Las últimas horas,* is surrounded by people who have hardly any reason to live or direction in life. From them he learns the secret sweet vitality of his own existence.

24 Domingo Pérez Minik, *Novelistas españoles de los siglos XIX y XX* (Madrid: Ediciones Guadarrama, 1957), p. 330.

NOTES TO CHAPTER 2

page 9

1 These aspects of style might be conveniently grouped under the heading of linguistic forms, as Wolfang Kayser has done in his *Interpretación y análisis de la obra literaria* (Madrid: Editorial Gredos, 1958), p. 157. (The Spanish transla-

tion is mentioned because it is the most recent edition and most readily available.) In our study of these linguistic forms we will be concerned only with those forms that appear with enough frequency to make a noticeable contribution to Baroja's style.

2 Ricardo León, *El amor de los amores* (Madrid: Editorial Hernando, 1929), p. 10.

3 Ricardo León, *Casta de hidalgos* (Argentina: Espasa-Calpe Argentina, 1952), p. 13. First published in 1908.

4 Baroja, *Zalacain el Aventurero,* I, p. 168.

5 Although the title of León's novel is an indication of his thesis, it also shows his liking for these words. The novel narrates the adventures of Jesús de Cebolla; *Las aventuras de Jesús de Cebolla* would have been an adequate title.

6 Baroja, *Rapsodias,* V, p. 863.

7 Ramón del Valle-Inclán, *La lámpara maravillosa* (Madrid: Artes de la Ilustración, 1922), pp. 77–78.

8 Azorín, *Clásicos . . ., Obras . . .,* II, pp. 794–795.

9 Baroja, *Rapsodias,* V, p. 867.

10 Baroja's attitude toward the importance of the sound of words and their musicality is significant both for much of Spanish literature which preceded the Generation of 98 and much of the literature written by his contemporaries. Many of the Generation of 98 were interested in the sound of words and their musicality. Ramón del Valle-Inclán expresses a view diametrically opposed to Baroja's in this matter in a chapter of his *La lámpara maravillosa* significantly called "El milagro musical." "El poeta ha de confiar a la evocación musical de las palabras todo el secreto de esas ilusiones que están más allá del sentido humano apto para encarnar en el número y en la pauta de las verdades demostradas. . . . A veces la música de una palabra logra despertar estas larvas, y otra las hace remover, y otra les da alas, pero jamás aprendemos nada. . . . El secreto de las conciencias sólo puede revelarse en el milagro musical de las palabras." (pp. 53–55).

11 Baroja, *Pequeños ensayos,* V. p. 988.

12 *Ibid.,* p. 987.

13 *Ibid.*

14 Baroja, *Pequeños . . .,* V, p. 986.

15 Baroja, *Aurora roja,* I, pp. 538–39.

16 *Ibid.,* p. 615.

17 Baroja, *La caverna del humorismo,* V, p. 395.

18 The tendency of certain words to lose vital significance has preoccupied many writers of this century. Joseph Conrad in his "Preface" to *The Nigger of the Narcissus* (New York: Random House, 1957), p. ix, speaks of "the commonplace surface of words: of the old, old words, worn thin, defaced by ages of careless usage." The same preoccupation is expressed in Luis Romero's novel, *La noria* (Barcelona: Ediciones Destino, 1954), p. 263, in the following manner: "Saca un duro del bolsillo (cinco pesetas, de papel o de lo que sea, siempre serán un duro, hasta que una nueva generación marchite la palabra) y se lo entrega a la vieja."

19 Baroja, *Pequeños . . .,* V, p. 985.

20 Baroja, *El mundo es ansí,* II, p. 784.

21 Baroja, *Vitrina pintoresca,* V, p. 835.

22 "Y es que a Pío Baroja, por otra parte, no le abandona nunca un íntimo pudor, algo como un miedo a incurrir en la afectación erótica." (José M. Salaverría, "Las inquietudes de un novelista," *A B C,* February 4, 1927, Mercadal, I, p. 110). Many of the quotations in this study come from García Mercadal's two volume

anthology of articles written about Baroja. These will be indicated by the name Mercadal plus the volume and page number.

[23] Baroja, *La caverna* . . ., V, p. 400.

[24] Baroja, *Divagaciones apasionadas,* V, p. 495.

[25] Baroja, *El mundo* . . ., II, p. 786.

[26] Baroja, *Los amores tardíos,* I, p. 1334.

[27] Baroja, *El mundo* . . ., II, p. 829.

[28] "Eso que no hay en el escritor vasco, y que por su mera ausencia vale como una grande virtud positiva, es la retórica. No voy ahora a desenvolver esta cuestión: estoy cierto de que los mejores se hallan en ello de acuerdo conmigo, y no me corre prisa buscar la connivencia con los peores.

Quien acierta a escribir sin retórica es un gran escritor: *tertium non datur.*

Porque retórica no puede significar ampulosidad ni rebuscamiento: caben estilos ampulosos y rebuscados sin retórica. Yo diría: todo estilo o trozo de estilo inexpresivos son retórica. Cuando las palabras o los giros no responden exclusivamente a la necesidad de expresar un pensamiento, imagen o emoción vivazmente actual en el alma del autor, quedan como materia muerta y son la negación de lo estético.

Una pregunta nos ocurre al punto: si no fué la urgencia de dar salida a un pensamiento, imagen o emoción, ¿qué movió a elegir esos vocablos y frases inanes? Evidentemente, el deseo de asemejarse a un autor o época ilustres y hacer creer a las gentes que somos ellos. Esto es, en ética como en estética, la esencia del pecado: querer ser tenido por lo que no es. Y la retórica es ese pecado de no ser fiel a sí mismo, la hipocresía en arte. El *casticista,* por ejemplo, es un retórico nato." (José Ortega y Gasset, "La prosa y el hombre," *El espectador, Obras* [Madrid: Espasa-Calpe, 1932], pp. 195–196.)

[29] Federico García Sánchiz, "Pío Baroja," *Heraldo de Madrid,* Mercadal, I, p. 80.

[30] Baroja, *Las inquietudes de Shanti Andía,* II, p. 1041.

[31] Emilio Carrere, "Canciones del suburbio," Mercadal, I, p. 235.

[32] H. Peseux-Richard, "Un romancier espagnol," *Revue Hispanique,* XXIII, No. 63 [1910], p. 182.

[33] Ignacio de Areilza, "La última novela de Baroja," Mercadal, I, p. 187.

[34] Cristóbal de Castro, "Baroja o Robinson," *El español,* March 24, 1945, Mercadal, I, p. 229.

[35] Peseux-Richard, p. 181.

[36] Baroja, in contrast to the *escritor castizo,* has no fear of a period or the beginning of a new paragraph.

" — ¿Por qué emplea usted ese período corto, que quita elocuencia y rotundidad a la frase?

— Es que yo no busco la rotundidad ni la elocuencia de la frase — les digo —; es más, huyo de ellas." (Baroja, *Juventud, egolatría,* V, p. 174.)

Baroja limits both paragraphs and chapters. "Después, mi preocupación es hacer la novela poco aburrida, para lo cual dejo los capítulos breves y los párrafos cortos." (Baroja, *Las horas solitarias,* V, p. 253.)

[37] This difference in the pattern of the sentences and its effects on the rhythm of the prose is considered one of the most salient features of the Generation of 98 as opposd to the *estilo castizo.* See Hans Jeschke's statement of this difference quoted on page 11.

[38] Baroja, *Juventud* . . ., V, p. 174. Baroja's reference to a nontraditional way of breathing may be considered a figurative statement and as sort of a personal intuition into one of the basic differences between his sentences and what he considered the traditional Spanish sentence. However, if we consider the statement in a more technical sense, in the light of phonetics, it tells us a great deal more about Baroja's sentences. His nontraditional way of breathing could tech-

nically refer to the length of the breath groups, to these natural, biological pauses which allow the speaker to inhale more breath before continuing. These breath groups in Baroja — Navarro Tomás refers to them as *grupos fónicos* — are shorter than the traditional breath groups and are not linked together in a series of rising and falling patterns of intonation.

[39] Juan de la Encina, "El laberinto de las sirenas," *La Voz,* December, 1923, Mercadal, I, p. 216.

[40] Jean Cassou, "Pío Baroja," Mercadal, II, p. 93.

[41] "En cambio Baroja es impaciente. Cuando esa impaciencia acumula los incidentes de tal forma que éstos sirven directamente a la intención y a la esencia de lo que el autor se propone, no hay nada que decir. Pero cuando se advierte que la rapidez es por simple fatiga (en la novela, al revés que en la vida, cuando estamos cansados, corremos) distrae nuestra atención y nos impacienta. Nos impacienta no en relación con la solución de la novela sino con nosotros mismos. Nuestra atención quiere prenderse en motivaciones y deducciones más genuinas, vivas y originales y detenerse antes de seguir y darlo todo por logrado. La prolijidad de Baroja, cuando la hay, no está en la acumulación de detalles triviales sino de movimiento frenéticos sin esencialidad, es decir, con un frenesí no motivado. En Baroja no hay miedo de prolijidad formal, al contrario. Lo querríamos más prolijo en el detalle porque en Baroja la palabra es siempre animada y viva." (Ramón J. Sender, *Unamuno, Valle-Inclán, Baroja y Santayana* [México: Ediciones de Andrea, 1955], pp. 111–112.)

[42] Julio Laborde, "Pío Baroja," *Comoedia,* Mercadal, II, p. 52.

[43] Areilza, Mercadal, I, p. 187.

[44] Baroja, *La nave de los locos,* IV, p. 321.

[45] Baroja, *La caverna . . .,* V, p. 439.

[46] All these affirmations seem to be pointed towards Buffon's famous affirmation that style is the man. Baroja himself considers this inexact.
"La frase «El estilo es el hombre», atribuída a Buffon, y que parece que no la escribió así, se me figura completamente inexacta. Lo que se podría decir es que cada hombre tiene un estilo, no en el sentido gramatical y retórico, sino en el sentido de que cada hombre tiene una manera de representarse el mundo y una manera de intervenir en él. Los animales tienen también un estilo." (*Ibid.,* p. 440.)

[47] Ortega y Gasset, "Baroja tropieza en Coria con la gramática," *El espectador, Obras,* p. 175.

[48] García Sánchiz, Mercadal, I, p. 78.

[49] Francisco de Miomandre, "Pío Baroja," prologue to the French edition of *Zalacain el Aventurero;* translation by Georges Pillement (Paris: Editions Excelsior, 1926), Mercadal, II, p. 29.

[50] Luis de Zulueta, "Padres e hijos," Marcadal, I, p. 152.

[51] Baroja, *La caverna . . .,* V, p. 439.

[52] Gregorio Marañón, "El academicismo de don Pío Baroja," *La Prensa,* April 28, 1935, Mercadal, I, p. 53.

[53] Baroja, *Vitrina . . .,* V, p. 834.

[54] Baroja, "Prólogo," I, p. xiii.

[55] José Sánchez Rojas, "La ciudad de la niebla," Mercadal, I, p. 77.

[56] Edmundo González Blanco, "Las horas solitarias," *La Esfera,* Mercadal, I, p. 127.

[57] Richard, p. 114.

[58] Baroja, *Paradox, Rey,* II, p. 203.

[59] Baroja, *La caverna . . .,* V, p. 403.

[60] Rafael Sánchez Mazas, "Baroja, de frac," *Ahora,* March 21, 1935, Mercadal, I, p. 113.

[61] B. Morales San Martín, "Memorias de un hombre de acción," *El Mercantil Valenciano,* May 15, 1935, Mercadal, I, p. 177.

[62] Areilza, Mercadal, I, p. 186.

[63] Jorge Pillement, "Pío Baroja," *Comoedia,* March 6, 1930, Mercadal, II, p. 82.

[64] Baroja, *La dama errante,* II, p. 231.

[65] Baroja, *La casa de Aizgorri,* I, p. 20. There are more of these similes in works which give more importance to the landscape such as this one and *El laberinto de las sirenas.*

[66] *Ibid.,* p. 27.

[67] *Ibid.,* p. 49.

[68] Baroja, *El mayorazgo de Labraz,* I, p. 59.

[69] *Ibid.,* p. 101.

[70] Baroja, *Los últimos románticos,* I, p. 904.

[71] Baroja, *Las tragedias grotescas,* I, p. 998.

[72] Swimming clouds lend a dynamic sensation to many of Baroja's descriptive landscapes.

[73] Baroja, *El mayorazgo . . .,* I, p. 79.

[74] Baroja, *La busca,* I, p. 291.

[75] *Ibid.,* p. 297.

[76] *Ibid.,* p. 369.

[77] Baroja, *Camino de perfección,* VI, p. 17.

[78] *Ibid.,* pp. 23–24.

[79] *Ibid.,* p. 109.

[80] Baroja, *César o nada,* II, p. 625.

[81] *Ibid.,* p. 630.

[82] *Ibid.,* p. 581.

[83] Baroja, *Las inquietudes . . .,* II, p. 1017.

[84] Baroja, *El árbol de la ciencia,* II, p. 521.

[85] Baroja, *El laberinto . . .,* II, pp. 1174–75.

[86] Baroja, *El laberinto . . .,* II, p. 1215.

[87] Baroja, *El cabo de las tormentas,* VI, p. 374.

[88] Baroja, *El caballero de Erláiz,* VII, p. 352.

[89] Notice that this essential something doesn't have to be completely physical. Many times the essential quality is freedom, but it is important to remember that when the term relates to animals it becomes more physical and less abstract.

[90] Baroja, *El aprendiz de conspirador,* III, p. 55.

[91] Baroja, *El mundo . . .,* II, p. 784.

[92] Baroja, *El árbol . . .,* II, p. 512.

[93] Baroja, *César . . .,* II, p. 619.

[94] Baroja, *El laberinto . . .,* II, p. 1201.

[95] *Ibid.,* p. 1224.

[96] *Ibid.,* p. 1301.

[97] Baroja, *Los amores . . .,* I, p. 1361.

[98] Baroja, *Las noches del buen retiro,* VI, p. 650.

[99] *Ibid.,* p. 636.

[100] Baroja, *El caballero . . .,* VII, p. 32.

[101] Baroja, *Locuras de carnaval,* VI, pp. 937–938.

[102] Carlos Bousoño, *Teoría de la expresión poética* (Madrid: Editorial Gredos, 1952), p. 102.

[103] Peseux-Richard, p. 124.

[104] The term *símbolo bisémico* or bimodal symbol is used according to Carlos Bousoño when the symbol exists in reality. If this symbol doesn't exist in reality but only serves to evoke a certain emotion, he uses the term *símbolo monosémico*. (Bousoño, pp. 101–108.)

These symbols are somewhat like those employed by Sherwood Anderson in *The Triumph of the Egg* in which the two-headed chickens and other preserved monsters were symbols of the grotesque humans which parade through the book. Baroja uses many similar devices.

[105] Baroja, *La ciudad de la niebla*, II, p. 393.

Again the sententious phrase cannot help but remind us of a similar bit of philosophy found in Sherwood Anderson's *Winesburg, Ohio*.

"The old man had listed hundreds of the truths in his book. I will not try to tell you all of them. There was the truth of virginity and the truth of passion, the truth of wealth and poverty, of thrift and of profligacy, of carelessness and abandon. Hundreds and hundreds were the truths and they were all beautiful. And then people came along. Each as he appeared snatched up one of the truths and some who were quite strong snatched up a dozen of them. It was the truths that made the people grotesque." ([New York: The New American Library of World Literature, 1956], p. 10.)

[106] Baroja, *La ciudad . . .*, II, p. 440.

[107] Baroja, *Camino . . .*, VI, p. 20.

[108] Baroja, *Aventuras, inventos y mixtificaciones de Silvestre Paradox*, II, p. 135.

[109] *Ibid.*, p. 117.

[110] Baroja, *El mundo . . .*, II, p. 784.

[111] Baroja, *El laberinto . . .*, II, p. 1174.

[112] *Ibid.*, p. 1175.

[113] *Ibid.*

[114] This isn't to say that all symbols found in Baroja's novels are pessimistic and sad. There are a few, and these are more likely to be found in his first novels, which are optimistic and hopeful. The red dawn which appears at the end of *La casa de Aizgorri* seems to be an optimistic symbol. It remains an optimism projected into the future and has little effect on the novel.

"Mariano, después de mirar hacia allí, en voz baja y trémula, como si en la franja roja estuviera parte de su dicha, le contesta conmovido: — No, Agueda, Esa es la luz de la aurora. Es el día nuevo que nace." (I, p. 49.)

Given the sad ending of the novel called *Aurora roja*, the symbol cannot be a very optimistic one in that novel. The same symbol appears once again in *El árbol de la ciencia*. "Hoy, después de siglos de dominación semítica, el mundo vuelve a la cordura, y la verdad aparece como una aurora pálida de los terrores de la noche." (II, p. 511.)

[115] Baroja, *Los amores . . .*, I, p. 1376.

[116] *Ibid.*, p. 1377.

[117] Baroja, *Aventuras, inventos . . .*, II, p. 37. The same inscription is repeated in the following works: *Zalacain el Aventurero*, I, p. 252; *Los amores tardíos*, I, p. 1326; *Canciones del suburbio*, VIII, p. 1057.

[118] Baroja, *Los pilotos de altura*, II, p. 1352.

[119] *Ibid.*, p. 1365.

[120] *Ibid.*, p. 1371.

[121] *Ibid.*, p. 1417.

[122] *Ibid.*, p. 1453.

[123] Baroja, *Rapsodias*, V, p. 863.

[124] Baroja, *Pequeños . . .*, V, p. 985.

[125] Ortega y Gasset comments on the abundance of such words in Baroja's novels. "Pues bien; los improperios son palabras que significan realidades objetivas determinadas, pero que empleamos, no en cuanto expresan éstas, sino para manifestar nuestros sentimientos personales. Cuando Baroja dice o escribe «imbécil», no quiere decir que se trata de alguien débil, *sine baculo,* que es su valencia original, ni de un enfermo del sistema nervioso. Lo que quiere expresar es su desprecio apasionado hacia esa persona. Los improperios son vocablos complejos usados como interjecciones, es decir, son palabras del evés.

La abundancia de improperios es el síntoma de la regresión de un vocabulario hacia su infancia o, cuando menos, de una puericia persistente y que se inyecta en el léxico de las personas mayores." (Ortega y Gasset, "Teoría del improperio," *El espectador, Obras,* pp. 202–203.)

[126] Baroja, *El hotel del cisne,* VIII, p. 210.

[127] Baroja, *Rapsodias,* V, p. 881.

[128] Baroja, *El hotel . . .,* VIII, p. 237.

[129] Marañón, Mercadal, I, p. 55.

[130] Baroja, *El tablado de Arlequín,* V, p. 47.

[131] Baroja, *Artículos,* V, p. 1099.

[132] Baroja, *Vitrina . . .,* V, p. 835.

[133] *Ibid.,* p. 837.

[134] A complete examination of all the works of English and American literature in Baroja's library in Itzea, Vera del Bidasoa revealed no markings. Most of these works were read in French and Spanish translations.

[135] Baroja, *Las veleidades . . .,* I, p. 1198.

[136] Baroja, *Prólogo,* I, p. XIII.

[137] Baroja, *Los enigmáticos,* VIII, p. 360.

NOTES TO CHAPTER 3
pages 44—50

[1] "A superficial glance at almost any one of Baroja's novels discloses that a good half of their space is devoted to conversation." (Dwight L. Bolinger, "Pío Baroja: A Critique" [unpublished Ph.D. dissertation, University of Wisconsin, 1936], pp. 8–9.)

[2] Baroja, *Las figuras de cera,* IV, p. 174. Significantly Baroja's dialogues produce none of these results.

[3] Benito Pérez Galdós, *Fortunata y Jacinta* (2d ed.; Argentina: Espasa-Calpe Argentina, 1951), pp. 321–22.

[4] Baroja, *Mala hierba,* I, p. 457.

[5] Marañón, Mercadal, I, p. 55.

[6] *Ibid.*

[7] *Ibid.,* p. 54.

[8] Baroja, *La caverna . . .,* V, p. 431.

[9] Baroja, *El árbol . . .,* II, pp. 558–61.

[10] Notice how one of Galdós' characters abuses the synonymous phrase.

"Pez. — Al punto a que han llegado las cosas, amigo don Francisco, es imposible, es muy difícil, es arriesgadísimo aventurar juicio alguno. La revolución de que tanto nos hemos reído, de que tanto nos hemos burlado, de que tanto nos hemos mofado, va avanzando, va minando, va labrando su camino, y lo único que debemos desear, lo único que debemos pedir, es que no se declare verdadera incompatibilidad, verdadera lucha, verdadera guerra a la muerte entre esa misma revolución y las instituciones, entre las nuevas ideas y el Trono, entre las reformas indispensables y la persona de Su Majestad." (Benito Pérez Galdós, *La de Bringas* [Madrid: Editorial Hernando, 1952], p. 63.)

[11] See Marañón's article in *La Prensa*. We have quoted the pertinent selection from this article in the preceding chapter, pages 71–72.

[12] Baroja, *Las figuras* . . ., IV, p. 174.

[13] Baroja, *El amor* . . ., IV, p. 60.

[14] Baroja, *La nave* . . ., IV, p. 458.

[15] Baroja, *Las figuras* . . ., IV, p. 189.

[16] Baroja, *La nave* . . ., IV, p. 337.

[17] *Ibid.*, p. 369.

[18] *Ibid.*, p. 426.

[19] Baroja, *Las figuras* . . ., IV, p. 302.

[20] Bolinger, p. 150.

[21] Baroja, *Las noches del Buen Retiro,* VI, p. 589.

[22] *Ibid.*

[23] *Ibid.*, p. 611.

[24] *Ibid.*, p. 615.

[25] *Ibid.*, p. 617.

[26] Baroja, *Las figuras* . . ., IV, p. 270.

[27] *Ibid.*, p. 277.

[28] We have already noted the constant use of word deflators such as *un tanto, no del todo, ¿qué quiere usted?, sin embargo, yo no creo, me parece.*

[29] Baroja, *La caverna* . . ., V, p. 437.

[30] "El andaluz era uno de los hombres que más me exasperaban; tenía la manía de alargar todas las frases, hasta a los refranes les adicionaba un pequeño suplemento de palabras. Así, por ejemplo, para decir: «No es tan fiero el león como le pintan», decía: «No es tan fiero el león como *la gente le suele* pintar.» Cualquiera hubiese creído que ganaba algo por cada palabra de más que pronunciaba.

A mí aquel hombre me ponía frenético. Alguna vez le indiqué que no alargara las vulgaridades ni empleara tanto circunloquio, y él me contestó:

— Le voy a decir lo que Periquito Martínez le dijo a Frasquito García una vez en el paseo de Baza.

Después de un preámbulo insulso, el hombre habló y habló sin decir nada, y concluyó diciendo: «Porque con eso del hablar pasa como con el comer y rascar, que ya se sabe que el comer y el rascar todo es *hasta ponerse* a empezar.»" (*Ibid.*, pp. 436–37.)

[31] Gaziel, "El error de Pío Baroja," *La Vanguardia,* February 27, 1925, Mercadal, I, p. 167.

[32] Pío Caro Baroja, p. 56.

[33] Gómez-Santos, p. 40.

[34] *Ibid.*, p. 65.

[35] *Ibid.*, p. 81.

[36] Baroja, *La nave* . . ., IV, p. 442.

[37] Baroja, *Las mascaradas sangrientas,* IV, p. 479.

[38] Bolinger, pp. 8–9.

[39] Baroja, *El cura de Monleón,* VI, pp. 806–07.

[40] Baroja, *La nave* . . ., IV, p. 457.

[41] Baroja, *El cantor vagabundo,* VIII, p. 477.

[42] Baroja, *Divagaciones* . . ., V, p. 498.

[43] Henry James and many other theorists thought that the dialogue should stand out from the other parts of the narrative in sharp relief.

[44] J. B. Trend has called his style that of one who speaks in his own home next to his own fireplace. (Mercadal, II, p. 172.) This observation seems accurate enough, but we musn't forget that it is Baroja who speaks and that it is Baroja's house and by Baroja's fireplace. Whether he is talking to friends in his diurnal *tertulia* or whether he is writing a novel or an essay, he is still exercising the great faculties and devices, consciously or unconsciously, of an artist in the fine art of communication.

[45] Baroja, *La nave* . . ., IV, p. 433.

NOTES TO CHAPTER 4
pages 63—66

[1] It is also possible to compare Pío Baroja's novelistic atmosphere or climate with that of other masters. In the creation of atmosphere in a novel or a short story he has often been compared to Edgar Allen Poe. At least in regard to his first works, he frankly admits the authenticity of this comparison. "Hay en *Vidas sombrías* cuatro o cinco cuentos imitados de Poe, alguno que otro en que se nota al lector de Dostoievski y detalles y modos de decir aprendidos de Dickens." (Pío Baroja, *Páginas escogidas* [Madrid: Casa Editorial Calleja, 1918], p. 28.)

[2] Antonio Machado, *Poesías completas* (Buenos Aires–México: Espasa-Calpe Argentina, 1952), p. 41.

[3] Baroja, *El mayorazgo* . . ., I, pp. 53–54.

[4] Uribe Echevarría, p. 140.

[5] Baroja, "Soledad," *Indice*, Nos. 70–71 [1953–1954], p. 1.

[6] Carlos Bousoño, in his *Teoría de la expresión poética* receives the same acute feelings of sadness, solitude, and hopeless dejection upon reading the short poem from Machado's *Soledades*. He also explained the process through which this feeling was created. His explanation is more scientific and more precise, but it corroborates, in every way, the procedure deduced from the comparison of the two passages.

The most important element of the poem, according to the explanation of Bousoño, is the intensifying reiteration of certain word connotations or associations. This is accomplished through the use of carefully selected words which tend to connote or to be associated with certain emotions or feelings. In this case words such as *crepúsculo, ascuas, morado, negro, cipresal, humean, sombra* and so on throughout the poem reiterate and greatly reinforce the feeling of hopeless and depressed dejection which the *símbolo bisémico, agua muerta,* elicits. Carlos Bousoño calls these words which reiterate the connotations or associations *signos de sugestión.*

In his work Bousoño gives a precise and quite detailed account of just how he feels that these sensations are produced. (Bousoño, pp. 113–19.)

[7] Along with Antonio Machado, Miguel de Unamuno and Azorín use an abundance of such words. These examples come from *Sobre el marasmo actual de España.*

"Atraviesa la sociedad española honda crisis; hay en su seno reajustes íntimos, vivaz trasiego de elementos, hervor de descomposiciones y recombinaciones, y por de fuera un desesperante marasmo." (Miguel de Unamuno, *Obras selectas* [Madrid: Editorial Plenitud, 1950], p. 132.)

"Los unos adoran al tozudo y llaman constancia a la petrificación; los otros plañen la penuria de *caracteres,* entendiendo por tales hombres de una pieza." (*Ibid.,* p. 133.)

These are from Azorín's *Castilla.*

"Leopoldo Alas ha dedicado — en su novela *Superchería* — unas páginas a pintar una de estas fondas pequeñas y destartaladas de viejas ciudades." (Azorín, *Castilla, Obras completas,* II, p. 679.)

"A la izquierda se ve una desvencijada escalera, entre tabiques deslucidos, . . ."
(*Ibid.,* p. 678.)

[8] Baroja, *El mayorazgo* . . ., I, p. 56.

[9] None of the Generation of 98 — Azorín, in particular — felt kindly towards their schoolmasters.

[10] Baroja, *El mayorazgo* . . ., I, p. 75.

[11] "Dos callejas angostas conducían a la plazuela en la cual se hallaba la antigua casa solar de Labraz: una de ellas terminaba en la muralla, delante de un arco que tenía la imagen de un Cristo, de noche iluminada por una lámpara de aceite; la otra callejuela daba vuelta al ábside de la iglesia vieja, erizado de gárgolas y canecillos, que, lanzándose en el aire, abrían sus fauces como amenazando morder los muros próximos.

En los huecos de balcones y ventanas tejían sus redes las arañas; alguna golondrina entraba en la casa y volaba, piando, azarada, ante la presencia de Micaela y Ramiro.

En algunos rincones oscuros de las guardillas, colgados de las desconchaduras de la pared por la uña de sus membranas aladas, dormían los murciélagos." (*Ibid.,* p. 123.)

[13] The term ideology here is used to indicate the manner or content of thinking characteristic to a group of people. Most of the terms indicating these ideologies will have the suffix *ism.*

[14] Luis Carvajal expresses this indifference to the different ideologies in *El cantor vagabundo.*

" — ¿Ideología? Yo no tengo ideología. Ideología no es más que pedantería." (Baroja, *El cantor* . . ., VIII, p. 481.)

"Todo es igual; no cambia más que la retórica. Fascismo, comunismo, todo eso no es nada." (*Ibid.,* p. 482.)

"¿Qué tienen como norma los comunistas? El mismo odio por el pensamiento que los católicos y los fascistas. Ya lo dijo Santo Tomás; ya lo dijo Karl Marx; luego es verdad." (*Ibid.,* p. 484.)

"Con esta idea de su superioridad y con el desprecio de los demás, el judío es hombre de pocos escrúpulos. Es el jesuíta de la acera de enfrente." (Baroja, *Vitrina* . . ., V, p. 737.)

"Lo principal para el judío intelectualista es llegar a ser algo y mandar; arrivismo, dominación y talento práctico. En esto sigue pareciéndose al jesuíta. Para llegar, todos los procedimientos son buenos; la cuestión es tener éxito." (*Ibid.*)

"El católico, como el judío socialista — los dos espiritualmente judíos —, quieren unificar el mundo, hacer operaciones aritméticas con los hombres y constituir Gobiernos ecuménicos." (*Ibid.,* p. 738.)

[15] "Conseguida la categoría de Colegiata para la iglesia, los vecinos de Labraz costearon una nueva, y en la pared de la entrada de ésta, en el lado de la Epístola, colgaron un caimán, que fué durante mucho tiempo asombro y admiración de todos los comarcanos y motivo de discusiones para los eruditos de Labraz; pues no se sabía de dónde procedía aquel caimán, ni si lo habían traído o había llegado él a Labraz por su propia voluntad." (Baroja, *El mayorazgo* . . ., I, p. 82.)

[16] "La única ventana de la capilla, cubierta por un espeso cortinaje azul, filtraba tan débil claridad, que todo aparecía velado en la penumbra azulada. Alguna umbela del retablo perfilaba sus ramos retorcidos, y sobre el fondo negro de las tablas pintadas se distinguían los nimbos de oro de las figuras como una constelación de soles apagados.

Oíanse murmullos de rezos, cuchicheo de conversaciones, roce de faldas, estruendo de toses y, de cuando en cuando, el chirriar de un postigo que se abría y se cerraba, lanzando a intervalos un dardo de luz que se hundía en el misterio lóbrego de la nave." (*Ibid.*, p. 88.)

[17] "En algunos callejones estrechos tenían que ir todos en fila. En estos pasadizos oscuros se veían efigies de santos en hornacinas, con su farolillo delante y su guirnalda de flores secas." (*Ibid.*, p. 91.)

"Dieron vuelta a la casa y salieron a la calle Mayor. La noche estaba fría y serena; el cielo, muy estrellado; las calles, oscuras; sólo alguna lámpara, colgada de una cuerda, se balanceaba ante una hornacina, iluminando alguna piadosa imagen." (*Ibid.*, p. 119.)

[18] *Ibid.*, p. 92.

[19] *Ibid.*, p. 74.

[20] "Había llegado el otoño; después de algunos días de lluvias torrenciales, el sol brillaba más pálido en los campos segados; vapores tenues flotaban en el cielo; los árboles amarilleaban y clareaban, viéndoseles las ramas negras, y en la tierra las hojas amarillas y rojizas se agitaban con furor, e iban y venían y correteaban formando torbellinos negruzcos.

De noche el viento gemía en las chimeneas, golpeaba puertas y ventanas, roncaba y silbaba con furia." (*Ibid.*, p. 106.)

[21] *Ibid.*, p. 162.

[22] *Ibid.*, pp. 101–102.

[23] "De pronto, Cesárea vaciló, dió un grito sordo y cayó en la cama hacia un lado. Su cara adquirió un tinte de cera; resonó en la alcoba un gorgoteo largo, siniestro; pocos instantes después quedó muerta." (*Ibid.*, p. 111.)

[24] *Ibid.*, pp. 112–13.

[25] *Ibid.*, p. 144.

[26] *Ibid.*, p. 129.

[27] "Recordé que aquel Swiveller era un tipo de Dickens de *El almacén de antigüedades,* y le pregunté al inglés si no creía que el novelista autor de *Pickwick* era un escritor admirable.

— Sí — me dijo muy serio —, era un buen samiota. Bebamos a su salud.

— ¿A la salud de uno que no existe? — pregunté yo.

— ¿No existe en sus obras más que la mayoría de los hombres que viven, más que tanto coleóptero que nada significa?

Bebimos a la salud de Dickens el vino rosado de la amistad.

El segundo *toast* fué en honor de Ribera, aquel gran espíritu sombrío, a quien el inglés admiraba, más que nada, por poseer uno de sus cuadros.

Concluímos la última botella con este brindis, y el inglés me dijo, en confianza, que la literatura española le parecía despreciable.

— Pero Cervantes . . .

— ¡Pech!

— Quevedo.

— ¡Psé! Entre los escritores españoles, los únicos que me gustan son el autor de *La Celestina,* el hidalgo de la oda a su padre y aquel clérigo que cuenta que llegó a un prado.

Verde e bien sencido, de flores bien poblado, logar cobdiciaduero para ome cansado." (*Ibid.*, pp. 57–58.)

[28] *Ibid.*, p. 61.

[29] *Ibid.*, p. 65.

[30] *Ibid.*, pp. 77, 81.

[31] *Ibid.*, p. 112.

[32] As pointed out in the introduction, many times different elements serve a multiplicity of purposes in the novel, but the analysis can only point them out one at a time, thus destroying the synthetic perfection and artistic beauty of the work.

33 "Escribimos estas líneas a gran distancia del lugar dichoso en donde, durante largos años, nos hemos encontrado la víspera de Navidad, en un alegre círculo de amigos. La mayoría de los corazones que palpitaban entonces a nuestro lado dejaron de latir; las manos que gustábamos estrechar están descarnadas; las pupilas que buscábamos han perdido su brillo, y, sin embargo, el recuerdo de la vieja mansión, de la gran sala, las bromas, las risas, las voces alegres, los rostros sonrientes, todo, hasta las circunstancias más frívolas de estas reuniones felices, se presentan en tropel en nuestro espíritu cuando vuelve esta fiesta." (Baroja, *El mayorazgo . . .,* I, p. 157.)

34 "La madre de la mujer, sin valor para asistir a su hija, esperaba impaciente; la cuñada del amo, sentada en el fogón, cuidaba de las ollas y andaba de un lado a otro, siempre en movimiento." (*Ibid.,* p. 157.)

35 "Después de calentarse entró frotándose las manos en el cuarto, y poco después salió seguido del marido, que daba muestras del mayor azaramiento.
— Pero ¿cree usted, señor médico . . .?
— Sí, hombre, va bien. No tengas cuidado.
Y se puso a dar zancadas en la cocina, silbando tonadillas de sus buenos tiempos de estudiante." (*Ibid.,* pp. 157–158.)

36 "Mugían los bueyes en el establo; ladraban los perros de las casas cercanas; el aire silbaba en la chimenea. De cuando en cuando se oía el sonar de las esquilas de un rebaño que un pastor llevaba a guardar al pueblo." (*Ibid.,* p. 158.)

37 *Ibid.*

38 *Ibid.,* p. 159.

39 *Ibid.,* p. 158.

40 Baroja, *Camino de . . .,* VI, p. 11.

41 The theme of suicide is found in many of the works of Unamuno, specifically in his *Nivolas.*

42 To substantiate the general statement about the frequency of suicides in Baroja's novels, here are a few instances in which they occur. The novel *La veleta de Gastizar* is darkened by the news that León, the son of *la señora de Aristy,* has committed suicide. (III, p. 1001.) In *Susana y los cazadores de moscas,* the room which the protagonist, Miguel Salazar occupies in Paris is less expensive because it has to be shared with the ghost of a person who has committed suicide there before. (VII, p. 13.) He also mentions this fact later on in the novel and the word *triste* appears again, " — Sí; sobre todo, muy triste. No le digo a usted más sino que vivo en un cuarto donde se ahorcó una vieja, y que dicen que se aparece algunas noches su fantasma." (*Ibid.,* p. 30.) In *El amor, el dandismo y la intriga* it is mentioned in connection with the ingratitude of the kings. "Louis XVIII daba pensiones a los bonapartistas y republicanos, y dejaba abandonado a Fauche-Borel, agente de los Borbones durante más de treinta años, que, viéndose en la vejez, sin amparo, acabó suicidándose." (IV, p. 33.) There are at least two suicides mentioned in *Agonías de nuestro tiempo.* Neither one of these is related to the narration; they merely form part of the sad atmosphere. (I, pp. 1141, 1250.) The thought of suicide comes forcibly to Joe's mind as he looks at the river Seine. "Los unos piensan en los miles de mujeres de los cafés, de los teatros y de los bailes; en los ojos sombreados por el *khol* y en labios pintados. Los otros, en los hambrientos y en los apaches, dispuestos a cualquier fechoría; los unos se imaginan las cenas al lado de cortesanas hermosas e incitantes; los otros, las aventuras de los cadáveres de los suicidas al resbalar por las aguas turbias y cenagosas del río, con los brazos abiertos en cruz, huyendo de las miserias de la existencia." (*Ibid.,* I, p. 1060.)

43 Baroja, *Camino de . . .,* VI, p. 14.

44 The same episode of the coffin intended for a little girl appears in Azorín's *La voluntad.* Both novels were published in 1902. Baroja and Azorín were good

friends at this time, and an incident in real life with which they were both acquainted seems to have precipitated the passage in their respective novels.

[45] *Ibid.*, pp. 79–80.

[46] "De pronto, el misterio y la sombra parecieron arrojarse sobre su alma, y un escalofrío recorrió su espalda, y echó a correr hacia el pueblo. Se sentía loco, completamente loco; veía sombras por todas partes. Se detuvo. Debajo de un farol estaba viendo el fantasma de un gigante en la misma postura de las estatuas yacentes de los enterramientos de la catedral: la espada, ceñida a un lado y en la vaina, la visera alzada, las manos juntas sobre el pecho en actitud humilde y suplicante, como correspondía a un guerrero muerto y vencido en el campo de batalla. Desde aquel momento ya no supo lo que veía las paredes de las casas se alargaban; se achicaban; en los portones entraban y salían sombras; el viento cantaba, gemía, cuchicheaba. Todas las locuras se habían desencadenado en las calles de Toledo." (*Ibid.*, p. 80.)

[47] Yécora is the name Baroja gives to Yecla, the town where Azorín attended school with the Escolapian fathers.

[48] Baroja *Camino de . . .*, VI p. 11.

[49] *Ibid.*, p. 19.

[50] *Ibid.*, p. 75.

[51] *Ibid.*, p. 74.

[52] A definite part of this religious air is a rather primitive sort of superstition. Herein is further proof that Baroja makes no distinction between the different ideologies. There had been thirteen nuns in the church of Santo Domingo el Antiguo for a long time. Other novices have joined their ranks, but according to the *portera* someone always dies so that there would be just thirteen. (*Ibid.*, p. 75.)

[53] *Ibid.*, pp. 76–77.

[54] "Tenía la idea del cristiano, de que el cuerpo es una porquería, en la que no hay que pensar. Todas estas fricciones y flagelaciones de origen pagano le parecían repugnantes. Ver a un atleta en un circo le producía una repulsión invencible." (*Ibid.*, p. 23.)

[55] It seems that Sundays are more in line with the antivital atmosphere which Baroja creates because nothing is done on those days and the streets seem a little more saddened and the sounds of life are almost completely absent.

[56] *Ibid.*, p. 77.

[57] "El café grande, con sus pinturas detestables y ya carcomidas, y sus espejos de marcos pobres, daba una impresión de tristeza y desolación." (*Ibid.*, p. 80.)

[58] "Allí todo es nuevo en las cosas, todo es viejo en las almas. En las iglesias, grandes y frías, no hay apenas cuadros ni altares, y éstos se hallan adornados con imágenes baratas traídas de alguna fábrica alemana o francesa.
Se respira en la ciudad un ambiente hostil a todo lo que sea expansión, elevación de espíritu, simpatía humana." (*Ibid.*, p. 86.)

[59] *Ibid.*, p. 87.

[60] The scene from Yécora is obviously based on Azorín's school days in Yecla with the Escolapian fathers. Telling of these days in *Las confesiones de un pequeño filósofo,* Azorín mentions Baroja's novel and tells of the imprint the terrible town of Yecla has made on his spirit. "«Yecla — ha dicho un novelista — es un pueblo terrible.» Sí que lo es; en este pueblo se ha formado mi espíritu." (*Obras completas,* II, p. 54.) Baroja sympathizes with Azorín's unhappy school days in Yecla because his own experiences with the Catholic fathers and the university professors who taught him were far from pleasant. As a young student in Pamplona he was frightened by a priest.
"Otra impresión, para mí terrible, fué una que recibí en la catedral. Yo estudiaba el primer curso de latín y tenía nueve años.

Habíamos salido del Instituto y habíamos estado presenciando unos funerales. Después entramos tres o cuatro chicos, entre ellos mi hermano Ricardo, en la catedral. A mí me había quedado el sonsonete de los responsos en el oído, e iba tarareándolo.

De pronto salió una sombra negra por detrás del confesionario, se abalanzó sobre mí y me agarró con las manos del cuello, hasta estrujarme. Yo quedé paralizado de espanto. Era un canónigo gordo y seboso, que se llamaba don Tirso Larequi." (*Juventud* . . ., V, pp. 194–95.)

In *Juventud, egolatría,* in *Intermedios,* and more extensively in his *Memorias* he criticizes the vacuity, the stupidity, and the general incompetence of nearly all his professors. Thus it is Baroja's own subjective feelings toward certain aspects of schools and churches which causes him to use them to depress the emotional climate of many of his novels.

61 "Pero de noche . . ., de noche era horroroso. Al subir después de cenar, a las nueve, desde el refectorio, frío y triste, al pasillo donde desembocaban las celdas, al arrodillarse para rezar las oraciones de la noche y al encerrarse luego en el cuarto, entonces se sentía más que nunca la tristeza de aquel presidio. Por las hendiduras de la persiana, cuyo objeto era espiar a los muchachos, se veía el corredor, apenas iluminado por un quinqué de petróleo; ya dentro de la cama, de cuando en cuando se oían sonar los pasos del guardián; del pueblo no llegaba ni un murmullo; sólo rompía el silencio de las noches calladas el golpear del martillo del reloj de la torre, que contaba los cuartos de hora, las medias horas, las horas, que pasaban lentas, muy lentas en la serie interminable del tiempo.

¡Qué vida! ¡Qué horrorosa vida! ¡Estar sometido a ser máquina de estudiar, a llevar como un presidiario el número marcado en la ropa, a no ver casi nunca el sol!" (Baroja, *El camino* . . ., VI, p. 93.)

62 "El cielo iba poniéndose negruzco, plomizo, violado por algunos sitios; una gran nube oscura avanzaba. Empezó a llover, y Ossorio apresuró su marcha. Iba acercándose a un bosquecillo frondoso de álamos, de un verde brillante. Ocultábase entre aquel bosquecillo una aldehuela de pocas casas, con su iglesia de torre piramidal terminada por un enorme nido de cigüeñas. Tocaban las campanas a misa. Era domingo.

Fernando entró en la iglesia, que se hallaba ruinosa, con las paredes recubiertas de cal, llenas de roñas y desconchaduras.

....

Y la iglesia quedó negra, vacía, silenciosa . . ." (*Ibid.,* pp. 36–37.)

63 *Ibid.,* p. 41.

64 Dawn in *Aurora roja* was a symbol of optimism, as it was in *La casa de Aizgorri.*

65 *Ibid.,* p. 36.

66 Remember Baroja's frequent use of the simile to animate, to give a dynamic and moving quality to his landscape.

67 *Ibid.,* p. 98.

68 "¡Oh, qué primavera! ¡Qué hermosa primavera! Nunca he sentido, como ahora, el despertar profundo de todas mis energías, el latido fuerte y poderoso de la sangre en las arterias. Como si en mi alma hubiese un río interior detenido por una presa, y, al romperse el obstáculo, corriera el agua alegremente, así mi espíritu, que ha roto el dique que le aprisionaba, dique de tristeza y de atonía, corre y se desliza cantando con júbilo su canción de gloria, su canción de vida; nota humilde, pero armónica en el gran corro de la Naturaleza Madre." (*Ibid.,* p. 110.)

69 "Estoy ahora aquí, sentado. ¡Qué sitio más agradable! Enfrente, por encima de las tejas, veo la torre de un convento, torcida, con su veleta adornada con un grifo largo y escuálido que tiene un aspecto cómicamente triste. Me ha parecido conveniente hacerle una salutación, y le he dirigido la palabra: «¡Yo te saludo, pobre grifo, jovial y bondadoso — le he dicho —; yo sé que, a pesar de tu actitud fiera y rampante, no eres, ni mucho menos, un monstruo; sé que tu lengua bífida

no tiene nada de venenosa, como la de los hombres y que no te sirve más que para marcar sucesivamente, y no con mucha exactitud, la dirección de los vientos! ¡Pobre grifo, jovial y bondadoso, yo te saludo y reclamo tu protección!» " (*Ibid.*, p. 113.)

[70] *Ibid.*, p. 111.

[71] *Ibid.*, p. 127.

[72] *Ibid.*, p. 129.

[73] *Ibid.*

[74] "La carretera, encharcada, llena de agujeros y de zanjas, estaba por aquella parte intransitable. El agua corría por encima de ella, formando arroyuelos, y los hierbajos brotaban entre las piedras." (Baroja, *El aprendiz . . .*, III, p. 13.)

[75] "Los tres viajeros avanzaron por la carretera hasta un camino estrecho que subía a Peñacerrada. Era una calzada sinuosa, entre dos paredes llenas de maleza; un verdadero río de fango y de inmundicias." (*Ibid.*, p. 14.)

[76] "El joven levantó su sombrero de copa y se niclinó finamente. Luego hizo avanzar al caballo por el camino; fué hundiéndose el animal, hasta dar con el vientre en el cieno, y siguió hacia adelante, chapoteando en aquella cloaca, hasta dar en una empalizada que cerraba la muralla." (*Ibid.*, p. 15.)

[77] The action of the novel here refers to those events which actually took place during the novel and does not include the story of Aviraneta's childhood which he tells to Pello in his farmhouse called Ithurbide.

[78] "La tarde estaba lluviosa y gris. Entre la niebla apenas se veía. Pello iba dirigiendo el tílburi, obedeciendo las indicaciones de Aviraneta.
— El tiempo se nos mete en aguas — murmuró Aviraneta.
— Sí; parece que sí.
— A ti eso no te preocupa; pero a mí, mucho.
— ¿Por qué?
— Por el reuma." (*Ibid.*, p. 75.)

[79] "Comenzó a llover; se oía el redoblar de las gotas de agua que azotaban los cristales de las ventanas; todas las trompetas del viento sonaban el [*sic*] unísono, silbando, cantando, mugiendo; alguna ventana chirriaba en el enmohecido gozne con un quejido lastimero, y terminaba dando un golpazo.
A veces, el viento, rugiente, parecía que iba a arrancar la casa y a llevarla en el aire; luego volvía a su moscardoneo manso y en algunos momentos se detenía, y entonces resonaba el rumor de la lluvia y el del mar." (*Ibid.*, p. 78.)

[80] "Desecho este proyecto poco conveniente para un artrítico, y me voy a la cama." (Baroja, *Las horas . . .*, V, p. 240.)

[81] Baroja, *Nuevo tablado de Arlequín*, V, p. 85.

[82] Baroja, *Familia, infancia y juventud*, VII, p. 572.

[83] "Siguió Leguía por la callejuela a una plaza triste, mísera y llena de charcos. Los balcones y ventanas de las casas estaban cerrados con tablas y con paja; dominaba un silencio angustioso, sólo interrumpido por las ráfagas de viento, que hacían golpear la puerta de la iglesia en la apolillada jamba.
Leguía encontró la posada, o lo que había sido posada, y entró en ella. Pasó a un zaguán, oscuro y húmedo, que comunicaba con un patio pequeño, cubierto de estiércol. Una escalera, estrecha y negra, subía al piso principal. Leguía llamó, dió palmadas; no apareció nadie. Sólo un gato maullaba, desesperado." (Baroja, *El aprendiz . . .*, III, p. 16.)

[84] *Ibid.*, p. 32.

[85] *Ibid.*, p. 33.

[86] Since the different towns described by Baroja are located in many different geographical regions of Spain, it would seem logical that they would differ greatly one from another, which, in reality, they do.

[87] *Ibid.,* p. 52.

[88] *Ibid.,* p. 61.

[89] There is certainly a difference in the Carlist wars in Baroja's novels and those few glimpses he gives us of the wars of 1812 fought against the French. In the second novel of the Aviraneta series, *El escuadrón del brigante*, it seems that there is a unity of purpose and a solid front of heroism opposing the French, and that the personal differences of the Spaniards and their own private interests are almost completely erased while they are facing the common enemy.

[90] Baroja, *El aprendiz . . .,* III, p. 86.

[91] *Ibid.,* p. 87.

[92] *Ibid.,* pp. 76–77.

[93] "Los caballos, cansados, marchaban muy despacio. El tiempo, aunque de invierno, estaba muy hermoso; en el cielo, azul, pasaban algunas nubes grandes, blancas como el mármol.

Al comenzar la tarde, Corito y la vieja decidieron tomar un bocado, porque estaban desmayadas. Leguía les ayudó a desmontar, y se sentaron los tres al borde de la carretera, cerca de un arroyo de agua muy pura que bajaba espumeante por entre las peñas.

Corito estaba encantada y alegre; el aire del campo daba un tono de carmín a sus mejillas, y en sus labios jugueteaba la risa. El ver a Leguía con su corbatín y su sombrero de copa en medio de aquellos breñales le producía una alegría loca. La vieja refunfuñó, porque entre las provisiones no había más que pan y queso." (*Ibid.,* pp. 16–17.)

[94] *Ibid.,* p. 1377. Almost anything which describes a complete and closed circle seems to have a special poetic interest for Baroja, the Generation of 98, and many of the writers of this century. This grinding out of useless circles must be one of the things which interests Baroja in the old-fashioned carrousel.

"Y, sin embargo, vuestro sino es cruel; cruel, porque, lo mismo que los hombres, corréis desesperadamente y sin descanso, y, lo mismo que los hombres, corréis sin objeto y sin fin . . ." (Baroja, *Paradox, rey,* II, p. 216.)

Azorín saw in this vicious circle the poetic tragedy of life.

" «Vivir — escribe el poeta — es *ver pasar.*» Sí; vivir es ver pasar: ver pasar, allá en lo alto, las nubes. Mejor diríamos: vivir es *ver volver*. Es ver volver todo en un retorno perdurable, eterno; ver volver todo — angustia, alegrías, esperanzas —, como esas nubes que son siempre distintas y siempre las mismas, como esas nubes fugaces e inmutables.

Las nubes son la imagen del Tiempo. ¿Habrá sensación más trágica que aquella de quien sienta el Tiempo, la de quien vea ya en el presente el pasado y en el pasado lo por venir?" (Azorín, II, p. 705.)

Antonio Machado was also captivated by the eternal circle of the treadmill.

> "Yo no sé qué noble,
> divino poeta,
> unió a la amargura
> de la eterna rueda
> la dulce armonía
> del agua que sueña,
> y vendó tus ojos
> ¡pobre mula vieja! . . ."

(*Poesías . . .,* p. 55.)

Later on in the century, the treadmill becomes the title and the theme of Luis Romero's novel. Part of the emotional force which comes from this tragic circle must result from its being the symbol, par excellence, of nothingness. This is expressed adequately by Truman Capote.

"And Joel realized then the truth; he saw how helpless Randolph was: more paralyzed than Mr. Sansom, more childlike than Miss Wisteria, what else could he do, once outside and alone, but describe a circle, the zero of his nothingness?" (*Other Voices, Other Rooms* [New York: The New American Library, 1960], p. 125.)

[95] Azorín noted this quality; he uses the word *indeterminismo*, as one of the most important and vital qualities of Baroja's art, in his introduction to Baroja's *Obras completas*. (I, p. xii.)

[96] Baroja, *Las veleidades . . .*, I, p. 1256.

[97] Baroja, *El gran torbellino del mundo*, I, p. 1108.

[98] "El estanque ha sido la belleza y la gracia del jardín durante largo tiempo.
En el agua, cristalina y pura, las ninfeas y los asfodelos brillaban con sus flores carnosas y palidas; los cisnes blancos trazaban estrías en el líquido de cristal; reinaba la tranquilidad y la pureza.
El estanque dormía como las lagunas de los montes en sus lechos de roca, o como los pantanos que se forman en el fondo de los bosques.
Una planta exótica, la raíz de un árbol, hizo de cuña en las paredes y abrió un boquete; las hojas muertas obturaron el cauce de entrada, y en el estanque, antes serenidad y perfume, comenzó la fermentación y la pestilencia.
Las plantas del fango se desarrollaron; las flores malsanas, de corolas espesas, comenzaron a exhalar sus perfumes embriagadores y estupefacientes. Al hálito puro y sano del agua viva sucedió el aliento febril del agua inmóvil. Las raíces, viciosas y retorcidas como serpientes, salieron de los rincones, y los peces rojos aparecieron muertos en la superficie." (Baroja, *Las veleidades . . .*, I, p. 1250.) The impression as well as the poetical procedure remind us of the poem of Machado quoted at the beginning of this chapter.

[99] *Ibid.*, p. 1287.

[100] *Ibid.*, p. 1284.

[101] Baroja, *El gran torbellino . . .*, I, p. 1052.

[102] *Ibid.*, p. 1105.

[103] The *signos de sugestión* are missing here, but the very objects which provoke them are present — the charlatans — and therefore this impression has the same atmospherical effectiveness.
"Hay quien cree que la mentira no ha de ser eterna. Es una afirmación un tanto sospechosa — piensa Joe —. El caso es que, por ahora, el mundo de los charlatanes vive con la misma fuerza de siempre. Cuando no los hay en la religión, los hay en la política, en la literatura, en el arte y en la ciencia. Así vamos saltando del cubismo al expresionismo, del psicoanálisis a la metapsíquica. Es decir, de farsa en farsa y de mixtificación en mixtificación." (Baroja, *Las velei-dades . . .*, I, p. 1229.)

[104] *Ibid.*, p. 1209.

[105] Baroja, *El gran torbellino . . .*, I, p. 1043.

[106] *Ibid.*, p. 1076.

[107] "En algunos pueblos de las costas septentrionales tienen la fantasía de dejar en el mismo corral, entre las gallinas y los cerdos, algunas de esas gaviotas blancas, *Larus Canues*, grandes y salvajes, con las alas cortadas.
Las gaviotas blancas asustan con su ferocidad a los perros, a las gallinas y a los cerdos, y no se domestican.
Cerca de Esbjerb, Joe ha visto una gaviota grande metida en un corral, que se imponía a los demás animales y les quitaba la comida.
Se cree que estas aves de pluma blanca deben de ser mansas, dóciles, buenas. Una gaviota parece que se ha de domesticar mejor que un buho, y no hay nada de eso. Joe recuerda haber visto en su niñez un buho grande, con una ala rota y los ojos fulgurantes, casi completamente domesticado.
La gaviota blanca no se domestica nunca. Su cuerpo, y al parecer también su espíritu, están hechos para el aire libre, para los temporales y para las tormen-tas." (*Ibid.*, p. 1121.)

[108] *Ibid.*, p. 1194.

[109] Baroja, *Las veleidades . . .*, I, p. 1238.

[110] *Ibid.*, p. 1206.

[111] Again movement, here that of the cyclists, is associated with life, with that which is biologically vital.

[112] Baroja, *El gran torbellino . . .*, I, p. 1090.

[113] "El otoño ha sido regular. El invierno empieza a ser muy frío. Se va encareciendo la vida por día. Gracias al racionamiento podemos vivir.
    La calefacción en el hotel es mediocre; en el quinto piso, y de noche, sobre todo, apenas se nota. Por la madrugada, en la cama, sentiría frío si no tuviera el calorífero eléctrico regalado por Evans." (Baroja, *El hotel . . .*, VIII, p. 213.)

[114] *Ibid.*, p. 208.

[115] " — Yo soy un ciudadano que va llegando al final de su vida, ya próximo — dice Pagani —. Padezco insomnios, vértigos y zumbidos de odos. Como hombre nervioso, todo me intranquiliza e inquieta: tomar el tren, esperar a una persona, cobrar una letra en un Banco. Para mí estas pequeñas diligencias son verdaderos suplicios, y no tengo ya la menor condición para la vida práctica." (*Ibid.*, p. 208.)

[116] *Ibid.*, p. 210.

[117] Death, in Baroja's novels, is a unique aspect of life. Death in his novels seems to be particularly unadorned. It never seems to be the death of a hero for a cause, nor the death of a religious man in odor of sanctity. It is merely the end of a biological existence. It is the time in life when the biological will and the power to live becomes less than that demanded by the struggle for life. This death never seems to be accompanied by the hope of a recompense in another life nor punishment in Hell. It is, in essence, what Miguel de Unamuno fears most, complete non-existence, complete nothingness.

[118] War has served this same function in many of Baroja's novels. In the *Memorias de un hombre de acción* and other novels the Carlist Wars served as an atmospherical background. The Spanish Civil War of 1936 and World War II make a frame which marks the beginning and end of *Laura, o la soledad sin remedio.*

[119] Baroja, *El hotel . . .*, VIII, p. 209.

[120] *Ibid.*

[121] Cela, *La colmena*, pp. 11–12.

[122] José Suárez Carreño, *Las últimas horas* (Barcelona: Ediciones Destino, 1954), p. 298.

NOTES TO CHAPTER 5
pages 95—96

[1] Baroja, *Camino de . . .*, VI, p. 108.

[2] Baroja, *La busca*, I, p. 263.

[3] "Dos años llevaba en la casa guardando la soldada; su ideal era que sus hijos pudiesen estudiar en un Seminario y que llegasen a ser curas." (*Ibid.*, p. 263.)

[4] "Al día siguiente de su llegada, el muchacho ayudó a servir la mesa a su madre." (*Ibid.*, p. 266.)

[5] "Uno de los comisionistas, que padecía del estómago y se pasaba la vida mirándose la lengua en el espejo, solía levantarse furioso, cuando pasaba alguna de estas cosas, a pedir a la dueña que despachase a un zascandil que hacía tantos disparates." (*Ibid.*, p. 267.)

[6] *Ibid.*, p. 277.

[7] *Ibid.*, p. 284.

[8] *Ibid.*, pp. 287–288.

[9] *Ibid.,* p. 294.

[10] *Ibid.,* p. 327.

[11] " — ¿Cómo te llamas?
— El *Expósito.*
— ¿Y por qué te llaman *Expósito?*
— ¡Toma! Porque soy inclusero.
— Y tú, ¿no has tenido nunca casa?
— Yo, no." (*Ibid.,* p. 335.)

[12] *Ibid.,* p. 359.

[13] Bousoño's phrase is defined in the preceding chapter, page 172.

[14] Baroja, *La busca,* pp. 358–59.

[15] *Ibid.,* p. 372.

[16] *Ibid.,* p. 373.

[17] His displacement has prevented him from having any illusions about life. His needs and wants seem to be basic, physical, biological ones such as food, sunshine, work, and affection.

[18] Bolinger, pp. 167–68.

[19] Uribe Echevarría, p. 128.

[20] "Baroja ha hecho de su obra una especie de asilo nocturno donde únicamente se encuentran vagabundos." (Ortega y Gasset, "Ideas sobre Pío Baroja," *El Espectador, Obras,* p. 168.)

[21] Uribe Echevarría, p. 112.

[22] " — Mira, chico: tengo la certeza, la absoluta certeza de que es la mujer más noble, más honrada y más pura de todo el mundo.

Una noche, a la salida del teatro, Fausto, venciendo su natural timidez, se decidió a seguir al militar y a la cómica, y los vió entrar en una casucha de una callejuela de no muy buena fama.

— ¿Y me ve usted todos los días con esa señorita y me pregunta por qué la acompaño? Entonces usted es tonto — y el militar, sin añadir nada más, le volvió la espalda.

No había medio de que Fausto se convenciera de la conducta escandalosa de la cómica y de que dejase de pensar en ella. El único modo lo dió la casualidad, la casualidad en forma de amor, casando a la dama, en Valencia, con un traspunte. Fausto entonces se juró a sí mismo olvidar a la pérfida; pero fué tan benévolo, que ni siquiera le lanzó una imprecación en verso ni dejó de creerla pura como la azucena." (Baroja, *Los últimos . . .,* I, pp. 819–820.)

[23] "Soportando al enfermo y al médico, en una pobre y miserable condición de domesticidad, vivió don Fausto más de diez años. No estaba enterado de nada de cuanto pasaba en la casa; alguna que otra vez quiso dar un consejo referente a la marcha de la industria, pero le demostraron que no tenía idea de lo que era el negocio y que debía callarse.

Durante una época hubo momentos en que don Fausto casi se sintió celoso; había un dependiente joven, rubio, un hortera satisfecho de sí mismo, que estaba siempre al lado de Clementina. Un día don Fausto recibió un anónimo, diciendo que su mujer le engañaba con el dependiente. Don Fausto consultó el caso con el suegro, y dijo que le iba a enseñar el papel a su mujer. El italiano miró a su yerno con curiosidad, sonrió con una sonrisa verdaderamente cínica, y dijo:

— No le digas nada a Clementina; le vas a dar un disgusto.

— Don Fausto no dijo nada, rompió la carta y se olvidó de lo que decía." (*Ibid.,* p. 827.)

24 Baroja, *Las tragedias grotescas,* I, p. 965.

25 *Ibid.,* pp. 984–986.

26 "Entre aparentar y ser hay mucha menos distancia de lo que generalmente se cree. Los valores morales no tienen la comprobación de los físicos o los químicos; un valor moral o intelectual es siempre recusable dentro de lo posible.

Las famas de Shakespeare, Miguel Angel o Velázquez pueden ser resultado de una convención; seguramente lo son en parte; pero, aunque lo fueran en todo, siempre serían las más altas del mundo artístico.

Si se pudiera medir exactamente la fuerza dinámica de los hombres, con seguridad los más fuertes no serían los más conocidos ni los más ilustrados. Las necesidades del medio social son las que crean los grandes hombres.

¡Aparentar! ¡Ser! Para don Fausto comenzaban a confundirse estos conceptos. Si se hubiera visto despreciado como marido engañado y consentido, se hubiera encontrado a sí mismo miserable; pero se veía considerado, rico, con una cinta roja en el ojal, y se sentía grande." (*Ibid.,* p. 989.)

27 *Ibid.,* pp. 994–95.

28 The idea that there is no direct relationship between happiness and exterior circumstances finds expression in the first part of the novel.

29 Baroja, *Los últimos . . .,* I, pp. 811–12.

30 "Don Fausto quería lucir su cinta roja, y al día siguiente por la mañana salió con esta intención. Por todas partes en donde se presentaba veía que la cinta roja le daba grandes preeminencias; el portero, al verle, le saludó más cariñosamente que de ordinario, y el mozo del café de Mulhouse le sirvió con mayor premura y le felicitó al mismo tiempo y le estrechó la mano." (Baroja, *Las tragedias . . .,* I, p. 990.)

31 *Ibid.,* pp. 992–93.

32 Baroja, *Aurora . . .,* I, p. 634.

33 " — No, no — replicó Yarza —. París es un pueblo podrido, peligroso . . . París es un pedestal para el francés que vale y un disolvente enorme para los demás países. Aquí se desgasta uno, pierde su carácter . . . A nosotros mismos nos tragará París.

— ¿Cree usted? — preguntó Rita entre burlona y desdeñosa —. ¿Y eso qué importa? La vida no es eterna.

— Yarza preferiría vivir en algún poblachón español y aburrirse allá — repuso Clementina burlonamente.

— Sí, señora; es cierto.

— Y casarse con una mujer de mantón y comer gazpacho y sopa de aceite — añadió Rita.

— También es verdad.

— ¿Y por qué eso? — preguntó Gálvez.

— Es que quiere hacer penitencia — dijo Pilar.

— No — replicó Yarza — Es que hay que vivir apoyado en algo, en verdades o en mentiras, en principios aceptados porque sí, por la fuerza de la raza, o en convicciones, porque si uno se desprende de todas las preocupaciones heredadas llega un momento en que se queda uno sin amparo, azotado por todos los vientos." (Baroja, *Las tragedias . . .,* I, p. 934.)

34 "En Baroja no es menos fuerte el ansia de verdad que en Unamuno y Ganivet, pero intelectualmente más temperada y resignada. Se atreve a mirar la realidad del mundo tal como es, o lo intenta, en todo caso, sobriamente, realísticamente, con todo el romanticismo del sentimiento. Se precia, ocasionalmente, de materialista en cuanto concibe el materialismo no tanto como un sistema filosófico, sino como un *procedimiento científico que no acepta fantasías ni caprichos* (*Juventud, Egolatría*). Como escéptico y fenomenólogo, sin saberlo, renuncia a una interpretación del mundo, porque sabe que de ahí necesariamente resulta una construc-

ción, y también que la mentira y el piadoso engaño de sí mismo hacen propiamente la vida posible, pues la *mentira es lo más vital que tiene el hombre.*" (Jeschke, p. 83.)

[35] Baroja, *Las figuras* . . ., IV, p. 174.

[36] Baroja, *La caverna* . . ., V, pp. 406, 408.

[37] Baroja, *La dama* . . ., II, p. 249.

[38] Baroja, *La ciudad de* . . ., II, p. 393.

[39] Baroja, *La sensualidad* . . ., II, pp. 908–09.

[40] "A veces, en medio de mis trabajos, se me ocurre pensar en mi vida y en la de los demás; por ejemplo, en la de Joshé Mari, y obtengo una conclusión: que la tradición no es algo que incline al bien, como se quiere decir; pero sí algo vital, algo que da energía a la vida, porque impide que la inteligencia arruine la personalidad, empeñándose en resolver problemas irresolubles." (*Ibid.*, p. 984.)

[41] *Ibid.*, pp. 950, 989.

[42] *Ibid.*, p. 882.

[43] "Me hubiera gustado leer algo que me hubiese aclarado mis vacilaciones y mis dudas. Entre los libros que tenía mi tío, llevados allí de la Mota del Ebro para adornar su despacho, había la *Historia Natural,* de Buffon, en varios tomos.
En uno de ellos encontré estas dos frases, que me sorprendieron:
— ¿Por qué el amor hace la felicidad de todos los seres y la desgracia del hombre? ¿Es que únicamente lo físico es lo bueno en esta pasión? ¿Es que lo moral no vale nada?»
Y la otra frase era: «Queriendo fijarse en el sentimiento, el hombre no hace más que abusar de su ser y abrir en su corazón un vacío que nada es capaz de llenar.»
Estas dos tesis acerca del amor tan del siglo XVIII me parecieron muy acertadas. Yo veía claramente que así debía ser; comprendía que lo contrario no eran más que perturbaciones producidas por la abstinencia." (*Ibid.*, p. 883.)

[44] *Ibid.*

[45] Interest in the vital illusions built around the character Don Juan has been intensified in Spain during this century. Creative works such as Unamuno's *El hermano de Juan, o el mundo es teatro,* Pérez de Ayala's *Tigre Juan* and *El curandero de su honra,* Azorín's *Don Juan,* Jacinto Grau's *El burlador que no se burla* are examples of this interest. Marañón's *Don Juan: Ensayos sobre el origen de su leyenda,* Maeztu's *Don Quijote, don Juan y la Celestina* are manifestations of this interest expressed in essays.

[46] Baroja, *La sensualidad* . . ., II, p. 879.

[47] *Ibid.*, p. 916.

[48] *Ibid.*, p. 919.

[49] *Ibid.*, p. 994.

[50] *Ibid.*

[51] *Ibid.*, pp. 929–30.

[52] Baroja's considering of the Catholic faith as a vital illusion recalls a chapter from *The Brothers Karamazov.* Ivan has written a poem called the "Grand Inquisitor." In this poem the Grand Inquisitor plainly tells Christ that this religion is just a vital fiction which he himself cannot believe but that it is necessary for the masses.
"The most painful secrets of their conscience, all, all they will bring to us, and we shall have an answer for all. And they will be glad to believe our answer, for it will save them from the great anxiety and terrible agony, they endure at present in making a free decision for themselves. And all will be happy, all the millions of creatures except the hundred thousand who rule over them. For only we, we who guard the mystery, shall be unhappy. There will be thousands of millions of happy babes, and a hundred thousand sufferers who have taken upon themselves the

curse of the knowledge of good and evil. Peacefully they will die, peacefully they will expire in Thy name, and beyond the grave they will find nothing but death. But we shall keep the secret, and for their happiness we shall allure them with the reward of heaven and eternity." (Fyodor Dostoyevsky, *The Brothers Karamazov*, trans. Constance Garnett [New York: The Modern Library, 1940], p. 308.)

53 Baroja, *La sensualidad* . . ., II, p. 929.

54 *Ibid.*, p. 939.

55 *Ibid.*, p. 986.

56 "El instinto de que todo en la vida está compensado, es un instinto muy popular que nace de un anhelo de justicia. Así, en los cuentos, los enanos feos son muy listos; los gigantes, muy torpes y muy brutos. En las religiones, los que sufren en el mundo gozan en el cielo, y al contrario. En la literatura romántica, Lucrecia Borgia, muy guapa, es de espíritu abominable; en cambio, Cuasimodo, muy feo, es de alma casi celestial.

En contra de estos buenos trascendentalismos morales, religiosos y literarios, los demás no hemos podido vislumbrar en tales buhardillones mundanos más que desorden caótico, oscuridad, casualidad; la rifa hecha por la Fortuna sin seso, con su clásica rueda, de los bonitos juguetes salidos antes de su cuerno, y hasta un poco de olor diabólico, que sería de azufre si el diablo no hubiese sustituído modernamente un olor tan sencillo y tan rudo por otros perfumes y esencias más penetrantes y enervadores, elaborados en las mejores fábricas alemanas de productos químicos." (Baroja, *Las veleidades* . . ., I, p. 1197.)

57 "En nuestra época de nacionalismo se ha desarrollado el orgullo étnico de manera tan absurda, que todo el mundo ha echado una mirada retrospectiva hacia sus antepasados, pensando que quizá de ellos y de su lejana influencia pudiera venir algo tranquilizador.

«Así, en una época destructora por excelencia — ha pensado Joe —, en la cual se han descompuesto y han cambiado la Geometría y la Física y hasta las ideas clásicas sobre el Espacio y el Tiempo, podemos creer en serio en unos mitos tan vagos como la raza y la sangre. Verdad es que el hombre únicamente cree en serio en los mitos.» (Baroja, *El gran torbellino* . . ., I, p. 1095.)

58 *Ibid.*, pp. 1187–88.

59 *Ibid.*, p. 1154.

60 See page 161.

61 Baroja, *Las veleidades* . . ., I, p. 1238.

62 *Ibid.*, p. 1247.

63 Baroja, *El cura* . . ., VI, p. 876.

64 *Ibid.*, pp. 880–81.

65 This tendency of the dialogue to reduce itself to monologue has been discussed in the chapter on dialogue.

66 Baroja, *El árbol de* . . ., II, p. 507.

67 *Ibid.*, p. 510.

68 *Ibid.*, pp. 510–11.

69 *Ibid.*, p. 511.

70 "Hay, por último, los que quieren volver a las ideas viejas y a los viejos mitos, porque son útiles para la vida. Estos son profesores de retórica, de esos que tiene [*sic*] la sublime misión de contarnos cómo se estornudaba en el siglo XVIII después de tomar rapé; los que nos dicen que la ciencia francesa, y que el materialismo, el determinismo, el encadenamiento de causa a efecto es una cosa grosera, y que el espiritualismo es algo sublime y refinado. ¡Qué risa! ¡Qué admirable lugar común para que los obispos y generales cobren su sueldo y los comerciantes puedan vender impunemente bacalao podrido." (*Ibid.*, p. 512.)

71 *Ibid.*

[72] *Ibid.*, p. 514.

[73] Baroja, *La ciudad* . . ., II, p. 443.

[74] *Ibid.*, p. 444.

[75] Baroja, *La feria de los discretos*, I, p. 804.

[76] Baroja, *El cantor* . . ., VIII, p. 596.

[77] Baroja, *Las veleidades* . . ., I, p. 1224.

[78] Baroja, *El cura* . . ., VI, p. 822.

[79] Baroja, *El amor* . . ., IV, p. 15.

[80] Baroja, *Nuevo tablado* . . ., V, p. 133.

[81] D. L. Shaw, "A Reply to *Deshumanización* — Baroja on the Art of the Novel," *Hispanic Review*, XXV (1957), p. 111.

[82] Baroja, *El cantor* . . ., VIII, p. 596. The reader comes to enjoy a heightened sensitivity to these same things.

[83] Baroja, *El caballero* . . ., VII, p. 386.

[84] Baroja, *La intuición y el estilo*, VII, p. 1001.

[85] "«Kant no se pregunta qué es o cuál es la realidad, qué son las cosas, qué es el mundo. Se pregunta, por el contrario, cómo es posible el conocimiento de la realidad de las cosas del mundo.»

A mí no me parece esta posición extraña, sino muy natural y muy lógica. En un orden metafísico, es la misma que la que tiene el bacteriólogo cuando comienza por probar su microscopio, o el astrónomo sus aparatos. Estos investigadores necesitan saber las garantías de exactitud que tienen sus instrumentos de trabajo. Esto naturalmente, no es una suspicacia. Es la desconfianza lógica sobre los medios de conocer enfrente de los dogmáticos, que creen que un juego de palabras es una demostración axiomática." (*Ibid.*, p. 986.)

NOTES TO CHAPTER 6
page 123

[1] Bolinger, p. 147.

[2] "Estimo superfluo, desde luego, insistir más sobre este punto. Todos sus lectores asiduos saben — unos, los más, por comprensión directa; otros, los menos, de un modo vagamente intuitivo — que la mayor fuerza de atracción en sus obras reside en esas legiones de seres vivos que bullen y palpitan en ellas. No es necesario, pues, hacer hincapié en este extremo." (Francisco Pina, *Pío Baroja* [Spain: Editorial Sempere, 1928], pp. 50–51.)

[3] Para Baroja la novela no es un conjunto predeterminado de sucesos que se escalonan en armónica trabazón a cargo de tales o cuales personajes escogidos previamente y con funciones señaladas, ni es tampoco el relato de una historia, hazaña o aventura más o menos importante y de mayor o menor interés. Para él ha sido siempre — sobre todo — un desfile heterogéneo de seres humanos, cuyos antecedentes y circunstancias quedan expuestos en las páginas de sus libros, al mismo tiempo que los ambientes en que se desenvuelven." (Ballesteros de Martos, quoted by Pina, p. 51.)

[4] "Pero como en todas, lo más sugestivo, lo más extraordinario, lo más poderoso que hay en *Las figuras de cera* es ese continuo desfile de personajes, descritos a maravilla, que revelan una facultad observadora, inquisitiva y creadora, que se puede calificar de genial. Nadie hasta ahora la ha superado, y es difícil que nadie la pueda superar. Ni Balzac, ni Dickens, ni Galdós llegaron a tanto, si bien tuvieron cualidades artísticas que a Baroja faltan y que establecen las diferencias, porque de categorías no es prudente hablar." (*Ibid.*, pp. 51–52.)

[5] Bolinger, p. 161.

[6] *Ibid.*

7 *Ibid.*, p. 162.

8 Baroja, *Páginas escogidas*, p. 42.

9 *Ibid.*, p. 122.

10 *Ibid.*, p. 260.

11 *Ibid.*, p. 320.

12 Baroja, *El mayorazgo* . . ., I, p. 70.

13 Baroja, *Los caminos del mundo*, III.

14 Juan Uribe Echevarría mentions the portrait of the latter in a chapter of his book called *Camino de perfección, Novela-Clave del 98.*
"Ossorio visita al gobernador civil de la ciudad, que es su amigo. En la pensión alterna con dos curas simpáticos: don Manuel y don Pedro Nuño. Bajo la sotana de este último Baroja nos retrata a don Juan Valera, casticista, enemigo del neo-cristianismo de Tolstoy y de las novedades literarias de los escritores nórdicos."
"Como yo he escrito siempre de una manera un tanto descuidada, pinté un tipo de cura de Toledo que, en el fondo, era una contrafigura del autor de Pepita Jiménez." (Uribe Echevarría, p. 142.)

15 Juan Uribe also documents this relationship.
"En El Paular conoce a Max Schulze, alemán de Nüremberg, aficionado a España y fanático de Nietzsche.

Este Max Schulze es la contrafigura de Paul Schmitz *(Dominik Müller),* escritor suizo, de Basilea, con quien Baroja hizo excursiones por El Paular y Toledo. Schmitz, amigo también de Azorín, Maeztu y otros escritores del 98, les dió a conocer las doctrinas de Federico Nietzche que tanta influencia ejercieron en los escritores mencionados." (*Ibid.*, p. 139.)

16 "El escritor puede imaginar, naturalmente, tipos e intrigas que no ha visto; pero necesita siempre el trampolín de la realidad para dar saltos maravillosos en el aire. Sin ese trampolín, aun teniendo imaginación, son imposibles los saltos mortales." (Baroja, *La nave* . . ., IV, p. 320.)

17 Pina, p. 47.

18 Ortega y Gasset, "Ideas sobre . . .," *Obras,* p. 191.

19 Benjamín Jarnés, "Baroja y sus desfiles," *Revista de Occidente,* XLII (1932), quoted in part by Uribe Echevarría, p. 127.

20 Baroja, *César* . . ., II, p. 575.

21 Baroja, *Las inquietudes* . . ., II, p. 1040.

22 Baroja, *La nave* . . ., IV, p. 364.

23 Baroja, *Las figuras* . . ., IV, p. 185.

24 Baroja, *Los caminos* . . ., III, p. 365.

25 *Ibid.*

26 Sender, p. 101.

27 Baroja, *La caverna* . . ., V, p. 411.

28 "No todo el mundo puede ser sano, ni todo el mundo ser bueno. Yo aún no lo puedo ser, y como no lo puedo ser, al enviarte esta dote a ti, hermana mía, para que puedas vivir con tu marido, pienso que ésta es mi venganza, la venganza del abandonado, la venganza del sarnoso contra el sano, la venganza del miserable con el descendiente de la familia considerado y mimado." (Baroja, *Las inquietudes* . . ., II, p. 1123.)

29 "Yo pensaba que Machín era, sin duda, un hombre violento, capaz de cosas buenas y de cosas malas, dispuesto lo mismo a salvar a una persona exponiendo su vida que a asesinarla; pero ni al mismo Larragoyen, que era una persona sensata, le pude convencer de esto." (*Ibid.*, p. 1121.)

30 *Ibid.*, p. 1130.

[31] Baroja, *El gran torbellino* . . ., I, p. 1182.

[32] It does not seem very virtuous to spend an unlimited fortune on such a capricious enterprise as a gigantic landscape garden.

[33] Baroja, *El mayorazgo* . . ., I, pp. 69–70.

[34] "No; porque, aun encontrándola, no sabríamos si era absoluta o no; para mí no hay más que verdades agradables y verdades desagradables . . . Las agradables hay que aceptarlas siempre; las otras, rechazarlas . . . Yo no sé pintar, es cierto; pero me he hecho la ilusión de que pinto bien y vivo. ¿Para qué me voy a convencer de que no sé pintar?

— Usted quiere entonces — repuso Bengoa — que vivamos adormecidos con nuestras ilusiones en un continuo sueño.

— En un sueño continuo, eso es; pero en un sueño agradable.

— Sin conseguir nada, sin realizar nada.

— Eso, eso . . . ¡Conseguir!, ¡realizar! Es la muerte. Todos esos ingleses y franceses y yanquis es lo que quieren: conquistar las cosas, realizarlas . . . ¡Desdichados!

— ¿Por qué?

— Porque sí. Esas manzanas de oro del jardín de las Hespérides están por dentro agusanadas. Vale más verlas y decir: ¡Oh, qué hermosas manzanas! ¡Oh, qué manzanas tan hermosas! Pero no hay que probarlas, porque están podridas." (*Ibid.*, pp. 119–20.)

[35] Baroja, *El laberinto de las sirenas,* II, p. 1224.

[36] Baroja, *La sensualidad* . . ., II, p. 934.

[37] Baroja, *La casa de* . . ., I, p. 41.

[38] Baroja, *Las inquietudes* . . ., II, pp. 1071–72.

[39] Baroja, *Camino de* . . ., VI, p. 113.

[40] Ortega y Gasset, "La deshumanización del arte e ideas sobre la novela," *Obras,* p. 949.

[41] *Ibid.*, pp. 948–49.

[42] *Ibid.*, p. 949.

[43] Ortega y Gasset, "Espíritu de la letra," *Obras,* p. 989.

[44] Baroja, *La nave* . . ., IV, pp. 319–20.

[45] " — El tamaño quizá influye también — añadió Aviraneta —. Si las figuras fueran mayores o menores que el natural, probablemente no darían tanto la impresión de cosas muertas; pero esos gabanes usados, esas gorras, esos sombreros, que los han llevado seguramente gentes vivas, nos sugiere un poco la vida del difunto.

— ¡Qué macabros están ustedes! — exclamó el pintor.

— No, macabros, no. Insistimos un poco para aclarar — replicó Ochoa —. Indudablemente tiene usted razón, don Eugenio. El tamaño influye mucho. Es el del natural; por tanto, el del muerto. Aumentándolo o achicándolo, bastaría probablemente para quitar esa impresión. Un muñeco no da nunca esa sensación desagradable, porque no hay la posibilidad de confundirle con una persona. ¿Por qué la posibilidad de la confusión es tan desagradable?

— Es la posibilidad del fantasma, del espectro — dijo Aviraneta —. Un fantasma como una mosca o como un monte no podría ser fantasma asustador." (Baroja, *Las figuras* . . ., IV, pp. 235–36.)

[46] Baroja, *El amor* . . ., IV, p. 26.

[47] Baroja, *La caverna* . . ., V, p. 417.

[48] Baroja, *César* . . ., II, p. 573.

[49] Pina, p. 50.

[50] Baroja, *Las figuras* . . ., IV, p. 232.

51 Baroja, *Silvestre Paradox*, II, pp. 11–12. These accessories so necessary to the individualization of characters are, of course, nothing more than a vestige of vital illusion.

52 Baroja, *Las figuras* . . ., IV, p. 247.

53 Baroja, *La nave* . . ., IV, pp. 338–39.

54 Baroja, *Las figuras* . . ., IV, p. 189.

55 Pachi in *Las coles de cementerio* provides a fine example of these little displaced creatures who have their own particular system of values. He is allowed to cultivate a small portion of the cemetery and from it he makes a living for seven orphan children. Baroja, VI, p. 1028.

NOTES TO CHAPTER 7
pages 143—150

1 Baroja, *La ciudad* . . ., II, pp. 329–30.

2 Pina, pp. 41–42.

3 Marguerite Rand, *Castilla en Azorín* (Madrid: Revista de Occidente, 1957), pp. 146–47, 176–77.

4 Azorín, *Castilla, Obras completas*, II, p. 698.

5 It is perhaps worthwhile to note that the verb *eran* placed in this context of great movement and vitality seems to acquire some activating potential. "A medida que avanzábamos, las filas de barcos eran más nutridas." You could almost say here that *eran más nutridas* here really means, or means the same as, *iban creciendo.*

6 Laín Entralgo denies this autonomy of the description of the landscape in Baroja and other members of the Generation.
"En las imágenes, en las metáforas, en los juicios estimativos de Baroja late una actitud del escritor ante la vida histórica del país a que el paisaje castellano pertenece." (Laín Entralgo, p. 28.)
"La naturaleza, el nativo temperamento y la peculiar biografía del artista, una idea de la historia que acaeció y de la vida que bulle sobre la tierra contemplada: he ahí los tres elementos que se conjugan en los paisajes castellanos de Baroja, de Unamuno, de *Azorín*, de Machado." (*Ibid.*)

7 This movement is mentioned by Laín Entralgo. "Más movediza, más cambiante que la de *Azorín* y, por descontado, mucho más espontánea y metafórica." (*Ibid.*, p. 27.)

8 Although it would not have the same intensity of esthetic and emotional appeal outside of *La ciudad de la niebla* and outside of Baroja's works as a whole, it has an appreciable amount of esthetic appeal in a completely isolated position.

9 The device, the mention of the illusion, and the use of the two illusions which are inherent in the situation being described are quite similar to a device described in *Teoría de la expresión poética* of Carlos Bousoño. Carlos Bousoño has called this device a *superimposición situacional* which means that a situation which is illusory is taken for real. This is, of course, the case in all optical illusions. Baroja has done nothing more than place the perceiver in contact with the illusion; the *superimposición situacional* is inherent in the illusion. (Bousoño, pp. 172–81.)

10 Baroja, *La intuición* . . ., VII, pp. 1088, 1094.

11 Juan B. González, "Aspectos de la obra de Pío Baroja," *Nosotros*, Mercadal, II, p. 290.

12 Sender, pp. 111–12.

13 James T. Farrell, in a speech given at the Ethical Society in St. Louis in 1959, expressed this same interest in the ephemeral. Nothing is of less value because it is ephemeral.

14 Baroja, *La dama* . . ., II, p. 232.

[15] Bolinger, p. 109.

[16] Thus, Baroja's preference for the mountainous Basque country as opposed to the monotony of Castilla. "Sobre su extensión monótona vierte el cielo unas veces la luz de un azul uniforme.... La tierra recorrida por Alvarito no era igual, ni monótona, ni uniforme; no semejaba a un mar..." (Baroja, *La nave* ..., IV, p. 411.)

[17] Baroja, *La caverna* ..., V, p. 399.

[18] Laín Entralgo, p. 26.

[19] Baroja, *Páginas* ..., p. 21.

[20] Azorín, *Madrid, Obras completas,* VI, p. 216.

[21] Bolinger, p. 105.

[22] Baroja, *El mayorazgo* ..., I, pp. 53–54.

[23] It has been understood that this city is La Guardia. This seems to have no implications for the study of Baroja's descriptive technique.

[24] This use of stationary objects in the description seems to be a matter of chance. The first page has an excellent example of a description in which the objects described are moving. The movement does add a great deal to the dynamic quality of the passage.

"Avanzaba la noche; el cielo estaba negro; la luna llena salía del seno de un nubarrón negruzco para volverse a ocultar; el viento soplaba fuertemente, y aquel correr de las nubes daba un extraño y fantástico aspecto al paisaje.

Tan pronto dominaba la oscuridad como brillaba la luz clara de la luna y aparecían en el suelo las grandes sombras de los matorrales."

These are the first lines of *El mayorazgo de Labraz.* (Baroja, I, p. 58.) It is interesting to note that movement in the sky causes the illusion of movement and vitality on the land. This is not pointed out, but it is felt by both the author and the reader.

[25] It is quite possible that such a technique could be learned by critical watching of good movies in which the camera was moved with intelligence and sensibility. Baroja, unlike Azorín, did not frequent the movie house. He had to learn this technique from actual observation. He abhorred describing anything he had never seen and laughed at Galdós and other authors for this practice. They wrote about realistic details which they had not seen but only imagined.

"No podían tener los neorrománticos los ímpetus y la audacia de sus antecesores del principio del siglo; pretendían defenderse con una mayor observación, con más fidelidad en las descripciones de los tipos y de las costumbres.

Los detalles realistas abundaban en las obras de estos autores. Eran detalles realistas imaginados, no vistos y vividos." (Baroja, *Rapsodias,* V, p. 866.)

[26] Baroja, *El mayorazgo* ..., I, p. 53.

[27] *Ibid.*

[28] Baroja, *La veleta* ..., III, p. 863.

[29] This complete autonomy does not always hold true, as can be seen in the next few pages of the novel. They have arrived at the inn and Lacy contemplates the storm.

"Un olor de raíces y de tierra húmeda *venía* del suelo. A veces *había ráfagas de viento huracanado.* El follaje amarillo y rojizo de los árboles *se desprendía,* dejando las ramas desnudas; algunas hojas grandes, *al volar* por el aire, *parecían murciélagos* de vuelo tortuoso o *nubes de mariposas* que *al agitarse daban* el vértigo.

La hojarasca seca del camino *corría de aquí para allí* como en un sábado de brujas, *galopando* en *frenéticos escuadrones, volando* por encima de las copas de los árboles, *aplastándose* sobre los troncos y *quedando* inmóviles en los charcos." (*Ibid.,* III, pp. 867–68.)

The underlined words and phrases indicate that all the elements of motion are included here. Moreover, the simile which compares the huge leaves which were flying through the air to bats in tortuous flight or to clouds of butterflies whose agitation cause vertigo, adds a great deal to the sensation of movement and vitality. The passage has a superabundance of devilish movement. But the artistic autonomy of the passage is curtailed somewhat by linking the total picture to Lacy's thoughts:

" — Dejan la vida en la inmovilidad para irse a la libertad y a la muerte — se dijo Lacy a sí mismo —. Así hacemos nosotros los hombres; unos para caer en el fango como ellas, otros para quedar olvidados en la cuneta del camino." (*Ibid.*, III, p. 868.)

It is true that the comparison comes after the description and does not intervene directly in it, but it does seem to take away some of the artistic purity of the description. It is only artistically justified in part by the fact that the entire book is a prediction of the storm or the fate which is to befall the liberals when they invade Spain in the next novel. Here Lacy predicts his own death.

30 Gonzalo Torrente Ballester, *Panorama de la literatura española contemporánea* (Madrid: Ediciones Guadarrama, 1956), p. 188.

This directness and authenticity of the landscape is mentioned by most of the critics.

"He dicho y escrito, por otra parte, muchas veces que Baroja ha elaborado los retratos mejores, más finos, más sensibles de nuestra literatura moderna y que sus paisajes son maravillosos por lo directos, por la ausencia total de cartón que se nota en ellos." (José Pla, *Don Pío Baroja,* Mercadal, I, p. 239.)

31 Baroja, *El laberinto . . .,* II, p. 1176.

32 It should be made clear that the term artistic autonomy refers to the description as such and not to the work as a whole. The story deals with landscape gardening on a gigantic scale, carried out by a millionaire. One could easily find many such stories. Edgar Allan Poe's *The Domain of Arnheim,* (*The Works of Edgar Allan Poe* [New York and London: Funk and Wagnalls Company, 1904], VII), is quite similar to *El laberinto de las sirenas.* This, however, does not seem to detract from the directness, authenticity, or artistic autonomy of both man-made and natural landscape.

33 Baroja, *El laberinto . . .,* II, p. 1171.

34 *Ibid.*

35 *Ibid.*

36 Baroja, *La familia . . .,* VI, p. 259.

37 Baroja, *La leyenda de Jaun de Alzate,* VI, pp. 1147–48.

38 "Ya crieban los albores e vinie la mañana, ixie el sol, Dios, ¡qué fermoso apuntava!" (R. Menéndez Pidal, *Cantar de Mio Cid* [Madrid: Espasa-Calpe, 1946], III, p. 1042, 11. 456, 457.)

39 It is easy to discern that the only raison d'être of these two poems from *Canciones del suburbio* is to express this poetic reality.

SENSACIONES DE OTOÑO

El Guadarrama.
"Muralla del Guadarrama,
cielo azul, resplandeciente,
aire de tarde, relente,
viento que silba y que brama,
olor de jara y retama,
de tomillo y de romero;
montes de color de acero,
ceñuda tranquilidad,
reposo, serenidad,
lento anochecer severo."

Rioja.
"Pálida niebla de otoño,
blanco cendal de la tierra,
manchas de nieve en la sierra
de Cantabria y de Toloño.
Ebro turbio y cenagoso;
olmos de hojas amarillas,
Cárdenas y Najerillas
por el campo deleitoso;
horas de sol de sesteo,
vino blanco riojano,
conversación mano a mano,
versos del viejo Berceo."

(Baroja, *Canciones del suburbio,* VIII, p. 1003.)

NOTES TO CHAPTER 8

pages 162—164

[1] *Yoísmo* is a term indicating the projection of the author, or facets of the author, into the literary work.

[2] "De cada nueva etapa nos dejará un libro nuevo, lleno de cosas inesperadas, sombrías y, en el fondo, encantadoras; y al cerrarlo, una y otra vez repetiremos, parodiando el título de una de sus mejores novelas: Baroja es así." (Marañón, p. 66.)

[3] "Puesto que la mentalidad de Pío Baroja es tan exuberante, impresionable y expansiva, le hubiera convenido dedicarse al ensayo y al artículo de periódico, labor que ha rehusado obstinadamente. En el ensayo o el artículo hubiera logrado vaciar el exceso de ideas y sensaciones que se le acumulan. Un modo de «desangrarse» y poder quedar así más ligero, más desembarazado para la obra de pura imaginación. Por el contrario, Pío Baroja parece que llegase al momento de la novela con el espíritu y los nervios sobrecargados; con una balumba de cosas por decir; con el ánimo dispuesto a opinar sobre lo divino y lo humano, y a discutir con todo y contra todo." (Salaverría, p. 109.)

No one can deny, of course, that there is a great similarity between Baroja's novels and his essays. It would be a simple matter to include some of his articles in his novels or vice versa.

[4] Peseux-Richard, p. 187.

[5] "El mismo, sin embargo, ¿es un novelista? ¿Se puede dar el nombre de novelas a esas intrigas postizas que sirven de pretexto a un interminable desfile, a veces divertido, a veces monótono y frío de siluetas, de croquis, de simples notas, de vulgares sucesos, desenfardo incesante de carnets y de fichas, en las que el ingenio real se mezcla con la bufonada pretenciosa? Pero esos libros ¿tienen verdaderamente otro objeto que el de exponer los diversos estados de su alma?" (Laborde, p. 55.)

[6] "Es evidente que Baroja no sabría plegarse a las reglas habituales de un género, y nuestros editores mirarían con perplejidad estos dos gruesos volúmenes, donde el primer plano está ocupado, la mayor parte del tiempo por personajes accesorios que no tienen otro interés que descubrirnos poco a poco al hombre extraño que domina la obra." (Pillement, p. 77.)

[7] González, p. 295.

[8] "En cuanto a la personal representación, puede sentarse que los aventureros de Baroja son otros tantos yoes o momentos diversos del yo autor. Su movilidad nace del disgusto con la vida circundante, y sus acciones son diversos ensayos de una energía afanosa de mejorar, de superar lo torcido o vicioso actual. Dotados de una agudeza especial, sienten dolorosamente y se rebelan." (*Ibid.*, p. 298.)

This statement occurs again in *Juventud, egolatría.* "El escritor tiene siempre delante de sí como un teclado con una serie de yoes." (Baroja, *Juventud, . . .*, V, p. 156.)

[9] Baroja, *La caverna . . .*, V, p. 452.

[10] Granjel, p. 165. Ramón Sender seems to become a little annoyed when Baroja speaks of the narcissism of Valle-Inclán. He points out that Valle-Inclán has never written a page about himself while Baroja occupies the center of almost everything he writes.

"Pío Baroja ha publicado ocho volúmenes de memorias y anuncia otros. Tres mil páginas que no eclipsarán las confesiones de Rousseau ni el diario de Amiel, pero que tienen su encanto. Por supuesto, no habla bien de nadie. Tampoco francamente mal, con la excepción de Valle-Inclán, Unamuno y el pintor Solana. Ataca preferentemente a sus colegas muertos (de los vivos a ninguno, lo que podría ser revelador) y es curioso que el centro y objeto preferente de sus iras

siga siendo la "vanidad narcisista de Valle-Inclán," cuando este poeta no escribió
una sola página sobre sí mismo." (Sender, p. 95.)
    Baroja should be, and is, the first to admit this. He is continually defending his
right to be more concerned with himself in the novel than with other people.
    "No creo que la tendencia a lo autobiográfico indique siempre vanidad o
egolatría.
    Al querer hablar de la juventud de mi tiempo comenzaba a referirme, sin pro-
ponérmelo de antemano, más a la mía que a la de los demás, y me desenmascaré
ante mis ojos." (Baroja, *Rapsodias*, V, p. 864.)

11 Baroja, *Las figuras* . . ., IV, pp. 195–96.

12 Baroja, *La caverna* . . ., V, p. 401. These words are uttered by the learned Doctor
Schadenfrente in *La caverna del humorismo*, but it seems evident that they express
a very personal sentiment held by Baroja.

13 *Ibid.*, pp. 402–403.

14 " — «La copia es crítica y no creación», dice Ortega y Gasset; yo no lo creo.
No creo que se pueda copiar simplemente en el arte, sin poner algo. Si Holbein,
Durero, el Ticiano y *el Greco* vivieran, podrían copiar los cuatro la misma figura,
esforzarse en hacer un retrato parecido, y, sin embargo, cada uno le daría un
carácter irremisiblemente suyo." (*Ibid.*, p. 414.)
    Interpretation, for this same reason, does not escape this projection of the ego.
Therefore it becomes a lesser creation.
    "No hay diferencia en el fondo; todos son igualmente interpretadores, y la
interpretación es una creación más o menos subalterna." (*Ibid.*, p. 403.)

15 *Ibid.*, p. 438.

16 "Con relación a los ensayos, pasa igual; son tan viejos como el mundo, que no
tienen de nuevo más que el título. Montaigne puso un rótulo nuevo a un género
viejo y le añadió ingenuidad y gracia.
    «Yo quiero — dice — que se me vea en mi manera de ser, sencilla, natural y
ordinaria, sin estudio y sin artificio, porque soy yo lo que pinto. Mis defectos se
señalarán a lo vivo; mis imperfecciones y mi forma, cándida, tanto como mi reve-
rencia pública me lo permite.» " (Baroja, *Artículos*, V, p. 1108.)

17 Baroja, *Rapsodias*, V, p. 868.

18 "El niño ríe por alegría; es el primer escalón. El humorista ríe con tristeza; es el
último escalón." (Baroja, *La caverna* . . ., V, pp. 425–26.)

19 "Se necesita también la vejez." (*Ibid.*, p. 427.) Baroja was forty-seven when he
was writing this work.

20 "Entonces, hágase usted también humorista. Convierta usted en risa sus motivos
de queja. A usted, como a todo el mundo, le aceptaremos todo menos el ser aburrido." (*Ibid.*, pp. 432–33.)

21 The first of these three types is the spectator as we have already seen. The second
type is exemplified by those characters who flee from life and from themselves.
Granjel has discussed them in a chapter called "Abúlicos y Nietzscheanos,"
(Granjel, pp. 183–97.) The third type is made up of men of action. (*Ibid.*, pp.
170–71.) Granjel links the different types of characters to a certain phase of
Baroja's life. He considers the protagonist as spectator to be a product of Baroja's
more mature life and the protagonist who flees from life to be a product of his
earlier years.
    "Antes de adoptar la actitud del espectador que prefiere a la acción la contem-
plación y el comentario, la postura vital de Baroja fué muy otra; entonces, era en
su juventud, incapaz de desprenderse de la sociedad en que vivía y a la que le
ataban no pocas esperanzas, la vida de Baroja estuvo gobernada, de uno u otro
modo, por aquella misma sociedad, a la vez denostada y deseada. Recuerdos de
tal actitud aparecen incluso, acabamos de verlo, en el pasado de los personajes
símbolo de su madurez, pero junto a ellos, y a estos últimos he de referirme ahora,
hay otros cuya figurada existencia es auténtica perduración literaria de esa juven-

tud partida por tan encontrados sentimientos, y a quienes, como le sucedió al propio Baroja, repele y atrae el mundo en que viven." (*Ibid.,* p. 183.)

Granjel seems to rely more on his personal experience than on his literary experience — the reading of Baroja's novels — as a basis for this integration of Baroja's protagonists with the extra-novelistic Baroja. We find an indication of the dangers of such a close integration of protagonist and author in Granjel's insistence on making Baroja's momentary belief in a certain political trend the most important phase of César Moncada's character. At least three times Granjel points out that César Moncada incarnates Baroja's belief in the political philosophies of the *regeneristas.* (*Ibid.,* pp. 192, 196, 197.)

[22] He divides his protagonists in a number of interesting ways. One division makes a distinction between the men of action and the would-be men of action. Bolinger's main division separates the proxy from the Hamlets. According to Bolinger, the proxy appeared after 1908 and has more of the attributes which can be more properly attributed to an observed person. The Hamlets have less of the exterior Baroja and more of his ideals and aspirations. Larrañaga would be a good example of the first type and Zalacaín of the second, (Bolinger, p. 163). Bolinger further stresses the fractionary aspects of Baroja's *yoísmo.*

"The many shades of Baroja's personality may be appreciated when we see that the devious Aracil, the conqueror Caesar, the defeatist Thierry, and the neurotic Larrañaga are all more or less derived from him." (*Ibid.,* p. 164.)

He feels that, whether the character is invented or not, the traits have to come from somewhere. The most logical place, he surmises, is from the author himself. In the same vein Francisco Pina believes that Baroja bares his complete moral soul in his protagonists.

"Baroja deja entrever íntegramente en sus libros su verdadero ser moral, desnuda completamente en ellos su personalidad, y así, no hay mejor manera de conocer al hombre que leer sus producciones." (Pina, p. 54.)

[23] Baroja, *Artículos,* V, p. 1275.

[24] Baroja, *Las figuras . . .,* IV, p. 191.

[25] Baroja, *Artículos,* V, p. 1290.

[26] Baroja, *Susana . . .,* VII, p. 14.

[27] Baroja, *El tablado . . .,* V, p. 29.

[28] Baroja, *La nave . . .,* IV, p. 325.

[29] Sender, p. 135.

[30] The negation throughout the work serves to frame, to help delimit and define this fractionary poetic essence. It tells us many of the necessary ingredients which form part of it: isolation, atemporality, uselessness, formlessness, lack of direction. It never names, classifies, or defines this substance. This essence remains intangible within Baroja's sensibility. Being ineffable it must be communicated through poetry.

[31] A careful reading of all the poems in Baroja's *Canciones del suburbio* will show conclusively just how foreign a sonnet comparing temporal love to the fleeting beauty of a rose would be to his poetic sensibility. The form of a sonnet was too exacting for Baroja. Furthermore the theme is much too traditional and overworked. It reeks of literature. Such a sonnet carries still another thorn for Baroja's sensibility. It pithily affirms a universal truth and a moral lesson. Azorín states in his prologue to *Canciones del suburbio* that the substance of Baroja's poetry — within or without the novel — is popular and not literary. He also remarks on Baroja's independence, his avoidance of the accepted, his aversion for that which is falsely traditional. (Baroja, *Canciones . . .,* VIII, p. 978.)

[32] It is true that in general Baroja does not become very enthusiastic about many writers. Sender has stated that he speaks poorly about all his contemporaries, but he does show a tremendous respect for Dostoyevsky, Dickens, Stendhal.

[33] Azorín in his prologue to *Canciones del suburbio* considers this old or by-passed quality, this ambience of yesteryear, to be of great significance in Baroja's singular book of poetry.

"No bastaba el tipo primario; era preciso también que las figuras se movieran en un ambiente de lejanía y casi de ensueño; no tendría el libro de Baroja el valor que tiene si no le circundara ese ambiente de lo pretérito. Al hacerlo así, al escribir Baroja en pasado y no en presente, se logra un efecto que de otro modo acaso no existiera: lo que parece más ajeno a la verdadera poesía cobra de pronto un hechizo verdaderamente poético. No es preciso que, en abono de nuestro aserto, citemos al gran maestro medieval de la poesía Francisco Villón." (Baroja, *Canciones* . . ., VIII, p. 978.)

[34] Baroja, *El laberinto* . . ., II, p. 1253.

[35] Baroja, *Las figuras* . . ., II, p. 239.

[36] Baroja, *Paradox, rey*, II, pp. 169–70.

[37] Baroja, *La caverna* . . ., V, p. 483.

[38] This thought is expressed many times in *La caverna del humorismo.*
"En este horno de turba del humorismo aprovechamos el mineral rico y las escorias, el metal nuevo y la chatarra." (*Ibid.,* p. 410.)
" . . . para la pintura todo es noble." (*Ibid.,* p. 414.)

[39] Baroja, *El tablado* . . ., V, p. 83.

[40] Baroja, *Juventud,* . . ., V, p. 168. Baroja was told that he would never be anything by one of his teachers in Pamplona, Gregorio Pano.

[41] Baroja, *La casa* . . ., I, p. 32.
Although similar passages abound, this one seems to follow Baroja's ideals because of the limitation in the number of sounds and its brevity. Compare with a similar passage from Ricardo León.
"Junto a la huerta, por una senda, venían unos campesinos; pasaban detrás largas carretas gruñidoras, un caballo montesino, chiquito y vigoroso, con su jinete; una viejecita encorvada bajo la pesadumbre del cuévano . . . El vientecillo de la noche agitaba los árboles con manso rumor. Un perfume intenso, que embriagaba como un soplo de oxígeno puro, ascendía de la hierba recién segada. Las últimas golondrinas se acogían a sus nidos. La nota aflautada de los sapos sonaba monótona en la espesura, como un eco de las melancolías de la noche." (León, p. 69.)

[42] *Ibid.,* p. 3.

[43] Baroja, *La ciudad* . . ., II, p. 331.

[44] *Ibid.,* p. 332.

[45] Baroja, *Las figuras* . . ., IV, p. 241.

[46] Baroja, *Vitrina* . . ., V, p. 810.

[47] Gómez Santos makes many references to Baroja's humming and whistling popular tunes. (Gómez Santos, pp. 48, 58, 63, 75, 156.)

[48] Baroja, *Juventud,* . . ., V, p. 163.

[49] Cela, *Don Pío Baroja*, pp. 62–63.

[50] Azorín, "Baladas perdidas," *Canciones del suburbio* by Baroja, VIII, p. 978.
Both these evaluations have been mentioned by Anthony Kerrigan in his introduction to the translation of *Las inquietudes de Shanti Andía.*
"Late in his career, Baroja also issued a first book of verse, *Canciones del suburbio* ('Songs of the Suburb'), a book which Azorín calls a condensation of his originality, and which Cela considers an index of the man and his style and the single best book by which to know him." (Pío Baroja, *The Restlessness of Shanti Andía,* trans. by Anthony Kerrigan [Ann Arbor: The University of Michigan Press, 1959], p. 18.)

[51] "But the artist appeals to that part of our being which is not dependent on wisdom: to that in us which is a gift and not an acquisition — and, therefore, more permanently enduring. He speaks to our capacity for delight and wonder, to the sense of mystery surrounding our lives; to our sense of pity, and beauty, and pain; to the latent feeling of fellowship with all creation — and to the subtle but invincible conviction of solidarity that knits together the loneliness of innumerable hearts, to the solidarity in dreams, in joy, in sorrow, in aspirations, in illusions, in hope, in fear, which binds men to each other, which binds together all humanity — the dead to the living and the living to the unborn.

It is only some such train of thought, or rather of feeling, that can in a measure explain the aim of the attempt, made in the tale which follows, to present an unrestful episode in the obscure lives of a few individuals out of all the disregarded multitude of the bewildered, the simple and the voiceless. For, if any part of truth dwells in the belief confessed above, it becomes evident that there is not a place of splendor or a dark corner of the earth that does not deserve if only a passing glance of wonder and pity." (Conrad, p. VIII.)

[52] "Me parecen todos ellos decadentes y, al mismo tiempo, defectuosos, productos de vejez y de neurastenia.

Si yo supiera corregirlos — he intentado hacerlo, sin éxito —, lo haría; pero no tengo norma clara para ello. Si intento mejorarlos, pierden su carácter y se hacen afectados, y si los dejo tal como están, quedan toscos." (Baroja, *Canciones . . .,* VIII, p. 980.)

NOTES TO CHAPTER 9
pages 181—186

[1] Rosalie Wahl has written a doctor's dissertation on Pío Baroja's literary doctrine. ("The Literary Doctrine of Pío Baroja" [unpublished Ph.D. dissertation, New York University, 1959]).

[2] Baroja, *La caverna . . .,* V, p. 409.

[3] It is significant that many of his characters who are almost completely swallowed up in the antivital elements seem to migrate towards the Levante, the Mediterranean coasts, when they make their bid for freedom and life. We remember that Fernando Ossorio of *Camino de perfección* and Don Juan from *El mayorazgo de Labraz* found new life and vitality in the Mediterranean sunshine of the Levante.

[4] " — Para mí — decía la voz desconocida — esos reconocimientos continuos que hacen en los partos son perjudiciales. Yo no conozco este caso, pero ¿quién sabe? Quizá esta mujer, en el campo, sin asistencia ninguna, se hubiera salvado. La Naturaleza tiene recursos que nosotros no conocemos.

— Yo no digo que no — contestó el médico que había asistido a Lulú —; es muy posible." (Baroja, *El árbol . . .,* II, p. 569.)

[5] Baroja, *La estrella del capitán Chimista,* VI, p. 138.

[6] Baroja, *Los pilotos . . .,* II, p. 1341.

[7] "Los días de fiesta, aunque me esforzaba por quedarme en casa, no tenía bastante voluntad, y me iba a buscar a Aviraneta. Ese réprobo amigo de usted, como sabía mi flaco, me llevaba a una fonda de un navarro, un tal Iturri, de la calle de los Vascos, y me convidaba a una cena suculenta. ¡Qué bien se guisaba en aquella casa! ¡Qué merluzas, qué angulas, qué perdices rellenas he comido allí! Ante unas comidas como aquéllas, ¿qué quiere usted, amigo mío?, yo era un hombre al agua." (Baroja, *La Isabelina,* III, pp. 1016–17.)

[8] Baroja, *Los enigmáticos,* VIII, pp. 453–54.

9 " — Mi última consecuencia — contestó él — es que no hay sabiduría en la vida, y que aunque la hubiera no serviría para nada expresada en principios o en máximas. — Luego añadió —: También podría suceder que hubiera una sabiduría para cada persona, pero indudablemente no creo que haya una sabiduría comunicable." (Baroja, *Los enigmáticos,* VIII, p. 429.)

10 "¡Aufa! ¡De aquí para allá! ¡A jugar! ¡A correr! ¡A andar en rondas caprichosas por el aire! ¡Bastante tiempo hemos padecido esclavizadas, obligadas a estar quietas!" (Baroja, *La leyenda de Jaun de Alzate,* VI, p. 1132.)

11 *La leyenda de Jaun de Alzate* illustrates the enduring qualities of the countryside. Jaun rejects both the old Basque gods and the new Roman Catholic idols. "No hay más que la Naturaleza." (Baroja, *Ibid.,* p. 1165.)

12 Maxim Gorky, *Creatures That Once Were Men,* trans. by J. M. Shirazi (New York: The Modern Library, 1925), p. 103.

13 "Nadie duda que al mismo tiempo que egoísmo hay en el hombre un principio de simpatía por los demás, que en las religiones se llama caridad y entre los positivistas altruísmo, con esta palabra que creo inventó Augusto Comte. Hay que reconocer que es una gota de agua al lado del mar." (Baroja, *La intuición . . .,* VIII, p. 984.)

14 *Ibid.*

15 Capote, p. 81.

16 Baroja, *La influencia del 98,* V, p. 1240.

17 Machado, *Campos de Castilla* (1907–1917), *Poesías completas,* p. 92.

18 Rosalie Wahl, pp. 95–105.

19 "Encuesta en torno a Baroja," *Indice,* p. 23.

20 José Suárez Carreño, *Las últimas horas* (Barcelona: Ediciones Destino, 1954), p. 298.

21 Lino Novás Calvo, *Cayo canas* (Buenos Aires: Espasa-Calpe Argentina, 1946), pp. 9–43.

22 Baroja, *Paradox, Rey,* II, pp. 172–73.

Bibliography

A. Works by Baroja

PRELIMINARY NOTE. Baroja's works are listed below in the order in which they appear in his *Obras completas* (Madrid: Biblioteca Nueva, 1946–1951). Each work is listed separately with the bibliographical information according to the first edition. The Roman numeral at the end of the bibliographical entry refers to the volume of the *Obras completas* where the work is found.

La casa de Aizgorri. Madrid: Rodríguez Serra, 1900. I.

El mayorazgo de Labraz. (Biblioteca de novelistas del siglo XX.) Barcelona: Henrich y Cía., 1903. I.

Zalacain el aventurero. Barcelona: Domenech, 1909. I.

La busca. (La lucha por la vida.) Madrid: Fernando Fe, 1904. I.

Mala hierba. (La lucha por la vida.) Madrid: Fernando Fe, 1904. I.

Aurora roja. (La lucha por la vida.) Madrid: Fernando Fe, 1904. I.

La feria de los discretos. (El pasado.) Madrid: Fernando Fe, 1905. I.

Los últimos románticos. (El pasado.) Madrid: Hernando, 1906. I.

Las tragedias grotescas. (El pasado.) Madrid: Hernando, 1907. I.

El gran torbellino del mundo. (Agonías de nuestro tiempo.) Madrid: Caro Raggio, 1927. I.

Las veleidades de la fortuna. (Agonías de nuestro tiempo.) Madrid: Caro Raggio, 1927. I.

Los amores tardíos. (Agonías de nuestro tiempo.) Madrid: Caro Raggio, 1927. I.

Aventuras, inventos y mixtificaciones de Silvestre Paradox. (La vida fantástica.) Madrid: Rodríguez Serra, 1901. II.

Paradox, Rey. (La vida fantástica.) Madrid: Hernando, 1906, II.

La dama errante. (La raza.) Madrid: Hernando, 1908. II.

La ciudad de la niebla. (La raza.) Madrid: Hernando, 1909. II.

El árbol de la ciencia. (La raza.) Madrid: Renacimiento, 1911. II.

César o nada. (Las ciudades.) Madrid: Renacimiento, 1910. II.

El mundo es ansí. (Las ciudades.) Madrid: Renacimiento, 1912. II.

La sensualidad pervertida. (Las ciudades.) Madrid: Caro Raggio, 1920. II.

Las inquietudes de Shanti Andía. (El mar.) Madrid: Renacimiento, 1911. II.

El laberinto de las sirenas. (El mar.) Madrid: Caro Raggio, 1923. II.

Los pilotos de altura. (El mar.) Madrid: Caro Raggio, 1929, II.

El aprendiz de conspirador. (Memorias de un hombre de acción, I.) Madrid: Renacimiento, 1913. III.

El escuadrón del brigante. (Memorias de un hombre de acción, II.) Madrid: Renacimiento, 1913. III.

Los caminos del mundo. (Memorias de un hombre de acción, III.) Madrid: Renacimiento, 1914. III.

Con la pluma y con el sable. (Memorias de un hombre de acción, IV.) Madrid: Renacimiento, 1915. III.

Los recursos de la astucia. (Memorias de un hombre de acción, V.) Madrid: Renacimiento, 1915. III.

La ruta del aventurero. (Memorias de un hombre de acción, VI.) Madrid: Renacimiento, 1916. III.

Los contrastes de la vida. (Memorias de un hombre de acción, X.) Madrid: Caro Raggio, 1920. III.

La veleta de Gastizar. (Memorias de un hombre de acción, VII.) Madrid: Caro Raggio, 1918. III.

Los caudillos de 1830. (Memorias de un hombre de acción, VIII.) Madrid: Caro Raggio, 1918. III.

La Isabelina. (Memorias de un hombre de acción, IX.) Madrid: Caro Raggio, 1919. III.

El sabor de la venganza. (Memorias de un hombre de acción, XI.) Madrid: Caro Raggio, 1921. III.

Las furias. (Memorias de un hombre de acción, XII.) Madrid: Caro Raggio, 1922. III.

El amor, el dandismo y la intriga. (Memorias de un hombre de acción, XIII.) Madrid: Caro Raggio, 1923. IV.

Las figuras de cera. (Memorias de un hombre de acción, XIV.) Madrid: Caro Raggio, 1924. IV.

La nave de los locos. (Memorias de un hombre de acción, XV.) Madrid: Caro Raggio, 1925. IV.

Las mascaradas sangrientas. (Memorias de un hombre de acción, XVI.) Madrid: Caro Raggio, 1928. IV.

Humano enigma. (Memorias de un hombre de acción, XVII.) Madrid: Caro Raggio, 1928. IV.

La senda dolorosa. (Memorias de un hombre de acción, XVIII.) Madrid: Caro Raggio, 1929. IV.

Los confidentes audaces. (Memorias de un hombre de acción, XXI.) Madrid: Espasa-Calpe, 1931. IV.

La venta de Mirambel. (Memorias de un hombre de acción, XX.) Madrid: Espasa-Calpe, 1931. IV.

Crónica escandalosa. (Memorias de un hombre de acción, XXI.) Madrid: Espasa-Calpe, 1935. IV.

Desde el principio hasta el fin. (Memorias de un hombre de acción, XXII.) Madrid: Espasa-Calpe, 1935. IV.

Aviraneta o la vida de un conspirador. Madrid: Espasa-Calpe, 1931. IV.

Juan Van Halen, el oficial aventurero. Madrid: Espasa-Calpe, 1933. IV.

El tablado de Arlequín. Valencia: Sempere, 1904. V.

Nuevo tablado de Arlequín. Madrid: Caro Raggio, 1917. V.

Juventud, egolatría. Madrid: Caro Raggio, 1917. V.

Las horas solitarias. Madrid: Caro Raggio, 1918. V.

Momentum catastrophicum. Madrid: Caro Raggio, 1919. V.
La caverna del humorismo. Madrid: Caro Raggio, 1919. V.
Divagaciones apasionadas. Madrid: Caro Raggio, 1924. V.
Tres generaciones. (Conferencia leída en la Casa del Pueblo de Madrid.) May 17, 1926. V.
Intermedios. Madrid: Espasa-Calpe, 1931. V.
Vitrina pintoresca. Madrid: Espasa-Calpe, 1935. V.
Rapsodias. (Discursos y crónicas.) Madrid: Espasa-Calpe, 1936. V.
Pequeños ensayos. Buenos Aires: Sudamericana, 1943. V.
Artículos. (A series of articles first published as a work in *Obras completas.)* Madrid: Biblioteca Nueva, 1948. V.
Camino de perfección. Madrid: Rodríguez Serra, 1902. VI.
La estrella del capitán Chimista. (El mar.) Madrid: Caro Raggio, 1930. VI.
La familia de Errotacho. (La selva oscura.) Madrid: Espasa-Calpe, 1932. VI.
El cabo de las tormentas. (La selva oscura.) Madrid: Espasa-Calpe, 1932. VI.
Los visionarios. (La selva oscura.) Madrid: Espasa-Calpe, 1932. VI.
Las noches del Buen Retiro. (La juventud perdida.) Madrid: Espasa-Calpe, 1934. VI.
El cura de Monleón. (La juventud perdida.) Madrid: Espasa-Calpe, 1936. VI.
Locuras de carnaval. (La juventud perdida.) Madrid: Espasa-Calpe, 1937. VI.
Vidas sombrías. Madrid: Miguel Pereda, 1900. VI.
Otros cuentos. (A series of stories first published as a work in *Obras completas.)* Madrid: Biblioteca Nueva, 1948. VI.
La leyenda de Jaun de Alzate. Madrid: Caro Raggio, 1922. VI.
El "nocturno" del hermano Beltrán. Madrid: Caro Raggio, 1929. VI.
Todo acaba bien . . . a veces. Madrid: Biblioteca Nueva, 1948. VI.
El horroroso crimen de Peñaranda del Campo y otras historias. Madrid: Caro Raggio, 1928. VI.
Susana. San Sebastián: B.I.N.S.A., 1937. VII.
El tesoro del holandés. (La Novela del Sábado. Includes also: *Yan-Si-Pao o la svástica de oro* y *Los buscadores de tesoros.)* Sevilla: II. de Del Reguero, 1939. VII.
Laura o la soledad sin remedio. (Colección Horizonte.) Buenos Aires: Sudamericana, 1939. VII.
El caballero de Erláiz. Madrid: La Nave, 1943. VII.
El escritor según él y según los críticos. (Desde la última vuelta del camino, I.) Madrid: Biblioteca Nueva, 1944. VII.
Familia, infancia y juventud. (Desde la última vuelta del camino, II.) Madrid: Biblioteca Nueva, 1944. VII.
Final del siglo XIX y principios del XX. (Desde la última vuelta del camino, III.) Madrid: Biblioteca Nueva, 1945. VII.
Galería de tipos de la época. (Desde la última vuelta del camino, IV.) Madrid: Biblioteca Nueva, 1947. VII.
La intuición y el estilo. (Desde la última vuelta del camino, V.) Madrid: Biblioteca Nueva, 1948. VII.
Reportajes. (Desde la última vuelta del camino, VI.) Madrid: Biblioteca Nueva, 1948. VII.
Bagatelas de otoño. (Desde la última vuelta del camino, VII.) Madrid: Biblioteca Nueva, 1949. VII.
El puente de las ánimas. Madrid: La Nave, 1945. VIII.
El hotel del cisne. Madrid: Biblioteca Nueva, 1946. VIII.
Los enigmáticos. Madrid: Biblioteca Nueva, 1948. VIII.

El cantor vagabundo. (Saturnales.) Madrid: Biblioteca Nueva, 1950. VIII.

La dama de Urtubi. (La Novela Corta.) Madrid: Retrato en portada, 1916. VIII.

Elizabide, el vagabundo. Madrid: Caro Raggio, 1918. VIII.

El charcutero. Madrid: Caro Raggio, 1918. VIII.

Las familias enemigas. Barcelona: Pal-Las, 1939. VIII.

La caja de música. Barcelona: Pal-Las, 1939. VIII.

Los herejes milenaristas. Barcelona: Pal-Las, 1939. VIII.

Teatro. (Two plays first published as a work in *Obras completas.*) Madrid: Biblioteca Nueva, 1951. VIII.

Ensayos. (A series of essays first published as a work in *Obras completas.*) Madrid: Biblioteca Nueva. 1951. VIII.

Otros ensayos. (A series of essays first published as a work in *Obras completas.*) Madrid: Biblioteca Nueva, 1951. VIII.

Canciones del suburbio. (Prólogo de Azorín.) Madrid: Biblioteca Nueva, 1944. VIII.

Las veladas del Chalet Gris. (First published in *Obras completas.*) Madrid: Biblioteca Nueva, 1951. VIII.

Páginas escogidas. Madrid: Casa Editorial Calleja, 1918.

B. Works about Baroja, referred to in this book

Bolinger, Dwight L. "Pío Baroja: A Critique." Unpublished Ph.D. dissertation, University of Wisconsin, 1936.

Caro Baroja, Pío. *La soledad de Pío Baroja.* Mexico: Pío Caro Baroja, Editor; 1953.

Cela, Camilo José. *Don Pío Baroja.* Mexico: Ediciones de Andrea, 1958.

Díaz-Plaja, Guillermo. *Modernismo frente a 98.* Madrid, 1951.

Eaton, J. D. "Propagandist Novel: 'Red Dawn.'" *The Saturday Review of Literature,* I, No. 24 [1925], pp. 443–444.

García Mercadal, José. *Baroja en el banquillo.* Zaragoza: Librería General, 1947.

Gómez-Santos, Marino. *Baroja y su máscara.* Barcelona: Editorial A H R, 1956.

Granjel, Luis S. *Retrato de Pío Baroja.* Barcelona: Editorial Barna, 1953.

"Hemingway Visits Baroja in Madrid," *Time,* XLVIII, No. 18 [1956], p. 47.

Indice, Año 9, Nos. 70–71 [1953–1954]. (This has the most up-to-date and inclusive bibliography on Pío Baroja.)

Jeschke, Hans. *La Generación de 1898 en España.* Translated by Y. Pino Saavedra. Santiago: Editorial Universitaria, 1953.

Kerrigan, Anthony. Introduction to *The Restlessness of Shanti Andía* by Baroja. Ann Arbor: The University of Michigan Press, 1959.

Laín Entralgo, Pedro. *La Generación del Noventa y Ocho.* Buenos Aires: Espasa-Calpe Argentina, 1947.

Ortega y Gasset, José. *El Espectador. Obras.* Madrid-Barcelona: Espasa-Calpe, 1932.

————. "Espíritu de la letra." *Obras.* Madrid-Barcelona: Espasa-Calpe, 1932.

————. "La deshumanización del arte e ideas sobre la novela." *Obras.* Madrid-Barcelona: Espasa-Calpe, 1932.

Pérez Ferrero, Miguel. *Pío Baroja en su rincón.* Santiago de Chile: Ediciones Ercilla, 1940.

Pérez Minik, Domingo. *Novelistas españoles de los siglos XIX y XX*. Madrid: Ediciones Guadarrama, 1957.

Pina, Francisco. *Pío Baroja*. Spain: Editorial Sempere, 1928.

Sender, Ramón J. *Unamuno, Valle-Inclán, Baroja y Santayana*. Mexico: Ediciones de Andrea, 1955.

Shaw, D. L. "A Reply to *Deshumanización* — Baroja on the Art of the Novel," *Hispanic Review*, XXV [1957], pp. 105–111.

Torrente Ballester, Gonzalo. *Panorama de la literatura española contemporánea*. Madrid: Ediciones Guadarrama, 1956.

Uribe Echevarría, Juan. *Pío Baroja: técnica, estilo, personajes*. Chile: Ediciones de los Anales de la Universidad de Chile, 1957.

Valbuena Prat, Angel. *Historia de la literatura española*. Barcelona: Editorial Gustavo Gili, 1957. Vol. III, pp. 451–593.

Wahl, Rosalie. "The Literary Doctrine of Pío Baroja." Unpublished Ph.D. dissertation, New York University, April 15, 1959.

C. Other Sources

Anderson, Sherwood. *Winesburg, Ohio*. New York: The New American Library, 1956.

Auerbach, Erich. *Mimesis*. Princeton, New Jersey: Princeton University Press, 1953.

Azorín [José Martínez Ruiz]. *Obras completas*. Madrid: Aguilar, 1948. Vols. I, II, VI.

Baker, Carlos. *Hemingway*. Princeton, New Jersey: Princeton University Press, 1956.

Bousoño, Carlos. *La teoría de la expresión poética*. Madrid: Editorial Gredos, 1952.

Capote, Truman. *Other Voices, Other Rooms*. New York: The New American Library, 1960.

Castro, Américo. *La realidad histórica de España*. Mexico: Editorial Porrúa, 1954.

Cela, Camilo José. *La colmena*. Barcelona-Mexico: Editorial Noguer, 1957.

Conrad, Joseph. *The Nigger of the Narcissus*. New York: Random House, 1957.

Díaz-Plaja, Guillermo. *Defensa de la crítica*. Barcelona: Editorial Barna, 1953.

—————. *El poema en prosa en España*. Barcelona: Editorial Gustavo Gili, 1956.

Dostoyevsky, Fyodor. *The Brothers Karamazov*. Translated by Constance Garnett. New York: The Modern Library, 1940.

Gorky, Maxim. *Creatures That Once Were Men*. Translated by J. M. Shirazi. New York: The Modern Library, 1925.

Joyce, James. *Dubliners*. New York: D. W. Huebsch, 1916.

Kayser, Wolfgang. *Interpretación y análisis de la obra literaria*. Madrid: Editorial Gredos, 1958.

León, Ricardo. *El amor de los amores*. Madrid: Editorial Hernando, 1929.

—————. *Casta de hidalgos*. Argentina: Espasa-Calpe Argentina, 1952.

Lewis, R. W. B. *The Picaresque Saint*. Philadelphia and New York: J. B. Lippincott Company, 1959.

Machado, Antonio. *Poesías completas*. Buenos Aires-Mexico: Espasa-Calpe Argentina, 1952.

Menéndez Pidal, R. *Cantar de Mío Cid*. Madrid: Espasa-Calpe, 1946.

Novás Calvo, Lino. *Cayo canas*. Buenos Aires: Espasa-Calpe Argentina, 1946.

Pérez Galdós, Benito. *Fortunata y Jacinta*. 2d. ed. Argentina: Espasa-Calpe Argentina, 1951.

————. *La de Bringas*. Madrid: Editorial Hernando, 1952.

Poe, Edgar Allan. *The Works of Edgar Allan Poe*. New York and London: Funk and Wagnalls Company, 1904. Vol. VII.

Rand, Marguerite. *Castilla en Azorín*. Madrid: Revista de Occidente, 1957.

Romero, Luis. *La noria*. Barcelona: Ediciones Destino, 1954.

Shapiro, Karl. "T. S. Eliot: The Death of Literary Judgment," *Saturday Review*, XLIII, No. 9 [1960], p. 12.

Suárez Carreño, José. *Las últimas horas*. Barcelona: Ediciones Destino, 1954.

Unamuno, Miguel de. *Obras selectas*. Madrid: Editorial Plenitud, 1950.

Valle-Inclán, Ramón del. *La lámpara maravillosa*. Madrid: Artes de la Ilustración, 1922.